Negotiating Identity in the Ancient Mediterranean

The Mediterranean basin was a multicultural region with a great diversity of linguistic, religious, social, and ethnic groups. This dynamic social and cultural landscape encouraged extensive contact and exchange among different communities. This book seeks to explain what happened when different ethnic, social, linguistic, and religious groups, among others, came into contact with each other, especially in multiethnic commercial settlements located throughout the region. What means did they employ to mediate their interactions? How did each group construct distinct identities while interacting with others? What new identities came into existence because of these contacts? Professor Demetriou brings together several strands of scholarship that have emerged recently, especially in ethnic, religious, and Mediterranean studies. She reveals new aspects of identity construction in the region, examining the Mediterranean as a whole, and focuses not only on ethnic identity but also on other types of collective identities, such as civic, linguistic, religious, and social.

DENISE DEMETRIOU is Assistant Professor of History at Michigan State University.

T0370802

Negotiating Identity in the Ancient Mediterranean

The Archaic and Classical Greek Multiethnic Emporia

DENISE DEMETRIOU

CAMBRIDGE
UNIVERSITY PRESS

University Printing House, Cambridge CB2 8BS, United Kingdom

One Liberty Plaza, 20th Floor, New York, NY 10006, USA

477 Williamstown Road, Port Melbourne, VIC 3207, Australia

314-321, 3rd Floor, Plot 3, Splendor Forum, Jasola District Centre, New Delhi - 110025, India

103 Penang Road, #05-06/07, Visioncrest Commercial, Singapore 238467

Cambridge University Press is part of the University of Cambridge.

It furthers the University's mission by disseminating knowledge in the pursuit of education, learning and research at the highest international levels of excellence.

www.cambridge.org
Information on this title: www.cambridge.org/9781009296762

First published 2012
First paperback edition 2022

A catalogue record for this publication is available from the British Library

Library of Congress Cataloging in Publication data
Demetriou, Denise, 1976–
Negotiating identity in the ancient Mediterranean : the archaic and classical Greek multiethnic
emporia / Denise Demetriou.
   pages   cm
Includes bibliographical references and index.
ISBN 978-1-107-01944-7
1. Mediterranean Region – History – To 476.   2. Ethnic groups – Mediterranean Region –
History – To 476.   3. Culture conflict – Mediterranean Region.   4. Mediterranean Region –
Commerce.   5. Group identity – Mediterranean Region.   6. National characteristics,
Mediterranean.   7. Mediterranean Region – Social conditions.   8. Mediterranean Region –
Civilization.   I. Title.
DE86.D46   2012
938 – dc23   2012015657

ISBN 978-1-107-01944-7 Hardback
ISBN 978-1-009-29676-2 Paperback

Contents

Illustrations

Acknowledgements

This book began as a Ph.D. dissertation at Johns Hopkins University not quite ten years ago. In the meantime, I have accumulated many debts that I owe both to individuals and institutions without whose support the writing and publication of this book would not have been possible. Here I would like to express my thanks to all of them.

At Johns Hopkins, I was lucky to have not one but two exceptional advisors, Alan Shapiro and Irad Malkin. Their expertise and critical insights have inspired this work and have shaped my thinking about the ancient Greek world. For this and their constant support and good humor throughout the years, I owe them my deepest gratitude. My thanks also go to two other members of my committee, Marcel Detienne and the late Ray Westbrook, whose guidance gave me a comparative perspective as well as a better understanding of the sources.

Several grants, fellowships, and institutions have supported the completion of this project. The J. Brien Key Fellowship (sponsored by Johns Hopkins University) enabled a research trip to France, Spain, and the U.K. to examine archaeological material from several of the sites discussed in this book. I am particularly grateful to the Mary Isabel Sibley Fellowship for Greek Studies and the Loeb Classical Library Foundation for their grants that afforded me the time to revise my manuscript at the wonderful library of the American School of Classical Studies in Athens. I would also like to thank the last two directors of the school, Steven Tracy and Jack Davis, as well as the School's secretary, Bob Bridges, for providing me with a home away from home and the resources to complete my project.

For their help with the acquisition of images illustrated in the book, I would like to thank Marta Santos Retolaza (Museu d'Arqueologia de Catalunya-Empúries), Sevdalina Popova (Archaeological Museum "Prof. Mieczyslav Domaradzki," Septemvri), Angela Carbonaro (Musei Capitolini), Emma Darbyshire (Fitzwilliam Museum, Cambridge), Amy Taylor (Ashmolean Museum, Oxford), Nikolaos Kaltsas (National Archaeological Museum, Athens), Maria Englezou, Eleni Zavvou, and Athanassios Themos (Epigraphic Museum, Athens), Alexandra Villing (British Museum), Kathleen Scott (JARCE), and Claire Weatherhead (Bloomsbury Academic).

I am grateful to Lucio Fiorini, Astrid Möller, and Marta Santos Retolaza for allowing me to reproduce some of their site plans. Mario Torelli, Sara Saba, and Pierangelo Buongiorno have been incredibly generous with their time and effort in helping me acquire permissions to reproduce some of the images in this book. My sincere thanks go also to my friend and colleague Jon Frey for his technical assistance with the images, and Jackie Belden Hawthorne for all the time and effort she put into creating the maps included in this book.

My very special thanks are due to my colleagues in both the History and Classics Departments at Michigan State University, who have provided me with a most supportive and friendly environment, as well as the resources to be able to complete this project. The History Department, in particular, has generously financed the cost of several images and maps illustrated in the book.

I am indebted to Antonis Ellinas, Mark Piskorowski, Sara Saba, and Bronwen Wickkiser, who have not only been my good friends over the years but also astute readers. They, together with the two anonymous reviewers of Cambridge University Press, gave me their most helpful comments on portions of or the entire book. Milan Griffes, an exceptional undergraduate student, has helped me correct many errors in the manuscript. All errors that remain are, of course, my own. Michael Sharp and Josephine Lane at Cambridge University Press deserve special thanks for their interest in the project as well as for their superb cooperation throughout the editorial process.

Had it not been for my mentor, Rebecca Sinos, who first taught me ancient Greek at Amherst College, I would now be a chemist. Her classes opened for me a door to the fascinating world of classics and she has been an inspiration ever since.

Finally, I have no adequate way to express my gratitude to my family. They taught me to be intellectually curious and have given me, with their unwavering support and encouragement throughout my life, the freedom to pursue my interests, even when that meant moving abroad. My parents have experienced with me the anxieties and hopes of this project; it is to them that I dedicate this book.

Abbreviations

All translations are my own unless otherwise indicated. In general, I prefer to transliterate rather than anglicize Greek names and words, but I am not consistent about this; instead, I often use the more familiar spellings in English.

Abbreviations of journals follow the conventions set by *L'année philologique*. Abbreviations of corpora of inscriptions and standard works follow the conventions set by S. Hornblower and A. Spawforth (eds.) (1996) *Oxford Classical Dictionary*, 3rd edition. Oxford: xxix–liv. References to editions of papyri follow the conventions in J. F. Oates, R. S. Bagnall, S. J. Clackson, A. A. O'Brien, J. D. Sosin, T. G. Wilfong, K. A. Worp (eds.) (2001) *Checklist of Editions of Greek, Latin, Demotic, and Coptic Papyri, Ostraca and Tablets*. 5th edition. Bulletin of the American Society of Papyrologists Supplement 9. Atlanta. In addition, I have used the following works:

CID	Rougement, G., J. Bousquet, A. Bélis, F. Lefèvre (eds.) (1977–2002) *Corpus des inscriptions de Delphes*. 4 vols. Paris.
CIG	(1828–77) *Corpus inscriptionum graecarum*. 4 vols. Berlin.
Dürrbach, *Choix*	Dürrbach, F. (ed.) (1921–3) *Choix d'inscriptions de Délos*. 2 vols. Paris.
ET	Rix, H. (ed.) (1991–2) *Etruskische Texte*. 2 vols. Tübingen.
IEph	Engelmann, H., H. Wankel, and R. Merkelbach (eds.) (1979–84) *Die Inschriften von Ephesos*. 8 vols. Bonn.
IEryth	Engelmann, H., and R. Merkelbach (eds.) (1972–3) *Die Inschriften von Erythrai und Klazomenai*. 2 vols. Bonn.
IMilet	Herrmann, P., W. Günther, N. Ehrhardt (eds.) (1997–2006) *Inschriften von Milet*. 3 vols. Berlin.
IosPE	Latysew, B. (ed.) (1885–1916) *Inscriptiones antiquae orae septentrionalis Ponti Euxini graecae et latinae*. 3 vols. St. Petersburg.
Iscr. di Cos	Segre, M. (ed.) (1993) *Iscrizioni di Cos*. Monografie della scuola archeologica di Atene e delle missioni italiane in Oriente. Vol. 6. Rome.
IScM I	Pippidi, D. M. (ed.) (1983) *Inscriptiones Daciae et Scythiae Minoris antiquae. Series altera: Inscriptiones Scythiae Minoris graecae et latinae*. Vol. 1. *Inscriptiones Histriae et vicinia*. Bucharest.
IOlbia	Knipovich, T. N. and E. I. Levi (eds.) (1968) *Inscriptiones Olbiae*. Leningrad.

IPriene	Hiller von Gaertringen, F. (ed.) (1906) *Inschriften von Priene.* Berlin.
Obbink-Parker	Parker, R. and D. Obbink (2000) "Aus der Arbeit der 'Inscriptiones Graecae' VI. Sales of Priesthoods on Cos I," *Chiron* 30: 415–49.
OGIS	Dittenberger, W. (ed.) (1903–5) *Orientis Graeci inscriptiones selectae.* 2 vols. Leipzig.
Tit. Calymnii	Segre, M. (1944–5 [1952]) "Tituli Calymnii." *ASAA* 22–23: 1–248.
WZHalle	Wissenschaftliche Zeitschrift der Martin-Luther-Universität Halle-Wittenberg.

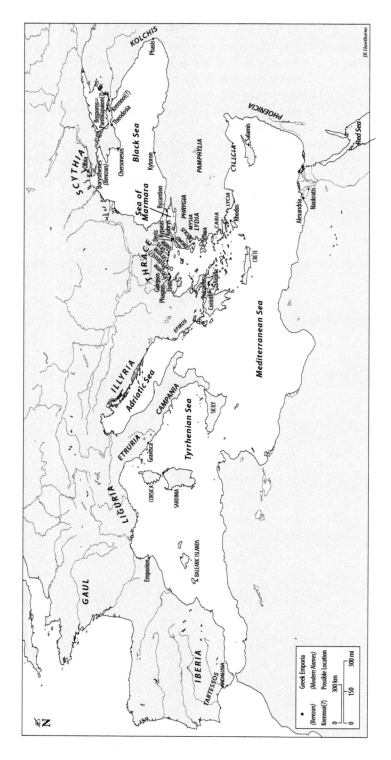

Map 1 Map of the archaic and classical Greek emporia in the Mediterranean. Created by Jackie Belden Hawthorne.

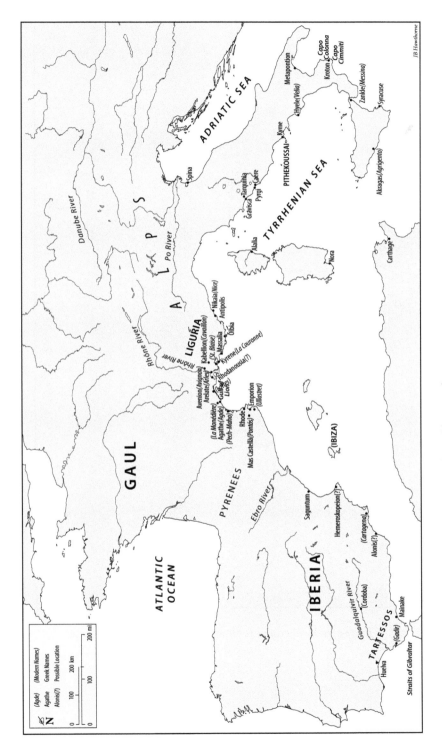

Map 2 Map of the western Mediterranean. Created by Jackie Belden Hawthorne.

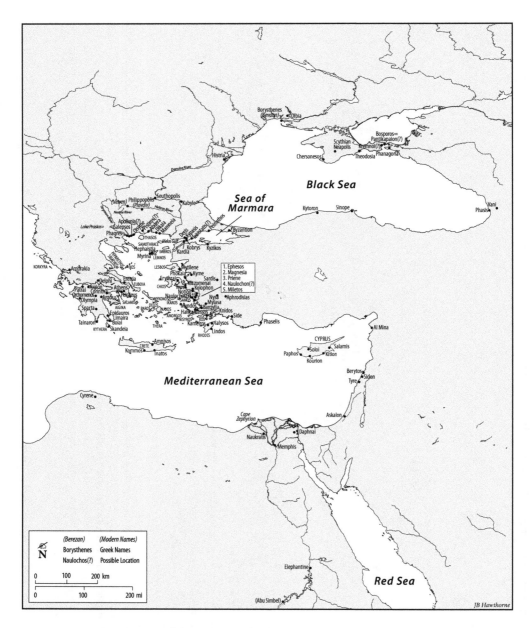

Map 3 Map of the eastern Mediterranean. Created by Jackie Belden Hawthorne.

Introduction

This book starts from two premises. First, the Mediterranean basin during the first millennium BC was a multicultural region with a great variety of linguistic, religious, social, and ethnic groups. Second, this diverse and dynamic social and cultural landscape encouraged extensive contact and exchange and fostered permanent modes of interaction among many different groups. Building on these two ideas, this book studies the construction of identity in the archaic and classical periods from a Mediterranean perspective. The underlying questions are: What happened when different ethnic, social, linguistic, and religious groups, among others, came into contact with one another? What means did they employ to mediate their interactions? How did each group construct distinct identities while interacting with others? What new identities came into existence because of these contacts?

This study of human interactions in the Mediterranean brings together several strands of scholarship that have emerged and become popular recently in the field of ancient Greek history, especially in ethnic, religious, and Mediterranean studies, in order to provide a new understanding of the archaic and classical Mediterranean. The book breaks with much of the historiography on the study of ancient identity, thereby revealing new aspects of identity construction in the region, first because it deals with the Mediterranean as a whole and second because it focuses not only on ethnic identity but also on other types of collective identities, such as civic identity based on an individual's city-state, linguistic identity determined by language, religious identity decided by membership in a cult, and social identity based on social status. In what follows, I present the benefits in approaching the subject of identity construction from a Mediterranean perspective and the necessity and importance of examining other types of identities besides ethnicity, and I lay out the book's methodological approach.

Mediterranean perspectives

In the last three decades, numerous journals and books with the word "Mediterranean" in their title have appeared, and the field of Mediterranean studies has experienced a resurgence in popularity in many disciplines, including that of classics.[1] This recent explosion of interest in the ancient Mediterranean came after a hiatus that lasted for almost half a century. After Braudel's *magnum opus* on the Mediterranean in the age of Philip II, published originally in 1949, nothing much appeared until the 1980s that treated the Mediterranean as a subject of study, despite the wide-ranging debates that Braudel's work sparked in the field of history. One of the major reasons for the recent reemergence of Mediterranean Studies lies in the unprecedented connectedness we experience in the contemporary world, which has created an intellectual milieu interested in looking more at linking institutions rather than at isolated states.[2] It should come as no surprise that in the discipline of classics, the response to the increasing need to approach the field from a global perspective, whether imposed institutionally, by academic trends, or today's globalized culture and society, has been to emphasize the connections, mobility, and networks throughout the Mediterranean basin.[3]

The attention to Mediterranean Studies has not appeared without criticism. Whether modern historians can treat the Mediterranean as a single field of inquiry or not is a notoriously difficult subject. Is it the production of certain crops, such as the vine and the olive, that unites the Mediterranean or the extent of their consumption? Is it, instead, transhumant pastoralism? Is it a dependence of local economies on each other? Or is there some semblance of a cultural unity that ancient historians can discuss, especially before the Roman conquests?[4] One of the more impressive undertakings has been Horden and Purcell's *The Corrupting Sea*, a remarkable work that has

---

[1] Morris 2005 presents numbers and statistics on these titles and discusses various journals' Mediterranean scope.

[2] Similar academic trends exist in other fields. A case in point is "transnationalism," a hot topic in modern history, sociology, and political science. Transnationalism emphasizes the movement of ideas, people, technologies, and institutions across national boundaries; it involves the study of migration patterns, ethnic diasporas, trade networks, and other institutions that connect nations; it questions the efficacy of nation-states as a framework for analysis, given the contemporary historical situation; and it tries to explain the nation-state in terms of cross-cultural influences. A useful recent synopsis is Iriye and Saunier 2009. For the adoption of the rubric of transnational history in modern history see Tyrrell 2007 and Espagne, Geyer, and Middell 2010. Transnationalism is purely concerned with modernity. It is interesting to note, however, that Braudel 1949 actually approximated a kind of transnational history. Though not considered transnational in its scope because it treated a pre-modern era when dynastic rule prevailed rather than the nation and it was concerned with cultural and regional history, rather than national and international history, Braudel's work combined comparative approaches and pioneered cross-cultural history.

[3] Morris 2005 also attributes the increase in popularity of Mediterranean Studies to globalization.

[4] Harris 2005: 1–42, especially 20–9, reviews the historiography on the question of Mediterranean unity. See also Carpentier and Lebrun 1998, Grove and Rackham 2003, and Abulafia 2003.

created a framework based on historical ecology for studying the history of the Mediterranean region over several millennia in order to determine the extent and basis on which the pre-modern Mediterranean can be treated as a single field of inquiry.[5] The project's agenda, clearly influenced by our own global universe, involves "decentering" the Mediterranean and emphasizing instead the fluidity and connectedness of the region in order to interpret it.[6]

Even if the connectivity of the Mediterranean is taken for granted, and this, too, has been questioned because of the inability to define and provide consistent limits for the Mediterranean, no satisfactory answer has been given to the questions above, and especially not to the last one.[7] The point, however, should be that in ancient Mediterranean thought the Mediterranean basin *was* treated as a unit connected by the sea. In Plato's *Phaedo*, Socrates says: "the earth is very large, and we inhabit a small portion of it, from Phasis to the pillars of Heracles, and we live around the sea like ants and frogs around a swamp; many other peoples live in many such parts of it."[8] This statement is significant because it reveals that at least some ancient Greeks already conceived of the Mediterranean sea – the swamp, as Plato likens it – and the lands that surrounded it as a unit. Ancient Greek authors who wrote sailing manuals described the connectedness of the Mediterranean and the cities on its coasts in terms of navigation: discussing sailing from harbor to harbor, these texts transport the reader slowly around the different city-states located in the Black Sea, the Red Sea, the Bosporus, the coasts of Europe, Asia, and Libya; in other words, all the areas that Plato includes within the limits that he offers for the world, namely Phasis on the Black Sea and the pillars of Heracles (Straits of Gibraltar) in the western Mediterranean. The notion of a Mediterranean unit, therefore, was not only present in ancient thought, but also observable on the ground (or sea!), and is thus a legitimate subject of study.

Who precisely the subject is in Socrates' statement that "we live around the sea like ants and frogs around a swamp" is unclear and perhaps we should not take it to refer only to Greeks. Certainly ancient Greeks were cognizant of the

---

[5] Horden and Purcell 2000. The authors' responses to reviews and critiques of their project are: Horden and Purcell 2005 and 2006, and Purcell 2005a. At the time of writing, *Liquid Continent*, a sequel to the *Corrupting Sea*, was scheduled to appear in the fall of 2012.

[6] Horden and Purcell 2006; Morris 2005.

[7] Morris 2005: 35–7 discusses the "studied imprecision" with which the Mediterranean is described by Braudel, Horden and Purcell, and the general editors of various journals that publish studies on the Mediterranean.

[8] Plato, *Phaedo* 109b: Ἔτι τοίνυν, ἔφη, πάμμεγά τι εἶναι αὐτό, καὶ ἡμᾶς οἰκεῖν τοὺς μέχρι Ἡρακλείων στηλῶν ἀπὸ Φάσιδος ἐν σμικρῷ τινι μορίῳ, ὥσπερ περὶ τέλμα μύρμηκας ἢ βατράχους περὶ τὴν θάλατταν οἰκοῦντας, καὶ ἄλλους ἄλλοθι πολλοὺς ἐν πολλοῖσι τοιούτοις τόποις οἰκεῖν.

fact that non-Greeks inhabited the same regions as they did. Thus, with some of the earliest writings, such as those of Homer, Hekataios, the lyric poets, and Herodotus, we hear descriptions of the non-Greek populations of the Mediterranean lands. Sailing around the wine-dark sea inevitably brought different groups into contact with each other: seaborne communication, in terms of movement of both people and knowledge, was easy, and land was frequently traversed by both people and ideas. Soldiers, pirates, pilgrims, slaves, athletes, artists, craftsmen, prophets, oracle emissaries, philosophers, law-givers, guest-friends, judges, diplomats, and traders, to mention but a few, traveled throughout the area, and their travels created the connections that linked the Mediterranean lands.

Although Greek perceptions of the ancient Mediterranean are the only ones that survive in discursive form, given the unfortunate fragmentary nature of literature from other Mediterranean populations, non-Greek populations shared the Greek maritime perspective, and perhaps also the Greek notion of the Mediterranean as a unit. The multiethnic landscape of the archaic Mediterranean was created by expeditions – a direct consequence of the maritime outlook of Mediterranean populations – that resulted in countless new city-states along the Mediterranean and Black Sea shores, especially from the ninth to the sixth centuries BC. This kind of immigration, regardless of whether it was forced or peaceful, also created permanent contacts among different groups. Greeks and Phoenicians founded city-states all along the coast of North Africa, Iberia, the south coast of Italy, and on Sardinia, Sicily, and Corsica. A strong Phoenician presence is also attested on Cyprus, the Balearics, and in various cities in the Greek world, such as Kommos on Crete, Eretria, and Athens, whereas Greeks also established settlements in France, all around the Black Sea and the Illyrian coast, and they were present in Phoenician communities in the East.[9] The Etruscans established communities on the Greek island of Lemnos, the northeastern coast of Italy, and had a strong presence in Sardinia and Iberia, while Etruscan city-states in Etruria were hosts to Phoenicians and Greeks.[10] In some cases, city-states were founded jointly by various groups, as for example Pithekoussai, which was probably founded by Phoenicians and Greeks and had a strong Etruscan presence.[11] Even the kingdom of Egypt, which is usually

[9] The bibliography on this subject is vast. I offer here only a few starting points. For Phoenician colonization, see Moscati 1968, Niemeyer 2000, and Aubet 2001. For Greek colonization, see Tsetskhladze and De Angelis 1994, Graham 2001, and Tsetskhladze 1998, 1999, and 2006.

[10] Cristofani 1983; Paoletti and Perna 2002.

[11] Although usually called the first western Greek colony, there is evidence to suggest that Pithekoussai was actually jointly founded by Euboian Greeks and Phoenicians and that Etruscans were present from the very origins of the settlement (Ridgway 1994).

thought to have been more isolated, participated in these movements: Egyptians lived in Athens, and Greek, Phoenician, Carian, and other mercenaries fought in Egyptian armies and were subsequently settled in Egypt.[12] The many settlements founded along the Mediterranean coast were axiomatically multiethnic because they brought into permanent contact the migrant groups with indigenous populations and with each other.

These few examples, though by no means exhaustive, demonstrate the maritime outlook of the various Mediterranean groups and the ease of mobility enabled by the Mediterranean Sea. The islands, promontories, and jutting peninsulas facilitated sailing from port to port, even if dangers were never absent, and the many different groups inhabiting this region could not have existed in isolation from each other. On the contrary, an appropriate vision of the Mediterranean region is one that regards it as a cosmopolitan area at least from the archaic period onwards. Horden and Purcell's recent emphasis on the connectivity that the sea provided to the region, the same one that Socrates describes in the quotation above, has not, however, addressed the issue of how this connectivity affected Mediterranean populations. It is not enough to show that the lands of the Mediterranean were connected. What is important is to move beyond this static image and to shift our attention to the question of how Mediterranean populations changed over time as a result of these interconnections.

This is one of the motivating questions for this book. While this is not the first time that it has been asked, this time the question tackles a different issue, namely, identity construction in the Mediterranean as a whole. More specifically, recent comparative works on the history of Mediterranean populations have identified similarities in their political, religious, and material culture, in addition to their common maritime outlook, discussed above: the groups of this region had similar political structures based around small city-states, similar polytheistic religious systems that were easily translatable among different groups, and artifacts or artistic and architectural styles that comprised a common material culture. Further, these works point out that it was precisely cross-cultural borrowing and adaptation that led to the creation of a common Mediterranean culture. I build upon this scholarship by showing how different groups used this common culture both to mediate among themselves and to construct distinct identities.

Each of these trans-cultural phenomena that characterized the Mediterranean basin played an important role in creating a middle ground in

---

[12] Ionian, Carian, and Phoenician mercenaries were in the service of the Egyptian pharaohs from the seventh century on, as graffiti written by these mercenaries attests. Bernand and Masson 1957; *SEG* 37, 994.

which different groups could coexist. In terms of the political landscape, from the archaic to the Hellenistic periods, Phoenicians, Etruscans, Greeks, and Latins, among others, all had political structures based on small city-states.[13] Each of these groups may have used a different word to describe its own polity, but Hansen's comparative work on the city-state has identified a common definition: a city-state is a self-governing but not necessarily independent, highly institutionalized and centralized micro-state, consisting of one town and its immediate hinterland, settled with a stratified population whose political identity is focused on the city-state itself even though ethnically it is affiliated with the population of neighboring city-states.[14] The similarities among city-state cultures extend even to the administration and types of offices – e.g., councils of elders and voting assemblies – and have led some scholars to argue that the origin of the Greek polis in the archaic period may be found in Phoenician polities and that of the Roman *res publica* in the Oscan and Etruscan communities of the Italian peninsula.[15] The shared understanding of polities in the ancient world also helps explain the joint establishment of new city-states undertaken by various groups, such as the foundation of Pithekoussai, discussed above. The common Mediterranean political structures, therefore, allowed for mediation among different groups. The question remains, however, of how these groups maintained distinct identities while living in multiethnic states and what new political and civic identities they created through their interactions with each other.

In addition to common political structures, ancient Mediterranean populations also had similar religious systems, which played an important role in reaching accommodation among different groups. Religious exchange often involved simple borrowings of sculptural styles for statues of divinities or architectural techniques for temples. At other times, gods themselves were exchanged. Mediterranean pantheons had gods with specific characteristics and functions that made it easy to recognize others' gods, integrate them

---

[13] For the Phoenicians see Moscati 1968, Niemeyer 2000, and Aubet 2001; for the Etruscan city-state see Heurgon 1957, Cristofani 1983, Massa-Pairault 1996, Torelli 2000a and 2000b; for the Greek city-state see the multiple volumes published by the Copenhagen Polis Centre, among which are Hansen and Raaflaub 1995 and 1996, Hansen 1996a, Nielsen 1997, and Hansen 2000a and 2006b; for the Italian city-state see Drews 1981 and Cornell 1991, 1995 and 2000. See also the other essays in Hansen 2000c and 2002, including Larsen 2000 on Neo-Babylonian city-states and Marksteiner 2002 on Lycian city-states.

[14] Hansen 2000a: 19. Greeks called it a polis, the Romans *civitas*, in Oscan it was *touta*, in Etruscan probably *meθlum*, and in Phoenician 'M.

[15] Gschnitzer 1990 and 1993; Cornell 2000; Demand 2004. Contrary opinions do exist. See for example Raaflaub 2004 who questions whether there were Phoenician influences on the Greek polis.

into one's own pantheon, or even create new hybrid divinities in a process called syncretism or hybridization, a popular subject again in recent years.[16] Herodotus – and he is not the only ancient writer who does this – often describes foreign gods in terms of their Greek analogues or provides the Greek translation of their names.[17] Cross-cultural interactions also led to the adoption of foreign gods into one's own pantheon, as is evidenced by the Athenian state's adoption of Thracian Bendis or the Roman introduction of the Phrygian Magna Mater, to name but two examples. Regardless of their hometown or cultic affiliation, patrons could worship in the same sanctuary. For instance, Etruscans and Carthaginians used the temples at Pyrgi, the port of the Etruscan city Caere, and pan-Hellenic sanctuaries like Delphi enjoyed a reputation far beyond the limits of the Greek world and were frequented by non-Greeks: the Lydian king Croesus consulted the oracle, Etruscan city-states built treasuries there, and the Egyptian pharaoh Amasis was the biggest donor when Delphi asked for contributions to rebuild the temple of Apollo after it had burned.[18]

All these examples show that the polytheistic nature of Mediterranean religions with their highly differentiated divinities created a space in which there was a universal religious language shared by the various groups inhabiting this region.[19] Yet, in a recent volume on ancient religions that points out similarities among pantheons and religious practices in this region, the sole essay on Mediterranean religion only goes so far as to say that what ancient religions had in common was the fact that they were in constant contact.[20] Even more surprising is that very few studies have dealt with religion in multiethnic settlements.[21] The questions that I ask in this book focus on religion in cosmopolitan settings: how did groups inhabiting the Mediterranean basin use their common religious universe to mediate among themselves? When and why did certain religious practices acquire particular salience in the self-definition of groups? How were rituals

---

[16] For example, Bonnet and Motte 1999, Porter 2000, Iles Johnston 2004, and De Angelis and Garstad 2006.

[17] In 4.59 Herodotus describes the Scythian gods by using Greek names and in 2.42 and 2.59 he translates the names of Egyptian divinities into Greek (Osiris is Dionysus, Zeus is Ammon, and Isis is Demeter).

[18] Pyrgi: Serra Ridgway 1990. Delphi and Lydia: Herodotus 1.153; Delphi and Egypt: Herodotus 2.180; Delphi and Etruria: Herodotus 1.167 and Strabo 5.1.7 and 5.2.3.

[19] Graf 2004: 3–16.   [20] Iles Johnston 2004; Graf 2004: 14–16.

[21] One exception is De Angelis and Garstad 2006, who contextualize Euhemerus' *Sacred History* in multiethnic Sicily, where syncretistic forces at work among Phoenicio-Punic, Greek, and indigenous populations created a unique pantheon. Another is Scholtz 2002/2003 and his projected work, entitled "Goddess at the Margins: Greek Religion between Cultures, across Boundaries," which focuses on religious mediation in multiethnic sites.

conditioned and shaped by the multiethnic nature of the space in which they were conducted?

The connectedness of the ancient Mediterranean is also evident in the material culture that circulated in this region. Artifacts and styles traveled widely and were adopted by various populations in the Mediterranean. For example, Egyptian scarabs are found throughout the Mediterranean in Punic, Phoenician, Etruscan, Greek, and other local contexts. This commodity was traded and, as its popularity increased across various cultures, it became part of a common Mediterranean material culture, spawning local workshops that emerged to produce scarabs on Cyprus and Rhodes, among other places.[22] If we consider a different example, namely, the distribution of Phoenician metal bowls or ivories, it is clear that these circulated throughout the Mediterranean outside the orbit of Phoenician settlements: they are found in non-Phoenician contexts in Iberia, Italy, Sardinia, and mainland Greece, among other regions. Just as in the case of Egyptian scarabs, local, non-Phoenician workshops also existed that produced ivory and metal goods in the style of their Phoenician originals.[23] These examples of the Mediterranean-wide distribution of artifacts and commodities, which could be easily supplemented with other cases, suggest that there existed a common material culture that could be used as a means of communication among Mediterranean populations. Yet, despite the existence of a common material culture, scarab workshops did not exist everywhere, and Phoenician ivories and metalwork were almost certainly popular primarily among elite circles. In other words, specific objects acquired particular importance for some people in certain places at given times and could become indicators of identities.[24] I am interested in examining instances both when artifacts signified identities and when they were used in processes of mediation.

Mediterranean identities

By this point, I hope to have demonstrated that in the archaic and classical periods the Mediterranean region was cosmopolitan inasmuch as there were permanent and extensive interactions among the groups inhabiting this region, which resulted in structural similarities among Mediterranean

---

[22] Kaczmarczyk and Hedges 1983; Gorton 1996.
[23] Moscati 1988: 436, 440, 443, 542–3, 547; Aubet 1971.
[24] See also Duplouy 2006: 151–83 who discusses the circulation of *orientalia* in elite circles and the importance of these objects as symbols of social identity, albeit in the Early Iron Age, an earlier period than the one studied here.

populations. I now turn to a consideration of how these groups used their common Mediterranean background – politics, religion, material culture, and maritime perspective – to define themselves and create new identities. Like Mediterranean Studies, identity has become an increasingly popular topic among scholars, resulting in a copious bibliography on identity in the ancient world. Yet, despite the ever-expanding list of titles that contain the word identity, the subject is rarely approached from a Mediterranean perspective and usually involves the study of ethnic identity, to the exclusion of other types of identity. I hope to remedy this by examining here various kinds of identities – civic, religious, linguistic, and ethnic, among others – throughout the Mediterranean.

It is important to note at the outset that the general analytical category of identity is a modern construct. Nonetheless, identity was part of social reality in the ancient Mediterranean: individuals and groups experienced different kinds of identities subjectively, whether these were self-representations or imposed by outsiders, and these identities conditioned some of their choices and decisions. While the use of categories of identity – religious, civic, ethnic, etc. – to analyze ancient societies represents the point of view of the modern observer, ancient social actors themselves did proclaim various kinds of identities that often converged with and at other times differed from modern ones. These two perspectives, usually discussed in studies on ancient identity or ethnicity, correspond to the anthropological distinction between etic (externally perceived) and emic (internally perceived) categories.[25] In other words, emic perspectives are based on the conceptual schemes and categories that are meaningful to the members of the group under study, whereas etic perspectives are based on the conceptual schemes and categories that are meaningful to the contemporary community of researchers.

An instance when the emic and etic classifications diverge concerns the names of the Mediterranean groups under study here – Greek, Etruscan, and Phoenician, among others. It is instructive first to point out that none of these groups used these names to describe themselves. Phoenician is a descriptor that Greeks used for the people who lived on the Levantine coast, and it has been adopted by modern scholars for the population of this area usually from the Iron Age onwards.[26] By contrast, although written

---

[25] The terms emic and etic were originally coined by Pike 1954, a linguistic anthropologist, and were subsequently taken up by cultural anthropologists in particular. The papers in Malkin 2001 are most useful in discussing how the etic and emic points of view pertain to studies of ancient identity. For similar discussions of these perspectives see J. Hall 1997: 18–19 and 2003: 23–4, and Ruby 2006: 33–4.

[26] Niemeyer 2000: 92–3 discusses the use of the name 'Phoenician' in scholarship.

sources produced by the Phoenicians are not many, they indicate clearly
that the Phoenicians identified themselves sometimes as Canaanites but
more frequently in terms of their individual city-states.[27] Similarly, Greek
is the Latin name given to a specific group of Greeks, called Graikoi, and is
used today to describe collectively all those who called themselves Hellenes,
at one point or another.[28] The name Etruscan derives from the Roman
name, Etrusci, given to the Mediterranean population that Dionysios of
Halikarnassos claimed called itself Rassena.[29] The name Rasna is, in fact,
attested in Etruscan epigraphic sources, where it seems to designate the
people of Etruria.[30] The emic categories in this example are Canaanite (or
Sidonian, Tyrian, etc.), Hellene, and Rasna, while the equivalent etic ones
are Phoenician, Greek, and Etruscan. To avoid confusion I will use emic
categories when referring to ancient viewpoints and etic ones when talking
about modern perspectives.

This particular example of the emic and etic categories has two important
implications. First, the image of a cosmopolitan Mediterranean presented
thus far needs to be complicated even more because the etic terms Phoenicians, Etruscans, Greeks, Iberians, etc., are misleading. They suggest that
these groups were monolithic cultures whereas the fact that Phoenicians
identified themselves mostly in terms of their city-states of origin – their
civic identities – as did other Mediterranean populations indicates that there
was diversity within these groups. In fact, each of these different cultures
had an incredible variety of dialects, scripts, gods, rituals, artistic styles, etc.
Joining a growing body of literature that insists on emphasizing the variety
of changing and competing identities available to members of these groups,
this book studies cross-cultural interactions in the Mediterranean in the
broadest sense possible.[31] To avoid the facile binary opposition between
Greeks and others, I examine the construction of identity among Mediterranean groups and, in particular, among different groups of Greeks.

Such simple distinctions between Greeks and barbarians are typical of
past scholarship. In part, they were motivated by intellectual currents that
privileged Greek civilization as the foundation of Western civilization,
appropriated Greek and Latin literature as "the Classics," and assumed
that "Hellenization," namely, the westward spread of the values of Greek
civilization, was due to the fact that the indigenous populations of the

[27] Moscati 1968: 3–4.
[28] Ancient sources (ps.-Apollodorus 1.7.3 and Stephanos of Byzantion s.v. Γραικός among others) suggest this group perhaps originally lived in Thessaly.
[29] Dionysios of Halikarnassos 1.25.   [30] Massa-Pairault 1996: 41–2.
[31] Malkin 2001; Dougherty and Kurke 2003.

Mediterranean lands were empty vessels waiting to be filled with the superior Greek culture. These problematic views stripped Mediterranean populations of their own indigenous cultures and ignored the dynamic nature of cultural exchange. In the last three decades, however, colonial, post-colonial, and cultural studies have brought a welcome shift away from these monolithic perspectives.[32] The result is a proliferation of works in ancient history and archaeology that reconsider the interaction between Greeks and others, especially in colonial contexts, and that study non-Greek Mediterranean populations in their own right.[33] These new studies emphasize overall the connections and interactions between colonizers and colonized in the ancient Mediterranean and, borrowing from the language used in colonial and post-colonial works in other fields, speak of the hybridity and creolization that results from permanent modes of interaction between groups.[34] While these works have opened up the path for studying modes of interaction between (usually) two groups, not much attention has been paid to modes of interaction among many groups. Binary oppositions are still current even as our culture of globalization is breaking down barriers and national frontiers.

The persistence of the Greek/barbarian dichotomy has been compounded by the fact that most studies on identity in antiquity have focused on ethnic identity, traditionally thought to be constituted by opposition to other ethnicities.[35] Most of the scholarship on Greek ethnicity, therefore, has concentrated on binary distinctions drawn between Greeks and others.[36]

[32] For example, Bourdieu 1977, Foucault 1978, Said 1978, A. D. Smith 1986, Spivak 1988, Anderson 1991, Bhabha 1994.

[33] A small sample of works that study the interactions of Greeks and others in colonial contexts are: Doescœdres 1990, Cartledge 1993, Tsetskhladze and De Angelis 1994, Tsetskhladze 1998, 1999, and 2006, Lyons and Papadopoulos 2002, Dietler and López-Ruiz 2009. The literature on non-Greek Mediterranean populations is difficult to summarize. References to these works are found throughout this book. A small but important and often controversial subset of these works sought to show that Greek culture, too, was altered by extensive interactions with non-Greeks, often reversing the model of "Hellenization" by assuming that the younger Greek civilization was an empty vessel filled by the older Egyptian and Near Eastern civilizations: Bernal 1987 and 1991; Burkert 1992; M. L. West 1997.

[34] For example, Van Dommelen 1997, Lyons and Papadopoulos 2002, Antonaccio 2001 and 2003, Malkin 2004.

[35] Barth 1969: 9–38. Barth's famous essay considers ethnicity as a socially constructed and subjectively perceived concept and defines an ethnic group not by describing the cultural content of the group but rather by identifying its ascriptive boundaries. The emphasis on drawing boundaries between different ethnic groups led to the understanding that ethnic identity can only be constituted by opposition to other ethnicities.

[36] Here I mention a small sample of books. Even their titles show clearly the binary opposition between self and other: E. Hall 1989; Cartledge 1993; Cohen 2000; T. Harrison 2002; J. Hall 2002; Mitchell 2007.

Further, the emphasis on ethnicity derives not only from modern concerns with multicultural societies or ethnic conflicts but also from the trajectory of scholarship on identity in antiquity. Hall's two seminal books on ethnic identity in the Greek world were so influential that most of the subsequent research on identity has likewise focused on ethnic identity.[37] However, the fact that Mediterranean groups usually identified themselves in terms of their city of origin suggests that civic identity was at times more salient than ethnic identity.[38] The second lesson, therefore, to be learned from the divergences between our modern categories of group identity and the ancients' own perceptions of their identity, as others have also shown, is that ethnic identity was neither the sole nor always the most important mode of self-representation.[39] Here, I investigate the construction of various collective identities – civic, regional, religious, social, ethnic, etc. – available to social actors in the ancient Mediterranean.

There are a few more observations to make about Hall's work on ethnic identity in order to clarify my own approach. Recognizing what a watershed moment the Persian Wars were for Hellenic identity, Hall proposed that the construction of ethnic identity before the wars was "aggregative" – sub-Hellenic groups (Dorians, Aeolians, Ionians, etc.) defined themselves by recognizing similarities, mainly by invoking descent from a common ancestor – whereas after the wars it was "oppositional" – Greeks defined themselves through opposition to the Persians.[40] Hall's further distinction between the "aggregative" and the "oppositional" modes of self-definition is that the former was based throughout history on ethnic criteria, which Hall defines as putative notions of common descent and territory, while the latter, though initially also conceived in ethnic terms, gradually came to be defined according to cultural criteria.[41]

---

[37] J. Hall 1997 and 2002; Malkin 2001; Derks and Roymans 2009.

[38] See also Morgan 2003: 10–15.

[39] Ruby 2006: 48–54 in a theoretical piece on the study of ethnicity in antiquity insists that there were different levels of collective identities available to ancient Mediterranean populations. Modern scholarship on ethnicity has also discussed the formation of individual sub-Hellenic identities, as for example McInerney 1999 and Larson 2007.

[40] J. Hall 1997: 47–8. For J. Hall, a myth of common descent and a connection with common territory are the most important characteristics that distinguish ethnic groups from other social entities, at least in the case of ancient Greece. Hall considered six different characteristics that distinguish an ethnic group, first offered by A. D. Smith 1986: 22–30. These are a collective name, a common myth of descent, a shared history, a distinctive shared culture, an association with a specific territory, and a sense of communal solidarity. Ruby 2006: 37–46 considers a collective name to be one of the defining characteristics of an ethnic group together with a myth of common descent.

[41] J. Hall 2002.

Hall's two successive modes of self-definition have been criticized because of the rigidity implicit in claiming that one mode replaced the previous one without considering the possibility that the two modes may have operated simultaneously. Malkin has argued that the "oppositional" model must have already existed before the Persian Wars either in isolated instances, such as when Ionians had to face Lydians or Persians, or when Greeks were in constant contact with non-Greek ethnic groups, while founding colonies, trading, and traveling throughout the Mediterranean. In these cases, the particular group of Greeks in question would have defined themselves as such not only because they recognized similarities, but also because they found themselves in opposition to foreigners, like Egyptians, Etruscans, Phoenicians, Iberians, etc. At the same time, the "oppositional" model must have operated concurrently with the "aggregative" one in the negotiations of sub-Hellenic identity. The Ionians of Asia Minor, for example, distinguished themselves from the Dorians and Aeolians also living there.[42]

At the heart of this debate lies also the issue of when Hellenicity emerged. Hall has pointed out many times that the term Hellas originally designated only the region of Thessaly in central Greece, but by the end of the seventh century BC it came to include the whole of the Greek world. Similarly, the term Hellenes designated an inclusive group of Greeks only by the beginning of the sixth century BC, at the earliest.[43] Further, based on his views that Hellenicity was defined culturally only after the Persian Wars, Hall has argued that before the fifth century BC there were many Greek cultures and thus no overall Greek ethnic identity.[44] He has reiterated this view elsewhere, adding that early Greeks coming into contact with non-Greeks throughout the Mediterranean could not have had a common Hellenic consciousness, partly because of the internal diversity of Greek dialects, religions, etc., and partly because their individual experiences varied from one location to the other.[45] Malkin has adopted a completely different view on this issue, arguing that while different groups of Greeks had varied experiences in different parts of the Mediterranean, there was always a virtual center in Delphi that held them all together and contributed to the emergence of a Hellenic identity.[46] Moreover, according to Malkin's most recent work, a sense of Greek identity emerged in the archaic period precisely when Greeks found themselves far apart from other Greeks. The process of colonization linked mother-cities to their colonies and engendered the creation of even more independent settlements, thereby constructing a network of Greek

---

[42] Malkin 2001: 1–23.   [43] J. Hall 2003: 27–30 and 2004: 37–8.   [44] J. Hall 2003: 30–2.
[45] J. Hall 2002: 90–124 and 2004.   [46] Malkin 2003a and 2007.

city-states, which resembled each other more closely than their foreign neighbors.[47] For the purposes of this book, which concentrates on the period between the end of the seventh and the middle of the fourth centuries BC, I follow Hall in accepting that an inclusive group of Hellenes existed by this period and that the term Hellas encompassed the whole of the Greek world. I also aim to contribute further to this debate by showing that a sense of Hellenic identity, not necessarily defined in ethnic terms, but rather in cultural ones, was often fostered early on in individual settlements that hosted a diversity of Greeks.

This book, therefore, studies the construction of civic, religious, linguistic, social, and ethnic identities because, I argue, an individual's and a group's identity was a conscious statement of self-perception, contingent upon the circumstances: in antiquity, identity was defined at times in terms of common descent, sometimes along linguistic lines, other times according to religious traditions, and often in political terms. Moreover, it studies the construction of identity from a Mediterranean perspective. Emphasizing Mediterranean connectivity highlights that with the creation of new communities founded upon common Mediterranean political, religious, and maritime perspectives, new collective identities were also articulated. By adopting such a wide perspective it is possible to see how different groups inhabiting the region managed their interactions and how they forged new visions of a world of which they were all a part, at the same time crafting new identities for themselves.

Methodology

To study identity construction in the ancient Mediterranean I examine the cultural dimension of trade networks, one of the mechanisms that connected the different regions of this area. More specifically, this book focuses on Greek commercial settlements, which the ancient Greeks called emporia. As the nodes of trade networks, these settlements had the specific purpose of facilitating cross-cultural trade and gave rise to interactions among different ethnic groups. In an essay that conceived of the Mediterranean as being laden with emporia, Gras gave the following definition for an emporion: "When one says emporion, one means an ethnic and cultural encounter that is socially successful because it serves economic purposes."[48] Socially

---

[47] Malkin 2011.

[48] Gras 1993: 106: "qui dit emporion dit donc confrontation ethnique et culturelle, réussie socialement dans un but économique."

successful, multiethnic emporia were permanent settlements where different groups were in contact long enough to leave substantial traces for a modern historian to examine. Encounters among various groups in emporia had profound effects on both host societies and trader communities and led to the articulation of new collective identities. The processes that created new identities were not limited to emporia. The connectedness of the Mediterranean meant that ideas traveled as quickly as people did. What happened in emporia did not stay there; rather it had echoes locally through relations with the hinterland, regionally along the specific trade networks that linked emporia, and in the Mediterranean as a whole. Thus, emporia provide a particularly useful prism through which to study the construction of identity in the ancient Mediterranean and how Mediterranean populations changed because of the connectedness that the sea afforded to this region.

In order to present as comprehensive a view of the negotiation of identity as possible, I examine five different Greek emporia located in geographically diverse locations: Emporion in Iberia, Gravisca in Etruria, Naukratis in Egypt, Pistiros in Thrace, and Peiraieus in Attica. Such a range has the advantage of treating the Mediterranean as a whole, not only geographically but also culturally, because it enables a study of the interactions of several Mediterranean populations, including Greeks, Thracians, Iberians, Etruscans, Egyptians, and Phoenicians. Greek emporia located in non-Greek lands brought specific groups of Greeks into contact with non-Greeks, and vice versa. Not only was the population of emporia very often multiethnic, but also the Greeks residing in emporia usually came from different poleis. Thus, the study of emporia allows an investigation of cross-cultural interactions among different groups of Greeks.

The temporal parameters of this study are determined by the dates when the specific emporia under consideration were established and popular; more precisely, the book focuses on the period from the end of the seventh to the middle of the fourth centuries BC. It is not surprising that these dates coincide with the period when Mediterranean populations expanded their horizons by planting settlements throughout the Mediterranean basin. This period was a formative one because these population movements made the region increasingly connected. It is particularly profitable to examine cross-cultural interactions during these centuries, which represent the most intense stages of connectedness.

The approach is interdisciplinary in that the sources examined are literary, epigraphic, and archaeological. Studies of identity in the ancient Mediterranean have concentrated almost exclusively either on written or on archaeological sources. Hall, for example, argues that ethnic identity is discursively constructed through genealogical myths. He privileges, therefore, literary sources in his studies and discredits the use of archaeology in trying to identify ethnic groups, although he accepts that groups did actively use artifacts to proclaim an ethnic identity once they had already constructed it discursively.[49] In contrast, Jones has argued that material culture is an active dimension of social practice with meanings that vary through time depending on an artifact's history, the position of social agents who used it, and the immediate context of its use. As such, material culture both contributes to the formulation of ethnic identity and is structured by it.[50] Others have also argued for the importance of archaeology in understanding the relevance of written texts and the connectivity of the Mediterranean, especially because archaeological sources are sometimes the only ones that survive to shed light on cross-cultural interactions.[51]

Here, I examine both written and material evidence available from each emporion under consideration in order to investigate the nature of interactions among different groups. While I privilege literary sources in discussing how different groups identified themselves, material evidence is an indispensible part of the discussion. In the first place, although it is difficult to discern expressions of identity in the material record when no textual evidence is available, the examination of archaeological evidence nonetheless provides important insights into cross-cultural interactions in the Mediterranean. For instance, it is possible to show the distribution and adoption of certain artifacts across the Mediterranean, indicate how material culture changed when groups came into contact, and discuss what aspects of it were used to express certain identities at specific moments in time when these identities acquired particular salience. In the second place, taking into consideration the material record allows the silent, and often non-Greek, populations of the Mediterranean to speak through artifacts, if not through texts. This is especially important since most of the written sources at the historian's disposal were produced by Greeks.

A working definition of emporia

An explanation is due of what emporia were since these settlements provide the body of evidence for this study. One of the problems that presents itself immediately when studying emporia is the fact that ancient authors are

---

[49] J. Hall 1997: 111–42 and 2002: 19–24.   [50] S. Jones 1997: 116–19.
[51] Morgan 2001: 75–112; Lyons and Papadopoulos 2002; Morris 2005: 46; Ruby 2006: 54–9; Antonaccio 2009.

not forthcoming in the information they give about this type of site and, consequently, modern scholars have found it difficult to provide a working definition for them.[52] This is not as detrimental to the study of emporia as it may seem at first glance; as a point of comparison, it is worth noting that it has also been notoriously difficult to define the polis based on what ancient authors wrote about it and yet studies on the polis or individual poleis continue to be at the forefront of the discipline. Witness the work of Hansen and various scholars brought together by the Copenhagen Polis Centre. For both emporia and poleis there are the further complications of how to translate these terms and whether the modern words used – city-state for polis and port-of-trade, commercial settlement, or trading post, for emporion – are coterminous with the ancient Greek words. Discussions of the applicability of the term city-state to describe the Greek polis and other polities found at various periods throughout the world abound, and I refer the reader to them.[53] Heuristic concepts like that of the city-state are useful as long as they reflect the mentality, to the extent it can be discerned, of the ancient Greeks who lived in poleis. As a translation, city-state corresponds with what we think the Greek polis was since it implies a self-governing, urban center.

The heuristic tool that has been employed to explain the phenomenon of Greek emporia is Polanyi's ideal "port-of-trade." Polanyi, an economic anthropologist, defined a port-of-trade in early societies as a coastal or river-ine location, situated at the interface of two groups with differing economic organizations, whose neutrality was an absolute prerequisite for its existence and operation. The port-of-trade was an instrument of long distance trade that enabled the exchange of goods under pre-market conditions, that is, fixed prices, accountancy, etc., through the mediation of the local inhab-itants who, according to Polanyi, were natives.[54] Greek emporia are often assimilated into the Polanyian port-of-trade, despite the fact that they do not fit the ascriptive criteria for ports-of-trade: they were neither neutral nor peripheral since they were self-governing, even if they happened to be dependent on one or more powers at a given time; they were not located in the margins between states; the trading partners' economic systems were similar; and, since they were poleis, as I will show, they had non-economic functions.[55]

[52] The next three paragraphs are reproduced from Demetriou 2011 with the permission of *Historia.*
[53] Hansen 2000c: 597–609 defends the use of city-state. Marcus and Feinman 1998: 7–9 provide a critique of the term, especially as it applies to non-Greek polities.
[54] Polanyi 1963.
[55] Figueira 1984. Möller 2001b insists on the validity of the term port-of-trade, and, more generally, Weberian ideal types, to describe Greek emporia, even though she has modified

The notion of the port-of-trade is problematic to use for Greek emporia, and the term does not translate accurately the word emporion. LSJ defines the word emporion as a trading-station, mart, factory, a market center in a region without a polis, or the district in a polis where merchants resorted. These definitions do not stack up well against more recent studies on emporia.[56] The first attempts to define an emporion based on the ancient sources took place within the context of a series of seminars organized in Bordeaux from 1989–1991, which resulted in a volume of collected essays on ancient Greek emporia.[57] These essays range from the semantics of the term emporion in the classical period,[58] Greek geographers,[59] and Strabo,[60] to regional studies of emporia,[61] specific case-studies,[62] and an essay about the role of emporia in the ancient economy,[63] among others.[64] The essays on the semantic field of the term emporion agree that the word always indicated a location, usually maritime, where commercial exchange took place.[65] Bresson's essay concluded that an emporion was either an administered institution that was part of a polis, or any location where commerce took place, whether a polis, a village, a fort, or a settlement devoted to facilitating exchange.[66] In this way, an opposition was set up between communities that had an emporion and communities that were emporia.

Hansen subsequently challenged this dichotomy and offered the best analysis yet of the uses and meaning of the word emporion in the archaic and classical periods.[67] By comparing the settlements ancient Greek authors classified as emporia, the language used to classify them, and what we know about these settlements from other literary and archaeological sources, Hansen was able to describe emporia.[68] First, an emporion of the archaic and classical periods was a coastal location that enabled long-distance and

---

several points in Polanyi's description of the port-of-trade, since they do not fit the example of Naukratis.

[56] Faraguna 2002 reviews recent scholarship on ancient Greek trade and ancient Greek emporia.

[57] Bresson and Rouillard 1993.   [58] Casevitz 1993.   [59] Counillon 1993.

[60] Étienne 1993; Rouillard 1993.   [61] Perreault 1993; Laronde 1993.

[62] Duchêne 1993.   [63] Zaccagnini 1993.

[64] Teixidor 1993; Garlan 1993; Gras 1993; Descat 1993. The collection also includes a short conclusion summarizing the results of the different papers: Lévêque 1993.

[65] Casevitz 1993; Counillon 1993; Étienne 1993; Rouillard 1993.

[66] Bresson 1993: 215–17, 223–4 and 2002: 475–505. Wilson 1997: 199–207 accepted Bresson's distinction between communities that were emporia and ones that had emporia and argued that in the archaic period an emporion was defined as simply any community involved in commerce, whereas by the fourth century the word indicated a geographically delineated community, with its own administrators and juridical apparatus.

[67] Hansen 1997 and 2006a, which is an updated version of Hansen 1997.

[68] Hansen 2006a: 31.

cross-cultural trade.[69] This definition is not far from that given by Bresson and his collaborators, even if Bresson's distinction is controversial.[70] Second, the few sites that ancient sources say *had* an emporion were located on the Greek peninsula, whereas sites that ancient sources say *were* emporia are all foundations located in non-Greek lands. So, for example, Athens, Corinth, and Byzantion, among others, are said to have had an emporion, whereas Borysthenes, Emporion, and Naukratis, are called emporia.[71] Third, the settlements that ancient texts say were emporia are known from other sources to have been also poleis. Ancient Greeks must have described poleis as emporia when they considered their commercial character as their most important aspect, even though these poleis, just as their counterparts on the mainland, probably only had an emporion. Finally, the sites described as both emporia and poleis were actually dependent on another authority. Naukratis, for instance, was subject to the Egyptian authorities, and Galepsos, Oisyme, and Phagres were under Thasos' control.[72] Given these details that define emporia, it seems that the distinction the sources make between a site that was an emporion and a site that had an emporion simply reflects the ancients' understanding of the development of the Greek world rather than an actual difference between two types of emporia: they called emporia the newer settlements founded in the western Mediterranean and Black Sea, whose most important function was commercial, whereas when referring to the older Greek world of the Aegean circle they called an emporion the specified space in a polis dedicated to commercial exchange.

When referring to the emporia founded in non-Greek lands, a better English translation is commercial settlement, since the term captures the permanent and political nature of these poleis, which were called emporia. This expression, however, does not describe well sites like Peiraieus, the emporion of Athens, or the emporia of Corinth, since in these instances emporion refers to the actual space dedicated to cross-cultural trade within

---

[69] Scholars often mention the existence of inland emporia, even though of the thirty-one named sites ancient sources called emporia only one, Pistiros, in Thrace, has been identified as an inland emporion (Velkov and Domaradzka 1994; Hansen 2006a: 20–4). Various scholars, including myself, have instead located Pistiros on the North Aegean coast. If this is correct, it leaves no examples of inland emporia. See Bravo and A. S. Chankowski 1999 and Demetriou 2010a.

[70] Bresson and Rouillard 1993.

[71] Athens: e.g., Demosthenes *Against Apatourios, Against Phormio, Against Lakritos, Against Dionysodoros*; Corinth: Thucydides 1.13; Byzantion: Theopompos *FGrH* 115 F62; Borysthenes on the Black Sea: Herodotus 4.17; Emporion in Iberia: ps.-Skylax 2; Naukratis in Egypt: Herodotus 2.178–9.

[72] Naukratis: Herodotus 2.178–9; Galepsos, Oisyme, and Phagres: ps.-Skylax 67 and Bresson 1993: 202.

the larger polis. It is better to use the Greek word emporion, which can be defined as the location where commercial exchange took place in coastal, self-governing poleis. When situated in areas inhabited by both Greeks and non-Greeks, these poleis were dependent on a Greek or foreign power, whereas when located in the Aegean circle, they were independent. The emporion's main function of facilitating cross-cultural trade attracted a multiethnic population, which, in turn, necessitated the presence of special sanctuaries, laws, and customs.

As scholars have suggested, the concept of an emporion can be used as a heuristic tool to understand better some Greek settlements not called emporia by ancient sources but which nonetheless fit the definition of emporion just provided.[73] After all, ancient authors classify as emporia only thirty-one named sites and several unnamed ones, a number that seems unusually low if we consider that there existed over a thousand poleis in the archaic and classical periods, most of them coastal, and most reliant on trade.[74] Extreme caution is required when undertaking such an enterprise because the word emporion has been used indiscriminately to describe any settlement that engaged in commerce, whether or not it had the characteristics mentioned in the definition above and whether or not it was Greek. In the ancient Greek mind some Carthaginian, Phoenician, Egyptian, and possibly Arabian, Persian, and Illyrian settlements were sufficiently like Greek emporia that the ancient Greeks used the term freely to describe them, just as they applied the term polis to many non-Greek city-states in the Mediterranean.[75] For possibly the same reason, modern scholars have applied the term emporion to many non-Greek settlements that had a commercial function, even though they do not fulfill the definition of emporia provided above. As examples, I mention the Phoenician sites on the Andalusian coast of Spain, which have been dubbed emporia though they were neither multiethnic nor self-governing,[76] and Al-Mina, a port on

---

[73] Hansen 2006a: 1, 26–7, 31; Gras 1993: 103–11.

[74] Hansen 2006a: 2–3. Over 100 emporia are known from the Hellenistic and Roman periods. The total number of poleis attested from the archaic to the Hellenistic periods is about 1,500 (Hansen 2006b: 31).

[75] Carthaginian: ps.-Skylax 1 (unnamed), Thucydides 7.50 (Neapolis on the coast of North Africa); Phoenician: Herodotus 4.152 (Tartessos in Spain), Xenophon, *Anabasis* 1.4.6 (Myriandros in Syria); Egyptian: Aristotle, *Economics* 1352a-b3 (Kanobos). The Arabian (Herodotus 3.5), Persian (Aristotle, *Economics* 1346a), and Illyrian (ps.-Skylax 24) emporia are all unnamed and no details are given as to who founded them.

[76] Niemeyer 2000: 99 and 101; Aubet 2001. Part of the problem is that there is no Phoenician word that designates the Phoenician equivalent of the Greek emporion. Teixidor 1993 discusses the meaning of the word *mahuza*, which comes close to the Greek emporion.

the Levantine coast, which has been called a Greek emporion, although the evidence suggests at most a small and temporary Greek presence.[77]

Despite these instances when sites have been called emporia without enough attention to the actual implications of the Greek word, other settlements have been better understood by keeping in mind the definition of an emporion given above. In the Aegean circle there were many inland poleis that had a separate commercial harbor, whose situation can be likened to Athens and its port, Peiraieus. Kolophon, Kythera, and Priene, for example, were inland poleis in Ionia that had on the coast the ports of Notion, Skandeia, and Naulochon, respectively. By analogy to the Athenian situation, where the emporion was only a part of Peiraieus, one can speculate that these ports on the coast of Ionia also had a specially demarcated emporion.[78] Further, like Peiraieus, Notion, Naulochon, and Skandeia developed into urban centers. Yet, while the Ionian ports eventually became self-governing poleis dependent on the inland city they served, Peiraieus remained throughout its history an Athenian deme.[79] Still, it was probably the same forces, such as their importance as commercial centers and their wealth, which led to the political development of the three Ionian ports and gave Peiraieus much more independence in its administration than other Athenian demes. In the non-Greek lands of the Mediterranean, there are examples of multiethnic, self-governing poleis dedicated to facilitating cross-cultural trade, which fit the definition of an emporion and can thus legitimately be called emporia. Gravisca in Etruria, for example, bears striking similarities to known emporia, among which are Naukratis and Pistiros, as will be discussed in more detail in the chapter on Gravisca.[80]

Before describing the emporia that this book focuses on, a note on the archaeology of emporia is in order. First, emporia overall have not attracted as many excavations as other poleis of the Mediterranean. Second, it used to be the case that historians distinguished between two different types of colonies: those with an extensive hinterland and a focus on agriculture,

---

[77] Boardman 1990: 186 considers Al-Mina a Greek emporion, whereas Graham 1986: 51–65 and Perreault 1993: 62–8 have pointed out that archaeologically the Greek presence in Al-Mina was minimal.

[78] The emporion in Peiraieus was clearly demarcated by *horoi* (*IG* I³ 1101).

[79] Hansen 2006a: 26–7. Rubinstein 2004: 1077–80 and 1089–93 discusses the relationship between Notion and Kolophon, and Naulochon and Priene, as well as literary and epigraphic evidence indicating that Notion and Naulochon were poleis and not simply ports. Shipley 2004: 583–4 presents the evidence for the relationship between Skandeia and Kythera and the eventual emergence of Skandeia as a polis.

[80] Torelli 1988: 181; Cornell 1995: 109–12; Hansen 2006a: 2.

which were called *apoikiai* (and, therefore, poleis) and those with no hinter-land and a commercial focus, which were named emporia but not poleis.[81] One expected, therefore, emporia to have a smaller size than other settle-ments and thus to be detectable in archaeology. In fact, various foundations on the coast of France, such as Agathe and Olbia, have been called emporia because of their small size.[82] A closer look at these settlements, however, shows not only that they did exploit their hinterland but also that they were actually larger sites than originally thought.[83] Further, the assumption that a hinterland implied a polis is wrong; as Hansen states, many poleis did not actually possess a hinterland.[84] More importantly, almost all the empo-ria of the archaic and classical periods were poleis that had an emporion. This means that in theory one would expect the size of emporia to vary as widely as poleis, which range from 8 km^2 to 8,000 km^2.[85] As Hansen says, there is no reason to superimpose the archaeological distinction between urban centers with a hinterland and nucleated settlements without one on an already artificial distinction between a polis and an emporion.[86]

What can be detected in the archaeological record are the special charac-teristics that one would expect to find in an emporion, a site dedicated to facilitating cross-cultural trade. For example, an excellent harbor, a greater variety of pottery, and a large number of transport amphorae are all ele-ments in the material record that are more typical of emporia than other types of settlements. Sometimes dedications in sanctuaries might reflect the multiethnic nature of the population, attested in the various languages and different Greek dialects used for graffiti. Sometimes patterns emerge from pottery distributions that allow the historian to make an inference about the make-up of the population. One example discussed in the chapter on Naukratis is the exclusive presence of one type of Samian pottery, which can

---

[81] The tendency to categorize new settlements into agrarian *apoikiai* or commercial emporia has a long history: Gwynn 1918; Lepore 1968 and 2000: 22–3; Vallet 1968: 136–40, Tandy 1997. The question of whether a settlement was an emporion or an *apoikia* has often been asked without resolution. Pithekoussai, for example, has suffered especially from this question. See Ridgway 1984: 122–4; 1992: 107–9; Greco 1994; and D'Agostino 1999: 207, 212, 216. Some scholars see emporia as a first step in the development of a polis: Morel 1975 and Petropoulos 2005: 75–125. More recent scholarship has challenged the distinction between agrarian vs. commercial settlements. De Angelis 2002, for example, argues that agriculture and trade were complementary and that agriculture was central to Greek colonies as a basis of trade. See also the next chapter and Demetriou 2011.

[82] Lepore 1968; Vallet 1968: 136–40.

[83] Nickels 1982; Bats 1982; Clavel-Lévêque 1983a; Benoit 1985. See also Purcell 2005b: 120 and n. 11, my discussion in the next chapter, and Demetriou 2011.

[84] Hansen 2006a: 33 mentions Tarrha on Crete as an example.

[85] Hansen 2000b: 155–6.   [86] Hansen 2006a: 32–4.

be found only on Samos and in the Samian sanctuary of Hera in Naukratis. Such interpretations, however, can be made only on a site-to-site basis.

With these constraints in mind, the emporia I have chosen to investigate here fall into various categories. Four of them, namely Emporion, Gravisca, Naukratis, and Pistiros are all Greek emporia founded in non-Greek lands. With the exception of Gravisca, the other three emporia are named as such in ancient literary and/or epigraphic sources. I have included Gravisca in this book not only because other scholars have identified this site as an emporion, but also because, as will become clear from subsequent chapters, the material and epigraphic evidence corresponds to what we know from other emporia. Gravisca, therefore, contributes in our understanding of emporia as much as the site itself is understood better in being discussed as an emporion. Naukratis, Gravisca, and Pistiros are also clearly poleis that were dependent on foreign powers in their region. Naukratis was controlled by the Egyptian authorities, Gravisca by the Etruscan city-state of Tarquinia, Pistiros by Thracian dynasts, and Emporion might have been dependent on its mother city, Massalia. Regardless of the fact that these settlements were dependent on others, they were all self-governing. The fifth settlement considered here is Peiraieus, whose emporion provides a wealth of information on the presence of non-Greeks in a Greek emporion. No other place in the Mediterranean furnishes the same abundance of evidence for the archaic and classical periods. As such, it provides an important counterpoint to the other four emporia and an indispensible part of the study undertaken here.

Trade networks, in their capacity as vehicles for the multidirectional mobility of people, goods, and ideas, are particularly suitable for studying the construction of identity. Emporia, the nodes of these trade networks, connected the Mediterranean on three levels: the local – as redistribution centers that had contacts with their immediate surroundings –, the regional – as nodes on regional trade networks –, and the pan-Mediterranean – as export and import centers. In addition, their multiethnic nature makes them a perfect locus in which to examine the history of cross-cultural interactions and the effects that these exchanges had on various collective identities of Mediterranean populations. The process of constructing identities was complex; it involved a negotiation between self-definition and the ways outsiders defined a group. In a Mediterranean context, "self" and "other" are concepts whose definition changed as Greeks and non-Greeks started to form links, created new identities, and began to see themselves as part of a broader heritage.

1 | Emporion

The first Greeks to venture to the western Mediterranean, according to Herodotus, were the Phokaians of Asia Minor, who undertook long voyages and discovered the Adriatic and Tyrrhenian Seas, the Iberian peninsula, and the kingdom of Tartessos on the southwestern coast of modern Spain.[1] When the Phokaians reached Tartessos, they befriended the local king, Argantho-nios, who ruled for eighty years and lived for one hundred and twenty. The king liked the Phokaians so much that when he heard of the imminent Persian attack in Phokaia he invited them to leave Ionia and settle in his country. Unable to persuade them to move, he instead gave them money to build a wall around Phokaia in order to protect it from the increasing power of the Persians. The king gave generously, comments Herodotus, for the circumference of the wall was many stades long and made of great stones.[2] Sections of the Phokaian wall, which is indeed impressive, were accidentally unearthed when the Turkish authorities started the construction of a Government Administration Building. This discovery led to more excavations around ancient Phokaia to try to determine the extent of the fortifications, which revealed more traces and sections of the archaic walls.[3] According to the tradition preserved in Herodotus and Strabo,[4] the Phokaians eventually did leave their polis, after various adventures settled in their foundation Massalia (Marseille), and from there expanded their trading diaspora by founding several other settlements along the coast of the Gulf of Lion, like Agathe, Emporion, Rhode, and Olbia among others. For the Phokaians, the quasi-mythic story of their ancestors' relations with the local king of the indigenous kingdom of Tartessos may have legitimized their foundation of Emporion, even though Tartessos was located in the Guadalquivir valley in Andalusia, far away from Emporion, which was situated on the Catalan coast. In addition, the Tartessian script was not used for writing the Iberian language used in the area around Emporion.[5] In a sense, all of Phokaia

---

[1] Herodotus 1.163.
[2] Gómez Espelosín 2009: 289–90 points out similarities between this myth and epic tradition.
[3] Ozyigit 1994.   [4] Herodotus 1.164–7; Strabo 4.1.4.
[5] Untermann 1995; Rodriguez Ramos 2000 and 2002.

was linked with the local king through the inheritable institution of *xenia*, or "guest-friendship," one of the institutions in the ancient Mediterranean world that transcended ethnic boundaries.

The legend of the Phokaians' travels in the western Mediterranean reveals how cross-cultural interactions among different ethnic groups actively changed the Greeks' perceptions of the world they inhabited and their connections with other populations. Until the foundation of Massalia and Emporion, the far west of the Mediterranean represented the margins of the world for the Greeks. Once the peninsula became more familiar through the encounters with Iberians, Phoenicians, and Etruscans who lived and traded on its shores, it entered the mythical geography common to all Greeks, by way of Heracles, a hero whose travels and exploits throughout the Mediterranean encompassed both the expanding Greek world and the various populations Greeks came in contact with.[6] Thus, Aristotle calls the path Heracles followed when chasing the Kerynian hind, the "Heraclean road," which he says was a route that offered protection to travelers on their way to Iberia.[7] Another labor brought Heracles to Tartessos, where Herodotus places the first meeting of Phokaians and Iberians, to capture the cattle of Geryon.[8] The incorporation of the western Mediterranean into the myths of the Greeks is one of the ways in which encounters with other ethnic groups altered Greek culture. The myths surrounding the persona of Heracles, known from as early as the Homeric epics, were enriched by these additional stories that ultimately connected the Greeks with the western-most coasts of the Mediterranean basin. Interactions among Mediterranean populations, therefore, were conducive to the production of new identities for both mythical heroes and ethnic groups.

This chapter focuses on the interactions between Greeks and Iberians, with reference to Etruscans and Phoenicians, and on the various identities articulated by Greeks and Iberians especially in the settlement of Emporion, on the northeastern coast of Spain, said to have been a colony of Massalia. The words "Iberia" and "Iberians," which derive from the ancient Greek names for the region and the people inhabiting it, designate in modern scholarship a large region of the Mediterranean coast of what is today Spain, from Cartagena to north of the Pyrenees.[9] A brief history of cross-cultural

---

[6] Herodotus 4.8–10 considers Heracles to be the progenitor of the Scythians. Local populations adopted other Greek heroes as their own, as the Etruscans did in the case of Odysseus, for instance. The hero's connections with the colonial world in turn changed Greek myths regarding Odysseus. See Malkin 1998 and 2002: 159–72.

[7] Ps.-Aristotle, *On Marvelous Things Heard* 837a.

[8] Ps.-Apollodorus 2.5.10.   [9] Sanmartí 2009: 49.

exchange in this region will provide the context for the main discussion on the interactions between Greeks and Iberians in Emporion. Foreign imports existed alongside Iberian art and architecture and attest to contacts with the Bronze Age eastern Mediterranean.[10] In the beginning of the Iron Age the landscape of Iberia consisted of small political units, usually fortified, with low population densities of various ethnic or sub-ethnic groups.[11] Iberian religion, like other Mediterranean religions, was polytheistic, and divinities were worshipped with a variety of rites in sanctuaries.[12]

Starting from the end of the eighth century BC, when trade contacts with the Phoenicians and Etruscans intensified, Iberia became an integral part of the Mediterranean world. The Etruscans never founded any colonies in Iberia, instead restricting themselves to trading along the coast from southern France through Catalonia, with perhaps some Etruscan communities residing in indigenous settlements at Saint-Blaise and Lattes.[13] In contrast, by the end of the seventh century BC, Phoenicians had settled in colonies on the south and west coasts of Spain and Portugal, and there is some evidence that small communities of Phoenicians lived in indigenous Iberian settlements farther north.[14] By the sixth century BC, when Carthage began to control Phoenician settlements in the western Mediterranean, Greeks had also entered the picture, trading with Iberia and founding colonies on the northeast coast of the peninsula, and perhaps also in the southwest at Huelva.[15]

Although most of the discussion on ancient Iberia has concentrated on the colonial interactions between the Phoenician, Greek, or Etruscan colonizers and the Iberian colonized, it is important to note that ancient literary sources attribute, possibly falsely, some colonization movements to the Iberians themselves. Thucydides, for example, writes in his archaeology of Sicily that the Sikanoi, the first people to have inhabited Sicily, were Iberians who migrated to the island and took their name from the Sikanos River in Iberia, and Pausanias reports another tradition that Iberians migrated to Sardinia and founded the first city on the island, Nora.[16] The idea of a connection between the Sikanoi and Iberians probably derives from Hekataios who mentions a city in Iberia called Sikane, but such a colonizing movement from Iberia to Sicily is not obvious in the archaeological record and other literary sources report competing theories about the origins of the Sikanoi.[17] Further, the presence of Iberian products in Sardinia is scant and

---

[10] Olmos and Rouillard 1996; Ruiz and Molinos 1998.
[11] Almagro-Gorbea 1995; Chapman 1995; Ruiz and Molinos 1998: 97–141.
[12] Moneo 2003.   [13] Bouloumié 1987; Py 1995.   [14] Sanmartí 2009; Arruda 2009.
[15] Rouillard 1991 and 2009.   [16] Thucydides 6.2; Pausanias 10.17.5.
[17] Thucydides 6.2; Hekataios *FGrH* 1 F 45. Pareti 1956.

probably indicative of trade instead of Iberian colonization.[18] Nonetheless, these Greek – or Sikanian – perspectives locate the Iberians within a larger Mediterranean framework and at the very least reflect extensive trade interactions in the western Mediterranean, which resulted in the export not just of raw materials but also Iberian finished products.[19]

The presence of Etruscans, Phoenicians, Greeks, and indigenous groups of Iberians in the region of Iberia meant that there was significant contact among these populations resulting in cross-cultural borrowings and adaptations. These are reflected in architecture and artistic production and are worth noting briefly before turning to a discussion of collective identities in Emporion. The history of scholarship on Iberian archaeology has experienced the same intellectual movements described in the Introduction in relation to studies on Greeks and others: at first discussed as a primitive culture civilized by Phoenicians and Greeks Iberian culture was then interpreted within the academic debates on post-colonialism, and, at times, has been used to serve various nationalist and regional purposes.[20] More recent studies critical of old approaches have reassessed both what comprises "Iberian" culture and the effects of colonial encounters.[21] Thus, while urbanization in indigenous Iberian settlements from the sixth to the fifth centuries BC had been originally attributed to the effects of Phoenician and Greek colonization, it is now thought to have been also propelled by endogenous demographic growth.[22] Iberian architecture, long considered derivative of Phoenician or Greek techniques and styles, depending on which colonizer was in the vicinity of particular Iberian groups, is now presented as being new in its form and influenced more by changing modes of production resulting from trade relations with various groups than by actual Phoenician or Greek styles.[23] A similar line of argument has appeared regarding Iberian pottery and sculpture.[24] Iberian sculpture, for example, displayed both local characteristics,[25] such as the realistic portrayal of warriors, and Greek elements like palmettes, and volutes,[26] and Iberian pottery

---

[18] Santos Velasco 1997: 161–4. García y Bellido 1935 and 1954 argued that Iberians were present in Sardinia.

[19] Bruni and Conde 1991 argued that there was a significant presence of Iberians in Etruria.

[20] The introduction in Ruiz and Molinos 1998 is a good discussion of the historiography of Iberian archaeology.

[21] Cunliffe and Keay 1995; Olmos and Rouillard 1996; Balmuth et al. 1997; Aranegui-Gascó et al. 1997; Ruiz and Molinos 1998; Domínguez 1999a; Dietler and López-Ruiz 2009.

[22] Sanmartí 2009: 63–76.   [23] Belarte 2009: 98–107.

[24] Chapa Brunet 1982; Trillmich 1990; Croissant and Rouillard 1996; Aranegui-Gascó et al. 1997; Ruiz and Molinos 1998: 14–96; Domínguez 1999a and 2002; Olmos and Rouillard 2002; Truszkowski 2003; Abad Casal and Soler Díaz 2007.

[25] Chapa Brunet 1982: 374–89.

[26] Almagro-Gorbea 1982 and 1983: 453–61; Croissant and Rouillard 1996. Trillmich 1990: 607–11 argues that Iberian monumental architecture and stone sculptures exhibit both Greek

imitated Greek forms but not necessarily their decoration.[27] In areas further south where Phoenician trade was common and where Phoenicians settled in their own trading posts, Iberian sculpture incorporated Phoenician elements. The adoption of Greek or Phoenician aesthetic ideals, however, does not signify the Hellenization or "Phoenicianization" of local Iberians; in fact, it probably shows the "Iberianization" of Greek or Phoenician aesthetic ideals, as is evident from the mixed style of Iberian sculpture and pottery.[28]

More will be said about archaeology and the effects of the implantation of Emporion on the northeast coast of Iberia. This region of Iberia was inhabited by a group of Iberians known from Greek, Roman, and indigenous sources as the Indiketans, while the Greeks of Emporion were mostly Massaliote and Phokaian, who were also identified as Ionians and in later, Roman, periods, simply as Greeks. To understand the salience of the Massaliote, Phokaian, Ionian, and Greek collective identities, and the Indiketan and Iberian ones, expressed in this region, the history of Massalia, Emporion, and the trade network that connected them must be presented, as well as the nature of the interactions among these groups. I argue that the contacts encouraged by commercial affairs and the permanent settlement of Emporion led to changes in the settlement patterns of the Iberian landscape and produced new hybrid forms of artifacts, myths, language, and political constitutions for both Greeks and Iberians. At the same time, each of the two groups maintained a distinct identity expressed primarily in terms of religion. In particular, the cult of Artemis of Ephesos was important in asserting and defining a Massaliote, Phokaian, Ionian, and eventually Greek identity in Emporion and other Greek settlements in the western Mediterranean. The cult became important for these collective identities because of the cross-cultural interactions among Persians, Greeks, and Lydians in the eastern Mediterranean; in the context of the encounters of Greeks, Phoenicians, and Iberians in the westernmost colonies, these identities acquired a new significance for the Greeks who lived there.

The "Phokaian" trade network

Almost all the archaic and classical Greek settlements located in Iberia, Liguria, and Gaul, in other words, on the Mediterranean coasts of Italy,

---

and Phoenician trends but not the direct influence of Greek or Phoenician sculptors. Domínguez 1999a: 302–5 argues the contrary.

[27] Domínguez 1999a: 314.   [28] Domínguez 1999a: 305.

France, and Spain, are described in sources as either belonging to Massalia or as being Massaliote or Phokaian foundations. The discussion on identity formation in this region, therefore, must start with the origins of Massalia. The archaeological remains of the city, built on virgin soil, suggest a foundation date of 600 BC,[29] which contradicts Herodotus, Strabo, and some later sources that date the foundation of Massalia to 545 BC, when Harpagos attacked Phokaia and effectively forced the Phokaian refugees to flee from their hometown.[30] Most scholars accept that the original foundation of Massalia took place *c.* 600 BC and that a second wave of Phokaians arrived after the fall of Phokaia in 545 BC.[31] Indeed, the inhabited area of Massalia expanded considerably after 540 BC, perhaps reflecting the influx of refugees from Phokaia.[32]

Soon after the establishment of Massalia, Emporion and Rhode were founded on the northeastern shores of modern Catalonia, followed by Agathe (Agde), Alonis, Antipolis, Athenopolis, Avenion (Avignon), Azania, Hemeroskopeion, Kabellion (Cavaillon), Kyrene (La Couronne), Mainake, Nikaia (Nice), Olbia, Rhodanousia (Espeyran?), Sekoanos, the Stoichades Islands (Îles d'Hyères), Tauroeis (Le Brusc), and Troizen.[33] These may not all have been poleis but rather fortresses (ἐπιτειχίσματα) whose purpose was to protect Massaliote interests.[34]

Several of these settlements were part of a trade network that developed in this region, as, for instance, Massalia, Agathe, Olbia, Emporion, Arelate (Arles), and perhaps a few other sites attested archaeologically that have not been identified with any known Greek settlements. This trade network, dubbed "Phokaian" because all these poleis were associated with either Phokaia or Massalia by ancient authors, is also attested archaeologically. The distribution of Massaliote pottery in the Mediterranean coasts of France and Spain, consisting of fine wares and commercial amphorae used mostly to carry wine, is a good indicator of trade routes. From the period 550 to 500 BC, there is a high concentration of Massaliote amphorae between

---

[29] Gantès 1992: 72.

[30] Herodotus 1.164; Strabo 6.1.1; Thucydides 1.13–14; Pausanias 10.8.6; Isokrates, *Archidamos* 84; Ammianus Marcellinus 15.9; Aulus Gellius 10.7; Seneca, *To Helvia* 7.8. Some sources do date the foundation to *c.* 600 BC: ps.-Skymnos 211–14; Aristotle *apud* Athenaios, 13.576a; Justin *apud* Pompeius Trogus, 43.3.4.

[31] Harpokration s.v. Massalia and Malkin 1990b: 42–52. Brunel 1948: 5–26 did not accept this proposition.

[32] Gantès 1992: 73, map 2. Shefton 1994: 79 n. 33 also wonders whether this expansion relates to the refugees.

[33] Domínguez 2004b lists all these settlements with bibliographic references.

[34] Strabo 4.1.1–14 describes the defensive purpose of these sites.

Olbia and Emporion while the density drops south of Emporion, and even inland, along the river Rhône.[35] Further, coins minted in Emporion were often related to coins from Massalia and Phokaia: the first silver coins of the fifth century imitated Massaliote prototypes,[36] fourth-century Emporitan coins were struck on the Phokaian standard,[37] and in the third century they were possibly related to Massaliote weights.[38] This suggests that there was a trade network utilizing these coins that ran along the Gulf of Lion, from Olbia down to Emporion, which seems to have been the southernmost node.[39]

What is also interesting to note about this particular trade network are the contacts that it fostered not only between Greeks, whether they came from Phokaia or not, and the indigenous populations, but also among Greeks, Etruscans, and Phoenicians who were already trading in these same areas. In Massalia, for example, the predominance of Etruscan amphorae before the middle of the sixth century, when Massaliote amphorae took off, is striking, as it is also in settlements near Massalia, like Saint-Blaise, and near Agathe, like La Monédière.[40] Phoenician amphorae are not absent from these areas but they are found more frequently in the region near Emporion and the southern coasts of Iberia, where the Phoenicians had established their own trade network that comprised several settlements whose main function was to promote trade.[41] The kingdom of Tartessos, where the Phokaians met the king Arganthonios, for example, was a territory in the immediate vicinity of Gadir, one of the richest Phoenician colonies in the west.[42] Greek imports are present in Greek settlements founded in these areas but are few in number in indigenous settlements.[43] This general picture of the trade connections and the cross-cultural interactions they fostered in the coastal regions of Gaul, Iberia, and Liguria, is not different from that observed in the settlement of Emporion, located on a promontory just south of the Pyrenees.

---

[35] Bats 1990.   [36] Villaronga 1991: 85–6.

[37] Campo 1992: 196; García-Bellido 1994: 115–49, especially 118–21 and fig. 13 on p. 149.

[38] Villaronga 1991: 86 and 89.

[39] Shefton 1994: 72. Sanmartí-Grego 1992 has proposed instead that it was a stopping point along a commercial route that ran from Massalia to southern Iberia; this seems unlikely given the distribution of amphorae.

[40] Morel 1981a; Gras 1985a; 1985b; 2000; Py 1985 and 1995; Bats 1992; Bouloumié 1987.

[41] Bats 1992: 269. Phoenician amphorae are also prominent farther north, in La Monédière, in the fifth century. Aubet 2001: 257–355.

[42] Tsirkin 1986; Aubet 2001: 257–91, especially 285–91; Belén Deamos: 2009; Celestino Pérez 2009.

[43] Shefton 1994; Domínguez and Sánchez 2001.

A dynamic commercial settlement: Emporion

Emporion is exceptional in the whole of Catalonia because it is one of only two settlements – the other is nearby Rhode, another Massaliote colony, according to literary sources – that have yielded Greek material within a Greek context. Otherwise, little Greek material is found in Phoenician or Iberian contexts: Greek archaic terra-cotta statuettes are found only in Emporion and the Phoenician cemetery on Ibiza, sixth-century Greek pottery is predominant in Rhode and Emporion, and Greek writing derives almost exclusively from Emporion and Rhode.[44]

In the literary tradition, Emporion appears only in Greek geographical works since it was a convenient stopping point on sailing routes,[45] and in Roman historians who refer to Emporion because it was a battle-site during the second Punic War.[46] What the Greek geographers of the fourth century BC say is limited to its location in relation to other towns in Iberia and its foundation by Massalia. Thus, ps.-Skylax simply says that the Greek polis of Emporion was made up of Massaliote colonists,[47] ps.-Skymnos says that it was the Phokaian Massaliotes who colonized Emporion,[48] and Strabo and later grammarians and lexicographers echo these statements, calling Emporion a Massaliote foundation.[49] The Greeks in Iberia, therefore, are alternately called Massaliotes or Phokaian Massaliotes, suggesting that they claimed ties with both these cities.

The history of the relationship between Phokaian Massaliotes and Iberians in Emporion begins in Palaiapolis (Old Town), an islet off the coast of Catalonia. Stratigraphic studies show that Iberians occupied the area in the ninth century and again in the second half of the seventh century, during which times they cultivated contacts with Phoenicians and Etruscans, and later, in the beginning of the sixth century, with Greeks.[50] The implantation of Emporion in this area provided the most important stimulus for intensive contact between Greeks and Iberians. Excavations carried out in Palaiapolis

---

[44] Cabrera Bonet 1996: 46. Sanmartí et al. 2002: 99 and Rouillard 2009: 137 note that the percentage of Greek vessels is small compared to indigenous assemblages. Blech 1996: 111 treats Greek terra-cotta statuettes in Iberia. De Hoz 2004 counts only seven Greek inscriptions in all of Spain besides those from Emporion and Rhode.

[45] Ps.-Skylax 2.2–3, 3.3; ps.-Skymnos 204–7; Strabo 3.4.8–9, 17.3.2–3.

[46] Polybius 1.82.6, 3.23.3, 3.76.2, 31.21.1; Appian, *Spanish Wars* 2.7, 8.40; Livy 34.11–16.

[47] Ps.-Skylax 2: εἰσὶ δὲ οὗτοι Μασσαλιωτῶν ἄποικοι.

[48] Ps.-Skymnos 203–6: Μασσαλιῶται Φωκαιεῖς ἀπῴκισαν.

[49] Strabo 3.4.8, Aelius Herodianus 1.365, and Stephanos of Byzantion s.v. Emporion: κτίσμα Μασσαλιωτῶν.

[50] Aquilué et al. 2000: 11–15; Aquilué et al. 2002: 306–11; Sanmartí 2009: 59.

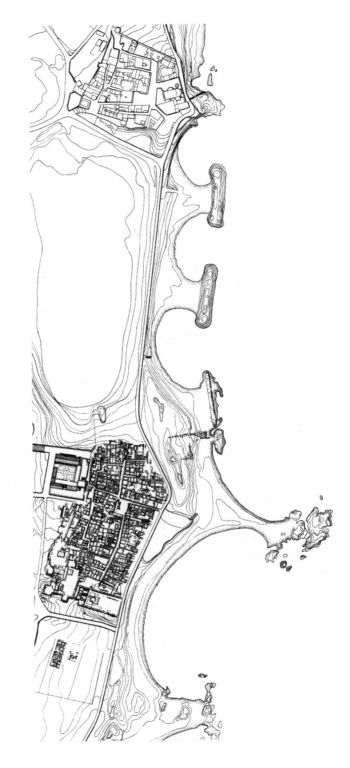

Figure 1 Plan of Emporion with Palaiapolis (right) and Neapolis (left). Reproduced from Marcet and Sanmartí-Grego 1989: 66.

suggest a foundation date in the second quarter of the sixth century BC.[51] Palaiapolis was shortly thereafter abandoned, and the Greeks moved the settlement to a facing site on the coast, dubbed "Neapolis" (New Town) by scholars (Figure 1).

The nature of the settlement of Emporion has been understood in terms of the traditional historical narrative of Greek colonization, described in the Introduction, that distinguished between two different types of colonies: *apoikiai* that cultivated extensive agricultural lands in their hinterland and emporia that exercised no control over a hinterland and had a commercial role.[52] Thus, some scholars proposed that Emporion was at first an emporion and did not become a proper polis until the fifth century, when "Neapolis" became an urban center that cultivated relations with the periphery, earning the settlement influence over its hinterland.[53] Despite Hansen's work on emporia, which has defined settlements called emporia as coastal self-governing Greek poleis located in non-Greek lands that enabled cross-cultural trade, even the most recent references to Emporion continue to consider it as a commercial colony without a hinterland, and distinguish it from an *apoikia*, which was an agrarian colony.[54] For this reason, it is important to discuss briefly the political and commercial nature of Emporion in order to demonstrate that Emporion was a self-governing polis whose main function was to facilitate cross-cultural trade, in accordance with Hansen's definition of emporia, as well as Emporion's extensive relations with its hinterland, so as to demonstrate that the distinction between colonies with or without hinterland is no longer helpful.[55] In addition, Emporion's interactions with the hinterland by necessity involved the cultivation of permanent relations with the indigenous population and are thus relevant to this study.

First, was Emporion a polis? Defining a polis and identifying one in the archaeological record is a notoriously difficult task.[56] The work carried out by the Copenhagen Polis Centre has defined a polis as "a small institutionalized self-governing society, a political community of adult male citizens,

---

[51] Almagro Basch 1966: 14. Sanmartí-Grego 1982: 281–94 dates the foundation of Palaiapolis to 600 BC and "Neapolis" to 580–575 BC based on a handful of Greek vases discovered at the two sites. See also Bosch-Gimpera 1977. Recent excavations (Aquilué 2002: 301–27, especially 311) support a foundation date of *c.* 575 BC for Palaiapolis. "Neapolis" has remained unoccupied since the Middle Ages and has been excavated extensively, whereas the settlement's original site on the islet, now a promontory, has been inhabited continuously.

[52] Gwynn 1918; Lepore 1968 and 2000: 22–3; Vallet 1968: 136–40.

[53] Sanmartí-Grego 1990: 389–410, especially 398.   [54] Hansen 2006a; Rouillard 2009: 134–5.

[55] De Angelis 2002 and Demetriou 2011 argue that the distinction between commercial and agrarian colonies is artificial.

[56] So much so that Camp 2000: 47 wrote that he knows a polis when he sees one, quoting supreme court Justice Potter Stewart's famous opinion on pornography.

who along with their families lived in a fortified (usually) city or in its hinterland along with two other sets of inhabitants, free non-citizens and slaves."[57] This definition suggests that defensive walls, an urban center, a hinterland, a community of citizens, and the power to make political decisions are some of the criteria that determine whether a settlement is a polis, although the absence of one or more does not indicate the opposite. Emporion exhibits all these criteria from an early date, suggesting that it was a polis at the same time as it was an emporion.[58]

The literary sources – the earliest is ps.-Skylax in the fourth century – preserve the tradition that Emporion was a polis founded by Massalia.[59] In this period, Emporion was certainly an urban center with fortification walls,[60] minting its own coins with the legend EM,[61] and shortly thereafter, in the third century, manufacturing bricks stamped with the letters ΔHM, which stand for δημόσιος, a word that denoted public ownership.[62] Even earlier, in the sixth and fifth centuries, there is evidence that Emporion was an urban center with a territory and a political apparatus that enabled it to make collective political decisions.[63] First, permanent fortifying structures appeared in the settlement in the middle of the fifth century BC when a defensive wall was built around a rectangular area that housed all the urban sanctuaries of the city, and may also have served as part of the city fortification.[64] Habitations inside the urban center, which is about 4 ha in area, existed already in the sixth century BC.[65] Second, a temple, an example of monumental architecture, was erected in this same period, although the

---

[57] Hansen 2006b: 40–4.

[58] Peña 1992 and Domínguez 1986 also think that it was both a polis and an emporion.

[59] Ps.-Skylax 2: πόλιν Ἑλληνίδα ᾗ ὄνομα Ἐμπόριον (A Greek polis with the name Emporion); Polybius 3.39.7: ἀπὸ δ' Ἐμπορίου πόλεως (from the polis of Emporion); Stephanos of Byzantion s.v. Emporion: Ἐμπόριον, πόλις Κελτική, κτίσμα Μασσαλιωτῶν (Emporion: a Celtic polis, a Massaliote foundation). The insistence in the sources that Emporion was a colony of Massalia has led scholars to accept without doubt that Emporion was a political entity from the very beginning, and to search for evidence of its political organization in Strabo 4.1.4–5 and Livy 34.9, with recourse to references to Massalia in Aristotle's *Politics* (Domínguez 1986: 3–12). What Strabo and Livy describe in terms of the constitution of Emporion, discussed below, cannot be dated with certainty.

[60] Sanmartí-Grego et al. 1992: 102–3.

[61] Head 1911: 2; Villaronga 1977: 2; R. J. Harrison 1988: 78.   [62] Peña 1992: 141.

[63] The lack of material from Palaiapolis and the short-lived occupation there necessitates that the discussion focus on "Neapolis," which has yielded the only near-contemporary evidence to the establishment of the settlement.

[64] Sanmartí-Grego et al. 1992: 103–4. For walls as indicators of a polis see Camp 2000 and Gat 2002. The walls of Emporion are illustrated in Figure 3 below.

[65] Aquilué et al. 2002: 316–17.

god in whose honor the temple was built is unknown.[66] Third, Emporion started minting coins in the first half of the fifth century. By the fourth century, the mint at Emporion was striking coins with the legend EM, and later in the third century Emporion produced drachmae with the legend EMΠOPITⲰN.[67] Minting coins is secure evidence for the qualification of an urban center as a polis, since it suggests the political coalescence of a community.[68] This community of citizens who lived in the fortified urban center of Emporion is attested making other political decisions as well. Another fragmentary inscription on lead discovered at Emporion, in a palaeo-Christian basilica adjacent to a Hellenistic stoa, contains the words νόμος (law) and ἐσκατοικίσαι (to found a settlement).[69] This text was most recently dated back to the fifth century BC.[70] If this date is correct, this lead inscription, with its mention of laws and foundations, corroborates the political nature of Emporion in the fifth century. Only a political entity could have laws and discuss in an official manner a possible colonizing expedition.

The question is whether Emporion could have functioned as a political entity earlier, in the sixth century BC. The answer is yes. First, the city-ethnic Emporitai, which signifies both the political community of Emporion and its citizens, is attested on a lead inscription from Emporion dating to 550–530 BC and later on a fifth-century BC lead inscription from Pech-Maho.[71] The key term that appears on both inscriptions is ἐμπορῖται. It is extremely rare, occurring only five times in Greek texts, each time referring to the

---

[66] Fragments of antefixes and parts of what was probably an akroterion have survived. See Sanmartí-Grego 1990: 400–2.

[67] Villaronga 1977: 2; Head 1911: 2; R. J. Harrison 1988: 78

[68] Hansen 1996b: 12–13 considers the presence of a mint as a criterion for defining a settlement as a polis.

[69] Almagro Basch 1952: 34–6, no. 21. The word ἐσκατοικίσαι is not attested anywhere else. The text reads:

καὶ . . . αυ
έει ὑμέων τη
ι Πυθαγορ . . . σε
Ἀγαθοκλη . . . με
. . . ενος Νυμ(.)ρίτην
. . . κο ἐσκατοικίσαι
νόμος ὑμέας τοῦ
. . . μεθα καὶ τῆς γρ . . .

[70] Peña 1992: 140–1 says that Santiago has dated it to the fifth century. Almagro Basch 1952: 35 originally dated it to the first century BC, and Lejeune and Pouilloux 1988: 532 suggested a date in the fourth or third century BC.

[71] The *editio princeps* of the inscription from Pech-Maho is Lejeune and Pouilloux 1988 and of that from Emporion is Sanmartí-Grego and Santiago 1987. For more bibliography on these two texts, see below.

citizens of Emporion.[72] It also occurs in a fourth-century BC inscription from Pistiros in Thrace.[73] The word ἐμπορῖται on that inscription indicates the resident traders of a settlement called Pistiros, which was an emporion. Hesychios also equates ἐμπορῖσαι, most likely a corruption of ἐμπορῖται, with μέτοικοι, settlers.[74] Therefore, while ἔμπορος designates a trader who usually travels from place to place, as can be seen from the evolution of the word in Greek literature, ἐμπορῖται signified the inhabitants of an emporion.[75] Likewise, the Pech-Maho and Emporion lead inscriptions must use the word *emporitai* to designate traders who live in a specific emporion. With this synonymy in mind, Musso protested that if the correct reading on the inscription from Emporion were ἐμππορίταισιν the word would merely refer to resident traders somewhere, rather than specifically residents of Emporion.[76] However, unlike the ἐμπορῖται of Pistiros, who are further described as Maroneians, Thasians, and Apollonians, neither the Pech-Maho nor the Emporion inscription suggest that the Emporitans were a composite group of traders from different poleis. This implies that the Emporitans were one specific group, located at a single place. The find-places of the inscriptions, "Neapolis" and Pech-Maho, one of the stops along the trade network, help identify this place as Emporion. The word *emporitai* then, as used in the two inscriptions, not only describes traders who had settled somewhere permanently, but also designates citizens of Emporion. These epigraphic texts offer the strongest evidence that already within a generation after the first implantation of the settlement, Emporion was a polis in the political sense of the word since city-ethnics indicate a body of citizens.[77]

Second, there exists important evidence that the body of citizens of Emporion took decisions collectively as a polity. One of the most important decisions a political community could take was how to organize its hinterland. This subject relates directly to the interactions between the citizens of the polis and the populations inhabiting the outlying territories and is therefore important for the discussion of interethnic contacts. The relations between Emporion and its hinterland, and for that matter of all the

[72] Strabo 3.4.8 (twice), 3.4.9 (twice), and Stephanos of Byzantion s.v. Emporion.
[73] Velkov and Domaradzka 1994. This inscription will be discussed in its entirety in Chapter Four.
[74] Hesychios s.v. ἐμπορῖσαι. Hansen 1997: 90 makes the same argument.   [75] Knorringa 1926.
[76] Musso 1998: 156–9 would prefer to read ἀππορίταισιν (amphorae), although the E in Ἐμππορίταισιν is certain.
[77] Hansen 1996c: 195 persuasively argues that if the toponym from which a city-ethnic derives designates an urban center – and Emporion was one – and if this urban center was not a *kome* or a *demos*, then the toponym designated a polis, and the city-ethnic was used collectively to describe a polis and its citizens.

settlements along the Phokaian trade network in the western Mediterranean, are a pivotal issue in discussions that distinguish between *apoikiai* with territory and emporia without territory mentioned in the Introduction. The prime examples of commercial colonies without hinterland cited in scholarly literature are the various Phokaian colonies in the west, like Massalia, Olbia, Agathe, Hyele (Velia in Campania), and Emporion.[78] Recent cadastral studies carried out using aerial photography and satellite-imaging on precisely these same sites have challenged the idea that Phokaian settlements had no hinterland. They show that these sites, including Emporion, took the political decision to organize their hinterland and develop relations with the indigenous inhabitants early on in their history.[79] Yet, the opposition between agrarian and commercial colonies remains popular in scholarship.

The accepted view has been that Emporion, Agathe, and Olbia were commercial colonies both because of their small size – 4 ha, 4.25 ha, and 3 ha, respectively – and their supposedly limited territory.[80] The recent cadastral studies have challenged this picture by showing that Emporion from its very beginning formed an extensive zone of influence through contacts with the indigenous population inhabiting the region, exploited its hinterland for produce, and had indigenous *oppida* established around the settlement.[81] For instance, by the fifth century, there were roads that ran from the urban settlement outward to the countryside, which had even earlier been divided into parcels, and silos for cereal storage were scattered all over the area as well as in indigenous *oppida*.[82] Indigenous settlements existed in this area from the Bronze Age, but by the sixth century several more appeared in the areas surrounding Emporion.[83] A similar situation

---

[78] Vallet 1968: 136–40; Morel 1981b. Pompeius Trogus *apud* Justin, 43.3 and Strabo 4.1, who emphasize the maritime character of the Phokaians and attribute it to the aridity of the Phokaian hinterland, are ultimately responsible for this scholarly trend, since both of these ancient authors describe Phokaia and its colonies Massalia and Hyele as having a small and poor countryside.

[79] The following two paragraphs are reproduced with the permission of *Historia* and summarize the argument presented more fully in Demetriou 2011: 263–6. Nickels 1982 and 1983: 405–28, especially 418–21, 423–5; Bats 1982; Clavel-Lévêque 1983a and 1999; Benoit 1985; Plana-Mallart 1994a; Guy 1999.

[80] Domínguez 1986: 4; Morel 1981b.

[81] Ruiz de Arbulo 1984: 115–40, especially 127–8, 131–2. For a summary of the evolution of the scholarship on this issue see Plana-Mallart 1994a: 399–424, especially 399–402, 1994b and 1999; Guy 1999.

[82] Adroher et al. 1993: 34–41; Plana-Mallart 1994a: 413–19, 1994b, and 1999: 211–15. For a similar situation in Sicily, see De Angelis 2002, who interprets the presence of silos in domestic contexts at Megara Hyblaia as evidence that the colony was not only concerned with the consumption but also the trade of agricultural products.

[83] Plana-Mallart 1999: 201, 213–15. See also Ruiz and Molinos 1998: 242–3 and 267.

is visible in both Agathe and Olbia,[84] and also in the Andalusian coast of Spain, where Phoenicians established a trade diaspora. The establishment of Phoenician towns stimulated growth in the area, attracted indigenous *oppida* that grew around it and participated in commercial operations.[85] An appropriate model for understanding these changes in the Iberian landscape is one that involves a nucleation of indigenous settlements around a major economic center.

The extent to which the indigenous *oppida* were dependent on Emporion is not clear. Plana-Mallart, noting the regular distribution of these *oppida* in the countryside suggested that perhaps they marked the frontiers of the territory of Emporion and that they functioned as intermediaries in commercial transactions between the Greeks and other local populations.[86] By the fourth century, there was at least one sanctuary of Demeter and Kore in Mas Castellà (Pontós) in the hinterland controlled by Emporion, originally an Iberian *oppidum* abandoned in the late fifth or early fourth century BC.[87] This sanctuary is located in a field full of silos for cereal storage and probably acted as a mediator between Emporion and Rhode and the local Iberians.

The indigenous *oppida* that sprang up around Emporion continued to cultivate products, such as vines, which had been grown in this area from the middle of the seventh century BC, before the Greeks established their settlement, but did so at a more intense rate, reflecting trade and perhaps the increasing consumption of wine by the local elites. Interestingly, most Greek vases imported in the Iberian peninsula were vases related to wine consumption. Wine, as Dietler has shown, should be considered a prestige item whose consumption had various implications: it facilitated interactions especially among elites and was an instrument of power.[88] As such, these imported vases could be indicators of an elite Iberian status. Indigenous Iberians, however, might not have used these vases in the same way the Greeks did. Indeed, many of them were deposited as offerings in graves, suggesting that perhaps Iberians interpreted Dionysiac scenes on the vases in funereal terms.[89] The flexibility of Mediterranean polytheistic religions

---

[84] In Agathe, by the fourth century BC the land was subdivided into parcels according to the same measurements used in the sixth-century settlement, and storage silos were discovered in indigenous *oppida* installed around the Greek town: Garcia 1987: 67–93; Clavel-Lévêque 1999: 182–3, 193–4. Benoit 1985 and Bats et al. 1995: 376 show that the extent of the territory of Olbia was about 305 ha and that roadways connected it with the urban center.

[85] Aubet 2001: 326–9; Ruiz and Molinos 1998: 242–3.   [86] Plana-Mallart 1999: 214.

[87] Adroher et al. 1993. De Polignac 1995: 106–27 and Cole 1994 discuss the location of Demeter's sanctuaries in general.

[88] Dietler 1990. Domínguez 1995 argues that wine was not necessarily consumed in this fashion.

[89] Sánchez in Domínguez and Sánchez 2001: 455–8.

allowed such (mis)understandings of religious iconography and created a middle ground on which both Greeks and Iberians could co-exist. Other crops, like the olive, seem to have been introduced into this region by the Greeks, thereby changing its ecology. The traditional cultivation of cereals and legumes also expanded after the implantation of the Greek settlement, no doubt to serve the increasing indigenous and Greek population in the region, which was stimulated by the commercial nature of Emporion.[90] Other changes in local *oppida* are visible. For example, Ullastret, a sixth-century indigenous settlement in the vicinity of Emporion, had a higher number of Greek imports than other Iberian sites; it also adopted a rectilinear plan, perhaps influenced by the Greek town planning of Palaiapolis, built a fortification wall, something missing from other Iberian settlements, and produced pottery with imitations of Attic motifs that became popular throughout Iberia.[91] These changes may have been instigated indirectly by the presence of Emporion, which provided the socio-economic environment that stimulated demographic growth in Iberian settlements and subsequently led to social complexity in the region.

The new cadastral studies that explore the hinterland of the Greek settlements established in the Mediterranean coast of Iberia, Gaul, and Liguria are extremely important because they show, first, that the dichotomy between agrarian and commercial settlements is no longer applicable in studies of colonization and, second, they reveal how the implantation of new settlements affected the topography of these areas and altered significantly the settlement patterns in their vicinity. As dynamic urban centers that exploited the hinterland and promoted interactions between indigenous populations and settlers, emporia also encouraged the growth of indigenous urban centers and therefore reconfigured relations among various groups.

Emporion was a dynamic polis, whose name also indicates that its function was mainly commercial.[92] Evidence to suggest that Emporion was an emporion comes from diverse sources. First, excavations have revealed the

---

[90] Buxó 2009: 160–4.

[91] Ruiz and Molinos 1998: 86; Domínguez 1999a: 312; Domínguez in Domínguez and Sánchez 2001: 73–6; Belarte 2009: 102–4; Sanmartí 2009: 63–4.

[92] It is not infrequent that the name of a place derives from its primary function. There were numerous settlements called Emporion in the ancient Mediterranean. Stephanos of Byzantion s.v. Emporion adds to his primary definition that it is a Celtic polis and a foundation of the Massaliotes and that there are three more poleis called Emporion in Macedonia, Sicily, and Campania. Tanais on the Black Sea had Emporion as an alternate name (Alexandros Polyhistor *FGrH* 273 F 134). Strabo 6.1.5 says that a harbor was called Emporion (ἐπίνειον καλούμενον Ἐμπόριον) and in 17.3.2 he makes explicit the relation between the word and what it signifies in his description of North Africa, where he explains that the name "Emporic" given to the gulf on the coast of Libya is because of all the Phoenician commercial settlements implanted on its shores.

position of the ancient port located between the old and new settlements.[93] Second, as is typical of trading ports, the provenance of the commercial amphorae, whose very existence is evidence for trade, is varied and includes Iberia, Chios, Corinth, Athens, Eastern Greece, Etruria, Phoenicia, and Massalia,[94] while other types of vases are East Greek, Athenian, Corinthian, Laconian, Etruscan, and Phoenician.[95] In addition to the archaeological material, epigraphic sources also attest to the trading nature of Emporion. The two lead inscriptions mentioned above, which contain the earliest attestations of the city-ethnic Emporitai, are important because they demonstrate Emporion's commercial focus. The sixth-century lead inscription from Emporion provides the earliest evidence that exists for the noun *emporion*, since it uses the city-ethnic Emporitai, which implies that the name of the settlement was Emporion. Although the nouns ἔμπορος (trader) and ἐμπορία (trade) occur already in the Homeric and Hesiodic poems, the word ἐμπόριον makes its first appearance in literary sources in Herodotus.[96] Before the publication of the lead inscriptions from Emporion and Pech-Maho, several scholars had disputed the existence of the concept of an emporion in the archaic period because of its late attestation,[97] and some even offered an unlikely identification for the settlement in Iberia with a town called Pyrene.[98] The name Emporion, however, probably reflects the settlement's function of coordinating commercial operations.

---

[93] Almagro Basch 1966: 14.   [94] Bats 1998: 623.

[95] Cabrera Bonet 1996: 43–54; Domínguez in Domínguez and Sánchez 2001: 60–71.

[96] For a collection of all occurrences of these nouns and other related ones, see Knorringa 1926.

[97] Hansen 1996c and 1997 and Wilson 1997. Hansen 2006a revised his position after the publication of the lead inscriptions from Emporion and Pech-Maho.

[98] Hind 1972. This identification is based on Avienus, *Ora Maritima* 559–66, who says "[I]t is said there once stood near the slopes of the Pyrenees and near an island rising loftily a city of wealthy households. And here the inhabitants (*incolae*) of Massilia often used to exchange their wares in business. But to Pyrene it is a voyage of seven days in a swift ship from the Pillars of Hercules and the Atlantic Ocean and the confines of the western shore." Based on the similarity of this text to ps.-Skylax's description of Emporion, especially in relation to the emphasis on commerce, the Massaliote ties, and the seven-day journey, Hind identified Emporion as the settlement known as Pyrene. However, Lloyd 1976: 143 pointed out that *incolae* does not refer to colonists, but rather inhabitants, and the distance from the straits of Gibraltar to Emporion should be covered in a shorter time than seven days. Pyrene, therefore, probably cannot refer to the same town as Emporion. Avienus' *civitas Pyrenae* must be the same as Herodotus' Pyrene. Herodotus 2.33 claims that it is a polis lying on the river Danube, which, he says, has its source in the lands of the Celts. As scholars recognize, and Herodotus himself confesses (3.115), neither he nor Hekataios nor any other source had accurate information on the geography of the western Mediterranean. The most likely interpretation of this passage is that Herodotus considered the Danube to have run all the way from Spain across continental Europe. This would locate Pyrene in Spain, but not necessarily at Emporion. For other suggestions as to Pyrene's location and criticism of these, see Lloyd 1976: 140–5.

Besides the two lead inscriptions mentioned already and quoted below, there is a second lead letter from Emporion, dating to the late fifth or early fourth century, written in the Ionic dialect:[99]

Recto	Verso
[–]λι[–]	[– παρ]ὰ Τιελαρ[–]
[–]δίς[τ]ό[σσον–]	[–]ασ.ασλ [–]
[–] ὤν[ησ]θ[ε–]	[–] ἄνδρα νᾳ[ύκληρον–]
[–]ον ὀνῆσ[αι–]	
[–] ἤν τις [θεληι–]	
[–] αὐτῶι δ[ὲ –]	
[–] οὐ[[η]]κ ἡδύ[–]	
[–] νος ἐς Ἀ[. . . ἦλθε–]	
[– ἔπρη]ξε κεῖνο[–]	
[–] ἄλλοι καὶ Ὀ[–]	

The poor condition of this letter renders a translation impossible. However, several key words, such as ὀνῆσαι (profit), ὤνησθε (profit), and ἄνδρα ναύκληρον (boat-owner), suggest the content was commercial. Its later date supports the idea that it was not only the first implantation, Palaiapolis, which was a trading settlement, but also "Neapolis," contrary to some arguments that have been proposed.[100] Emporion, therefore, was a commercial settlement whose main function was to facilitate cross-cultural trade throughout its history.

The other two lead inscriptions provide evidence for earlier trading at Emporion. The first inscription was discovered in Emporion and dates from 550 to 530, whereas the second is from Pech-Maho and dates from 480 to 460.[101] Both have been categorized as private letters, sent by one individual to another.[102] The lead letter discovered in Emporion is written in an Ionian

[99] Cf. Sanmartí-Grego and Santiago 1989: 36–8; Santiago 1990b: 176.
[100] Sanmartí-Grego 1982 regards only the first implantation, Palaiapolis, as a trading settlement.
[101] Slings 1994 argues that both these letters date from the middle of the fifth century BC. Scholars have not generally accepted his proposal, with the exception of López García 1995: 101.
[102] Chadwick 1990 argues convincingly that the Pech-Maho lead is not actually a letter but a legal document between parties. Other lead letters have been discovered from the Black Sea region (Bravo 1974; Vinogradov 1998), Corcyra (Calligas 1971; Vélissaropoulos 1982), and the environs of Emporion. The Black Sea letters deal with a variety of subjects: three sixth-century letters record the sale of a slave-girl, directions on how to deal with certain goods (food, pottery, dyes, iron, leather, clothing, etc.), and an order for payment; a fifth-century letter records a conflict between the sender and one of the addressee's relatives. The sixth-century tablets from Corcyra are contracts recording loans. Some of the letters from Corcyra are

Figure 2 Lead letter from Emporion negotiating a price for transporting goods, *c.* 550–530 BC.

dialect (Figure 2):[103]

---

1   [–]ὡς ἐν Σαιγάνθηι ἔσηι, κἄν[–]
    [–] Ἐμππορίταισιν οὐδ' ἐπιβα̣[–]
    [–] νες ἢ ἔκοσι κοῖνος οὐκ ἐλα̣[–]δ[–]
4   [– Σαιγ]ανθηῖον ὠνῆσθαι Βασπεδ[. . .]π[–]
    [–]αν ἄρσαν παρακομίσεν κἄσ[..] εγ[–]
    [–]ωνι τί τούτων ποητέον [..]ν[–]
    [–]α καὶ κέλευε σὲ Βασπεδ[..] ἐλκ̣[εν–]
8   [εἴρεσ]θαι [εἴ] τις ἔστιν ὃς ἕλξει ἐς δ[.]οστ[–]
    [–ἡ]μέτερον· κἂν δύο ὦἲσι, δύο προ[έσ]θ[ω –]
    [διπ]λ[ό]ος δ' ἔστω · κἂν αὐτὸς θέλη[ι –]
    [– τὦ]μυσυ μετεχέτω · κἄμ μὴ ὁ[–]
12   [–]τω κἀπιστελάτω ὁκόσο ἄν[–]
    [–]ν ὡς ἂν δύνηται τάχιστα[–]
    [–κεκ]έλευκα · χαῖρε.

---

contracts recording loans. Some of the letters from Emporion are inscribed in Greek and others in an undeciphered Iberian language (Almagro Basch 1952: 31–6, nos. 19–21 [Greek]; 66–8, no. 5 [Iberian]; De Hoz 1993); they are believed to have been of a commercial nature (Sanmartí-Grego 1988). The common use of lead letters to record contracts, sales, or pledges for payments throughout diverse areas of the Greek world at such early periods as the sixth century also constitute evidence for the literacy of ancient traders (Wilson 1997–8).

[103] Sanmartí-Grego and Santiago 1987, 1988a, and1988b; Santiago 1990a and 1990c; Slings 1994; López García 1995; Musso 1998.

Since you are in Saigantha…with the Emporitans, no less than twenty, and of wine, no less than ten. <Order> Basped of Saigantha to buy (a ship) sufficient to transport as far as…which of these we should do…and order Basped to transport you and inquire whether there is anyone who will transport to our…And, if there are two, let him send two, and let <the pay> be double; and if he himself is willing, let him share in half. But, if he does not agree, he should…send me a letter telling me how much, as soon as possible. These are my orders. Farewell.

This letter from Emporion instructs the recipient to ask Basped, whose name suggests he was an Iberian, to transport his merchandise – possibly wine – in exchange for half a share, presumably of the profits from the sale of this merchandise. If Basped was not satisfied with these terms, he could send a letter with a counteroffer before the sender looked for another transporter.

The Pech-Maho lead tablet has two inscriptions on either side. The earlier is in Etruscan (Face A) while the later inscription (480–460 BC) is in Greek (Face B). There is also a Greek name inscribed vertically on Face A:[104]

	Face B	Face A
1	ἀκάτι […] ἐπρίατο [Κύ]πρι[ος παρὰ τῶν] *vac.*	Ve[n]elus : [–]is
	Ἐμποριτέων · ἐπρίατο τε[ ] *vac.*	Zeke : kisnee : heki[
	ἐμοὶ μετέδωκε τὤμυσυ τ[ρίτ]ο ἠ[μι]οκταγ-	veneluz : ka : utavu[
4	ίο · τρίτον ἡμιεκτάνιον ἔδωκα ἀριθμῶ-	heitva : kiven : mis[
	ι καὶ ἐγγυητήριον τρίτην αὐτός · καὶ κε-	mataliai : me[
	ῖν' ἔλαβεν ἐν τῶι ποταμῶι · τὸν ἀρρα-	zik : hinu : tuz[
	βῶν' ἀνέδωκα ὅκο τἀκάτια ὁρμίζεται ·	
8	μάρτυρ · Βασιγερρος καὶ Βλερυας καὶ	Ἡρωνοίιος
	Γολο.βιυρ καί Σεδεγων · ο[ὗ]τοι μαρτ-	
	vac. υρες εὖτε τὸν ἀρραβῶν' ἀνέδωκα,	
	vac. [ε]ὖτε δὲ ἀπέδωκα τὸ χρῆμα τρίτον	
12	*vac.* [ἠμ]ιοκτάγι[ο]ν. αυαρυας Ναλβε..ν.	

So-and-so (Ky)pri(os?) bought (a) boat(s) [from the] Emporitans. He also bought…He passed over to me a half share at the price of 1.5 hectai (each). I paid 2.5 hectai in cash, and two days later personally gave a guarantee. He received the former (i.e. the money) on the river. I handed over the pledge where the boats are moored. Witness(es): Basigerros and Bleruas and Golo.biur and Sedegon; these

---

[104] Unfortunately, I am not able to illustrate this lead inscription. Cf. Lejeune and Pouilloux 1988; Lejeune et al. 1988; Pouilloux 1988; Colonna 1988; Chadwick 1990; Ampolo and Caruso 1990–1; Lejeune 1991; Effentere and Vélissaropoulos 1991; Rodríguez-Somolinos 1996; De Hoz 1999; Castellano i Arolas 2007.

(were) witnesses when I handed over the pledge. But when I paid the money, the 2.5 hectai, .auaras, Nalb..n.

Heronoios

Although the Etruscan text is fragmentary, the name of Massalia can be identified on it. It is unclear whether the context of the Etruscan inscription is commercial but merely the presence of two texts on the same tablet is strong evidence that the interethnic exchanges that took place in Emporion were not limited to those between Greeks and Iberians. The reuse of the tablet shows the trade connections both between Massalia and Emporion and between Greeks and Etruscans. The Greek text is a legal document that recounts a sale of boat(s) at Emporion. The buyer of the boat(s) sold a share (of the profits) to the author of the document, who then paid his debt in installments in front of witnesses, who were probably Iberians, given their names. The Emporion and Pech-Maho inscriptions demonstrate the multiethnic nature of trading settlements in general, and of Emporion more specifically, because they show the cooperation of Greeks and Iberians in commercial affairs: in the letter from Emporion, a Greek directs an intermediary to ask an Iberian man to name his price for transporting goods on ships; the lead from Pech-Macho records a transaction that had Iberians as witnesses.

The text from Pech-Maho is important also because it contains the earliest attestation in Greek of the word ἀρραβῶν, meaning pledge.[105] This word is of Semitic origin; it is probably Phoenician and appears in Hebrew as well ('erabon).[106] The borrowing of words from Phoenician sources is significant in the context of trade, which promotes cross-cultural interactions. It is perhaps possible to imagine that the frequency of contacts promoted by trade aided in the creation of a hybrid language that borrowed terms from the languages of the traders involved in the commercial transactions. In turn, of course, this must have facilitated further trade. The word ἀρραβῶν later entered the Greek vocabulary as is evidenced by the frequency with which it is used by many authors, as a simple search on the *TLG* shows. The Greek language, therefore, did not remain static but rather was changed by cross-cultural trade. The fact that this Semitic word is found on a bilingual tablet inscribed in Greek and Etruscan in the western reaches of the Mediterranean Sea demonstrates how far and wide the effects of trade connections were felt.

---

[105] The word appears next in Isaios, *On Behalf of Kiron* 23.   [106] LSJ s.v. ἀρραβῶν.

Greco-Iberian encounters

The establishment of a Greek settlement on the north Iberian coast changed not only the settlement patterns surrounding the urban center but also the urban settlement itself and resulted in the articulation of new identities and new political formations. In his description of Emporion, Strabo calls the urban center a δίπολις (twin-city) and proceeds to describe the topography of the polis, which reveals vital details about the relations between Greeks and Iberians in the urban center itself. Here is Strabo's full text regarding this double nature of Emporion:

ᾤκουν δ' οἱ Ἐμπορῖται πρότερον νησίον τι προκείμενον, ὃ νῦν καλεῖται Παλαιὰ πόλις, νῦν δ' οἰκοῦσιν ἐν τῇ ἠπείρῳ. δίπολις δ'ἐστί, τείχει διωρισμένη, πρότερον τῶν Ἰνδικητῶν τινας προσοίκους ἔχουσα, οἳ καίπερ ἰδίᾳ πολιτευόμενοι, κοινὸν ὅμως περίβολον ἔχειν ἐβούλοντο πρὸς τοὺς Ἕλληνας ἀσφαλείας χάριν διπλοῦν δὲ τοῦτον τείχει μέσῳ διωρισμένον· τῷ χρόνῳ δ' εἰς ταὐτὸ πολίτευμα συνῆλθον μικτόν τι ἔκ τε βαρβάρων καὶ Ἑλληνικῶν νομίμων, ὅπερ καὶ ἐπ' ἄλλων πολλῶν συνέβη. (Strabo 3.4.8)

The Emporitans formerly lived on a nearby island, now called "Old Polis," but now they live on the mainland. It is a *dipolis* divided by a wall. Formerly it had some of the Indiketans as neighbors. Although these had their own polity, they also wished to have a common enclosure with the Greeks for reasons of security. This enclosure was double, separated in the middle by a wall. In time, they united together in the same constitution, mixing some barbarian and some Greek customs, as has happened in many other cases.

The word δίπολις (twin-city) occurs only in geographers' works, especially in Strabo and ps.-Skylax. The two authors, however, use it differently. On the one hand, ps.-Skylax uses it as an adjective only to describe islands that had two poleis, as is the case of Mykonos, Ikaros, Ikos and Skiathos.[107] Similarly, he uses the word τρίπολις (*tripolis*) to designate islands that had three poleis, such as Amorgos and Peparethos, and the word τετράπολις (*tetrapolis*) for islands that had four poleis, such as Euboia.[108] On the other hand, Strabo uses δίπολις in an entirely different manner. For Strabo, δίπολις designates a polis that for some reason, either natural or man-made, is divided into two parts. He describes Nysa with this word because a gorge divides it into two, and he so describes an island off Knidos because

---

[107] Ps.-Skylax 58.

[108] Ps.-Skylax 58. *Etymologicum Magnum* s.v. *dipolis* employs the word to describe the island of Lemnos and even names the two poleis that the island had, namely, Hephaistia and Myrina. The scholia to Apollonios of Rhodes also describe Lemnos as a *dipolis* and name its two poleis.

it is connected with the mainland with moles; the sea, therefore, divides the polis in two: half is on the island, the other half on the mainland.[109] Likewise, Strabo calls Emporion a *dipolis* because a wall divides it in two (τείχει διωρισμένη), making it a twin-city. Strabo, therefore, uses the word *dipolis* as a geographical term that does not have any political connotations.

The double aspect of Emporion appears also in Livy:

iam tunc Emporiae duo oppida erant muro divisa. unum Graeci habebant, a Phocaea, unde et Massilienses oriundi, alterum Hispani . . . tertium genus Romani coloni ab divo Caesare post devictos Pompei liberos adiecti. nunc in corpus unum confusi omnes, Hispanis prius, postremo et Graecis in civitatem Romanam adscitis. (Livy 34.9)

Already at that time, Emporiae were two towns divided by a wall. The Greeks from Phokaia, from where the Massaliotes also came, had one, and the Spaniards had the other. A third element was the Roman colonists settled there by the deified Caesar after Pompey's sons were defeated. At the present day all have been fused into one municipal body by the grant of Roman citizenship, in the first instance to the Spaniards and then to the Greeks.

By Livy's time, the name of the settlement had changed from the singular Emporion to the plural Emporiae to refer to the union of the Greek "Neapolis" with the Roman city established to its west in the first century BC.[110] This union was marked by the construction of a new wall surrounding both the Greek and Roman towns.[111] Nonetheless, both Livy and Strabo refer to an earlier twin-city, co-inhabited by Greeks and Iberians. The details of Strabo's text, on which Livy probably based his account, correspond closely with the topography of "Neapolis."

After its move from Palaiapolis to the mainland, Emporion seems to have grown southwards from the ancient port. In terms of the layout of the city, the material culture discovered in the houses east of the earliest, fifth-century fortification wall, is mainly composed of domestic wares of Iberian manufacture not found in other parts of the settlement, suggesting that Iberians inhabited this area in the sixth and fifth centuries when Emporion was established and became an urban center.[112] This fifth-century wall, originally built as a defensive wall by the Greeks, probably became the one that Strabo says separated Greek Emporion from the indigenous habitation

[109] Strabo 14.1.43 and 14.2.15.
[110] Peña 1985: 69–83, especially 71–6. Peña 1988a: 11–45 reprints (pp. 11–18) the text of Peña 1985, but continues (pp. 18–27) to discuss the double-city in Emporion during the second century and then (pp. 27–45) Emporion's second-century juridical status (Peña 1988b reprints this last part).
[111] Marcet and Sanmartí-Grego 1989: 123.
[112] Marcet and Sanmartí-Grego 1989: 79; Sanmartí-Grego 1992: 32.

that grew to the east of the wall.[113] As the indigenous settlement migrated towards Emporion, the Iberians demanded for reasons of protection to be incorporated into the Greek urban center. Archaeologically, it is clear that the topography of the settlement changes in the fourth century. At this time, the polis fortifications, while still using the fifth-century wall, were extended to the east and included both a tower that formed part of the gateway into Emporion and a bastion to the far east, discovered where the coastline is today (Figure 3).[114] These 375–350 BC extensions enclosed the indigenous Iberian habitation, previously outside the walls, together with the Greek city in one urban, albeit divided, entity.[115] Strabo used the word *dipolis* to describe the moment of formation of a Greek and Iberian urban entity, when a common defensive wall was built around both the Greek and indigenous parts. From Strabo's perspective in the first century BC or that of his sources, it may have seemed that the original fortifications divided the two groups.[116]

The situation encountered in the polis of the living is mirrored also in the polis of the dead. The earliest necropoleis of the area show ethnic differentiation both geographically and culturally. In the sixth and fifth centuries, some necropoleis, such as Martí, Bonjoan, and de las Corts, situated to the south of "Neapolis," housed only Greek graves, identified as such because they contain mostly Greek artifacts, while others, to the northeast of "Neapolis," are thought to contain only Iberian graves since the material culture interred with the bodies consists mostly of Iberian wares.[117] These graves also show that Greeks and Iberians had different funerary practices: Greeks preferred inhumations, whereas Iberians preferred cremations. With the exception of a few graves, both Iberian and Greek, that contained richer grave goods, the only other differentiation visible is within the Greek burials, some of which contained black-figured lekythoi, particularly of the Haimonian group. Twenty-six of these vases were discovered in early fifth-century funerary contexts in the Bonjoan cemetery at Emporion, and a total of ninety-six black-figured lekythoi were found in Emporion, but only nineteen more have been discovered throughout the rest of Iberia.[118] This discrepancy in the numbers found in Emporion and the rest of Iberia suggests that this particular type of vase could have acted as an indicator

---

[113] Santiago 1994: 68.

[114] Marcet and Sanmartí-Grego 1989: 74–5; Sanmartí-Grego et al. 1992: 102–12.

[115] Sanmartí-Grego et al. 1992: 111.

[116] Dueck 2000: 182. Strabo's main source in his descriptions of Iberia is Poseidonios, who lived during the second and first centuries BC.

[117] Almagro 1953–5: I 333–98.

[118] Domínguez 1999a: 319; Domínguez in Domínguez and Sánchez 2001: 88, 460, and 462.

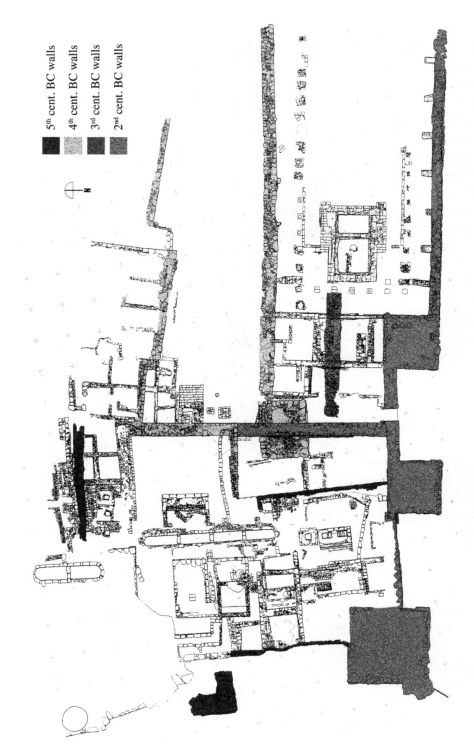

Figure 3 Plan of the fifth, fourth, third, and second-century fortification walls of Emporion. Modified from Marcet and Sanmartí-Grego 1989: 74.

5th cent. BC walls

4th cent. BC walls

3rd cent. BC walls

2nd cent. BC walls

N

of social identity within the Greek population of Emporion, although it is unclear what identity exactly they marked.[119]

When the fortifications of Emporion were extended in the fourth century, the situation in the necropoleis changed radically. Many indigenous cremations are found in what used to be exclusively Greek necropoleis, such as Martí, Bonjoan and Car Park (so called because today it is the parking lot that serves the site).[120] In the same way that the Iberians joined the Greeks in the city of the living, they also joined them in their necropoleis. More importantly, by the fourth century, when Greek and Iberian burials coexisted in the same cemeteries, the artifacts discovered from both Greek inhumations and Iberian cremations demonstrate no significant differences.[121] Moreover, locally produced monochrome grey pottery is present in both Greek and Iberian burials in the Martí cemetery.[122] Whereas in the beginning of the history of the settlement burial goods divided along ethnic lines, by the fourth century, Greeks and Iberians shared common burial practices and common goods that were produced in the area. The permanent implantation of Emporion in this region of Iberia, therefore, had profound effects both on local Iberians and Greeks, who eventually came to be incorporated in the same urban space. Once the settlement became multiethnic so did the necropoleis, though the two groups retained different funerary practices. At the same time, they started to use locally produced pottery, which might have articulated a common Emporitan identity.

Strabo's description of Emporion as a *dipolis* is not limited to geography; it extends to inter-ethnic politics between the Greeks and Iberians living there, and, therefore, has significant implications for the interactions and identities of both groups. First, it seems that despite frequent interactions between the two component parts of Emporion's population, the two communities remained separate and maintained differences. These differences, in addition to being cultural, such as the funerary practices or the use of domestic wares, were also political. Thus, Strabo points out that though the Indiketans, the local group of Iberians living in the region around Emporion, wanted to have a common defensive wall with the Greeks for security reasons, they still lived in a separate quarter divided by a wall and they "had their own polity (ἰδίᾳ πολιτευόμενοι)."[123] The two communities maintained not only a separate geographical identity emblematized by the wall that separated them but also a distinct political identity.

---

[119] Domínguez 2004a: 440.   [120] Almagro 1953–5: I 27–216.
[121] Almagro 1953–5: I 59, 90, 96–7, 123–4, 126 (Inhumations no. 23, 90 and 103; Cremations no. 20 and 29); Domínguez 2004a: 438–42.
[122] Almagro 1953–5: I 38–9.   [123] Strabo 3.4.8.

It was only with time, Strabo says, that Greeks and Iberians founded a common constitution: "In time, they united together in the same constitution, mixing some barbarian and some Greek customs (νομίμων), as has happened in many other cases."[124] Their eventual composite constitution – another instance of a new cultural product resulting from close contacts among different ethnic groups – implies that up until the moment of its formation Greeks and Iberians maintained distinct political identities. The exact point at which the mixed constitution emerged is not known. What archaeology helps us to determine is that, if the δίπολις can be dated to the second quarter of the fourth century and if Strabo is reliable in his report, then the common constitution must date at the earliest to the Hellenistic period. Despite the late date, Strabo's perspective is interesting. First of all, he presents Greek and Iberian relations as those between Greeks and barbarians, an issue that Strabo is interested in throughout his work.[125] More importantly, it is the customs (νόμιμα), such as elements of the constitution, the terminology for magistrates, names and numbers of tribes, and the sacred calendar, that he qualifies as Greek and barbarian. He ignores the fact that νόμιμα varied both on an intra-Hellenic level – Ionians had different νόμιμα from Dorians – and also locally. Emporion could have modeled its νόμιμα on those of its purported mother-city Massalia.[126] In fact, Strabo describes Massalia's laws (*nomoi*) as being specifically Ionian.[127] The νόμιμα of Emporion, however, were neither Massaliote, nor even Phokaian or Ionian, but rather Greek, according to Strabo. In the context of Emporion, where a group presenting itself cohesively as Greeks from Massalia found themselves in contact with non-Greeks, the contrast is that between Greeks and non-Greeks, especially since it is Strabo in the first century BC who contextualizes and describes the contrast in these terms. It is doubtful that the Greeks of Emporion had a strong Hellenic identity in the archaic period, which would have caused them to view the distinction between themselves and the local Iberians in terms of Greeks vs. barbarians. In fact, as is discussed in the next section, the Greeks of Emporion described their collective identity as Phokaian and Ionian rather than as Greek.[128]

Archaeological and epigraphic sources, which reveal several characteristics of the early relations between Greeks and Iberians in Emporion, can supplement Strabo's text. Unfortunately, the indigenous Iberians living in Emporion did not write down their own narratives; they used writing only

---

[124] Strabo 3.4.8.   [125] Dueck 2000: 75–84.
[126] Domínguez 1986 discusses the political organization of Emporion.   [127] Strabo 4.1.5.
[128] Domínguez 2004a: 429–56, especially 446–56, also concludes that the Greeks living in the towns of the Phokaian trade network mostly declared a Phokaian identity.

for graffiti inscribed on pottery as a mark of ownership, or to record perhaps commercial transactions.[129] Incidentally, Greek influence is visible in the Iberian script. In fact, Iberians in the northeastern part of the peninsula adopted the Ionian alphabet, whereas those who lived in the southwestern areas adopted the Tartessian semi-syllabic system, itself probably derived from the Phoenician script. These foreign alphabets, however, were devoid of ethnic connotations; the Iberians simply used them to write their own Iberian languages.[130] This alone should suggest that the use of the Greek or Phoenician alphabet was a choice of the indigenous population.

The content of the inscriptions could reveal more about the nature of the Greco-Iberian relations but, unfortunately, as long as the Iberian language remains undeciphered, the Iberian side also remains silent. The indigenous response to the Greek presence in Iberia, therefore, can only be seen through the archaeological record and Greek discursive sources. I have already discussed the presence of Greek elements in Iberian sculpture and pottery in general, presented the specific changes in the landscape and geography of the Emporitan hinterland, and showed that indigenous *oppida* in this region, as for example, Ullastret, adopted Greek urban planning. In the settlement of Emporion itself, similar co-optations of Greek and Iberian artifacts and techniques existed that resulted in hybrid products, which are typical of multiethnic settlements. For example, by the fourth century BC, houses in "Neapolis" exhibited cross-cultural influences in their layout and constructions since they contain Greek, Iberian, Punic, and, later on, Roman elements.[131] Similarly, Iberian pottery from this region, which some have called Indiketan after the name of the particular group of Iberians inhabiting this region, was a unique product of Greco-Iberian contacts: using typically Iberian shapes, the potters decorated the vases with both Iberian (floral, vegetal, and geometric designs) and Greek (ivy and palmettes) motifs done in white paint.[132] This particular type of Indiketan pottery rose in popularity towards the end of the fifth century BC, as did the grey Emporitan ware, produced in Emporion and also Ullastret. The Emporitan grey monochrome pottery and the Indiketan white-painted vases seem to have replaced other forms of Iberian pottery from the northeast coast of Iberia, which declined in numbers.[133] These were the new local productions, resulting from the dynamic interactions between Greeks and Iberians in Emporion, which created a new 'Iberian' culture.

---

[129] Almagro Basch 1952: 75–83; R. J. Harrison 1988: 140–8; De Hoz 1979. These graffiti are further evidence of the presence of Iberians in the Greek settlement.
[130] De Hoz 1998.　　　[131] Tang 2005: 148–9.　　　[132] Martín 1988.
[133] Ruiz and Molinos 1998: 267–8.

The lead tablets from Emporion and Pech-Maho are important also because they reveal the nature of relations between Greeks and Iberians. Both these texts suggest that the indigenous Iberians took part in the commercial affairs of the Emporitan Greeks. What is striking is the extent of Iberian participation in commercial affairs already by the middle of the sixth century and the fact that Greeks and Iberians were on equal footing.[134] The lead tablet from Emporion, for example, records an offer by a Greek to the Iberian Basped: he gives Basped half a share of the profits if he would transport some merchandise in a ship that Basped had bought; if Basped did not agree to this price, he could make a counter-offer. This indicates that Basped had sufficient means to buy his own ship to use in potentially lucrative trading ventures. Similarly, the fifth-century Pech-Maho inscription is a legal document that attests that the buyer, probably a Greek, had fulfilled his obligation and paid for his shared ownership of boats in front of at least four witnesses, Basigerros, Bleruas, Golo.biur, and Sedegon, whose names are Iberian. These Iberians are important because they protected from fraud whoever (Greek, Iberian, Phoenician, or Etruscan) had sold the boat. These two texts reveal not only the close cooperation between Greeks and Iberians in Emporion, but also the equality of the two parties in their dealings.[135]

As contacts in this area intensified and became permanent with the implantation of Greek Emporion, Greeks and Iberians could feel long-term effects. The Greek polis, on the one hand, changed when it included the local Indiketans within the urban center, incorporated Iberian elements in its housing, and used Iberian pottery. The Indiketans, on the other hand, adopted selectively artistic motifs, technology, and writing systems. Eventually, new products appeared, which can be termed Emporitan, common to both Greeks and Indiketans, such as the creation of a common political constitution and common Emporitan pottery. Yet, despite these cross-cultural borrowings, adaptations, and articulations of new products, whether material or political, both the Greeks and Indiketans of Emporion maintained separate identities: Iberians retained elements of Iberian art, funerary practices, and their language, even when they adopted the Greek or Phoenician alphabets to write it, and, according to Strabo, the Indiketans and Greeks preserved for some years each their own political identity before the development of a common constitution. The Greeks also maintained distinct religious identities, as I discuss next.

---

[134] Sanmartí 2009: 68 thinks that these Iberian men were local chiefs acting as intermediaries in commerce.

[135] These texts also show that that prices were not fixed by the state but determined by the market.

Massaliote, Phokaian, and Ionian identities

The ancient texts discussing the circumstances of the foundation of Massalia and Emporion demonstrate the various levels of collective identity expressed by the Greeks. First, the Greeks of this area had strong cultural affinities with Massalia. All the sources that describe Emporion as a Massaliote foundation suggest that Emporion and Massalia cultivated a mother-city/colony relationship with each other.[136] The very high concentration of Massaliote amphorae in Emporion,[137] the Massaliote coins discovered there,[138] and the fact that in the third century BC coins minted in Emporion were related to the Massaliote standard,[139] all indicate not only the trade connections with Massalia but also the close cultural ties between these two settlements. It is also noteworthy that the sole city-ethnic attested in Emporion, besides the one derived from the name of the settlement itself (Emporitai) attested on the two lead inscriptions discussed above, is *Massalietes*.[140] The two occurrences of this city-ethnic are late in date: one of them is a bilingual stele in Greek and Latin that records the name of a person who sponsored some construction at the temple of Serapis; the other is a funerary stele dated palaeographically to the first century BC. The fact that Massaliotes were frequenting Emporion at this late date shows the close ties between the two settlements.

A Massaliote identity at Emporion may have centered on the cult of Artemis of Ephesos, which, as I will argue, acquired singular importance for Phokaians because of their interactions with the Persians on the Ionian coast. This cult was transferred to Massalia, Emporion, and other poleis associated with Massalia, and once it reached the western Mediterranean it was reinterpreted. It is Strabo who provides a tantalizing statement about Emporitan religion, revealing the links between Emporion and its metropolis Massalia:

ἐνταῦθα δ' ἔστι καὶ ἡ Ῥόδη πολίχνιον, Ἐμποριτῶν κτίσμα, τινὲς δὲ Ῥοδίων φασί· κἀνταῦθα δὲ καὶ ἐν τῷ Ἐμπορίῳ τὴν Ἄρτεμιν τὴν Ἐφεσίαν τιμῶσιν· ἐροῦμεν δὲ τὴν αἰτίαν ἐν τοῖς περὶ Μασσαλίαν. (Strabo 3.4.8)

The town Rhode, is there, too, a foundation of the Emporitans, though some say it is a foundation of the Rhodians. Both there [Rhode] and at Emporion, they worship Artemis of Ephesos. We will provide the reason in the discussion of Massalia.

---

[136] Ps.-Skylax 2; ps.-Skymnos 203–6; Strabo 3.4.8; Aelius Herodianus 1.365.29; Stephanos of Byzantion s.v. Emporion.
[137] Bats 1990. [138] Villaronga 1991: 86 and 89. [139] Villaronga 1998: 58.
[140] Almagro Basch 1952: 18–21, nos. 2 and 3.

This statement, explained in a later passage on Massalia quoted below, is doubly puzzling for scholars. First, it is strange that a Phokaian colony insists on the worship of an Ephesian cult, when colonies usually adopted the νόμιμα (customs), including the cults, of the mother-city. Second, no temple dedicated to Artemis of Ephesos has ever been identified in Emporion, Rhode, or even Massalia. It is commonly accepted, as far as Emporion is concerned, that the temple must have been established in Palaiapolis, where it remained even after the foundation of "Neapolis," and must now lie under the medieval church of San Martí that includes various ancient *spolia* in its construction.[141] Despite the recent stratigraphic excavations in Palaiapolis, however, no such evidence has appeared.[142] Marcet and Sanmartí-Grego proposed instead that the sanctuary of Ephesian Artemis was the fifth-century unidentified temple in "Neapolis."[143] The difficulty of such an interpretation, as Peña has recognized, is that the fifth-century temple was destroyed and rebuilt as a temple dedicated to Asklepios.[144] If the Emporitans still worshipped the Ephesian Artemis in his time, as Strabo seems to imply, then the temple would not have been rededicated to Asklepios.

The sole material evidence for the worship of Artemis in Emporion is numismatic, and even that is controversial, as it depends on the interpretation of the iconography of fourth-century coins minted at Emporion. The earliest coins of this series depict a female head facing left on the obverse and a standing horse on the reverse. The later coins also depict a female head on the obverse, this time facing right, and Pegasus on the reverse. The female head has been interpreted as Arethusa or Persephone,[145] and more recently as a local spring,[146] based on their similarity with Syracusan coins. Peña proposed that the female head is, in fact, Artemis and that Pegasus was a modification of the original standing horse, which in turn derived from Carthaginian coin iconography.[147] The problem is that even if Peña is correct in identifying the female head as Artemis, the fourth century BC date of the coins in question is rather late. The iconography on these Emporitan coins is nonetheless important because it demonstrates the co-optation of myths and symbols across cultures in the Mediterranean, as well

---

[141] This idea began with Almagro Basch 1966: 14 and was followed by subsequent scholars.

[142] Aquilué et al. 2002.

[143] Marcet and Sanmartí-Grego 1989: 21; see also Sanmartí-Grego et al. 1992: 102–12, especially 111.

[144] Peña 2000.

[145] Arethusa: Delgado y Hernández 1876: 114–234; Vives y Escuedero 1926: 19–20. Persephone: Amorós 1933: 3–51. Pujol y Camps 1878: 70 believed that some coins depict Arethusa while others depict Diana. See also Head 1911: 2.

[146] Olmos 1992: 103–20, especially 107–8 and 1995: 41–52, especially 46–7.

[147] Peña 1973 and 2000.

as the importance of trade in spreading far and wide what became a common Mediterranean language of myth. The standing horse on Carthaginian coins, for instance, was interpreted by the Greeks as one of the familiar characters in their myths, namely Pegasus, which they subsequently imprinted on their coins. While we often discuss the long-term results of Greek expansion in the Mediterranean, it is important to recognize that interactions facilitated by trade also changed Greek culture by introducing hybrid cultural products that became part of a common Mediterranean heritage.

Let us now turn to the relevant passage for the worship of the Ephesian Artemis in Strabo's description of Massalia:

κτίσμα δ' ἐστὶ Φωκαιέων ἡ Μασσαλία... ἐν δὲ τῇ ἄκρᾳ τὸ Ἐφέσιον ἵδρυται καὶ τὸ τοῦ Δελφινίου Ἀπόλλωνος ἱερόν· τοῦτο μὲν κοινὸν Ἰώνων ἁπάντων, τὸ δὲ Ἐφέσιον τῆς Ἀρτέμιδός ἐστι νεὼς τῆς Ἐφεσίας. ἀπαίρουσι γὰρ τοῖς Φωκαιεῦσιν ἐκ τῆς οἰκείας λόγιον ἐκπεσεῖν φασιν, ἡγεμόνι χρήσασθαι τοῦ πλοῦ παρὰ τῆς Ἐφεσίας Ἀρτέμι- δος λαβοῦσι· τοὺς μὲν δὴ προσαχθέντας τῇ Ἐφέσῳ ζητεῖν ὄντινα τρόπον ἐκ τῆς θεοῦ πορίσαιντο τὸ προσταχθέν. Ἀριστάρχῃ δὲ τῶν ἐντίμων σφόδρα γυναικῶν παραστῆναι κατ' ὄναρ τὴν θεὸν καὶ κελεῦσαι συναπαίρειν τοῖς Φωκαιεῦσιν, ἀφί- δρυμά τι τῶν ἱερῶν λαβούσῃ· γενομένου δὲ τούτου καὶ τῆς ἀποικίας λαβούσης τέλος, τό τε ἱερὸν ἱδρύσασθαι καὶ τὴν Ἀριστάρχην τιμῆσαι διαφερόντως ἱέρειαν ἀποδείξαντας, ἔν τε ταῖς ἀποίκοις πόλεσι πανταχοῦ τιμᾶν ἐν τοῖς πρώτοις ταύτην τὴν θεὸν καὶ τοῦ ξοάνου τὴν διάθεσιν τὴν αὐτὴν καὶ τἆλλα νόμιμα φυλάττειν τὰ αὐτὰ ἅπερ ἐν τῇ μητροπόλει νενόμισται. (Strabo 4.1.4)

Massalia is a foundation of the Phokaians... The Ephesion and the sanctuary of Apollo Delphinios were founded on the promontory. The latter is common to all Ionians, whereas the Ephesion is a temple of Ephesian Artemis. They say that at the moment when the Phokaians were leaving their home, an oracle came to them advising them to take and use a guide for their voyage from Ephesian Artemis. They went to Ephesos and sought some way to procure from the goddess what had been ordered. In the meantime, the goddess stood by Aristarche, one of the most honor- able women, in her dream and ordered her to sail with the Phokaians, taking one of the cult images. After this happened, and when the colony was established, they founded the temple and bestowed extraordinary honor on Aristarche by naming her a priestess. Everywhere in the daughter poleis they worship Artemis foremost among the gods, and they guard the same shape of the *xoanon* and the other customs, which were traditional in the metropolis.

The worship of the Ephesian Artemis, according to this passage, was not only conserved in Massalia, but also in its colonies.[148] There have been several attempts to interpret this difficult passage, which poses more

---

[148] Strabo 3.4.6 mentions a sanctuary dedicated to Artemis of Ephesos at Hemeroskopeion, a Massaliote foundation.

questions than it answers. What is the date of this event? Why did the oracle come to the Phokaians without their solicitation? What is the importance of Artemis of Ephesos for the Phokaians? How did they worship this goddess? And how did this cult change once it was transferred to the west?

Noting several similarities between the passage quoted above and Herodotus' description of the flight of the Phokaians in 545 BC when Harpagos threatened them, such as taking holy items from the sanctuaries,[149] scholars date the events Strabo recounts to the same time.[150] This implies that neither Strabo nor Herodotus refers to the original foundation of Massalia, which had taken place earlier, at approximately 600 BC, since ordinarily the sources preserve many more details regarding the original foundation of a settlement, including, for example, the name of the founder, his consultation of the oracle at Delphi, etc. There is no evidence that the Phokaians sent an emissary in 545 BC to consult the oracle, as was usual in colonizing expeditions.[151] The oracle, instead, was simply delivered to the Phokaians as they were about to set sail, suggesting that they may have been ready to flee from Phokaia. Given the similarity between Strabo's and Herodotus' accounts and the fact that the oracle came to the Phokaians unsolicited, Strabo's account probably records a second wave of migration that took place in 545 BC.

An interesting parallel is the story of the foundation of Boiai, a polis in Laconia. Pausanias recounts that three cities, Etis, Aphrodisias, and Side, whose inhabitants were all expelled, were anxious to know where they should settle. As in Strabo's account of the foundation of Massalia, Pausanias says that an oracle was delivered to the soon-to-be refugees telling them that Artemis would show them where to dwell. When the latter beached their ship on land, a hare acted as their ἡγεμών, the same word Strabo uses to describe Aristarche, who guided the Phokaians to Massalia.[152] The hare, which is strongly associated with Artemis,[153] finally stopped at a myrtle tree, where the refugees built the city of Boiai and set up the worship of Artemis under the suitable epithet Σωτείρα, Savior.

Artemis herself was worshipped as Artemis Hegemone in two other instances in which the goddess acted as a guide to deliver certain cities from tyrants: Antoninus Liberalis writes that Artemis delivered the city

---

[149] In Strabo 4.1.4 the Phokaians take with them an ἀφίδρυμα, while in Herodotus 1.164 they take τὰ ἀγάλματα τὰ ἐκ τῶν ἱρῶν καὶ τὰ ἄλλα ἀναθήματα (the statues and other dedications from the sanctuaries).

[150] Graham 1970: 140–1; Malkin 1990b: 51 n. 40.

[151] The Phokaians sought an oracle from Delphi twenty years earlier. The oracle commanded them to found Alalia, on Corsica: Herodotus 1.165.

[152] Pausanias 3.22.11–13.   [153] Callimachus, *Hymn to Artemis* 2, 95, 154–7.

of Ambrakia from a tyrant and received a cult in the name of Artemis Hegemone; Pausanias says that Chronios killed the tyrant Aristomelidas of Orchomenos, who had abducted a maiden and built a temple dedicated to Artemis Hegemone, who had guided him in this deed.[154] The word *hegemon* is synonymous with *archegetes*, typically used as an epithet for the founder of a colony, and for Apollo, the god of colonization.[155] When this epithet is used for Artemis, therefore, it must refer to the goddess' role in colonization as the story of the Phokaian emigration and the foundation of Boiai suggests. This role seems to have been particularly important in Ionia. Callimachus, for example, in his hymn to Artemis, also gives the epithet Hegemone to the goddess: the hero Neleus chose Artemis as his guide when he colonized Ionia and founded Miletos and other cities.[156]

A series of inscriptions from both Ephesos and Magnesia, though from the Hellenistic and Roman periods, also associates Artemis with colonization, by granting her the epithet ἀρχηγέτις τῆς πόλεως (city leader/founder).[157] The inscriptions from Ephesos record dedications made in honor of various officials. Those from Magnesia record that the temple of Artemis Leukophryne provided asylum to various Greek communities;[158] the institution of games and sacrifices in honor of the goddess;[159] and, the consecration of a new temple to Artemis Leukophryne.[160] Evidence from previous periods suggests that Artemis was a prominent deity in Ionia earlier than the Hellenistic period. A poem by Anakreon, for example, essentially a prayer to Artemis, describes the goddess as the deity who watched over the city of Magnesia, full of courageous people, and who did not shelter uncivilized (ἀνημέρους) men.[161] The poet here seems to contrast the courageous Greek citizens of Magnesia with the satrap Oroetes and other Persians who had taken over the city. In doing so, however, he reveals the central role Artemis played in Magnesia and also the use of the worship of this goddess as a symbol that opposed the Ionian Greeks with the Persians.

Artemis was not only important as the founder or patron deity of various cities on the Ionian coast; she also acted as the protector of Ephesos around 560 BC, when the Lydians conquered Ephesos under the command of

---

[154] Antoninus Liberalis, *Metamorphoses* 4.5 and Pausanias 8.47.6. In addition to these two cases, Pausanias (3.14.7) attests to a temple dedicated to Artemis Hegemone in Sparta and another one in Arcadia (8.37.1) but provides no commentary for them.

[155] Malkin 1987: 241–50.   [156] Callimachus, *Hymn to Artemis* 225–7.

[157] From Ephesos: *IEph* Ia 27; *IEph* IV 1387, 1398. From Magnesia: *Syll.*³ 557, 560, 562, 695; *IMagn* 37, 41, 53, 54, 56, 60, 63, 64, 79, 85, 89; *OGIS* 231, 232, 233, 319.

[158] *Syll.*³ 557, 560, 562; *IMagn* 37, 53, 54, 56, 62, 63, 79, 85.

[159] *IMagn* 41, 60, 64; *OGIS* 231, 232, 233, 319.   [160] *Syll.*³ 695.

[161] Anakreon fr. 348 (Campbell).

Croesus. The Ephesians' response was to place themselves under Artemis' protection by tying their city to the temple of Artemis with a thread. This made it impossible for the Lydians to attack them, as it would mean committing sacrilege. Though Croesus was nonetheless victorious, Ephesos remained intact and prospered. Fifteen years later, the citizens moved Ephesos to a lower site more difficult to defend but closer to the temple of Artemis.[162] Similarly, by 399 BC the city of Magnesia, still under Persian domination, imitated what the Ephesians had done by moving their city higher up in order to be closer to the temple of Artemis Leukophryne.[163]

In many ways, Strabo's story of the Phokaians fits the pattern established by Ephesos, Magnesia, and Boiai. Threatened by the Persians in 545 BC with total annihilation, the Phokaians decided to move their city, as the Ephesians had done earlier. The Phokaians, therefore, set out to migrate to Massalia for a second time and chose Artemis as their guide, given both her role as a protector of cities against external enemies and her role in colonization, especially when it was a forced emigration. The Phokaians needed a savior of this sort as their city was faced with extinction, and to escape from the Persians they actually emigrated to some of their existing colonies. And, as Malkin proposed, the protection Artemis afforded to the Ephesians was reason enough for the Phokaians to seek a guide from the Ephesian Artemis rather than from their own temple of Artemis.[164] There is no need to suggest, as some scholars have, that a group of Ephesians joined the Phokaian refugees and transferred with them the cult of Ephesian Artemis to Massalia.[165] Rather, the hostile interactions, first with the Lydians and then the Persians who attacked the Ionian communities on the coast of Asia Minor, endowed Artemis at Ephesos with a special role as a protector of whole cities from an enemy. It is perhaps because the Ephesian Artemis saved whole communities in Ionia from their non-Greek enemies that the cult eventually acquired a pan-Ionian character. In the fifth century, according to Thucydides, the major festival for all Ionians was not the pan-Ionian festival of Delos that honored Apollo but rather the Ephesia, which honored Artemis of Ephesos.[166] By transferring the cult of Ephesian Artemis to Massalia and other settlements in the western Mediterranean in the face of a foreign threat, the Phokaians were declaring their Ionian

---

[162] Herodotus 1.26; Aelian, *Varia Historia* 3.26; Polyainos, *Stratagems of War* 6.50.
[163] Diodorus Siculus 14.36.3.   [164] Malkin 1990b.   [165] Domínguez 1999b.
[166] Thucydides 3.104: ἦν δέ ποτε καὶ τὸ πάλαι μεγάλη ξύνοδος ἐς τὴν Δῆλον τῶν Ἰώνων τε καὶ περικτιόνων νησιωτῶν· ξύν τε γὰρ γυναιξὶ καὶ παισὶν ἐθεώρουν, ὥσπερ νῦν ἐς τὰ Ἐφέσια Ἴωνες (Once upon a time, there was a great assemblage of the Ionians and the neighboring islanders at Delos, who used to come to the festival with their wives and children as the Ionians now do at the Ephesia).

identity, as well as their civic identity, since the goddess had helped save Phokaia.

The Phokaians also worshipped a more explicitly pan-Ionian deity, according to Strabo. The opposition between the worship of the Ephesian Artemis and Apollo Delphinios is clear in Strabo's text. The temple of Artemis is described as specifically that of Artemis worshipped in Ephesos, even if it acquired certain pan-Ionic qualities of its own, while the temple of Apollo Delphinios is said to have been common to all Ionians, despite the fact that both literary and archaeological sources suggest that the cult of Apollo Delphinios was prominent not only among Ionians but among Dorians as well.[167] This incarnation of the god also seems to have been particularly prominent in Miletos, as well as in many of its colonies, and to have played a role similar to that of the oracle of Apollo at Delphi: the Milesian Apollo was the *archegetes*, the founder, of many colonies, especially those that originated from poleis in Asia Minor.[168] In addition to a pan-Ionian identity, the cult of Apollo Delphinios in Massalia might have represented the civic identity of the polis. Apollo Delphinios was more than a god of sea navigation, which the epithet Delphinios (of Dolphins) might suggest. Apollo Delphinios had two other functions: he was intimately connected with the political institutions of a polis and presided over *ephebic* rites.[169] In this context it is interesting to note that the temple of Apollo Delphinios was located in the Massaliote acropolis, a space often associated with the political infrastructure of a city.

Through Apollo Delphinios and Artemis of Ephesos, the Greeks in Emporion and the other settlements of the Phokaian network expressed various levels of collective identities that became important to them primarily because of their interactions with other Mediterranean populations. At the same time, once the goddess' cult was transferred to Massalia and the other

[167] Strabo 4.1.4. Graf 1979: 2–22, especially pages 3–4, where he lists all the poleis where Apollo Delphinios was worshipped; Salviat 2000: 25–31.

[168] Huxley 1966: 69; Parke 1967: 49; Fontenrose 1988: 104–5; Forrest 1957: 160–75. It is for this reason that Salviat 2000: 29 proposed that the oracle the Phokaians received arrived from the temple of Apollo of Didyma, not from Delphi, as Malkin 1987: 69–72 had argued, and that this is the reason for the existence of the cult in Massalia. The problem with both Salviat's and Malkin's interpretations is that the oracle delivered to the Phokaians is not, in fact, a foundation oracle. Malkin, however, is correct to point out that the oracle probably came from Delphi, because the Phokaians had previously received an oracle from the Pythia commanding them to found Alalia: Herodotus 1.165. If Strabo's story indeed records events that took place in 545 BC, there would have been no need for a foundation oracle, since Massalia already existed at that time. Regardless of the oracle's origin or purpose, what is significant for our purposes is that, at least in Strabo's view, or that of his sources, the temple of Apollo Delphinios was common to all Ionians.

[169] Graf 1979.

"Phokaian" colonies on the Mediterranean coasts of Liguria, Gaul, and Iberia, it was transformed yet again because of the interactions between the Greeks and the indigenous populations. Artemis of Ephesos became a salient feature of Massaliote identity and by the second century BC, when the Massaliotes faced conflicts with the indigenous populations, they set up a temple to Ephesian Artemis to serve as a marker of territorial control:

διόπερ οἱ Μασσαλιῶται πύργους ἀνέστησαν σημεῖα, ἐξοικειούμενοι πάντα τρόπον τὴν χώραν· καὶ δὴ καὶ τῆς Ἐφεσίας Ἀρτέμιδος κἀνταῦθα ἱδρύσαντο ἱερόν, χωρίον ἀπολαβόντες ὃ ποιεῖ νῆσον τὰ στόματα τοῦ ποταμοῦ. (Strabo 4.1.8)

On account of which, the Massaliotes set up towers as beacons, because they were in every way appropriating the country; indeed, for the same purpose, they established a temple of the Ephesian Artemis there, after first enclosing a piece of land which is made an island by the mouths of the river.

Even more than a symbol of Massaliote identity, the cult also acquired a proselytizing aspect, according to Strabo, which is unheard of in the history of Greek religion. The Phokaian colonies in Iberia, like Emporion and Rhode, not only worshipped Artemis foremost among the gods and conserved the shape of her statue and the other customs but also taught these rites to the Iberians, so that they sacrificed to the goddess in the Greek manner:

ὕστερον μέντοι ταῖς ἀνδραγαθίαις ἴσχυσαν προσλαβεῖν τινα τῶν πέριξ πεδίων ἀπὸ τῆς αὐτῆς δυνάμεως ἀφ' ἧς καὶ τὰς πόλεις ἔκτισαν, ἐπιτειχίσματα τὰς μὲν κατὰ τὴν Ἰβηρίαν τοῖς Ἴβηρσιν, οἷς καὶ τὰ ἱερὰ τῆς Ἐφεσίας Ἀρτέμιδος παρέδοσαν τὰ πάτρια, ὥστε ἑλληνιστὶ θύειν. (Strabo 4.1.5)

Later, however, because of their valor they took some of the surrounding plains, thanks to the same military strength by which they also founded their cities. These cities served as strongholds throughout Iberia against the Iberians. They even handed down to the Iberians the customary rites of the Ephesian Artemis, so that they sacrificed in the Greek manner.

Strabo again sets the opposition as that between Iberians and Greeks. He does not say the Iberians were taught to make sacrifices to Artemis in the Phokaian or Massaliote, or even Ephesian manner, as might be expected; rather, he specifies that the Iberians learned to sacrifice in the Greek manner (ἑλληνιστί). The word ἑλληνιστί is usually translated in this passage as "in the Greek manner," although in every other instance (282 times) it appears in texts it refers to the use of the Greek language. What would it mean to make sacrifices in the "Greek" manner? There were no overall "Greek" practices;

the worship of divinities varied on the local and regional level. City-states usually had clearly articulated cult practices, which varied from polis to polis, and often colonies adopted these from their mother-city. The customs due to the Ephesian Artemis were different from rites performed in honor of Artemis elsewhere. In the case of Massalia, however, one polis (Phokaia) adopted the cult practices of another (Ephesos). How was the goddess worshipped in Massalia, Emporion, and the other colonies? Strabo points out the conservatism of ritual practices when he says that the colonies kept the same shape of the *xoanon* and the other customs that were traditional in the metropolis.[170] Yet this statement is problematic. Which metropolis is Strabo talking about? Phokaia? Massalia? Or perhaps the metropolis of the cult, Ephesos? If it is Phokaia or Massalia, that might imply that the Ephesian Artemis was worshipped differently in these two cities than she was at Ephesos. Further, are we to think that some five hundred years after the transference of the cult nothing had changed in the manner the goddess was worshipped? No further details about the cult in the west are known, except that the local Iberians were taught to worship the goddess *hellenisti*. Perhaps we should not translate the word *hellenisti* as if to imply that there was a Greek manner in which to venerate Ephesian Artemis, since the word always indicates the language used; perhaps Strabo suggests that Greeks taught Iberians to perform sacrifices to the Ephesian Artemis in Greek.[171]

Archaeological evidence for the worship of Artemis in the region around Emporion is ambiguous. An indigenous temple in Ullastret, for example, was probably dedicated to a female divinity, identified as Artemis based on the dedications discovered in the temple, which resemble those of Artemis Orthia from Sparta.[172] It is tempting to see connections with Emporion and Massalia because of the peculiarity of Strabo's statement, but the evidence for the worship of Artemis in Ullastret is obviously not conclusive. The only other secure evidence for the worship of Artemis from the Iberian peninsula is one dedicatory inscription to Artemis from Cordoba, which is not in the vicinity of Emporion.[173] Otherwise, many other indigenous sanctuaries, temples, and domestic shrines have been excavated from the Emporitan region, but none of them show evidence of a worship of Artemis.[174]

Strabo does not explain these actions of the Phokaian Greeks in Iberia nor does he give a date for them. Even if these events took place much later than the foundation of Emporion, they are nonetheless indicative of the changing circumstances created by colonial encounters. The Phokaians adopted the

---

[170] Strabo 4.1.4.
[171] Cf. the Roman rites in honor of Ceres conducted in Greek, on which see Scheid 1995.
[172] Moneo 2003: 228–30. [173] Tovar 1971. [174] Moneo 2003: 205–66.

cult of the Ephesian Artemis and adapted it in order to declare both their civic identity, since the Ephesian Artemis rescued Phokaia, and their ethnic identity since the Ephesian Artemis had acquired pan-Ionian significance because of the hostile interactions between the Greeks in Ionia and their conquerors, the Lydians and the Persians. Once transferred abroad, the cult took on a new Massaliote identity and was used as a symbol of territorial control against the indigenous populations. The cult even counted Iberians among its worshippers who probably used the Greek language when they performed rituals in honor of the goddess. From Ionia to Iberia, therefore, Artemis' identity changed as she became a means of asserting and defining different levels of collective identities for the Greeks who were encountering new worlds in the western Mediterranean.

Conclusion

The history of Greco-Iberian relations in northeastern Iberia stretches as far back as the Bronze Age when Greek imports together with Phoenician and Etruscan products found their way to Iberian households and Iberian products traveled east. The Greeks founded Emporion first on an islet and later moved it to the facing coast. The Greco-Iberian encounters in the western Mediterranean transformed the landscape in northeastern Catalonia, as well as all the groups involved. The Greeks appropriated land and established a settlement there, thereby altering the topography of the Iberian coast and the hinterland by encouraging the nucleation of settlements around the Greek town, changing the ecology of the region with the introduction of certain crops and the intensification of the cultivation of others. Iberian art adopted certain Greek techniques and art forms and changed them to create new hybrid Iberian products that were used by both Greeks and Iberians. At the same time, the malleable Greek myths changed to incorporate the new areas and peoples encountered, and Greek architectural styles incorporated Iberian elements as the housing in Emporion demonstrates. The existence of flexible polytheistic religions also enabled the creation of a common Mediterranean culture that could be used by any group: Greeks adopted Carthaginian coin iconography while adapting it so that it made sense to a Greek audience, and Iberians saw Dionysiac scenes on Greek vases as carrying a funereal meaning and thus used them in funerary contexts. These cross-cultural borrowings are indicative of a larger process that created common identities inclusive of all the groups involved.

Despite the tight commercial network of interrelations between Greeks and Iberians, not to mention their close civic association, the two groups preserved their individual identities: Phokaian, Emporitan, Ionian, Indiketan, and Iberian. Both politics and religion emerge as vehicles for maintaining group identity. The Indiketan Iberians inhabiting the indigenous settlement that grew up near Emporion eventually asked to be surrounded by a common wall with the Greek city, even though another wall continued to divide their habitat from the Greek one, forming the *dipolis*. The Indiketans and Emporitans each maintained their own constitution until a later point, probably in the Hellenistic period, when the two finally formed a mixed constitution based on both Greek and Iberian νόμιμα. The cult of the Ephesian Artemis played a central role in Phokaian, and therefore Emporitan, identity. Artemis was the *hegemone* of Ionia and the *archegetis* of Magnesia and Ephesos; she was involved in colonization movements like her brother Apollo; finally, the goddess offered protection to whole cities threatened by external enemies. In the Massaliote and Emporitan imagination, it was the Ephesian cult that rescued Phokaia from extinction by guiding the Phokaian refugees to Massalia. In Massalia, Emporion, and Rhode, the cult of the Ephesian Artemis declared both their civic – the Ephesian Artemis rescued Phokaia – and Ionian identity – the Ephesian Artemis was of pan-Ionian significance.

The role of this commercial settlement in the negotiation of identity did not end with its decline and eventual abandonment. The final alternating sequence of the audiovisual presentation offered at the Museu d'Arqueologia de Catalunya at Empúries between ancient and modern is indicative of all the different levels of modern identity that Empúries emblematizes – Spanish, Catalan, and European. Ancient Greek vase-paintings depicting games are superimposed with the Barcelona Olympics, commercial amphorae with the modern port of Barcelona, and ancient coins produced in Emporion with the notes and coins of the euro: culture, politics, history, and religion were, and still are, used to assert collective identities.

2 | Gravisca

Herodotus is the earliest source that recounts that the Phokaians were the first to travel to the western Mediterranean and reach wealthy Tartessos. There they befriended the local king Arganthonios who not only became the benefactor of Phokaia, paying for the enormous wall that surrounded the city, but also invited the Phokaians to come and settle in his land, thus providing an *aition* for the later foundation of Phokaian cities in Iberia, such as Emporion. Herodotus may have glorified the Phokaian success but he did not forget to signal that the Samians reached Tartessos and made the greatest profit of all the Greeks by selling their cargo. Except, that is, for a certain individual by the name of Sostratos, son of Laodamas of Aigina; no one had ever been able to do as well as he.[1]

In 1970 Sostratos of Aigina may have left the realm of Herodotean myth and become reality, when half of a large stone anchor bearing an inscription was discovered in Gravisca, a Greek commercial settlement in Etruria (Figure 4). It reads: "Ἀπόλονος Αἰγινάτα ἐμι. Σόστρατος ἐποίησε hο [–]" (I am of Aiginetan Apollo; Sostratos . . . made me).[2] The date of the inscription – end of the sixth century or beginning of the fifth – and the Aiginetan script, together with the fact that the anchor was discovered in a commercial settlement far away from Aigina, suggest that Sostratos might be the same trader Herodotus mentions. A further connection between Sostratos and Etruria is the common mercantile mark on Attic pottery, *SO*, perhaps short for Sostratos. Largely unknown outside Etruria, this mark is inscribed on vases dating to 535–505 BC, a date that fits that of the inscription.[3] Sostratos is probably the earliest trader known from literature whose existence is confirmed by the material record.

Sostratos was an Aiginetan merchant who traded primarily Attic pottery with principally one area, Etruria, through Gravisca. Gravisca, however, was not simply a throughway for a single Aiginetan; it was an emporion of far greater importance. The first excavations at Gravisca, conducted in two seasons in 1969 and 1970, revealed two main sectors of the site: one consisted entirely of the Roman colony that dates to 181 BC, while the other

[1] Herodotus 4.152.   [2] Torelli 1971a: fig. 57.   [3] A. W. Johnston 1972.

Figure 4 Anchor from the Graviscan sanctuaries with an inscribed dedication by Sostratos to Aiginetan Apollo, end of the sixth century BC.

was a sanctuary with various temples and cults.[4] Ongoing excavations have identified another sacred area to the north of the sanctuaries (Figure 5).[5] The Roman colony is beyond the scope of this work and will not, therefore, be

[4] Torelli 1971a. For a summary of the results in English, see Ridgway 1974: 49–51.
[5] Fortunelli 2007.

Figure 5 Plan of the north and south complexes of the Graviscan sanctuaries.

considered; the sanctuaries, however, are vital in understanding the Greeks'
presence in Etruria, the nature of interactions among Greeks from different
poleis and between Greeks and Etruscans, and the role the sanctuaries played
in the social life of a multiethnic emporion.[6]

---

[6] Here I am concerned with the social aspect of religion, and more specifically, how it ultimately
encouraged and mediated interactions between different ethnic groups, rather than the

Greeks and Etruscans had been in contact (and conflict) for several hundred years before they encountered each other at Gravisca. The Etruscans were the heirs of the Villanovan culture, and inhabited the region roughly equivalent to modern Tuscany. By the eighth century BC when relations between the Etruscans and other Mediterranean populations intensified, Etruria was urbanized,[7] characterized by a city-state culture,[8] a polytheistic religion,[9] and a thriving artistic production.[10] The recent interest in Etruscology has increased our understanding of this particular civilization by focusing on indigenous sources and material culture rather than exclusively on Greek and Roman sources, which contain their own literary tropes that maligned the Etruscans.[11] For instance, the Etruscans were considered to be an early thalassocracy based mostly on piracy. Etruscan pirates were to said to have abducted the god Dionysus in the Homeric hymn to the god;[12] stolen a statue of Hera from Samos;[13] abducted women from Brauron;[14] and held territories on Sicily so that no one could safely sail there to trade.[15] Greek sources also mention that the Etruscans forcefully held multiple territories in the Mediterranean outside of their homeland, including Lemnos and Imbros,[16] and had colonies on Sardinia, Corsica, the Balearics, and even the coasts of Spain.[17] These descriptions of violent Etruscans wrongfully seizing lands, goods, or people, may not accurately represent historical reality and may indicate nothing more than the maritime perspective of the Etruscans or the competitive nature of the relations between Greek and Etruscan traders.

Archaeological and epigraphic evidence, however, indicates that the Etruscans were a maritime civilization.[18] The previous chapter discussed the strong presence of Etruscan products on the southern coast of France and Spain, and indicated not only that Etruscan goods were traded but also that they were traded by Etruscans.[19] At the very least, the representation of ships in Etruscan art and the identification of shipwrecks as being

economic role of sanctuaries, as either marketplaces or centers of production. Domínguez 2001 argues that religion in emporia was necessary because trade in the archaic period was a form of ritualized friendship.

[7] Riva 2010.   [8] Heurgon 1957; Massa-Pairault 1996; Torelli 2000a.

[9] Pfiffig 1975; Jannot 1995; Gaultier and Briquel 1999; De Grummond and Simon 2006.

[10] Pallottino 1975; Haynes 2000; Torelli 2000b; Camporeale 2004; Izzet 2007.

[11] For similar literary tropes that malign the Phoenicians see Winter 1995.

[12] Homeric Hymn to Dionysus 7.1–16.   [13] Athenaios 15.12.

[14] Plutarch, *On the Bravery of Women* 8.   [15] Strabo 6.2.2.

[16] Plutarch, *On the Bravery of Women* 8.

[17] Sardinia: Strabo 5.2.7; Corsica: Diodorus Siculus 5.13; Balearics and Spain: Stephanos of Byzantion s.v. Banaurides.

[18] For the Etruscans as a maritime civilization see Pallottino 1975; Cristofani 1983; Camporeale 2004.

[19] The lead from Pech-Maho contains an Etruscan text probably relating to commerce (Lejeune et al. 1988).

Etruscan ships is good evidence for the commercial and maritime character of the Etruscans.[20] Elsewhere in the Mediterranean, Etruscans exported
and traded their products since the eighth century BC, which can be found
in Italy, Sardinia, Sicily, Corsica, North Africa, France, Spain, the Greek
peninsula, Cyprus, Carthage, and Asia Minor.[21] The connections between
Sardinia and Etruria are particularly close, with Sardinian material culture
found in high concentration in Etruscan city-states and vice versa.[22] As
for more permanent interactions, it is now clear that Etruscan communities
existed in the Western Mediterranean, especially in southern France, Genoa,
and Pisa.[23] A hospitality token from Carthage that records the name of a
Carthaginian in Etruscan suggests not only that Carthaginians were present
in Etruria but also that there were permanent and official ties between the
two places.[24] We should also imagine that Etruscans reciprocated these visits
and lived in Carthage.

The picture in the Eastern Mediterranean is slightly different. Certainly,
bucchero vases inscribed in Greek and dedicated at sanctuaries were most
likely carried by Greeks, but there are also several Etruscan dedications discovered in Greek and Punic contexts, a fact which suggests the presence
of Etruscans in non-Etruscan lands. For example, one Etruscan dedication was discovered in the temple of Aphaia on Aigina and another in the
Athenian agora.[25] These few examples are indicative of a larger and more
permanent Etruscan presence in the eastern Mediterranean. The endur-
ing ties, at least with the Greeks, are also obvious from the two treasuries
dedicated at the sanctuary at Delphi by two Etruscan city-states, Caere
and Spina.[26] More surprising is the existence of an Etruscan community
on the island of Lemnos, which Plutarch claimed was held by the Etruscans, attested by several sixth century BC inscriptions in a language
that has been called both Etruscan and Etruscoid.[27] One of the longer

[20] Turfa and Steinmayer 1999 and 2001. Jannot 1995 and Pomey 2006 suggest the opposite.
[21] Cristofani et al. 1985; Gras 1985b; Camporeale 2004; Gori 2006.
[22] Paoletti and Perna 2002.   [23] Gori 2006.   [24] Messineo 1983; *ET*, Af 3.1.
[25] From the sanctuary of Hera at Perachora there is a bucchero *kantharos* with a Greek dedicatory
    inscription and from Pantikapaion on the Black Sea coast there exists a Greek dedication to
    Artemis of Ephesos inscribed on an Etruscan strainer. See Camporeale 2004: 95–6.
[26] Strabo 5.1.7, 5.3.2, 9.3.8; Pliny, *Natural History* 3.120.
[27] Plutarch, *On the Bravery of Women* 8. Thucydides 4.109 and Herodotus 5.26 also mention an
    Etruscan presence on Lemnos. A lot has been made of this inscription and what it may imply
    regarding the origins of the Etruscans. Some scholars (e.g., Massa-Pairault 1996: 19–22) have
    interpreted the Etruscan colony on Lemnos as confirming Herodotus' statement (1.94–8) that
    the Etruscans came from the East and explain the Etruscan community on Lemnos as the first
    to be established when the Etruscans were on their way west to found other city-states on the
    Italian peninsula. Others consider the colony as a foundation that originated from Etruria:

Figure 6 Funerary stele of an Etruscan warrior from Lemnos, sixth century BC.

texts is a funerary inscription that follows traditional Etruscan dating systems and mentions magistracies known from Etruria (Figure 6).[28] It also includes two toponyms, one of which can be identified with a town on

Pallottino 1975: 69–75; Cristofani 1983: 58–9. The latter argument is more persuasive.
De Simone 2009 discusses a recently discovered Etruscan inscription from Lemnos.
[28] Heurgon 1980.

the coast of Lemnos called Myrina and the other with Phokaia, demonstrating the extent of the network connecting Greeks and Etruscans in the Mediterranean.

The Etruscan maritime expansion was mirrored by the contemporary implantation of Greek and Phoenician settlements in the west, including in lands near Etruria, such as the bay of Naples, Sardinia, or Corsica. The colonial encounters in this region had permanent results for everyone involved, as is evident both in literary sources and the archaeological record. For example, the Etruscan alphabet was based on the Euboian Greek one and might have been learned in Pithekoussai or Kyme, jointly founded by Euboian Greeks, Phoenicians, and perhaps Etruscans.[29] The alphabet, however, was devoid of any ethnic significance. Much as in the case of the Iberians, who borrowed the Phoenician and Greek scripts to write their own language, the Etruscans also adopted and adapted the alphabet to write Etruscan. Other borrowings were relevant to the establishment of social identities. As many have noted, Etruscan elites adopted the Greek symposion, originally borrowed from the Near East, and the various drinking cups and plates used for eating and drinking. The appropriation of elite pursuits, such as the symposion, was a way for the Etruscan elites to maintain their elite identities and ties with their non-Etruscan equals, and differentiate themselves from Etruscan non-elites.[30]

Similarly, the appropriation of Greek myth and mythical heroes has been linked to Etruscan elites who embraced Greek culture as a way of maintaining their elite identity. The Etruscans, for example, adopted the Greek Apollo, Artemis, Heracles, and Odysseus into their pantheon, calling them Apulu or Aplu, Aritimi or Artumes, Hercle, and Utuse respectively. The role of the last hero, Odysseus/Utuse, as a mediating figure between Greeks and Etruscans in Etruria has been much discussed.[31] The hero was also said, as early as Hesiod, to be the progenitor of the Etruscans.[32] Just as the contacts with Iberia led to the incorporation of that peninsula into Greek myths through Heracles, Etruria was included through Odysseus. The malleability of Greek myth allowed Greeks to construct elaborate genealogies in order to relate themselves to other Mediterranean populations, thereby creating a common Mediterranean mythological background and positioning themselves within a larger collective. Interestingly, by the late classical period,

---

[29] Bonfante and Bonfante 2002: 52.   [30] Rathje 1990.   [31] Malkin 1998 and 2002.
[32] Hesiod, *Theogony* 1011–18. Even though M. L. West 1966: 398–9 thinks that the end of the *Theogony* is spurious, the implication of the lines is that in the Greek imagination the Etruscans were related to the Greeks.

Figure 7a and b Aristonothos Crater, mid-seventh century BC. Side A depicts a naval battle probably between a Greek and an Etruscan ship; Side B depicts the blinding of Polyphemos by Odysseus and his men.

Etruscans were doing the same by claiming Utuse as the legendary founder of certain Etruscan cities.[33]

The famous Aristonothos crater discovered in a tomb in Caere is another example of the cross-cultural borrowings in Etruria. The crater was painted on local clay by a Greek as the name Aristonothos shows, and on one side depicted a battle between two ships, one Greek and the other probably Etruscan, and on the other Odysseus blinding Polyphemos (Figure 7a and b).

---

[33] For example, Theopompos *FGrH* 115 F 354 says that Odysseus founded the city of Gortynaia in Etruria.

Figure 7 (*cont.*)

Scholars have read these scenes variously, but all interpret them within a colonial and post-colonial framework. Thus, the depiction of Odysseus blinding Polyphemos has been called an allegory of the Etruscan victory over the Greeks, symbolized also by the naval battle on the other side of the vase.[34] Alternatively, Polyphemos has been interpreted as a metaphor for the dangers faced by the Greek colonists.[35] Finally, both sides taken together could illustrate the ambivalent nature of the colonial experience, embodied in the glory of war seen in the naval battle and the fear of the native symbolized by the cannibalistic Cyclops.[36] This latter reading is

[34] Torelli 1996: 568–72.   [35] Martelli 1987: 264.   [36] Dougherty 2003.

sophisticated in the way it accounts for both conflict and collaboration in the colonial world and demonstrates the importance of the choice of images on vases produced in a colonial milieu.

The examples just mentioned are just a few selected to illustrate the general character of the interactions between Greeks and Etruscans and the specific changes brought about by these encounters. Gravisca exemplifies mainly the collaborative side of cross-cultural interactions between the two groups because it was founded in order to promote long-distance trade. It also allows a glimpse into the life of a Greek community permanently settled in Etruria. Gravisca is emblematic of the close encounters resulting from cross-cultural trade. Through the material record one is able to discern the creation of a mutually comprehensible world for various Greeks and Etruscans, especially through religion. While the Greeks were present in Gravisca, Etruscans used the sanctuary alongside them, and when the Greeks left, the Etruscans took over the various cults and adopted the divinities that had been worshipped there while at the same time giving them an Etruscan twist. The polytheistic frame of mind was instrumental in enabling Greeks and Etruscans to coexist by providing them with a common set of gods, and therefore, a common Mediterranean religious culture they could use to relate and react to one another. These gods may have had different names and may have been worshipped with local variations, but in the setting of a multiethnic *emporion* they were easily recognizable and adopted by both groups as their own. For their part, Greek dedicators sometimes expressed their civic identities by making offerings to divinities prominent in their *poleis* of origin. At the same time, living in Etruria and interacting with Etruscans led to the construction of new identities in Gravisca: the Greeks who came together here recognized that, irrespective of their origin, they all had certain Greek gods in common, creating what one might call a Hellenic identity.

Greek identities in Gravisca

One of the challenges Gravisca presents to the ancient historian is that it is mentioned sparingly in ancient sources. Practically no information exists, for example, that deals with the political status or establishment of the settlement. Strabo, the sole Greek source that mentions Gravisca, characterizes it as a πολίχνιον.[37] The term πολίχνιον, along with other

---

[37] Strabo 5.2.8.

words like πολίδιον, πόλισμα, πολισμάτιον, and πολίχνη, is a cognate of the term *polis*. In his study of site classification in Stephanos of Byzantion, Whitehead suggested that there was no difference among these classifiers and that the ancient lexicographer used polis-cognates interchangeably with the term *polis*.[38] Strabo's use of the term *polichnion* is consistent with the idea that politically there was no significant distinction between a *polichnion* and a polis,[39] but *polichnia* differed from poleis in their small size.[40] At least in Strabo's time, Gravisca was a small polis.

As was mentioned in the Introduction, Gravisca is not called an empo-rion in either literary or epigraphic sources. Nonetheless scholars have always treated it as an emporion, with good reason. Both ancient texts and the archaeological material discovered in Gravisca suggest that this site was a Greek polis dependent on the Etruscan authorities of Tarquinia, whose commercial port, facilities, and multiethnic population suggest that its main purpose was to facilitate trade. This fits precisely the definition of a Greek emporion. Moreover, several of Gravisca's characteristics are similar

---

[38] Whitehead 1994a: 121.

[39] The geographer ascribes to *polichnia* the same political characteristics as poleis: they could be foundations (e.g. 3.4.8, 7.1.48, 7.7.5, 7.6.1, 9.4.8, etc.) or *synoikismoi* composed of various settlements (9.5.17, 12.3.37, 12.6.1); they used their own or their metropolis' *nomima* (10.4.17); and were characterized as belonging to a certain region or people (4.1.12, 7.6.1). They had temples and sanctuaries, as well as residential areas with houses (5.2.6, 5.3.6, 9.2.7, 10.4.6, 13.3.5, 14.1.20), fortifications around the settlement (11.2.18, 12.3.10, 14.4.1), and harbors (13.1.63, 14.1.8, 14.5.18, 14.5.19, 5.2.6). Of the sixty-eight other *polichnia* that Strabo mentions, the majority (thirty-six) are classified as poleis by other authors: Hemeroskopeion (3.4.6), Rhode (3.4.8), Poplonion (5.2.6), Kollatia (5.3.2), Antemna (5.3.2), Fidenai (5.3.2), Alaisa (6.2.1), Chalastra (7a.1.24), Aineia, (7a.1.24), Tomis (7.6.1), Istros (7.6.1), Anchiale (7.6.1), Bouchetion (7.7.5), Krithote (7.1.56), Hyrmine (8.3.10), Andania (8.3.25), Daulis (9.3.13), Molykreia (9.4.8), Eleona (9.5.18), Chalkis/Hypochalkis (10.2.4), Tieion (12.3.8), Abonou teichos (12.3.10), Karana (12.3.37), Ikonion (12.6.1), Pedason (13.1.59), Herakleia (14.1.8), Pygela (14.1.20), Bargasa (14.2.15), Korykon (14.4.1), Aigaia (14.5.18), Bambyke (16.2.7), Beroia (16.2.7), Herakleia (16.2.7), Gabala (16.2.12), Herakleion (16.2.12), Tainaron (17.3.20); twenty-two are not classified elsewhere: Labikon (5.3.2), Teanou Sidikinon (5.4.10), Kefaloidion (6.2.1), Ouereton (6.3.5), Naulochos (7.6.1), Kisson (7a.1.24), Tempyra (7.1.48), Opisthomarathos (9.3.13), Alalkomenas (10.2.16), Prason (10.4.6), Ideessa (11.2.18), Herpa (12.2.5), Chrysa (13.1.63), Grynion (13.3.5), Keramos (14.2.15), Erai (14.1.32), Leukai (14.1.38), Garsaoura (14.2.29), Issos (14.5.19), Ornithon polis (16.2.24), Leire (16.4.4), Lynga (17.3.2); five are called *polichnia* by other authors: Myrmekion (7.4.5), Delion (9.2.7), Kallipolis (13.1.18), Kanai (13.1.68), Stratonikeia (14.2.25); four are not described with *polis*-cognates but rather as mountains, islands, or promontories: Kirkaion (5.3.6), Prote (8.3.23), Poseidion (16.2.12), Karmelos (16.2.27); and one is called a polis by Strabo in another passage: Makynia (*polichnion* at 10.2.4 and polis at 10.2.21).

[40] Strabo 7.7.5 and 17.3.2 describes two *polichnia*, Bouchetion and Tringa, as being small. In addition, many of the named *polichnia* in Strabo have diminutive names, such as Poplonion, Myrmekion, Tieion, Bouchetion, Kefaloidion (5.2.6, 5.3.6, 5.3.9, 6.3.5, 7.4.5, 7.7.5, 9.2.7, 10.4.6, 12.3.8, 12.6.1, 13.1.59, 13.3.5, 14.4.1, 17.3.20).

to Emporion, Naukratis, Pistiros, and Peiraieus, all known as emporia from ancient sources. The other emporia examined in this work also had a commercial function while their status was political, with the exception of the emporion of Peiraieus, which was an Athenian deme. Pistiros, in addition to being an emporion whose independence was guaranteed by the Thracian authorities, was also a polis; Naukratis was an emporion and a political entity dependent on the Egyptian government. All three settlements, Emporion, Naukratis, and Pistiros, were permanent, engaged heavily in trade, and had varying degrees of political independence. Given these comparisons, it is likely that Gravisca combined some level of political independence with a primarily commercial function but remained dependent on Tarquinia. Again, the mutually exclusive classification of settlements into either political or commercial entities, discussed in the previous chapter, can no longer be maintained.

Topographical studies have shown the extent of the site and its connections with the surrounding territories in the archaic and classical periods. Tombs from the sixth century, when Gravisca was first inhabited, are scattered on a road from Tarquinia to the east, around Gravisca, and along the coast to the south of the settlement,[41] and the ancient port was connected via a road with Tarquinia.[42] The construction of the road is strong evidence that Gravisca served as a port for the Etruscan town. Emporion was also connected to its hinterland with roadways. The difference is that whereas Emporion was associated with indigenous settlements that grew up around it and may have been dependent on the Greek polis, the Greek commercial settlement of Gravisca was established in Etruscan territory, and it was connected to a single Etruscan town. Although no residential or political sites around Gravisca have been excavated, it seems likely that Gravisca was subordinate to Tarquinia, and therefore, politically dependent on it, despite whatever independence it had to carry out commercial affairs.

Prospecting and excavations in and around the ancient port have clarified its position and structure, which were still merely conjectures when Gravisca was first excavated in the 1970s.[43] The distribution of ballast discovered underwater suggests that the outer port had two openings: the northern one was wide and, therefore, was probably the principal entry; the other was likely intended to relieve the rising waters whenever the northwesterly

---

[41] Torelli 1971a: 198–9.   [42] Torelli 1971a: 197–9; Quilici 1968: 116 and map on p. 115.
[43] Frau 1982a. In an article written shortly before actual excavations began in Gravisca, Quilici 1968: 118 follows Pasqui 1885: 519 n.3, who claims he noticed a mole underwater near the promontory of Porto Clementino and identified it as the medieval pier.

Mistral raged.[44] Aerial photography has shown further that the outer port acted as an antechamber to another basin, identified as the commercial port.[45] This division into an outer and inner harbor follows the plans of other major ports like that of Halikarnassos, Massalia, Syracuse, and Carthage, and probably served defensive as well as commercial purposes.[46] The existence of such an elaborate port, similar in structure to other commercial ports around the Mediterranean, suggests Gravisca rivaled them in importance as a trading settlement.

The elaborate and well-connected Graviscan port had a significant Greek presence, as is suggested by the unprecedented quantities of Greek votives from the sanctuary: most of the material from its foundation around 580 BC to the first decades of the fifth century is Greek. Although the Etruscan town and any other possible residential sector have not yet been excavated, the sheer quantity of Greek relative to Etruscan material suggests that Greeks were present permanently in this area. Moreover, as is typical of commercial settlements, the pottery discovered in Gravisca is of varied provenance: Massaliote, Corinthian, Laconian, Phokaian, Samian, Milesian, Chian, and Etruscan pots are common, and votive terra-cotta lamps – the largest quantity of Greek lamps in Etruria – are mostly East Greek, some Attic, and few of local production.[47] Transport or storage amphorae represent a high proportion (about 15 percent) of the imported pottery here and are mostly from Ionia (Samos, Chios, Lesbos, Klazomenai, and Miletos) with a few specimens from Athens, Corinth, Laconia, Massalia, Phoenicia, and Carthage.[48] Some of these vessels were inscribed with Attic or Etruscan numerals and commercial marks.[49] Commercial stamps are by themselves evidence of trade; in Gravisca they luckily also show who bought the imported products: stamps on pottery often resemble those on large vases discovered in Etruscan cemeteries, suggesting that the local Etruscan population was the recipient of a lot of the goods imported.[50] The wide range of products, the high proportion of amphorae in contrast to other vessels, and the obvious connection between pottery discovered in Tarquinia and that in the port of Gravisca, are all indicative of a site that served as an import and export center that traded regularly with its surroundings and promoted cross-cultural contacts.

[44] Georgi 1982: 23–7.   [45] Frau 1982b: 69–75.   [46] Frau 1982b: 49 and 71.

[47] Torelli 1971a: 262–85 and 1971b: 51; Valentini 1993; Boldrini 1994; Huber 1999; Pianu 2000; Galli 2004; Iacobazzi 2004; Bruni 2009.

[48] Slaska 1985: 19.   [49] A. W. Johnston and Pandolfini 2000: 39–41 and 48.

[50] A. W. Johnston and Pandolfini 2000: 48–9, with examples of marks that resemble those commonly found on pots discovered in Etruscan cemeteries.

Despite the fact that written sources do not discuss the establishment of this settlement, as they do, for example, in the case of Emporion or Naukratis, scholars have not shied away from suggesting possible founding cities for Gravisca. Solin, for example, has argued that Milesians had founded Gravisca based on his assessment that a high percentage of the inscribed names from Gravisca were Milesian.[51] Ehrhardt has pointed out, however, that Solin connected only three (Themistagoras, Eudemos, Paktyes) of the nineteen names to Miletos and showed that they were all widespread throughout Ionia and thus not indicative of a close connection to Miletos.[52] The most widely accepted theory regarding the foundation of Gravisca is that proposed by the original excavators of the site. Torelli attributed to the Phokaians, who were also present in Gravisca, the inauguration of its use as a Greek emporion. He based this proposal not on onomastic evidence but rather on the Massaliote commercial amphorae found in Gravisca, two pottery fragments belonging to one *dinos* that may have been produced in Phokaia, on the fact that the earliest sanctuary was dedicated to Aphrodite, a goddess who was also worshipped in Massalia, and on the close trade-connections between Etruria and the Phokaian trade network, described in the previous chapter.[53] Anyone could carry on a ship Massaliote pottery, however, and a connection between the cult of Aphrodite in Massalia and Gravisca cannot be proven. More recently, Haack has argued against a Phokaian foundation and suggested instead that it was Samians who founded Gravisca, because of the large number of dedicatory inscriptions to Hera, the similarity of the types of finds found in Gravisca and those found in Hera's temples, discussed below, and the importance the goddess had in Samos.[54] Indeed, the number of dedications to Hera (forty-three) far outweighs the number of dedications to other Greek divinities (six to Aphrodite, three to Apollo, one to Demeter, and one to either the Dioskouroi or Zeus).[55] However, these numbers are not necessarily an indication that a particular group of Greeks established Gravisca; a more likely suggestion is that Samians may have founded a sanctuary dedicated to Hera just as they did in Naukratis, but this, too, is a conjecture and not conclusive. Although a Greek founding polis cannot be identified for Gravisca, as it can in the case of Emporion, whose ties with Massalia and Phokaia are clear, this in no way limits the discussion of the construction of identities in this settlement in Etruria.

---

[51] Solin 1981. [52] Ehrhardt 1985. [53] Torelli 1982: 322–4.
[54] Haack 2007. [55] A. W. Johnston in A. W. Johnston and Pandolfini 2000: 17–18.

Gravisca was a commercial settlement that hosted people from various places in the Greek world, as is clear from the dedicatory inscriptions on votive offerings excavated from the sanctuary, which can reveal the origins of the dedicators from either the script used or the name. It affords the opportunity, therefore, to see how different Greek cultural groups interacted with each other when they came together in a town far away from their home, under peaceful circumstances. Unfortunately, none of the people who gave offerings in Gravisca identified themselves with a city-ethnic, something that occurs frequently in Naukratis and Peiraieus and is helpful in determining how these individuals defined themselves. To remedy this problem, I correlate the provenance of dedicators, surmised from onomastic or linguistic evidence, with the choice of divinity they worshipped in Gravisca. Such an exercise demonstrates that sometimes Greek traders used religion to declare a civic identity, even though, on the whole, any Greek could worship any deity regardless of his or her origin.

Most of the dedications in Gravisca are inscribed on Attic pottery, as might be expected from the popularity of Athenian ceramics throughout the Mediterranean and especially in Etruria.[56] No correlation exists, however, between the alphabet used and the provenance of the object dedicated. Whatever the ware, virtually all the inscriptions were in an Ionian script except for a few written in the Doric or Aiginetan script.[57] It seems, therefore, that the traders in Gravisca were principally East Greek.

To distinguish further among the merchants one must look at their names. Of all the dedications in Gravisca bearing names, only nineteen survive fully or can be reconstructed safely: Δηλιάδης, Λεόντιο[ς], Μόσχος, Ἀλέξανδρος, Ὑβλήσιος, Πακτύης, Ζώιλ[ος], Ἐρξήνω[ρ], Σύμαχο[ς], [Μ]έρισκος, Ὀμβρικός, Εὔδημος, Λήθα{ι}ος, Ἰράσας or Φράσας, Εὔαρχος, Θεμισταγόρας, Σώστρατος, Λείακος, Κυλιφάκ[η].[58] Some of these names, such as Alexandros, Leontios, Eudemos, Symachos, Moschos, Deliades, Themistagoras, and Euarchos, were common throughout the Greek world and are not therefore indicative of the traders' identities.[59] Others are equally silent about the traders' origins for the opposite reason: they do not occur anywhere other than Gravisca. These are [M]eriskos, Leiakos,

---

[56] See for example the various tables in Torelli 1982: 309–15. Table C tabulates inscriptions according to the deity they were dedicated to, while Table D lists the name of dedicators on East Greek and Attic cups of various dates. It is obvious that most of the inscribed dedications are on Attic cups, while East Greek cups are the next most popular. On the demand for Athenian vases in Etruria see Shapiro 2000 and Osborne 2001.

[57] A. W. Johnston and Pandolfini 2000: 24–7 and 47.

[58] See Table D in Torelli 1982: 314–15.

[59] Fraser and Matthews 1987–2005. See, however, the discussion below for a possible Aiginetan origin for Euarchos based on the Aiginetan script of the inscription.

and Irasas (or Frasas).[60] Yet others are rare and give a more secure indication of the dedicators' origins. The name Erxenor is attested only on Samos and Delos, with greater frequency in the former and only one occurrence in the latter.[61] Samos, therefore, is a likely provenance for this man.

The rest of the names provide insights into not only the composition of the population frequenting Gravisca, but also the prosopography of individual traders when compared to onomastic evidence from Naukratis. Consider Hyblesios. Torelli has proposed that he was from Phaselis, adducing evidence from Demosthenes' oration *Against Lakritos* that features a boat-owner (*naukleros*) called Hyblesios.[62] Demosthenes says that Lakritos hired the boat-owner Hyblesios to sail to Pontos in order to sell his wine.[63] Because Lakritos was from Phaselis, Torelli has argued that Hyblesios was also from Phaselis. Demosthenes, however, does not specify Lakritos' origin at all. Moreover, the assumption that a boat-owner had to be from the same polis as the trader who hired him is unwarranted. In the same oration, Demosthenes mentions that Hyblesios co-owned the boat with a certain Apollonides from Halikarnassos,[64] and we have already seen that in Emporion a Greek hired an Iberian boat-owner in order to sell his goods. If anything, trade networks in the ancient Mediterranean seem to transcend the polis; they were trans-political.

The name Hyblesios is extremely rare: it does not occur in any literary source other than Demosthenes, but it does appear on inscriptions from Samos.[65] Hyblesios, therefore, was probably from Samos and not Phaselis. It is noteworthy that the only other dedication bearing the name Hyblesios was inscribed on a vase excavated from the sanctuary of Hera in Naukratis.[66] As Torelli has noted, given the rarity of this name, the similar date of the two votives in Naukratis and Gravisca – around 550 BC –, and the fact that both dedications were made in commercial settlements, it is possible that the same Hyblesios, an itinerant trader, made both dedications.[67]

Hyblesios' offerings in Naukratis and Gravisca were both dedicated to Hera.[68] The dedication of objects in two separate temples of Hera is

---

[60] No entries can be found in Fraser and Matthews 1987–2005. Torelli 1982: 321 took Irasas to be a North African (Cyrenean) name, whereas A. W. Johnston in A. W. Johnston and Pandolfini 2000: 25 suggested instead that the word is not a name, but the participle ἱρέσας, derived from the verb ἱεράζω.

[61] Fraser and Matthews 1987–2005.

[62] Torelli 1982: 318–19. A. W. Johnston and Pandolfini 2000: 24 accept Torelli's identification.

[63] Demosthenes, *Against Lakritos* 18–20.   [64] Demosthenes, *Against Lakritos* 33.

[65] Fraser and Matthews 1987–2005: s.v. Hyblesios with references.

[66] Bernand 1970: no. 502.   [67] Torelli 1982: 318–19.

[68] Inv. 74/6; Bernand 1970: no. 502.

significant. Although a Greek anywhere from the Greek world could make
a dedication to the goddess, a Samian may have used her temples to express
his Samian identity when away from home, just as the Phokaians in Massalia
and her colonies used the Ephesian Artemis as a symbol of their civic identity. In Naukratis the temple of Hera was strongly identified with Samos:
Herodotus says that the temple was a Samian foundation,[69] and the majority
of the dedications in this sanctuary were the Samian-manufactured Hera-
cups found only in one other place, Hera's temple on Samos.[70] The parallel
example of the temple of Hera in Naukratis founded by Samos is what
makes it likely that Samos also founded the temple of Hera in Gravisca. It is
not necessary, however, that Samos founded the whole settlement, as Haack
argues.[71] First, some Greek multiethnic emporia, such as Naukratis, were
founded jointly by various Greek poleis. Second, different poleis could set
up sanctuaries, as they did in Naukratis, where the Aiginetans established a
temple dedicated to Zeus, the Milesians one to Apollo, and the Samians one
to Hera.[72] Whether the temple had any relation to Samos or not, it seems
that giving offerings to Hera, the most prominent divinity on Samos, both
in Naukratis and Gravisca, was probably a way for Samian traders, such as
Hyblesios, to express their civic identity.

Similarly, the dedications to Apollo in Gravisca suggest the god was
used as a marker of an Aiginetan civic identity. Three different dedicatory
inscriptions to the god were found in the sanctuaries. One of these bears
no name and is written in an Ionian script.[73] Another has the extremely
common name Euarchos on it, but the dedication is written in the Aiginetan
script and thus implies that the man came from Aigina.[74] The third and
final dedication is the famous stone anchor mentioned above (Figure 4):
Ἀπόλονος Αἰγινάτα ἐμι. Σόστρατος ἐποίησε ho [–] (I am of Aiginetan
Apollo; Sostratos ... made me). Scholars have convincingly argued that
Sostratos is very likely to be identical with or related to Herodotus' Sostratos
of Aigina, who traded his cargo in Tartessos.[75] An Aiginetan merchant,
therefore, gave an offering to a deity he specifically designated as "Aiginetan
Apollo." Apollo is the only divinity in Gravisca described with a city-ethnic;
this is true also in Naukratis, where Apollo is again the only deity whose
provenance – in that instance, Miletos – is emphasized.

---

[69] Herodotus 2.178.
[70] R. E. Jones 1986: 665. A typical Hera-cup is illustrated in the next chapter (Figure 11).
[71] Haack 2007.   [72] Herodotus 1.178–9.   [73] Inv. 75/11195.
[74] Inv. II 17049: Εὔαρχος μ' ἀ[νέθηκε Ἀπόλλο]νι.
[75] A. W. Johnston 1972; Harvey 1976; Torelli 1982: 317–18; A. W. Johnston 1991. For the
      opposite view see Gill 1994.

Scholars have carried the parallels between Naukratis and Gravisca too far, however. A few dozen years before the Graviscan dedication to Aiginetan Apollo, a man by the name of Sostratos gave an offering in the sanctuary of Aphrodite in Naukratis.[76] Given the fact that both Naukratis and Gravisca were commercial settlements, several scholars have suggested that the two Sostratoi belonged to the same Aiginetan family of traders. Torelli argued that the Sostratos attested in Naukratis was an ancestor of the Sostratos who made a dedication in Gravisca, while Mele proposed that the Herodotean Sostratos was the same as the one who gave an offering in Naukratis, and an ancestor of the man who dedicated the anchor in Gravisca.[77] Although a family of traders is theoretically likely since names were inheritable, the alphabet used in the Naukratite dedication is Chian, precluding any relation between the two Sostratoi.

Another name that occurs both in Gravisca and Naukratis is Zoilos. In Naukratis a Zoilos made several offerings at the temple of Aphrodite in the second quarter of the sixth century,[78] while a person with the same name inscribed a Little Masters cup and offered it in Gravisca sometime between 550 and 530 BC.[79] Although the dates of the two dedications do not correspond exactly, they are not so far apart as to preclude an identification of the two traders with one another. It is hard to determine where Zoilos came from: in Naukratis he does not identify himself with a city-ethnic; in Gravisca he used the Ionic alphabet. The name is attested widely in the Greek world, but with greatest frequency in Samos.[80] Perhaps Samos is Zoilos' place of origin, as Moretti has suggested, but there is no concrete evidence to confirm this.[81]

Several of the names on these offerings have been interpreted as representing non-Greeks in Gravisca, but none of these is without doubt a foreign name. The first is Lethaios, an uncommon name that also occurs on a contemporary Attic cup from Mende.[82] According to Johnston, who saw a photograph of the Mende cup, the script on the two vases is very similar,[83] implying that one and the same Lethaios may have made both dedications. His provenance is uncertain. As Torelli has pointed out, although the name

---

[76] Gardner 1888: no. 701. This dedication is illustrated in the next chapter (Figure 12).
[77] Torelli 1982: 317–18; Mele in Torelli 1988: 189.
[78] Gardner 1888: nos. 742, 743, 825; Bernand 1970: nos. 768, 882, 883, 894, 909, 965.
[79] Inv. II. 15335.
[80] The name is attested with frequency in Cyprus, Athens, South Italy, and Boiotia (Fraser and Matthews 1987–2005).
[81] Moretti 1984: 314.   [82] Inv. II 12822.
[83] A. W. Johnston and Pandolfini 2000: 25 and n. 15.

Lethaios does not occur anywhere else in Greece, it is the name of a Carian river that runs near Ephesos.[84] With so little evidence it is difficult
to decide whether Lethaios was a Carian or not. Another possible Carian
is Paktyes, who inscribed a dedication to Hera.[85] Herodotus mentions a
certain Paktyes entrusted with carrying Croesus' gold from Sardis, who
rebelled, appropriated the gold, and used it to hire soldiers to overthrow
Tabalos, Cyrus' appointed leader of Sardis.[86] However, since the name Paktyes was also common in Miletos and Ephesos, as Ehrhardt points out, it
does not necessarily designate a Carian.[87] Finally, Ombrikos has been sus-
pected of being non-Greek, because the name may be the ethnic for an
Umbrian.[88] Recent scholarship has argued instead that the name Ombrikos
is related to the Cretan Ὀμβρίων or Ὀμβρίας attested in literary sources
and inscriptions,[89] or to the name Ὀμριϙός attested on a Corinthian crater
from Cerveteri.[90] The names Lethaios, Paktyes and Ombrikos suggest the
possibility that non-Greeks were using the sanctuary of Hera in Gravisca as
early as the sixth century, even if they wrote their dedications in the Greek
language.

The last entry in the list of personal names mentioned above is of interest
because it has been thought to be the feminine name Kyliphake. According
to Torelli's reconstruction, the dedicatory inscription reads: "Κυλιφάκ[η
αἰ]ολοπ[όλ]ωι" (Kyliphake to the [goddess] of lively fillies).[91] Torelli translates the name Kyliphake as "Rotund Lentil," a name that he sees fit for
a sacred prostitute working at the sanctuary of Aphrodite. Apart from the
issue of sacred prostitution, which I will address briefly in the next section,
Torelli's reconstruction is improbable. First, αἰολοπώλος is not attested anywhere else as an epithet for Aphrodite. Second, taking into consideration the
fact that "Kyliphaktos" is the name of a vessel attested in an earlier Ionian
graffito,[92] Johnston reconstructed the inscription so that it would be similar
to other commercial inscriptions that list the type of vase for sale followed
by the price it should fetch: "Κυλιφάκ[το]ι ὀλοπ[οικίλ]οι" (all-decorated
kyliphaktoi).[93] Even if Kyliphake was not the colorful prostitute that Torelli

---

84 Torelli 1977: 408.   85 Inv. 74/8387; L. Robert 1937: 473 and 1963: 6.   86 Herodotus 1.153.
87 Ehrhardt 1985: 141.   88 Inv. 74/5. Fränkel 1912; Solin 1981: 186.
89 Moretti 1984: 314; Fraser and Matthews 1987–2005.
90 Torelli 1977: 408. Torelli also accepted that Ombrikos is an ethnic derived from Umbria.
91 Inv. 72/5369. Torelli 1982: 313. Previously, Torelli 1977: 428 had reconstructed the text as
    "Κυλιφάκ[ηι αἰ]ολοπ[ώλ]ωι," suggesting that Kyliphake was a "lively filly" and the recipient
    of the dedication. Moretti 1984: 315–16 objected to this reconstruction because it would
    indicate a dedication to a human being rather a divinity and altered the reconstruction:
    "Κυλιφάκ[ης αἰ]ολοπ[ώλ]ωι" (Kyliphakes to the lively filly). In this way, Kyliphakes was a
    male dedicator, and "lively filly" became an epithet for Aphrodite.
92 A. W. Johnston 1984.   93 A. W. Johnston and Pandolfini 2000: 27.

saw, other women probably did live in Gravisca, as the dedicatory evidence from the sanctuary of Aphrodite, discussed in the next section, suggests.

This short survey of the finds in the Greek sanctuary of Gravisca has revealed that most dedications were inscribed on East Greek and Attic vases and were written in an Ionian script. The analysis of the names attested on the votive offerings shows with certainty that Samians (Hyblesios, Erxenor, and Zoilos) and Aiginetans (Sostratos and Euandros) were present and frequented Gravisca, and that there is a possibility that Carians and Umbrians were using the Greek sanctuary as well. The remaining names are common throughout the Greek world and therefore cannot be indicative of the traders' provenance. A connection probably existed between Hera's temple on Samos and the goddess's sanctuary in Gravisca, as Hyblesios' dedication in the goddess's temple in Gravisca shows. Further, Apollo's cult in Gravisca is specifically described as being Aiginetan, and Aiginetans made two of the three dedications to this god. It would be wrong to claim that Samians used only Hera's temple in Gravisca and Aiginetans used only Apollo's temple. Others also used these sanctuaries: Lethaios, Ombrikos, and Paktyes – none of whom were Samians – gave offerings to the goddess. Unfortunately, the inscribed dedications in Aphrodite's temple do not bear any names that can be reconstructed with certainty and thus the provenance of the dedicators cannot be ascertained. The sample from Gravisca is too small but it is probably representative of the fluidity that characterized all cults in Gravisca, and more clearly so in Naukratis, as the next chapter shows: regardless of their origin, Greeks could frequent any sanctuary consecrated to any divinity. Nonetheless, certain cults may have served as symbols of identity for certain groups. Just as Artemis in Emporion was important for the Phokaians, so the cults of Hera in Gravisca and Naukratis were emblematic of a Samian identity, and Apollo's cult in Gravisca of an Aiginetan identity.

Trading religion

The multicultural Greek population of Gravisca did not exist in isolation. These Greeks lived in an emporion that was connected to one of the most important Etruscan city-states, Tarquinia, and, as was mentioned above, it promoted trade with the surrounding areas, mostly populated by Etruscans. Gravisca, therefore, encouraged interethnic contacts not only among Greeks who came from different poleis but also between the Greeks of Gravisca and the local Etruscans. In order to understand the Greek response to the Etruscans and the Etruscan reaction to the Greek presence in Gravisca it is necessary to examine how the Greek cults of Hera, Apollo, Demeter, and Aphrodite, who were worshipped here, functioned for both these groups. The Etruscans frequented the sanctuary during its Greek phase and continued to use it after the Greeks left Gravisca, though there it served exclusively Etruscan divinities. The ease with which the Etruscans adopted the Greek cults while giving them an Etruscan flavor is due partly to the flexibility of polytheistic religious systems and partly to the emergence of a common Mediterranean culture, initiated by the cross-cultural contacts trade promoted.

According to the excavators, the first phase of the sanctuary (600–480 BC) corresponds to the implantation of the Etruscan settlement in Gravisca, both built on virgin soil.[94] It is also the phase that has yielded a majority of Greek material culture and was thus identified as the Greek sanctuary. Dedications and votives have been discovered in various areas of this sanctuary. I will limit the discussion here to the cult-places of Hera, Apollo, Demeter, and Aphrodite, because the epigraphic and material evidence for the worship of these divinities is plentiful and contributes to the understanding of the role of these sanctuaries in the interethnic relations at Gravisca. It is important to note, however, that the worship of either Zeus or the Dioskouroi is also attested[95] and that the excavators have also suggested that one of the buildings (Building δ) was dedicated to Adonis. This identification is extremely tenuous, however, as it is based only on a stone case, identified as the tomb of Adonis, a small coral piece, and a late, 10 BC-AD 5 inscription that bears the letters A[-]ον, which have been read as Adon.[96] The poverty of finds dedicated to Zeus or the Dioskouroi, and the shaky identification of a cult to Adonis, cannot lead to any conclusions about the worship of these gods, and thus will not be discussed further.

A single dedication to the goddess Demeter was excavated from Area X (Figure 8), leading to the identification of the nearest building, Building β, as the cult-place of Demeter, but with a single epigraphic dedication this is difficult to maintain.[97] The worship of Demeter, however, is not only attested by the dedicatory inscription, but also by several thousand lamps, most of which were discovered in Building α.[98] Lamps are typical of the Greek goddess's worship in other Greek locations, as are sacrifices of piglets, which

---

[94] Torelli 1971a.

[95] Moretti 1984: 318 read the dedication, found in Room C (Figure 8) as: Διὶ Χορō[ν], whereas Torelli 1982: 311 proposed δι]οσ<σ>χόρο[ισι.

[96] Torelli 1997.   [97] Torelli 1997: 438–41.

[98] Galli 2004: 130–1 and graph 7 shows that approximately 82 percent (3626) of the lamps were discovered in Building α, and the majority of the rest of the lamps were found in Buildings β, γ, δ, and Zone X.

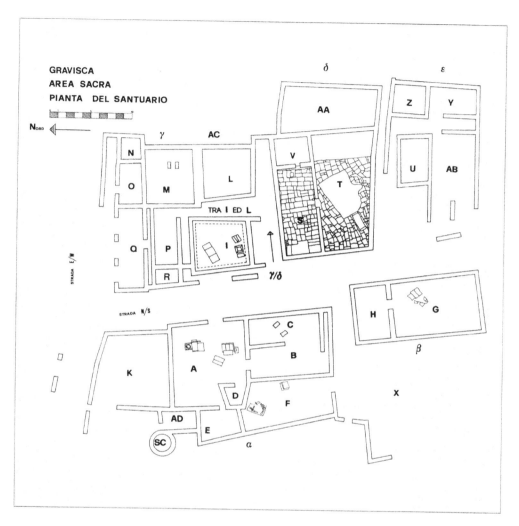

Figure 8 Plan of the south complex of the sanctuaries in Gravisca. Reproduced from Fiorini 2005: 6.

usually took place during the Thesmophoria. Indeed, the bones of a piglet as well as grain were also discovered in an early cist from Room A of Building α, which also contained the vast majority of lamps.[99] Extra-urban sanctuaries dedicated to Demeter have been identified as centers of mediation between Greeks and the non-Greek populations of the hinterland around Greek poleis.[100] As a multiethnic commercial settlement, Gravisca provided a

[99] Sorrentino in Colivicchi 2004: 177; 179–82. Bones of pigs were also discovered in Building β, identified as Demeter's cult-place, and throughout the sanctuary.
[100] De Polignac 1995: 106–27; Cole 1994.

similar social context in which the worship of Demeter could function as a mediating force, even though it was not an extra-urban sanctuary.

The religious complex to the north of the sanctuaries of Gravisca, in operation from the last quarter of the sixth century to the Severan period, has yielded material that resembles that from the sanctuary further south (Figure 5). In other words, the ceramics have a variety of origins, coming mostly from Ionia, but include also Corinthian, Attic, and bucchero-ware, and transport amphorae are Etruscan, Corinthian, and East Greek.[101] The history of this part of the sanctuary is the same as that of the sanctuary further south: Greeks used it predominantly in its first years of operation, and Etruscans took over subsequently. No epigraphic evidence has surfaced from this area, but the votive terra-cotta figurines, which include female statues, female heads, animal and fruit representations, could be related to the worship of Demeter and Kore.[102] Since there is no secure identification of the divinities worshipped in this section of Gravisca, this sanctuary and its material deposit will not be discussed in any detail.

Hera's cult is difficult to localize since the dedicatory inscriptions to this goddess were discovered throughout the various rooms.[103] Torelli proposed that Hera's cult in Gravisca was related to the goddess's temples on the Italian peninsula and that Hera was venerated here as a lunar deity and affiliated with Aphrodite.[104] The inscribed dedications, however, are mostly on cups and *oinochoai* that are fairly common as votives, and the inscriptions themselves are fragmentary and do not assign any epithets to the goddess. Any interpretation, therefore, is bound to remain a mere hypothesis until more evidence surfaces. What does seem to be the case is that Hera's cult in Gravisca may have had a Samian connection, and traders like Hyblesios may have used it because they were Samians, thereby expressing their civic identity.

The three dedicatory inscriptions to Apollo were also discovered far away from one another: Sostratos' dedication was cut in half and reused in later periods, forever obscuring the anchor's context; Euarchos' offering was

---

[101] Fortunelli 2007: 43–272.   [102] Fortunelli 2007: 273–84 and 309–34.

[103] A. W. Johnston and Pandolfini 2000: 17–19. In fact, Haack 2007 argues that the room identified as Aphrodite's cult-space (Room I in Figure 8) was actually Hera's. Her argument hinges on the fact that the dedications to Aphrodite may have belonged to the room next door (Room L in Figure 8) to the one now identified as being her cult-space (I). She also points out that the votive offerings found in Room I are just as typical of Hera as they are of Aphrodite. The fact that the dedicatory inscriptions to Hera were found scattered throughout the sanctuary whereas the dedications to Aphrodite, though fewer, were localized, suggests the identification of Room I with Aphrodite's cult-place is more likely.

[104] Torelli 1977: 435–8.

found in Room E (Figure 8); finally, the third inscription was found in Room AA (Figure 8).[105] Although these inscriptions do not locate Apollo's cult in Gravisca, more can be deduced from Sostratos' dedication. In the context of a coastal emporion, which by definition presupposes sea-travel, votive anchors were probably gifted to deities in order to ask or thank a god for safe travel. Anchors were common dedications to various divinities throughout coastal sites in the Mediterranean, ranging from the Propontis and the Aegean islands, to the Western Mediterranean:[106] Apollonios of Rhodes describes the dedication of the Argo's anchor at the temple of Athena at Kyzikos, while Arrian claims to have seen it at Rhea's sanctuary in Phasis;[107] in Metapontion, marble and stone anchors, dating from the seventh and sixth centuries BC, have been connected with the worship of Apollo Archegetes;[108] in Delos, numerous anchors are recorded in the temple inventories;[109] models of anchors were dedicated in Thasos, perhaps to Poseidon;[110] Hera's sanctuary in Kroton produced votive anchors;[111] an inscribed stone anchor was dedicated to Zeus Meilichios;[112] and, several fragments of anchors without any inscriptions were found in Aphrodite's cult-space in Gravisca.[113] Sostratos' dedication suggests that the trader thanked or asked Apollo for protection in his travels.

A nuraghic bronze model of a boat, a product of an indigenous Sardinian culture, was discovered in the sanctuary of Gravisca.[114] Nuraghic boats are actually one of the most common Sardinian finds in Etruscan tombs, indicating the close relations between Sardinia and Etruria.[115] Although the sanctuary of Hera cannot be localized, the excavators claimed that the bronze boat was a dedication to Hera. Despite the shaky grounds on which the boat was identified as an offering to Hera, it remains a distinct possibility because the goddess did often receive models of ships as dedications.[116] For example, the temple of Hera on Samos has also yielded twenty-two drawings of boats on wood and boat models.[117] Similarly, boat models can be found

---

[105] A. W. Johnston and Pandolfini 2000: 15 and 19.

[106] Gianfrotta 1975: 311–18, especially 313–14 and 1977; Romero Recio 2000: 22–60.

[107] Apollonios of Rhodes, *Argonautica* 1.955–60; Arrian, *Periplus of the Euxine Sea* 9.

[108] Adamesteanu 1971: 172.   [109] Deonna 1938: 197–8.   [110] Bon and Seyrig 1929: 348.

[111] Lattanzi 1991.   [112] Iacopi 1952: 167–8.

[113] Torelli 1977: 435. Haack 2007 would see these anchors as dedications to Hera, since she identifies the room as Hera's cult-place. As I have argued above, however, Haack's argument is not based on conclusive evidence.

[114] Lilliu 1971.   [115] Lo Schiavo 2002: 60–2; Bernardini 2002: 430–1.

[116] De Polignac 1997: 113–22, especially 115, and fig. 1 p. 114 for the distribution of boat models. See also Romero Recio 2000: 2–18, who discusses other divinities that received boats and models or drawings of boats as dedications.

[117] Kyrieleis 1980.

in other sanctuaries of Hera, such as the one in Kroton in Italy, where votive anchors were also discovered,[118] or in Hera's sanctuaries situated on promontories or on the coast.[119] Dedications of models of boats must have functioned in similar ways as votive anchors: Hera, at least in her sanctuaries located near the sea, was considered as a deity that protected navigation. It is possible that she had a similar role in Gravisca, as de Polignac suggests, but the only evidence is the single nuraghic boat that may have been dedicated in her temple.[120] This find is nonetheless significant because it demonstrates how varied material culture was, particularly in emporia. Nuraghic objects were dedicated alongside the Attic, East Greek, Laconian, Corinthian, and bucchero pottery the Greeks from Aigina, Samos, and Ionia gave as offerings in the Graviscan sanctuaries. All these objects had become popular among Mediterranean populations.

Aphrodite's cult in Gravisca is the only one that can be located with certainty (Room I in Figure 8); it is also the cult that dates from the earliest period of the sanctuary's existence and the first one to receive a temple.[121] The first signs of construction date from 580 BC, when a rectangular structure was erected. Ten years later the first *naiskos* was burnt and then enlarged, only to be burnt again around 530–520 BC. At this time it seems that whatever remained, including the votive offerings, was buried and another building was built over the original *naiskos*. The inscribed votive offerings here were dedicated to Aphrodite and were discovered together with other objects: pottery; statuettes; unguent boxes depicting a seated goddess; a statuette of a woman kneeling in a sexual pose; worshippers; banqueters; representations of doves, monkeys, and porcupines; two archaic Greek bronze statuettes depicting an armed goddess; Egyptian faience bottles depicting Bes and Horus; many pieces of stone anchors; and, even an Etruscan inscription dedicated to Turan, the Etruscan goddess closest in aspect to Aphrodite.[122] The preponderance of dedications to Aphrodite and the unguent boxes suggest that their find-spot was dedicated to the goddess's worship; their early date and find-spot imply that Aphrodite's veneration was the earliest of all the cults in Gravisca.

Most of these votives are typical of those dedicated in the goddess's temples everywhere in the Greek world. To mention a few examples: female statuettes, perfume vases, terra-cotta lamps, bronze mirrors, animal representations such as doves and fawns dating from the sixth to the second

---

[118] Lattanzi 1991.   [119] De Polignac 1997: 115.   [120] De Polignac 1997: 115.

[121] Haack 2007 identifies this room as Hera's cult-place, despite the fact that all the inscriptions discovered here were to Aphrodite.

[122] Inv. 72/23122; Torelli 1977: 398–404.

centuries BC were discovered in Argos;[123] in Delos, the inventories of the temple from the Hellenistic period record that statues of the goddess, bronze mirrors, female statues along with jewelry were dedicated to the goddess;[124] finally, more explicitly sexual objects, such as representations of female and male genitalia and breasts with inscribed dedications to Aphrodite dating from the fourth century onwards were discovered in the sanctuary of Aphrodite on the north slope of the Acropolis and in Daphni.[125] The dedications found in Room I of the sanctuaries at Gravisca, therefore, are all appropriate for Aphrodite, the deity of sex. Some of these are also typically feminine dedications and provide evidence that female worshippers, who are not otherwise attested, frequented the Graviscan sanctuaries.

The appearance of Egyptian objects with Egyptian divinities depicted on them is not unusual either in temples of Aphrodite or in seaside sanctuaries, such as the one in Gravisca. For example, the temple of Hera on Samos has yielded several imported Egyptian figurines, including one that features Bes and another with the goddess Neith, in addition to the models of ships and votive anchors, mentioned above;[126] a cave at Inatos on southern Crete, where similar finds to the ones discovered in the sanctuary of Aphrodite at Gravisca were found – figures of men and women, naked goddesses, and pregnant women – also yielded a statuette of Bes, as has another site on Crete, Amnisos;[127] the temple to Apollo, Artemis, and Rhetia on the harbor of Emporio on Chios has produced Egyptian and Egyptianizing objects;[128] finally, the temple of Aphrodite in Naukratis yielded Bes figurines along with other Egyptianizing statuettes.[129] On the one hand, these Egyptian and Egyptianizing finds probably did not bear their original meanings in the Greek temples where they were offered but rather were dedicated in sanctuaries as *exotica*, thus earning the dedicator prestige and elevating his/her social status.[130] On the other hand, the particular example of Bes in these sanctuaries has a different significance. Though an Egyptian deity, Bes was translated by Greeks into their own religious language and adopted as a male kourotrophic deity.[131] That statuettes of Bes were dedicated in the same sanctuaries where votive anchors were dedicated, such as the temple

---

[123] Daux 1968: 1024–36.
[124] *IDélos* 1417 A col. II, 1–21; *IDélos* 1423; *IDélos* 1443 B. col. II, 92–103. Bruneau 1970: 336.
[125] Van Straten 1981: 114–15; 120–1.   [126] Kyrieleis 1981: 25–38.   [127] Marinatos 1996.
[128] Boardman 1967.
[129] Bes: London BM 1886.4–1.1455 and London BM 1888.6–1.105; Egyptianizing statuettes: London BM 1886.4–1.1422; London BM 1886.4–1.1453.
[130] Marinatos 1996: 138; Duplouy 2006:177–83. Scholtz promises to discuss the role of "marginal" goddesses worshipped at seaside locations in the Mediterranean.
[131] Sinn 1982.

of Hera on Samos and Aphrodite in Gravisca, should not be surprising. One of the common features of these coastal sanctuaries, especially ones established in multiethnic emporia, is that there was no specialization in the worship of divinities; rather, these sacred spaces were multifunctional, allowing worshippers who visited and lived there to venerate divinities in whatever manner they chose. That this was the case in Gravisca, as well as in Naukratis, will become evident shortly.

The one Etruscan dedication in this sanctuary, dating to 550–525 BC, demonstrates the flexibility afforded to worshippers by polytheistic religious systems. For an Etruscan, Aphrodite took the name Turan and was thus perfectly acceptable as a divinity to worship. Further, the object on which the Etruscan inscribed his dedication was not a bucchero-vase but rather a Laconian crater.[132] The distribution of foreign material culture across ethnic groups throughout sanctuaries in the Mediterranean, such as Egyptian faience, Attic pottery, bucchero-ware, nuraghic boats, or East Greek cups suggests that they had come to constitute a common material culture that could be used by any group. Without any implication that all groups was the same, it is important to realize that they did share a common Mediterranean culture, one characterized by polytheism, a city-state system, a maritime perspective entailing an extensive network of ports, and a common material culture. Different groups could draw upon this common material culture, perhaps especially in situations where peaceful interaction between groups was facilitated, as in the case of emporia.

Based on his recognition of Kyliphake as a prostitute, a faience statuette of a naked woman kneeling in a sexual pose, and a *pinax* depicting a scene of a woman in her toilette, also discovered from the temple of Aphrodite in Gravisca, Torelli claimed that the cult of Aphrodite in Gravisca was associated with sacred prostitution, as was mentioned above.[133] Caution is required with notions such as sacred prostitution, coined and used indiscriminately by modern scholars. Despite the ease and frequency with which scholars associate Aphrodite's sanctuaries with "sacred prostitution," there is no evidence to suggest the goddess's temples ever sponsored such

---

[132] Even though only one Etruscan inscription has survived from Aphrodite's cult area, it is very likely that other Etruscans used this sanctuary. If one Etruscan could offer a Laconian crater, so could many others, without necessarily inscribing them.

[133] Torelli 1977: 429–33. Other scholars who have discussed the practice of sacred prostitution are: Van Groningen 1960; Yamauchi 1973; Sourvinou-Inwood 1974; Musti 1976; Torelli 1976; Aloni 1982; Amantini 1984; Colonna 1984–85 and 1985; Spivey and Stoddart 1990; Vanoyeke 1990; MacLachlan 1992; Bonnet 1996; Musti and Torelli 1994; Kurke 1996 and 1999; Salmon 1997; Rosner 1998; Redfield 2003.

practices.[134] Further, the facile claim that Aphrodite's sanctuaries were centers of "sacred prostitution," has obscured an aspect of Aphrodite's worship, which is particularly important in understanding the role of the goddess's temples in emporia, harbors, and on the coastline: Aphrodite was a patron deity of navigation and seafaring.

Torelli briefly acknowledged that Aphrodite was worshipped in Gravisca for her function as a protector of sailors and harbors.[135] He notes that several anchors were dedicated in the goddess's sanctuary in Gravisca, but without any dedicatory inscriptions.[136] As mentioned above, these anchors were usual votive offerings given to a variety of deities, such as Apollo, Athena, Zeus, Rhea, Poseidon, and Hera. Even though, with the exception of Sostratos' anchor, the ones from Gravisca are not inscribed, dedicatory inscriptions on stone anchors are not unknown. One dedicated to Zeus Meilichios was found on the coast between Capo Colonna and Capo Cimmiti, and a fifth century BC archaic votive anchor, more germane for the discussion here, was offered to Aphrodite Epilimenia in Aigina.[137] This last find helps to understand the choice of Aphrodite as the first deity to have had a temple built in her honor in Gravisca, and also in Naukratis.

Aphrodite's role as a patron of navigation is generally accepted in scholarship, although it is usually only summarily mentioned.[138] Here I will discuss briefly the evidence that exists for Aphrodite's function as a protector of sailing, especially as it pertains to traders, in order to demonstrate the importance of Aphrodite's worship in emporia in general and in Gravisca

---

[134] Oden 1987, Pirenne-Delforge 1994: 100–26, Beard and Henderson 1997, and Budin 2008 have all questioned the existence of such a practice as "sacred prostitution," in the ancient world. The earlier studies focus primarily on Herodotus' infamous passage on Babylonian sacred prostitution (1.199) and discuss almost exclusively literary sources, leaving aside epigraphic and archaeological material. Budin attacks the issue both from the Near Eastern and the classical perspective, and surveys archaeological, epigraphic, and literary sources. Whereas Beard and Henderson argue that the myth of "sacred prostitution" is orientalist, Budin sees the creation of this myth as a result of both ancient and modern scholars' historiographic misinterpretation and faulty methodology. Others have disputed the existence of "sacred prostitution" in specific sites only: Corinth (Conzelmann 1967; Saffrey 1985; Calame 1989); Lokroi (Pembroke 1970; Van Compernolle 1976).

[135] Torelli 1977: 435. [136] Torelli 1977: 412–13.

[137] Zeus Meilichios: Iacopi 1952: 167–8; Aphrodite Epilimenia: Welter 1938: 489–519, 497 fig.11. Gianfrotta 1977: 292 n. 5 claims, citing Wolters 1925, that there is another inscribed possible anchor stock in Aigina that mentions Aphrodite Epilimenia. Wolters 1925: 46 does mention a boundary stone that demarcates a sanctuary of Aphrodite on the Harbor (Ἀφροδίτα ἐπὶ λιμένι). It is possible that Welter and Wolters are giving two different interpretations of the same stone and that Gianfrotta misunderstood and took these to be two different stones.

[138] Scholars who have discussed this role of Aphrodite are: Pirenne-Delforge 1994: 433–7; Graf 1985: 261; Romero Recio 2000: 39; 70–2; 88; 92; 99; 119–21. Demetriou 2010b discusses this role in more detail.

and Naukratis in particular. Aphrodite, born from the sea, was a divinity whose sanctuaries are attested archaeologically and epigraphically on the shore or near harbors.[139] Pausanias mentions examples of coastal temples dedicated to Aphrodite at Epidauros Limera, Tainaron, Aigion, and Patrai.[140] In Peiraieus, too, where Athens' emporion was located, there was at least one temple dedicated to Aphrodite.[141] In Kos, a Hellenistic sanctuary of Aphrodite was located on the coast and had shipyards right next to it.[142] In addition, several epigrams from the Hellenistic period refer to coastal temples of Aphrodite.[143]

Why were all these sanctuaries dedicated on the coast? The answer, in part, is that Aphrodite had special importance among sailors, whether these were traders, the navy, or fishermen. For example, one Hellenistic epigram states that the reason Aphrodite's temple was located on the shore was so that the goddess could make the voyages of sailors pleasant,[144] and three others mention that sailors should pray to Aphrodite on Cape Zephyrion in order that she may provide smooth-sailing.[145] The goddess's importance for safe sailing is attested much earlier, in one of Solon's poems, demonstrating that the goddess's patronage on the sea was part of her cult from the archaic period onward, as also the fifth century BC anchor from Aigina dedicated to Aphrodite Epilimenia shows. Solon's poem includes a prayer that he made to Aphrodite, asking her to send him unharmed back to Athens in his ship, when he was about to set sail from Cyprus after refounding the city of Soloi there.[146]

The goddess's function as a patron of navigation seems to have been ubiquitous throughout the Greek world, as is evidenced also by several cult epithets attested from different periods and places along the Mediterranean coast that point to her role as a protector of navigation and harbors. One of Aphrodite's epithets is Epilimenia, attested on the stone anchor from

---

[139] Schindler 1998: 29, appendix 1 and fig. 2. Hesiod, *Theogony* 188–95 describes the goddess's birth and travels first to Kythera and finally to Cyprus, where she set up her abode.

[140] Pausanias 3.23.10 (Epidauros Limera); 3.25.9 (Tainaron); 7.24.2 (Aigion); 7.21.10–11 (Patrai). Four different temples are mentioned here.

[141] See Parker 1996: 238: Garland 2001: 112–13; Pironti 2007: 245–7.

[142] Parker 2002; Parker and Obbink 2000. The shipyards are mentioned on one of two inscriptions that detail the sale of priesthoods for this cult, dedicated to Aphrodite Pandamos and Pontia: *Iscr. di Cos* E.D. 178, b. 105. The other inscription is published fully as the Obbink-Parker text in Parker and Obbink 2000.

[143] *Anthologia Palatina* 9.143, 144, 333, 791 (ed. Beckby); Poseidippos 39, 116, and 119 (ed. Austin and Bastianini). For an analysis of these and other epigrams in the context of Aphrodite's maritime powers see Demetriou 2010b.

[144] *Anthologia Palatina* 9. 144 (ed. Beckby).

[145] Poseidippos 39, 116, 119 (ed. Austin and Bastianini).   [146] Solon fr. 19 (ed. M. L. West).

Aigina mentioned above and a later Roman imperial period inscription from Corinth.[147] One of the most common names that Aphrodite receives because of her role in navigation is "Euploia" (Smooth-Sailing), attested from early fourth-century Peiraieus and Knidos, and later in Olbia, Mylasa, Cilicia, and Delos.[148] The goddess was also called "Galenaia" (Calmer),[149] "Epaktia (on the Shore),"[150] and "Pontia and Limenia" (of the Sea and Harbor).[151] Another common epithet for Aphrodite is "Pontia" (of the Sea) found on inscriptions from Kos, Nisyra, Erythrai, Olbia, Teiristatis in Thrace, Histria, and Kyzikos.[152]

Although Aphrodite's role as a patron of navigation extended to all those who sailed, there is plenty of evidence to suggest that traders comprised a significant part of these. Two inscriptions from the sanctuary of Aphrodite Pandamos and Pontia on Kos, for example, mention boat-owners and traders who performed sacrifices and gave payments to Aphrodite Pontia after they returned safely to Kos.[153] Further evidence exists for the veneration of Aphrodite by traders, whom they considered to be vital for successful trading ventures. Inscriptions attest to the fact that traders gave dedications to the goddess to thank her for her help both in navigation and trade. For example, thirteen boat-owners offered a dedication to Aphrodite in Messina on Sicily,[154] and on Delos a certain Damon, a trader from Askalon, offered a dedication to Aphrodite Ourania for saving him from pirates.[155] In fourth-century Halikarnassos, a trader called Phaeinos dedicated a statue to

---

[147] *SEG* 23, 170.

[148] Peiraieus (Pausanias 1.13; *IG* II² 2872), Knidos (Pausanias 1.1.3; Miranda 1989), Olbia (*IosPE* I², 168 – first century AD), Mylasa (Hauvette-Besnault and Dubois 1881: 108–76 BC), Cilicia (*CIG* 4443–19/8BC), and Delos (*IDélos* 2132 – after 166 BC).

[149] *Anthologia Palatina* 10.21 (ed. Beckby) and Callimachos fr. 5 (ed. Pfeiffer).

[150] This epithet has been reconstructed from a fragmentary inscription excavated in Lechaion, the port of Corinth, which dates to the Roman period: *SEG* 23, 170; Pallas 1958: 132.

[151] Hermione (Pausanias 2.34.11).

[152] Graf 1985: 261 has collected all of the occurrences of this epithet for Aphrodite. Kos (*Iscr. di Cos* ED 178–196/5 BC – and Obbink-Parker – late second century BC), Nisyros (*WZHalle* 16.384, 26 – third century BC), Erythrai (*EI* 213a – first century BC), Olbia (*IOlbia* 68 – third century BC), Teiristastis in Thrace (*MDAI(A)* 1884: 75 n. 8 – no satisfactory date has been given), Histria (*SEG* 24, 1133 – second century BC), Kyzikos (Hasluck 1910: 236 – first century BC).

[153] Obbink-Parker l.27–9; *Iscr. di Cos* ED 178, a. 21–3.

[154] *IG XIV* 401. The inscription is of unknown date. The heading under which the dedications were listed has been reconstructed as Ναύ[κλη]ροι.

[155] *IDélos* 2305. This inscription probably dates to the middle of the second century BC. Given that the trader was from Askalon, he was probably a Phoenician. There is from Kos a bilingual inscription in Phoenician and Greek, dating to 325–300 BC, which records the dedication of a monument to honor Aphrodite made by the king of the Sidonians on behalf of those sailing (ὑπὲρ τῶν πλεόντων). In the Phoenician text the goddess is named Astarte: *SEG* 36, 758. See also Parker 2002: 147–50; Bonnet and Pirenne-Delforge 1999: 271–2.

Aphrodite for the help she gave him when she accompanied him, as a trader, on his sea-voyage.[156] This verse epigram suggests that the trader gave first offerings from his earnings to the goddess because she traveled with him on his journey, perhaps to keep him safe, and also because she was responsible for his profits. One epigram that calls Aphrodite a "guardian of all navigation" (πάσης ναυτιλίης φύλαξ) also makes it clear that if Aphrodite made the trader rich he would consider her a shareholder of his ship, and by implication of the profits earned from its cargo.[157]

This aspect of Aphrodite's worship can also be seen in Polycharmos' story of the trader Herostratos, who sailed to Naukratis via Paphos in Cyprus, where he bought a statuette of Aphrodite from the goddess's temple. This transaction proved to be fortuitous, for when the ship was caught in a storm, the sailors turned for safety to Aphrodite's statue, and the goddess then performed a miracle and saved the crew. True to her function as a goddess of perfumes, myrtle, and love, Aphrodite used her typical attributes to provide safety for sailors: the goddess's statue began to sprout myrtle branches and these in turn produced an aroma that soothed the sailors' seasickness, helping them to make it to the shore. Herostratos promptly dedicated the Cypriot statuette at the temple of Aphrodite in Naukratis.[158] Plutarch recounts a similar story of Dexikreon, a Samian boat-owner about to sail to Cyprus, who was advised by the goddess to take potable water on board. The boat was immobilized as no wind blew, and everyone grew thirsty. Dexikreon was able to sell the water at a high price and, in order to thank Aphrodite – for saving him and for the profit he made – he dedicated a statue of the goddess at his home on Samos.[159]

Whether Aphrodite's purpose was noble or not, it is uncontroversial that the evidence presented thus far does point to a relationship between Aphrodite and traders. It is no coincidence, further, that the locations appearing in these stories are all major commercial hubs on maritime trade routes and that Aphrodite is associated with all of them, given her role as a patron of navigation.[160] Her function as a patron of sailing explains the special relationship that Aphrodite had with traders and is the clue to understanding the goddess's central role in emporia, and particularly in Gravisca and Naukratis. Aphrodite, intimately associated with the sea

---

[156] *SEG* 28, 838: [ἢ γαρ] ἐπεί ποτέ νιμ μέγαν ἔμπορον εἰς ἅλα ἔβησα[ς], [ἐ]ξ ὁσίων ὅσιος δῶμα συνέσχεν ἀνήρ. In translating this last line I use Veyne 1965: 945 n.1, who cites parallels.

[157] *Anthologia Palatina* 9.601 (ed. Beckby).   [158] Polycharmos *apud* Athenaios 15.675f–676c.

[159] Plutarch, *Greek Questions* 54.

[160] Based on the anecdotes regarding Herostratos and Dexikreon, Giuffrida 1996 argues that a temple of Aphrodite Euploia existed on Cyprus. Horden and Purcell 2000: 438–45 also discuss sea-routes that stopped at sanctuaries where gods who protected seafarers were worshipped.

through her birth, had sanctuaries dedicated to her located on the coast throughout the Greek world and she was worshipped under such epithets as *Euploia*, *Pontia*, *Limenia*, and *Epilimenia*. She provided safe sailing and also presided over ports, two elements without which Mediterranean trade would not function. This might explain the dedication of the stone anchors in Aphrodite's temple at Gravisca and the presence of Egyptian and Egyptianizing material in her temple here and also at Naukratis. In Gravisca, frequented by merchants and sailors who came from different places in the Greek world, it was possible to recognize that Aphrodite was something they all, as Greek traders, had in common, since Greeks everywhere worshipped Aphrodite as a goddess of navigation. In this multiethnic emporion, Aphrodite's worship may have acted as a focal point for all Greeks irrespective of their origin, especially since the settlement was located in an area that was predominantly non-Greek (Etruscan) and served an Etruscan city. Aphrodite, therefore, being important to all traders in emporia, may have helped mediate among the different Greek groups. Recognizing that they had this goddess in common might have led to the construction of a Hellenic collective identity among the Greeks of Gravisca; if it did, unfortunately, it did not leave any traces. In Naukratis, however, it did, and this will be discussed in the next chapter.

To emphasize Aphrodite's maritime powers and patronage on the sea is not to say that the goddess was only worshipped for this aspect in Gravisca and in emporia more generally. On the contrary, the stone anchors excavated from Aphrodite's temple in Gravisca, whose presence can be explained by reference to Aphrodite's pan-Mediterranean worship as a protector of sailors and traders, were not the only finds discovered from this sanctuary. Aphrodite's guardianship of sailors was never separated from her role as a deity of sex.[161] While the sexual pose of the kneeling statuette found in the cult-space dedicated to Aphrodite in Gravisca and the other typically feminine objects should not imply the practice of "sacred prostitution" since it is doubtful that such a practice ever existed, these objects may very well have been dedicated by women or men, prostitutes or not, and may have had a sexual meaning. It is important to note also that similar finds to the one in Gravisca, namely, dedications typical of sailors, such as votive anchors, and

---

[161] The close relationship between Aphrodite's role as a patron of sailing and sex is evident in Hellenistic epigrams, which use the metaphor of the "sea of love." Lovers are portrayed as sailors, shipwrecked, or tossing on a sea of love, and the goddess is called upon to rescue them from the metaphorical storm they are experiencing in their love life and lead them to a safe harbor. Examples of these epigrams are *Anthologia Palatina*, 5.11 and 17, 9.143, 10.21 (ed. Beckby). Demetriou 2010b: 69–73 discusses this connection. See also Slater 1999.

offerings that could have been made by women or men to worship a god for
other reasons, such as female and male statuettes, animal representations,
etc., were also discovered in Aphrodite's sanctuary in Naukratis, Hera's
temple on Samos, and the two sanctuaries on Crete, Inatos and Amnisos,
as was mentioned in the beginning of this section. In cosmopolitan settings
such as multiethnic emporia, Greek religion was more flexible and open
than it was in Greek poleis.[162] The usual exclusivity of cult was bypassed,
as is clear from the dedications in each sanctuary offered by Greeks who
came from a variety of poleis, and anyone could venerate a god in the
manner they chose, celebrating whichever one of the god's many roles was
appropriate. How this was achieved in practical terms will be discussed
in the next chapter, which provides more detail on this topic. The social
reality of multiethnic emporia created new common cults and practices
that gave cohesion to the population of these settlements and perhaps even
a common identity.[163] Religion, therefore, acted as a mediator among the
many different Greeks who were present in emporia such as Gravisca. As
part of a flexible polytheistic pantheon that was easily translatable between
cultures, Aphrodite also mediated between Greeks and Etruscans, as I argue
in the next section.

From Aphrodite to Turan

Greeks and Etruscans continued to use the Greek cult-places of Apollo,
Hera, Aphrodite, and Demeter at the sanctuary in Gravisca until about
480 BC. A second phase from 480 to 400 BC involved the reorganization
and expansion of the temples, while the next hundred years, down to 300
BC, marked a third phase and also saw a complete rebuilding of the temples
and enlargement of the sanctuary. During the final phase of the sanctuary,
300–250 BC, some construction took place but not on the scale of the
previous two phases. Traces of fire in some parts of the sanctuary point
to the third century as the time when the sacred areas of Gravisca were
abandoned. Shortly afterwards, in 181 BC, the Romans established the
colony of Graviscae, marking the end of the Greek and Etruscan occupation
of the site.[164]

For the history of ethnic interactions, the significant fact is that, whereas
the first phase of the sanctuary yielded primarily Greek material – Greek

[162] See also Scholtz 2002/2003, who discusses this in connection with the temple of Aphrodite in
Naukratis.
[163] Sourvinou-Inwood 2000.   [164] Torelli 1977: 413–27.

pottery and inscriptions written in Greek – the subsequent phases yielded no
Greek inscriptions, and Greek pottery was often inscribed in Etruscan.[165]
The dramatic decrease in Greek material and inscriptions suggests that
Greeks stopped frequenting the sanctuary at Gravisca sometime in the
beginning of the fifth century. One explanation for the reduction in trade
and the disappearance of the Greeks in this area might be the defeat of
the Etruscan fleet at the battle of Kyme in 474 BC and the subsequent block-
ade of the Straits of Messina by the Deinomenid tyranny of Syracuse.[166]
This Etruscan loss marked the beginning of the decline of Etruscan political
and economic power in the region, and may have motivated the Greeks of
Gravisca to move to a different location. Yet, the sanctuary still received
dedications. Etruscan inscriptions now decorated Attic imports, bucchero-
ware, and pottery of local production, all part of the Mediterranean material
culture that continued to be dedicated in this sanctuary. The most frequent
subjects depicted on the Attic vases found in these sanctuaries, just as on
those from the hinterland of Emporion and the rest of Iberia, are military
and Dionysian – scenes of symposia, *komos*, Dionysus, satyrs, maenads –
although other mythological subjects were also common.[167] Pandolfini
points out that Attic imports are predominantly used when the inscription specified the recipient divinity, whereas bucchero and local pottery
were used instead when the personal name of the dedicator was inscribed.
Further, with one exception noted below, Etruscan dedicators did not record
their name when they specified the god to whom they dedicated a vase.[168]
The material record, therefore, suggests that when Greeks stopped frequenting Gravisca and its sanctuaries, Etruscans had no compunction about using
the Greek sacred areas, albeit after rebuilding and expanding the temples.

Even more impressive is the continuity in Aphrodite's cult that was maintained by veneration of the Etruscan goddess Turan. Characterized as a deity
of love, Turan was in a sense Aphrodite's analogue in Etruscan religion. She
was one of the important Etruscan gods, gave her name to a month in the
Etruscan calendar, had a son, called Turnu, who like the Greek Eros is represented as a winged boy, and was often portrayed nude and sometimes as
a winged woman.[169] Numerous dedications to Turan ranging from 480 to
300 BC were discovered from the same spot that yielded the pottery dedicated to Aphrodite. One inscription is particularly interesting because it is

[165] Torelli 1977: 416.
[166] Giudice 2007: 264–76 draws the same conclusion based on her analysis of the trade and
distribution of Attic ceramics in the Italian peninsula and Sicily.
[167] Huber 1999: 176.   [168] A. W. Johnston and Pandolfini 2000: 74–5.
[169] Simon 2006: 60–1.

bilingual. An Attic *skyphos* dating from 470 to 460 BC bears a dedication to Turan written in Etruscan and fragments of what is probably the dedicator's name in Greek.[170] The Greek text cannot be reconstructed with certainty but is given as δειακος τε.[171] If the Greek text does record a personal name, this pot would be the sole example of a dedication that bears both the name of the divinity and the name of the dedicator. The inscription could be the mark of a bilingual man who wrote his dedication to Turan in Etruscan or of a Greek dedicator who bought an already inscribed pot and added his name.

While the concentration of the dedications to Turan in a single room (Room I in Figure 8) helps identify this as the goddess's cult-place, other votive material excavated from the same room, dating to the last two phases of the sanctuary's life, that is, from 400 to 250 BC, makes this identification more solid. For example, several statuettes representing a female – dubbed "Aphrodite" – whose identity is established by her nudity or the doves that the goddess holds, as well as other female statuettes, swaddled babies, and a multitude of anatomical votive uteri, were all discovered in the very same area as the dedications to Turan and earlier to Aphrodite.[172]

The statuettes representing "Aphrodite" are all terra-cotta and probably produced locally, though some follow the artistic aesthetic of Hellenistic models. The name by which modern scholars call the divinity represented, that is, the Greek name of the goddess, "Aphrodite," is indicative of a Hellenocentric point of view. I suspect that the Etruscan worshippers in this sanctuary did not think they were offering statuettes representing Aphrodite; they probably thought they represented Turan. The goddess's representation as naked and her usual accoutrements, like doves, to the Hellenocentric eye signal Aphrodite, when in fact such representations were common on the Italic peninsula and were unrelated to Greek Aphrodite's cults.[173] Again, the popularity across cultures of certain objects and iconographies should be seen as representing a common Mediterranean material culture, which resulted from the intense contacts promoted by trade and other institutions that connected the Mediterranean lands.

Other dedications found in Room I of Building γ were swaddled babies and a multitude of anatomical votive uteri, hearts, breasts, hands, and ears, all of which are extremely common offerings in sanctuaries throughout

---

[170] Inv. 72/20095.   [171] A. W. Johnston and Pandolfini 2000: 21 no. 92, 26, and n. 24.

[172] Comella 1978: 26–8, 29–47, 67–82, 82–6. For a summary of the finds see the table on p. 90.

[173] For example, in Capua statuettes are depicted with pigs, doves, or pomegranates, all attributes of Greek Aphrodite. See Wilamowitz 1873.

the Mediterranean. In the Greek world, for example, swaddled babies are attested from the archaic period onwards from Ionia, Cyprus, Boiotia, and Magna Graecia; on the Italian peninsula they are numerous in Capua, South Italy, and Etruria.[174] Anatomical offerings, such as the ones discovered in Turan's cult-place in Gravisca, have been excavated from many sanctuaries in the Greek world, ancient Etruria, Latium, and Campania, particularly from the latter part of the fourth century onwards.[175] In the Greek world, especially in the Hellenistic period, a great variety of body parts were dedicated in sanctuaries as votives. Heads, arms, abdomens, legs, ears, breasts, thighs, feet, eyes, noses, jaws, mouths, teeth, necks, chests, genitals, pubic regions, bladders, hands, fingers, hips, knees, hearts, uteri have been discovered in many shrines, not necessarily always dedicated to healing deities like Asklepios, Apollo, or Hygieia. To mention just a few examples, anatomical offerings of breasts, genitals, faces, legs, etc., have been discovered in temples dedicated to Aphrodite, uteri, legs, eyes, ears, feet, etc., were dedicated in Artemis' temples, and eyes, legs, and arms, have been excavated from Zeus's temples.[176] The same diversity of finds has been discovered in ancient Italy, where this type of ex-voto was extremely popular.[177] As in the Greek case, these votives were not associated with purely healing cults, like that of Aesculapius, a view prevalent among some scholars,[178] or shrines dedicated to divinities particularly appealing to lower social strata who could afford the relatively cheap anatomical votives, like Feronia, Diana, and Ceres. In fact, what anatomical offerings have in common on the Italic peninsula, is that they are found in temples consecrated predominately to female divinities, such as Etruscan Uni, and Roman Mater Matuta, Juno, Diana, and Ceres.[179] To this list we must now add Turan, given the vast number of anatomical offerings of uteri and breasts discovered in the sacred area identified by inscriptions as Turan's cult-place in Gravisca.

The room next door to where Turan was worshipped (Room M in Figure 8), also yielded votive material variously described as pertaining to the reproductive sphere, or the feminine world, that is, swaddled babies

---

[174] Hadzisteliou Price 1978: 40–3 with references.

[175] For anatomical offerings in Greek sanctuaries, see the appendix entitled "Votive offerings representing parts of the human body (the Greek world)" in Van Straten 1981. For a catalogue of anatomical offerings in ancient Italy that is not exhaustive, see Comella 1981: 717–803.

[176] Van Straten 1981: 105–43 with references.

[177] Glinister 2006: 13 states that her own database of anatomical terra-cotta figurines includes over 290 different sites.

[178] Potter and Wells 1985: 23–47, especially 34–40. The authors argue that the diffusion of anatomic votives spread in conjunction with the increasing popularity of Asklepios.

[179] Glinister 2006: 22–3 and 29.

and anatomical votives such as breasts and uteri. This room is the same one where the single dedication to Uni, who can be compared to Greek Hera, was excavated.[180] Uni's worship does not, however, exhibit spatial continuity with Hera's since the dedications to Hera dispersed throughout the Graviscan sanctuary cannot help localize the Greek goddess's cult. In any case, the dedications in this room do not differ significantly with respect to type from those offered to Turan. The sole variation is in the numbers of these votives: 74 uteri and 2 breasts were excavated from Turan's sanctuary compared to 145 uteri and 2 breasts from Uni's; 23 female heads and 51 standing female statues were deposited in Turan's cult-place, as opposed to 2 heads and 10 statues in Uni's; and 2 swaddled babies were offered to Turan, compared to 22 given to Uni. In addition, about 24 uteri were discovered in an altogether different area of the sanctuary, and another 41 in a cistern.[181]

Scholars have often explained the diffusion of anatomical offerings in ancient Italy as a result of Roman colonization.[182] Recent research shows, however, that anatomical votives in Etruria predate those of Rome, and their distribution is wider than previously assumed.[183] The other peoples of Italy, therefore, already used such votives, without the intervention of the Roman state. Although the increase in the numbers of these votives and the widening of their diffusion coincides with the rise of Roman power, it is more likely that the expanding Roman republic provided the infrastructure, such as road networks, to facilitate the spread of a Mediterranean culture than that it was responsible for imposing anatomical offerings on other Italian cultures.[184]

The votive offerings in the sanctuaries of Turan and Uni in Gravisca are representative of a Mediterranean culture common throughout the Etruscan, Greek, Italic, Phoenician, and Egyptian worlds. These votives show that Turan and Uni in Gravisca were venerated in a manner typical of a variety of cults in the ancient Mediterranean, as deities that presided over the realm of sex, whether that entailed fertility, successful reproduction, nourishment of infants, or sexual health. In the Greek world, for example, a great number of both male and female divinities worshipped as nursing or kourotrophic deities are recipients of dedications such as the ones discussed

---

[180] Comella 1978: 21–4, 66–82. Simon 2006: 61 describes Uni as the wife of Tinia, mother of Hercle, and a warlike deity. In Pyrgi, Phoenician Astarte was translated into the Etruscan Uni (and not Turan, as one might expect since both Astarte and Turan are usually translated into Aphrodite in the Greek pantheon). See Colonna 1984–85 and Serra Ridgway 1990.

[181] Comella 1978: 90.

[182] For a summary of this argument and further bibliography see De Cazanove 1991.

[183] Glinister 2006: 17.   [184] Glinister 2006: 26–7.

here, that is, anatomical votives, swaddled babies, birthing scenes, women offering their breasts, or holding or suckling babies.[185] Similar offerings were dedicated to the Egyptian divinities responsible for various tasks of childbirth and nurture. Hathor, for example, the goddess of sex and love, received anatomical offerings of genitals, figurines of nude women whose breasts or pubic region is emphasized by decoration, or women holding or suckling babies, dating from the Middle Kingdom to the New Kingdom.[186] In later periods, Egyptian divinities overseeing childbirth are Bes and Taweret, both attested in this role from at least the eighteenth century BC to the Graeco-Roman period.[187] Figurines that also have accentuated breasts and pubic regions and are sometimes depicted holding or nursing babies are the Assyrian and Phoenician "Astarte" figurines, appearing from the eighteenth century BC onwards.[188] In the archaic and classical period these figurines were also discovered in Aphrodite's temples on Cyprus, showing once again the commonness of these types of dedications throughout the Mediterranean.[189]

The finds from Turan's cult-place in Gravisca fit nicely with the dedications that Aphrodite received in her various temples in the Greek world. The Greek goddess often had similar kourotrophic functions, especially on Cyprus but also in Athens and elsewhere.[190] In the fourth century, terracotta figurines from Taras depict Aphrodite as Kourotrophos[191] and much earlier the women of Thebes invoke Aphrodite as *Meter* in Aeschylus.[192] The anatomical votives of female genitals and breasts excavated from Aphrodite's sanctuaries at Daphni and on the Acropolis were mentioned above. In the fifth century, similar representations of statuettes touching their breasts with both hands are among the commonest offerings throughout the Black Sea settlements and are thought to have been dedications to Aphrodite.[193] Other material evidence from the goddess' various temples on Cyprus ranges from statuettes of females holding their breasts and women nursing babies to swaddled babies, seated female figures holding swaddled babies, actual childbirth scenes, and even representations of Aphrodite holding or nursing

---

[185] The major kourotrophic divinities are Aphrodite, Apollo, Artemis, Athena, Demeter, Eileithyia, Ge, Hekate, Hera, Heracles, Hermes, Hestia, Leto, Meter, Nymphs, and Rhea. Even rivers are sometimes called *kourotrophoi*. For a full list of all nursing divinities see Hadzisteliou Price 1978: 189–95.

[186] Hornblower 1926; Pinch 1993: 199–245, pl. 46–53.

[187] Robins 1995; Montserrat 1996: 29–31.　　[188] Pritchard 1943: nos. 5–8.

[189] Walters 1903: A10 and Q12–15.　　[190] Hadzisteliou-Price 1978: 90–101.

[191] Taras: Taranto 20088. The identification of the seated goddess as Aphrodite is secure because the child she is nursing is a winged Eros.

[192] Aeschylus, *Seven Against Thebes* 140.　　[193] Ustinova 1999: 45.

Eros.[194] This aspect of the goddess's worship is not absent from emporia. Aphrodite's temple in Naukratis, for example, yielded a statuette of a seated Kourotrophos.[195] Although anatomical votives are absent from the earlier period when Aphrodite was worshipped in Gravisca, the female statuettes, as well as those of Bes, dedicated here might indicate that the Graviscan residents ascribed a nursing function to the goddess.

There is no need to claim that there was an absolute continuity between the worship of Aphrodite and Turan that extended from the physical space where the two goddesses were venerated to their religious aspects. Aphrodite and Turan, both rooted firmly in the polytheistic religions of the Mediterranean, one belonging to the Greek pantheon, the other to the Etruscan, shared enough characteristics and attributes that Etruscans and Greeks could easily identify them with one another. Thus, even when Greeks frequented the Graviscan sanctuary, Etruscans were able to recognize their goddess in Aphrodite and give dedications to her, calling her Turan. However, while the Greeks venerated Aphrodite for her protective power during sea-voyages, and also as the goddess of sex, the Etruscans saw Turan mostly as a nourishing and healing divinity.

The seemingly smooth transition between the worship of Aphrodite and that of Turan led Torelli to propose a similar continuity in the worship of Demeter and Vei from the first to the second phase in the life of the Graviscan sanctuary, even though the number of dedications is much smaller. Only one Greek dedication survives from 530 to 500 BC recording the veneration of the Greek goddess Demeter, whereas we have two Etruscan dedicatory inscriptions for the goddess Vei, one dating to approximately 500 BC, the other to 470–460 BC. Vei is a little known goddess, whose name is attested on a bronze plaque dedication in the Orvietan sanctuary of Cannicella.[196] It was the happenstance of excavating both the Greek and Etruscan dedications from the same find-spot (Area X in Figure 8) that led Torelli to relate the little understood Vei to the Greek Demeter.[197] However tempting it might be to see a continuity of cult between the two deities, the evidence is far from conclusive. There are so few inscriptions to Vei both in general and in the Graviscan sanctuary in particular that no correlation between Vei and Demeter can be drawn.[198] Until the figure of Vei is described more fully,

---

[194] Chytroi: Myres 1899: 5217–42 and 5276–81. Idalion: Cesnola 1885: pl. xxxviii; Myres 1899: 3. Golgoi: Masson 1971: 305–34; Cesnola 1885: pl. lxvi, 435. Kition: Walters 1903: A332–4; Heuzey 1891: nos. 171–4, pl. xv, 4–5. Amathous: Myres 1899: 109. See also Hadzisteliou Price 1978: 90–101 for a summary and references.

[195] Pryce 1928: 197, fig. 238.   [196] Colonna 1967: 547.   [197] Torelli 1977: 404–5.

[198] The poverty of evidence on Vei is evident also in Simon 2006: 47–8 and 61 and Turfa 2006: 97.

the mere coincidence of discovering her two dedications in the same place as the single dedication to Demeter cannot be used to suggest continuity in the two cults.

Conclusion

The excavated sanctuaries of Gravisca offer a unique look into the religious life of Greek emporia and the ways in which religion was used as a mechanism of mediation among different groups. The first cult established in Gravisca was dedicated to Aphrodite, as was the case in the emporion of Naukratis. I have argued that the goddess's intimate association with the sea, from which she emerged at her birth, granted Aphrodite the capacity to protect traders on their sea-voyages. The goddess's capacity to guarantee safe sailing gave her precedence of worship in emporia. Her cult may also have provided social cohesion for the Greeks living in Gravisca as they recognized that they all worshipped her as a patron of navigation. This realization may have been particularly salient as they were living in a mostly Etruscan area.

As a settlement frequented by Greeks originating from different poleis, as well as by local Etruscan inhabitants, Gravisca reveals how these different groups used religion to relate and react to one another. Onomastic evidence and the dialects used to inscribe dedications on votive offerings in the various sanctuaries, suggest that Aiginetans, Samians, and other Ionians frequented Gravisca. Regardless of their origin, all these used the various temples at Gravisca, dedicated to Hera, Apollo, Aphrodite, and probably Demeter and the Dioskouroi. Even if they recognized all gods as something all Greeks, whether from Samos or from Aigina, had in common, certain traders made dedications to specific gods that were important in their polis of origin, thereby perhaps asserting a civic identity. The Aiginetan Sostratos, for example, dedicated a stone anchor specifically to Aiginetan Apollo, and the Samian Hyblesios gave several dedications in both Gravisca and Naukratis to Hera's temples at these two emporia.

Etruscans used the Graviscan sanctuary during its Greek phase and afterwards. The dedication to Turan discovered in Aphrodite's cult-site is exemplary of the ease with which different groups recognized their own gods in each other's divinities. The Etruscan worshipper who inscribed the Greek (Laconian) crater and dedicated it to an Etruscan goddess in the sanctuary of a Greek goddess perceived Turan's attributes in Aphrodite. No religious boundaries prevented him from doing so. Turan was not the same as Aphrodite, nor did the Etruscan venerate a Greek god that was imposed on him. Instead, the Mediterranean polytheistic religions afforded their followers flexible systems, which could be easily adapted depending on the social circumstances and used for mediation.

After the Greeks abandoned the Graviscan emporion, Etruscans continued to use the sanctuary, worshipping only Etruscan deities. Aphrodite's worship, in particular, exhibits some continuity with Turan's veneration. The same sacred area was used to venerate the two goddesses. Whereas Aphrodite received all sorts of dedications, including votive anchors that honored the goddess in her capacity to protect traders and typically feminine objects like perfume vases and female figurines, Turan was the recipient of anatomical votives and female statuettes. Anatomical votive offerings also belonged to a material culture composed of Attic imports, Egyptian faience, Etruscan bucchero-ware, metal objects, etc., which became common among Mediterranean groups because of the cross-cultural interactions in this region.

3 | Naukratis

Whereas other emporia encountered thus far were famous as places where individual Greek traders, or even groups of traders, made large profits, Naukratis, in Egypt, was infamous because of its courtesans, who were far superior in beauty to others. Herodotus, who singled out Naukratis because it had charming courtesans (ἐπαφροδίτους ἑταίρας),[1] preserved the name of an individual prostitute, just as he did the name of the Aiginetan trader Sostratos, encountered in the previous chapter:[2] Rhodopis, or Doricho as some sources call her, was a Thracian slave working her charms in Naukratis, freed by Sappho's brother.[3] Naukratis was also the most often discussed emporion in ancient sources, with the exception of Peiraieus, the port of Attica, to which I will turn in the final chapter. This was not only because of the allure of its courtesans: according to Herodotus, the most detailed source on this commercial settlement, Naukratis had once been the only emporion in Egypt, a statement echoed in the lexicographers of antiquity and the Middle Ages.[4] Nine Greek poleis administered the emporion of Naukratis and its unique temple called the Hellenion, and three other poleis founded sanctuaries there.[5]

The cross-cultural interactions that Naukratis promoted in Egypt were not an isolated instance. Unlike the rest of the Mediterranean world, Egypt was not a city-state culture, but rather a kingdom that had a highly centralized bureaucracy, legal codes, and a strong collective identity of its own.[6] Still, just like other Mediterranean cultures, Egypt had a polytheistic religion that, despite several differences, such as the theocratic rule of pharaohs, was not dissimilar from the religions of its neighbors.[7] The vast kingdom of Egypt was never cut off from the rest of the Mediterranean world.[8] From as early as the Old Kingdom, Egyptian pharaohs cultivated political and commercial contacts with their neighbors, especially the Red Sea coast, the

---

[1] Herodotus 2.135.   [2] Herodotus 4.152.

[3] Herodotus 2.134–5; Sappho fr. 138 (ed. Campbell). Ancient authors mention several other beautiful courtesans from Naukratis, such as, for instance, Archedike (Athenaios 13.596d; Aelian 12.63).

[4] Herodotus 2.179; Harpokration s.v. Naukrarika; Suda s.v. Naukraria; Photios s.v. Naukraria.

[5] Herodotus 2.178.   [6] Brewer and Teeter 1999: 69–83; Shaw 2004b.

[7] Assmann and Frankfurter 2004; Shafer et al. 1991.   [8] Shaw 2004a.

eastern Mediterranean, and the Aegean circle.[9] The connections between Egypt and the Minoan and Mycenaean civilizations are well known, as are the cross-cultural influences among these groups.[10] The earliest depictions of Ionians in Egypt were recently discovered in the tomb of Amenophis III, who reigned in the beginning of the fourteenth century BC.[11] By the seventh century BC contacts between Egypt and the rest of the eastern Mediterranean increased at an unprecedented rate. This should not be surprising as this is the same period during which Greeks and Phoenicians established settlements throughout the Mediterranean and trade and travel in the region intensified. The earliest permanent interactions between Egyptians and foreigners can be dated to this period, when mercenary soldiers from Ionia, Caria, Cyprus, and Phoenicia served in Egyptian armies, as will be discussed in more detail below, and pharaohs settled them in Egyptian towns.[12]

Egyptian official ideology viewed foreigners as representing disorder and chaos, which was opposed to the ordered Egyptian society maintained by the gods and pharaohs. These perceptions are reflected in the negative portrayal of foreigners in artistic media.[13] A good foreigner, in the Egyptian view, was one who conformed to Egyptian culture and who was subservient to the state because this ensured that a stable Egyptian society was maintained.[14] It is not surprising, therefore, to find that some of the foreign mercenaries living in Egypt often adopted Egyptian names, received Egyptian burials, and worshipped in Egyptian cults.[15] This situation is not dissimilar to that in fifth-century Athens, where the presence of foreigners was controlled by the Athenian state, and foreigners living there adopted various Athenian practices, as will be discussed in the final chapter.[16] On the contrary, the Greeks of Naukratis maintained Greek practices, as will become evident, but the settlement itself was regulated by Egyptian authorities.

From the seventh century onwards contacts between Egypt and the rest of the Mediterranean were sealed officially with intermarriages at the highest levels, as when Amasis purportedly married a daughter of the Greek ruling family in Cyrene in Libya, an act which by itself shows Egypt's political actions towards both Greeks and its North African neighbors.[17] This was also the time when Egyptian pharaohs started to offer dedications in Greek

---

[9] Artzu 1994; Fabre 2004a, 2004b, and 2007.   [10] Karetsou 2000.
[11] Souzourian and Stadelmann 2005.   [12] Bernand and Aly 1959; Peden 2001: 288.
[13] O'Connor 2003.   [14] Loprieno 1988; Valbelle 1990; Baines 1996; Bresciani 1997.
[15] Grallert 2001; Höckmann 2001; Kammerzell 2001.
[16] The same was true on Delos, a major emporion of the Hellenistic and Roman Mediterranean. See Trümper 2006.
[17] Herodotus 2.182.

sanctuaries and exchange gifts with their political counterparts in Greek cities. Amasis, for example, besides helping rebuild the pan-Hellenic sanctuary of Apollo at Delphi, as mentioned in the Introduction, also sent gifts to Polykrates, the tyrant of Samos, and statues of Athena to be placed in the temple of Athena Lindia, as a gift to Kleoboulos, the tyrant of Rhodes.[18] These gifts should probably be seen as attempts by the Egyptian government to cultivate political and military alliances that would aid them against the growing threat of Persia. Earlier attempts of the pharaoh Psammetichos I to woo the Corinthian tyrant Periander and Necho's use of Corinthian architects to build a fleet probably had the similar goal of securing naval assistance against the Phoenician navy in the service of the Babylonians.[19]

While the establishment of these permanent contacts was mostly between Egypt and the eastern Mediterranean, trade networks carried Egyptian products to the whole of the Mediterranean region.[20] Just to illustrate, I mention again that Egyptian scarabs have been found in Greek, Punic, Phoenician, Etruscan, Iberian, and other local contexts throughout the Mediterranean, and scarab production spread in various non-Egyptian contexts,[21] and that figurines of Bes acquired their own meaning in non-Egyptian contexts and can be found in many Greek and Etruscan sanctuaries.[22] Other examples, by no means exhaustive, that demonstrate the appeal of Egyptian products in the western, as well as the eastern, Mediterranean are the Egyptian alabaster jars with royal cartouches and Egyptian bronze statuettes discovered in what were probably elite Phoenician or Punic tombs in Andalusia and Carthage.[23] The popularity of Egyptian products among Greek elites is also reflected in texts. In the description of Menelaos' house in the *Odyssey*, for example, several prestige metal artifacts given as gifts are said to be from Egypt.[24] Egyptian artifacts, however, were not only sought by elites; demand for them also existed among non-elites. That this was the case can be easily recognized by looking at the distribution of bronze statuettes and faience objects in Etruscan and Greek tombs, as well as sanctuaries throughout the Greek world.[25]

---

[18] These gifts are recounted in Herodotus 2.180–2. Francis and Vickers 1984 discuss Amasis' gifts to Lindos.

[19] Aristotle, *Politics* 1315b and Herodotus 1.33–8.

[20] For general surveys of the relations between Greeks and Egyptians see: Austin 1970 and Burstein 1995.

[21] Kaczmarcyk and Hedges 1983; Gorton 1996.

[22] Sinn 1982. See also the discussion of Bes figurines in the previous chapter.

[23] Padró i Parcerisa 1980: II 31; Aubet 2001: 202–3, 332–4.

[24] Homer, *Odyssey* 4.120–37. For the role of eastern objects in constructing elite identities see Duplouy 2006.

[25] Von Bissing 1941; Webb 1978; Kaczmarcyk and Hedges 1983; De Salvia 1983.

The presence of Egyptian artifacts in Greek contexts and Egyptian influences in Greek art and architecture are well known and have been discussed by so many scholars and so frequently that it seems unnecessary to go into further detail here.[26] The appeal of Egyptian objects extended to include Egyptianizing artifacts produced not in Egypt but throughout the Mediterranean.[27] Faience workshops on Rhodes, for instance, produced Egyptianizing statuettes and vessels that were practically indistinguishable from faience objects produced in Egypt, and which were distributed throughout the Greek world, in both the eastern and the western Mediterranean.[28] The same held true for Punic workshops, which produced scarabs found in both Punic and other contexts.[29] Similarly, Egyptian bronzes, which were often dedicated in Greek sanctuaries in the eighth and seventh centuries BC, were so popular that eventually Greek artists were producing them.[30] What happened to Greek art when the Greek world came into contact with Egypt (and the Near East) is not dissimilar to what the Iberians and Etruscans experienced when they encountered the Greeks and Phoenicians. The demand for certain objects and their presence throughout the Mediterranean in different cultural contexts indicates the existence of a common material culture accessible to all groups inhabiting the Mediterranean, even if the various groups read and understood these objects in different ways.

It is interesting to note that the Greek representation of Greco-Egyptian relations did not always reflect the close interactions between the two civilizations. Stereotypically presented both in myth and historical writings as an antique country where writing, religion, and philosophy were invented and from which Greeks borrowed these cultural goods, Egypt remained static in Greek rhetoric.[31] This attitude has sometimes been read as respect for the older civilization to which the Greeks thought they owed, say, their

[26] Some recent studies that provide more extensive bibliography on Egyptian influences in Greek art and architecture, are Skon-Jedele 1994; Guralnick 1997; Bietak 2001; Tanner 2003.
[27] Burnett 1975.
[28] Webb 1978. Guralnick 1997 states that the only difference is that Rhodian faience is somewhat paler.
[29] Gorton 1996.
[30] The first bronzes from Samos, for example, are influenced by Egyptian techniques and motifs (Kyrieleis 1990).
[31] Herodotus' *excursus* on the Egyptians in Book 2 of his *Histories* exemplifies these ideas, which are shared by later Greek authors. See Vasunia 2001. In fact, it is these representations that have formed the basis of some of the most controversial scholarship that revolves around the notion that Greek civilization and culture derived from Egypt, which was older and wiser than the Greek world. I refer to Bernal's multi-volume project *Black Athena*. See Bernal 1987 and 1991 and for the response to Bernal's work see Lefkowitz 1996 and 2002–3, and Lefkowitz and Rogers 1996.

gods; other scholars, however, who have discussed the role Egypt played in the Greek imagination and the way it was portrayed in the Greek intellectual tradition, have pointed out the possible negative connotations of the Greek stereotyping of Egypt.[32] Yet, these literary perspectives do not acknowledge the socio-cultural, economic, or political aspects of the interactions between Greeks and Egyptians at any given point in time or place. It is the aim of this chapter to look more closely at Greco-Egyptian relations as they played themselves out in the emporion of Naukratis, in order to discern these particular actors' perceptions of each other and the construction of their own identities.

Cross-cultural trade in Naukratis facilitated two types of interactions. On the one hand, different Greek groups in Naukratis encountered each other and through these encounters defined their identity. Not only did they use their citizenship as one level of collective identity, but they also employed religion both to mediate among themselves and to express their civic identity. On the other hand, as an emporion in Egypt, Naukratis necessarily involved interactions between Greeks and Egyptians, which in turn produced a Greek response unlike any other. Faced with a bureaucratic kingdom and a strong Egyptian identity, the Greeks of Naukratis founded a common temple in 570 BC and called it "Hellenion," a unique name in the archaic period and symbolic of one of the earliest expressions of a Hellenic identity in the Greek world.

Founding Naukratis: a Greek city in Egypt

The date Naukratis was established, the group or groups that established it, and the political status of the settlement are all contested issues. The answers to these questions are all vital for understanding the context in which the interethnic relations unfolded. Herodotus and Strabo are the two ancient authors who give the most details about the establishment of Naukratis; they deserve to be quoted in full, as their reports constitute evidence that will be discussed throughout this chapter. Herodotus' account is the earlier:

Φιλέλλην δὲ γενόμενος ὁ Ἄμασις ἄλλα τε ἐς Ἑλλήνων μετεξετέρους ἀπεδέξατο καὶ δὴ καὶ τοῖσι ἀπικνεομένοισι ἐς Αἴγυπτον ἔδωκε Ναύκρατιν πόλιν ἐνοικῆσαι· τοῖσι δὲ μὴ βουλομένοισι αὐτῶν ἐνοικέειν, αὐτόσε δὲ ναυτιλλομένοισι ἔδωκε χώρους ἐνιδρύσασθαι βωμοὺς καὶ τεμένεα θεοῖσι. Τὸ μέν νυν μέγιστον αὐτῶν τέμενος καὶ ὀνομαστότατον ἐὸν καὶ χρησιμώτατον, καλεόμενον δὲ Ἑλλήνιον, αἵδε πόλιές εἰσι

---

[32] Froidefond 1971; Vasunia 2001.

αἱ ἱδρυμέναι κοινῇ· Ἰώνων μὲν Χίος καὶ Τέως καὶ Φώκαια καὶ Κλαζομεναί, Δωριέων
δὲ Ῥόδος καὶ Κνίδος καὶ Ἁλικαρνησσὸς καὶ Φάσηλις, Αἰολέων δὲ ἡ Μυτιληναίων
μούνη. Τουτέων μέν ἐστι τοῦτο τὸ τέμενος, καὶ προστάτας τοῦ ἐμπορίου αὗται αἱ
πόλιές εἰσι αἱ παρέχουσαι· ὅσαι δὲ ἄλλαι πόλιες μεταποιεῦνται, οὐδέν σφι μετεὸν
μεταποιεῦνται. Χωρὶς δὲ Αἰγινῆται ἐπὶ ἑωυτῶν ἱδρύσαντο τέμενος Διός, καὶ ἄλλο
Σάμιοι Ἥρης, καὶ Μιλήσιοι Ἀπόλλωνος.

Ἦν δὲ τὸ παλαιὸν μούνη Ναύκρατις ἐμπόριον καὶ ἄλλο οὐδὲν Αἰγύπτου· εἰ
δέ τις ἐς τῶν τι ἄλλο στομάτων τοῦ Νείλου ἀπίκοιτο, χρῆν ὁμόσαι μὴ μὲν
ἑκόντα ἐλθεῖν, ἀπομόσαντα δὲ τῇ νηὶ αὐτῇ πλέειν ἐς τὸ Κανωβικόν· ἢ εἰ μή γε
οἷά τε εἴη πρὸς ἀνέμους ἀντίους πλέειν, τὰ φορτία ἔδεε περιάγειν ἐν βάρισι περὶ τὸ
Δέλτα, μέχρις οὗ ἀπίκοιτο ἐς Ναύκρατιν. Οὕτω μὲν δὴ Ναύκρατις ἐτετίμητο.
(Herodotus 2.178–9)

Amasis, becoming a Philhellene, granted some Greeks certain rights, and in particular, he gave those who came to Egypt Naukratis, a polis in which to dwell. To those
among them who were going to sea and did not wish to settle there he gave lands to
erect altars and sanctuaries for the gods. The greatest of these sanctuaries, and the
most famous and most visited, is the so-called Hellenion, set up jointly by the following poleis: of the Ionians, Chios, Teos, Phokaia, and Klazomenai; of the Dorians,
Rhodes, Knidos, Halikarnassos, and Phaselis; of the Aeolians, only Mytilene. It is to
these poleis that the sanctuary belongs and it is they who appoint the *prostatai* of the
emporion. However many other poleis claim a share in the Hellenion, they do so
without any justification. The Aiginetans, however, founded separately a sanctuary
for Zeus on their own initiative, the Samians one for Hera, and the Milesians one
for Apollo.

From of old, Naukratis was the only emporion; there was none other in Egypt.
If someone arrived at any other mouth of the Nile, it was necessary to take an oath
that he had arrived there not of his own accord, and to sail in his ship to the Kanobic
mouth. Or if he could not sail against contrary winds, it was necessary to carry his
cargo in barges around the Delta, until he arrived at Naukratis. In such honor was
Naukratis held.

Strabo's account appears within his description of the Nile delta geography:

Μετὰ δὲ τὸ Βολβίτινον στόμα ἐπὶ πλέον ἔκκειται ταπεινὴ καὶ ἀμμώδης ἄκρα·
καλεῖται δὲ Ἀγνοῦ κέρας· εἶθ' ἡ Περσέως σκοπὴ καὶ τὸ Μιλησίων τεῖχος· πλεύσαν-
τες γὰρ ἐπὶ Ψαμμιτίχου τριάκοντα ναυσὶ Μιλήσιοι (κατὰ Κυαξάρη δ' οὗτος ἦν
τὸν Μῆδον) κατέσχον εἰς τὸ στόμα τὸ Βολβίτινον, εἶτ' ἐκβάντες ἐτείχισαν τὸ λεχ-
θὲν κτίσμα· χρόνῳ δ' ἀναπλεύσαντες εἰς τὸν Σαϊτικὸν νομὸν καταναυμαχήσαντες
Ἰνάρων πόλιν ἔκτισαν Ναύκρατιν οὐ πολὺ τῆς Σχεδίας ὕπερθεν. (Strabo 17.1.18)

After the Bolbitine mouth lies a low and sandy promontory that projects far into the
sea; it is called Willow-horn. Then there are Perseus' watchtower and the Milesians'

wall. For in the time of Psammetichos (who lived in the time of Kyaxares the Mede) the Milesians sailed with thirty ships into the Bolbitine mouth, disembarked, and built the aforementioned structure. In time they sailed to the Saitic region and having defeated Inaros in a sea-battle, founded the city Naukratis, not far above Schedia.

These two varying accounts have given rise to debates as to whether Naukratis was founded under the rule of Psammetichos I (664–610 BC), as Strabo appears to suggest, or under Amasis' rule (570–526 BC), as Herodotus seems to imply.[33] In addition, later literary sources offer divergent dates for the foundation of Naukratis. Polycharmos, followed by Athenaios, considers Naukratis to have been in existence in the year of the twenty-third Olympiad (688 BC), whereas Eusebios dates its establishment to the seventh Olympiad (749 BC).[34] The later the source, the earlier is the date of Naukratis' establishment. The material evidence, however, precludes the possibility of a Greek settlement already existing at the site of Naukratis in the eighth or early seventh centuries. The earliest Greek pottery dates to the late seventh century BC.[35] Such a date would suggest a significant Greek presence from this period onwards and would coincide with the reign of Psammetichos I.[36] A closer look at both Herodotus' and Strabo's texts shows that the two authors do not necessarily contradict each other. Most scholars today agree that Naukratis was established in the late seventh century BC as a Greek settlement in Egypt and that Amasis reorganized its structure in the sixth century BC.[37]

[33] For a mid- to late seventh-century foundation date see Petrie et al. 1886; Gardner 1888; Prinz 1908; Price 1924. For a sixth-century date see Hirschfeld 1887; Hogarth: 1898–9 and 1905; Gjerstad 1934 and 1959; Von Bissing 1951.

[34] Polycharmos *apud* Athenaios 15.676a-c; Eusebios, *Chronicle of St. Jerome* 88b (ed. Helm).

[35] Gardner 1888: 33–4 and 37; Cook 1937; Austin 1970: 23 n. 8; Möller 2000: 104 and 195.

[36] James 2003 argues that the settlement was founded around 570 based on the revised pottery chronologies of the Eastern Mediterranean with lower dates. In the case of Naukratis, bringing down the dates would mean that the earliest pottery dates not to the late seventh century but to the early or mid sixth century BC. In turn, this change would indicate that there is no disagreement between the archaeological evidence and Herodotus' account, and would yield a date for the foundation of Naukratis in the reign of Amasis. While several scholars (e.g., Francis and Vickers 1985; James et al. 1987; Fantalkin 2001 and his forthcoming article on "Naukratis as Contact Zone") consider the new chronologies plausible and have themselves argued for a lowering of the dates, these have not been fully accepted yet (cf. Boardman 1988; Cook 1989; Childs 1993). Even if the revised chronologies are correct, they do not affect the discussion in this chapter, which concentrates on the sixth-century and later settlement in Naukratis.

[37] In a forthcoming article, Fantalkin puts forth a different proposal. He argues that the foundation of Naukratis should be seen as the result of a treaty between Lydia and Miletos at the end of the seventh century BC. What is traditionally thought of as Amasis' reorganization is then understood in the context of Lydian imperial aspirations: the Lydian empire at the beginning of the sixth century BC was trying to cultivate good relations with Egypt, and the

Strabo's account, and those of the ancient authors who followed him, is problematic.[38] It is so similar to his report of the founding of Poseidonia,[39] which also involved first building a wall on the seashore before founding a city further inland, that Strabo may have followed the same pattern in constructing the two accounts without concern for accuracy.[40] In addition, the mention of Inaros is difficult to interpret. The only Inaros known to us is a Libyan who persuaded the Egyptians to break away from Persia after Xerxes' death in 465 BC.[41] Such a late date for the foundation of Naukratis is not likely at all since the earliest archaeological evidence from the site dates to the end of the seventh century. It may very well be that Strabo incorporated a later report about Inaros' revolt into his account of the foundation of Naukratis, which he intended to date to the reign of Psammetichos I.[42]

Herodotus' account does not necessarily go against a late seventh-century foundation of Naukratis. The historian says that it was the pharaoh Amasis who gave Naukratis to the Greeks, implying that the polis of Naukratis existed before it was given as a gift. Scholars agree that what Herodotus credits Amasis with is the reorganization of Naukratis by settling Greeks there, and the founding of the Hellenion by placing nine cities in charge of its administration.[43] As archaeological evidence shows, the Hellenion dates

Greek poleis that were within the sphere of influence of the Lydian empire became beneficiaries of these attempts when they were given the right to cooperate in commercial affairs in Egypt.

[38] Later authors, most likely derivative from Strabo, also name Miletos as the mother-city of Naukratis and claim that the foundation took place when Miletos was a thalassocracy: Stephanos of Byzantion s.v. Naukratis; Suda s.v. Naukratis.

[39] Strabo 5.4.13.   [40] Bresson 2000a: 51. Möller 2001a follows Bresson.

[41] Thucydides 1.104; Diodorus Siculus 11.71.3–6.

[42] Von Bissing 1951: 39–41 and Roebuck 1951: 219 n. 13. Drijvers 1999 has offered an alternative interpretation of the events Strabo describes. According to this scholar, the thirty Milesian ships that Strabo mentions were a mercenary army that had come to help Psammetichos I, who is known to have employed large forces of Greeks in his army (Herodotus 2.152–4; Diodorus Siculus 1.66.10–1.67). Psammetichos I rewarded the Milesians by permitting them to settle at a place called the Milesian wall, but they were unhappy there and wanted to join Naukratis, an already successful trading post. The Pharaoh did not allow them to do so and sent a certain Inaros to fight against them; only when they defeated him were the Milesians able to force their way into Naukratis. This interpretation of Strabo's account, although possible, is not based on any concrete evidence. No soldier identified himself as a Milesian from among the Greek mercenaries who inscribed graffiti on the colossal statue of Rameses II in Abu-Simbel, in Nubia, in 591 BC (*ML* 7), and the origin of the mercenary soldiers Psammetichos I employed is unknown.

[43] Bresson 2000a: 20–1. Möller 2000: 166–81 and 192–3 thinks that Herodotus actually dates to the reign of Amasis the foundation of Naukratis and not a later reorganization of the city. She argues that Herodotus deliberately attributed the foundation of Naukratis to Amasis and not Psammetichos I because he wanted to set Amasis firmly in the tradition of the pro-Greek Saite dynasty. While she might be right about Herodotus' portrayal of Amasis as a pro-Greek (see also Roebuck 1951: 213), a closer look at Herodotus 2.178 reveals that the historian clearly

to approximately 570 BC, the year that marked the beginning of Amasis' reign.[44]

Even if the date of Naukratis can be established with some certainty, especially with the help of archaeological evidence, the settlement's origins present a challenge, because Strabo's account states that Naukratis was a Milesian colony, while Herodotus gives the impression that Naukratis was not a colony since he says that Amasis granted the settlement to the Greeks and that nine Greek poleis founded a single sanctuary that they administered. To resolve this disagreement in the two accounts, scholars have typically conflated Herodotus and Strabo's texts, proposing that Milesians originally founded Naukratis and Amasis later assigned the settlement to the Greeks trading in the area.[45] They find supporting evidence not only in the presence of the temple dedicated to Milesian Apollo but also in the fact that in Roman times, Naukratis used the Milesian calendar and laws. The material remains, however, contain no indication of a Milesian preeminence at any point during Naukratis' history.[46] Moreover, the temple to Milesian Apollo dates from approximately the same time as the Hellenion, that is *c.* 570 BC, a generation after the foundation of the site.[47] It is also likely that in the Hellenistic period, Naukratis reinvented its own history by adopting the Milesian *nomima*.[48] In fact, there was a Hellenistic tradition of falsely naming Miletos as the mother-city of various Egyptian colonies, initiated by Miletos itself at about 200 BC. The first attestation of this claim is in an epigram that foreshadows the preambles of inscriptions of the Antonine and Severan eras: it calls Miletos "the earliest city to be founded in Ionia" and "the metropolis of many great cities in the Euxine Sea, in Egypt, and in many places in the world."[49] It is possible that by the second century BC Naukratis had co-opted a similar foundation myth and adopted Milesian customs to support this claim, and that Strabo followed this tradition in his account of the foundation of Naukratis.

Related to the issue of the foundation of Naukratis is the question of whether it was originally an Egyptian or a Greek town. In the cases of

---

points out that Amasis was not always pro-Greek but rather became one (γενόμενος) right around the time he gave Naukratis to the Greeks in Egypt. In fact, it is well known that before Amasis became pharaoh he waged a war against Apries and fought against Apries' Greek mercenaries (Herodotus 2.163).

[44] Möller 2000: 106; Höckmann and Möller 2006: 11–12.

[45] Petrie et al. 1886: 4; Gardner 1888: 9; E. M. Smith 1926: 12–26; Prinz 1908: 1–6; Sullivan 1996: 186–8.

[46] Lehmann-Hartleben 1923: 38; Prinz 1908: 38, 114.

[47] Gjerstad 1934 and 1959; Bresson 2000a: 25, and n. 52.   [48] Bowden 1996: 24–8.

[49] Peek 1966. Inscriptions: *CIG* 2878, *IMilet* 1, 7, nos. 233–6, 240, 260, 262. See also Austin 1970: 22 n. 5.

Emporion and Gravisca it was clear that the settlements in question were both Greek establishments founded in non-Greek lands. Since Naukratis existed already before Amasis gave it to the Greeks, a minority of scholars has considered that it was an Egyptian town originally, adducing either archaeological or linguistic evidence in support of their claim.[50] It is necessary to examine this possibility, as well as the alternate hypothesis that the settlement was divided into an Egyptian and a Greek sector, because both have important implications for the cross-cultural interactions facilitated in Naukratis.

The first excavators of Naukratis claimed the settlement was divided into two sectors: the southern Egyptian part and the northern Greek part.[51] What led the excavators to this conclusion was the false idea that no Greek pottery had been discovered in the lowest layer, a burnt stratum, of the southern part of the city. Möller clearly shows how the excavators misinterpreted the evidence.[52] Although it is difficult to interpret burnt layers, she points out that Petrie catalogued nothing but Greek finds from this stratum.[53] Moreover, Möller proposes that Hogarth misidentified as Egyptian local pottery shards of the Ptolemaic period found near the Ptolemaic buildings of this area.[54] This area is just east of Aphrodite's temple, which, as mentioned before, was a Greek foundation built on virgin soil. Stratigraphy, therefore, reveals that the lowest layers of southern Naukratis were originally Greek, not Egyptian.

Coulson and Leonard, who returned to Naukratis for further excavations in the 1970s, argued that the development of the city was chronological rather than ethnic, contrary to what Hogarth had implied.[55] They discovered that the northeastern and eastern sections of Naukratis yielded Greek material from the Hellenistic period, the western part produced predominantly Roman finds, and the southern part yielded nothing but Ptolemaic remains.[56] Nothing in this report suggested that the material unearthed from a particular area was principally Egyptian or older than the Ptolemaic period. Within the excavated areas, therefore, there is no indication that the settlement was ever spatially divided into a Greek and an Egyptian sector or that the older southern sector of the settlement, at least as much of it as has been excavated, was an Egyptian city before it was given to the Greeks. Does

---

[50] Hirschfeld 1887: 209–14; Hogarth 1905: 108; Gjerstad 1959: 160; Austin 1970: 29.
[51] Hogarth 1898–9: 43 and 1905: 106–8.   [52] Möller 2000: 116–19.
[53] Petrie et al. 1886: 21 and pl. 16.4.   [54] Möller 2000: 117.
[55] Leonard 1997: 22–30, esp. 23 and 29. Möller 2000 was not able to take their results into consideration.
[56] Coulson 1996: 11 and Leonard 1997: 28–30.

the lack of Egyptian strata in Naukratis mean that there were no Egyptians living there? Not necessarily. The problem in answering this question is that the excavated parts of Naukratis are limited to the areas given to the Greeks by Amasis.[57]

Similarly, the linguistic evidence employed by scholars who see Naukratis originally as an Egyptian polis is inconclusive. The argument revolves around the two names that Egyptian sources give to Naukratis, *Pr-mryt* and *Nkrd*. One suggestion is that the Greek name Naukratis in fact derived from an original Phoenician name that was later Egyptianized into *Nkrd*.[58] No literary or archaeological evidence, however, supports the idea that Phoenicians were present in Naukratis before the Greeks.[59] The suggestion was based on the false assumption that Aphrodite's sanctuary was actually a Phoenician temple of Astarte, but, as discussed above, this was originally a Greek temple. Others think that *Nkrd* is the original Egyptian name later adopted by the Greeks.[60] The name *Nkrd* is mentioned five times in Egyptian texts, none of which date from a period before the Greek presence in Naukratis: the oldest dates to 554 BC,[61] another to 380 BC,[62] and the remaining three to the Ptolemaic period.[63] If *Nkrd* were the name of the Egyptian town given to the Greeks we might expect to find its name in earlier documents. Nonetheless, Yoyotte argues that if the name of the town had been originally Greek, it would have been transcribed in Egyptian documents as *Nkrts* and not *Nkrd*, because Egyptian usually retains the final –s of Greek names.[64] Moreover, the component parts of the name would be *N* and *Krd*, where *N* stood for *n'iwt*, that is, "town."[65] In Yoyotte's view, therefore *Krd* was the name of a person who established Naukratis.[66] While these propositions are possible, it is important to note that Greek words related etymologically to "Naukratis," such as "ναυκράτωρ" (commander

---

[57] Bresson 2002. Bresson 2000a: 18 and 22 and 2000b: 66–7 thinks that Greeks and Egyptians lived side by side. At least at Emporion, Greeks and Iberians eventually lived in the same settlement. In Gravisca, the residential areas have not been excavated and the question of whether Etruscans and Greeks lived in the same city cannot be answered. At Pistiros, however, there were probably Thracians and Greeks living together, and, as is well known, Peiraieus was host to both Greeks and non-Greek traders who came from outside Athens.

[58] Lutz 1943.

[59] James 2003: 252–8 proposes that Phoenicians were present in Naukratis and operating the scarab factory.

[60] Yoyotte 1991–2: 640–2.   [61] Hermitage 8499.

[62] Gunn 1943: 58. The stele is discussed below.

[63] Michigan Stele (283/282 BC); *P.Louvre* E 3266, 7 (197 BC); *P.Cairo 2* 31169, col.1, 25 (*c.* 332–200 BC).

[64] Yoyotte 1991–2: 640–1.

[65] This is how *Nkrd* is spelled on the Stele of Nektanebis, also known as the Naukratite Stele.

[66] Yoyotte 1991–2: 641–2.

of the seas) and its compounds, occur in Greek sources contemporary to the Egyptian inscriptions bearing the name *Nkrd*: Hekataios, for instance, already uses the word ναυκρατέες in the sixth century.[67] It is equally possible, therefore, that Naukratis was originally a Greek name.

The word *Pr-mryt* is attested in the text inscribed on the Stele of Nektanebis I, an edict of 380 BC produced by the Pharaoh Nektanebis detailing taxes that Greeks had to pay to Egyptians on whatever was imported into Naukratis.[68] Several scholars assumed that this name was a translation of the name Naukratis either from Greek into Egyptian or from Egyptian into Greek.[69] In fact, *Pr-mryt* means simply, "house of the harbor," which is not the same as "commanding the sea," a possible translation of "Naukratis." Nonetheless, both the Greek and the Egyptian words indicate the maritime role of the commercial settlement. In fact, on the Stele of Nektanebis, *Pr-mryt* is later glossed: "*Pr-mryt*, called <Nau>kratis."[70] Thus, *Pr-mryt* was just a descriptive epithet for Naukratis. Linguistic arguments, therefore, are inconclusive as to the preexistence of an Egyptian site before the arrival of the Greeks in Naukratis.

Epigraphic sources are more likely to provide an answer as to whether Egyptians and Greeks lived together in Naukratis. Over 1500 inscriptions on pottery, and dozens on stone, were unearthed during the various Naukratis excavations. All of these were Greek, except for a few Egyptian ones. All were discovered within Naukratis except for eighteen Egyptian inscriptions, the majority of which were scattered within a radius of 6 miles from the settlement.[71] Most of the Egyptian dedications and other Egyptian objects that originate from Naukratis and its environs date to the Hellenistic period, at which time a temple dedicated to Amon-Rê-Baded existed just south of the temple to Aphrodite.[72] It is likely that this temple, in fact, dates to an earlier period, given that several sixth and seventh century buildings with the same structure have been discovered in Egyptian towns in the Nile Delta.[73] If so, this important evidence would indicate that there was a significant Egyptian presence in Naukratis contemporary with the implantation of the Greek settlement there. A few other inscribed objects also clearly date from earlier periods. One scarab discovered in the scarab factory bears two cartouches of Sheshanq I, thus dating to the middle of the tenth century BC.[74]

---

[67] Hekataios *FGrH* 1 F 5.   [68] Gunn 1943: 58.
[69] Greek to Egyptian: Von Bissing 1951: 33; Egyptian to Greek: Austin 1970: 30 n. 2.
[70] Gunn 1943: 58.
[71] Griffith 1888: 77–84. Two of the eighteen inscriptions may be from Naukratis.
[72] Yoyotte 1982–3, 1993–4: 684–92, and 1994–5: 671–82; Muhs 1994.
[73] Leclère 2008 discusses these buildings.   [74] Yoyotte 1993–4: 679.

Another scarab marked with a name might date to the late eighth century BC.[75] There is nothing, however, to preclude the possibility of these isolated objects having been treated either as antiques or heirlooms, in other words, as prestige objects carried by Greeks.

In addition to these scarabs, there are only two pre-Hellenistic Egyptian inscriptions. One is by someone who identifies himself as "a man from *Nkrd*," dating to 554 BC, discovered in Memphis.[76] The other is the Stele of Nektanebis, mentioned above and discussed in more detail below, which records import taxes the Greeks of Naukratis owed to the Egyptians. The publication of the inscription in Naukratis is not evidence that Egyptians lived there, but rather a reminder for the residents of Naukratis that the Egyptian government had authority over the Greek traders. It is interesting that the inscription was written in Egyptian when it was meant to be read by Greeks. In Egypt, the situation is the exact opposite of that in Pistiros in Thrace, where, as I discuss in the next chapter, the Thracian dynasts published legislation concerning the Greek traders in Greek. Egypt did not need to cater to the Greeks living there by writing in Greek since it had a unified collective identity compared to the Thracians, who were in any case broken up into several sub-ethnic groups.[77] Moreover, as will be discussed later, Egyptians placed emphasis on language in distinguishing among ethnic groups. The presence of an inscription in hieroglyphs would have made a strong impression on Greeks and it also would have marked clearly the difference between the Egyptian authorities and the Greeks living in Egypt.

Evidence that Egyptians lived in the excavated parts of Naukratis, therefore, is minimal. Much has been made of the faience workshop in Naukratis, from which molds for producing scarabs, heads, animals, busts, and amulets of Bes and Horus were discovered. These Naukratite molds are different from others found in Egypt, though the items produced here bore Egyptianizing motifs on the underside.[78] This does not necessarily mean that their producers were Greek, but the quantity of Greek pottery discovered from the factory, its late seventh-century date that coincides with the establishment of the Greek sanctuaries, and the fact that the scarabs produced here

---

[75] Yoyotte 1993–4: 679.

[76] Hermitage 8499. Two other inscriptions from the archaic period bear a connection to Naukratis since they mention the temple of Amon-Rê-Baded, which only existed in Naukratis, but their provenance is uncertain (Berlin 7780 and Cairo 14/2/25/2). Berlin 7780 was never edited, and the text had deteriorated already by the beginning of World War II. These three inscriptions suggest the presence of Egyptians and an Egyptian temple in Naukratis. See also Yoyotte 1991–2: 642 and 1993–4: 684.

[77] Herodotus 5.3.   [78] Petrie et al. 1886: 37 and pl. 38.

exhibit errors in the hieroglyphics, strongly suggest that they might have been Greeks.[79] At any rate, they were most probably not Egyptians. Even if the presence of the factory is not an indication that Egyptians lived in Naukratis, the distribution of the scarabs produced here, found in Cyrene, Rhodes, Chios, Samos, Olbia, Berezan, and Iberia, among others,[80] suggests they were intended for a wider Mediterranean market.

It seems that in the archaic and classical periods, the majority of Naukratis' residents were Greeks. This situation seems to have changed by the Hellenistic period, when the Egyptian temple was definitely in operation, suggesting a significant Egyptian presence at this time. Even if we cannot say with certainty that Egyptians lived in Naukratis together with Greeks, or whether any parts of Naukratis were an original Egyptian town given to the Greeks, it is clear that the two groups were in constant contact with one another, as is evidenced by the artistic influences, cross-cultural trade, and relations with the Egyptian government.

The last issue to be resolved that arises from Herodotus' and Strabo's accounts of the establishment of Naukratis is the political status of the settlement. Herodotus' text that calls Naukratis alternately emporion and polis and Strabo's implication that Naukratis was a Milesian *apoikia*, have sparked an intense debate about Naukratis' political status in its early stages, which is reminiscent of the debate on whether Emporion in Iberia was a Massaliote *apoikia* or an emporion. In both cases, part of the impetus was to deny the settlements in question a political status because of the perceived dichotomy common in scholarship between agrarian colonies and establishments set up for trade. Thus, some scholars have argued that Naukratis must have been a polis in the archaic period,[81] whereas others have said that it was not a polis before the late fifth century BC.[82] Hansen's recent and fundamental work on emporia, discussed in the Introduction and Chapter 1, reveals that all settlements that ancient sources called an emporion were self-governing but dependent Greek poleis located in non-Greek lands whose main purpose was to facilitate cross-cultural trade. Naukratis is, naturally, part of the evidence for this conclusion. It is instructive to review summarily the

[79] Petrie et al. 1886: 22; Möller 2000: 113–15. Some have argued that the scarab factory was operated by Phoenicians, but there is no evidence to this effect: Hogarth 1898–9: 50; Sullivan 1996: 187; James 2003: 252–8.

[80] Gorton 1996: 92.

[81] Lehmann-Hartleben 1923: 37–8; Von Bissing 1949: 1–2; Roebuck 1959: 134–5; Braccesi 1968; Austin 1970: 30–1 and 2004: 1238–40; Hansen 1996c: 184–5, 1997: 91–4, 2006a: 15–16, and 2007a: 127.

[82] Bresson 2000a: 15–17 and 2000b: 74–84.

evidence for the political character of Naukratis, especially in the archaic period.

By the Hellenistic period Naukratis was definitely a polis – it was an urban center with the ability to govern itself, as is evidenced by the presence of political architecture and minting of coins. Although the date of the coins had been disputed, it is now clear that they can be securely dated to the late fourth century BC, some time after Alexander's conquest of Egypt: the coins bear Alexander's head with the legend AΛE on one side and a female head with the legend NAY, presumably a personification of the city of Naukratis, on the other side.[83] In the same period, an inscription of the late fourth century calls Naukratis a polis: ἡ πόλις ἡ Ναυκρατιτ[ῶν] (the polis of the Naukratites).[84] Athenaios quotes a certain Hermeias who mentions the celebration of the birthday of Hestia Prytaneia in the prytaneion of Naukratis.[85] The mention of the prytaneion, the building that housed the hearth, the eternal flame without which a polis could neither exist nor be founded, should indicate that Naukratis was a polis by Hermeias' time, even if the latter projects the existence of the prytaneion to an earlier period.[86] The problem lies in identifying which Hermeias Athenaios quoted: was it Hermeias of Methymna, a fourth-century historian, Hermeias of Kourion, an iambic poet of the third century, or Hermeias of Samos, the author of a speech on love, who lived around 200 BC? Whichever of these candidates was our Hermeias, the numismatic evidence suggests that by the Hellenistic period Naukratis was certainly a polis.

Was it a polis before then? One of the points of contention is Herodotus' use of the word polis. Bresson proposed that the ancient historian used the word *polis* in the sense of an urban town and not in a political sense. Focusing on Herodotus' choice of words, ἔδωκε πόλιν ἐνοικῆσαι (he gave [them] a polis to inhabit), he argued that a polis in the Greek sense of the word cannot be "given"; a polis never exists as a geographical entity of its own, apart from the community of its citizens. He also compared this passage with two parallel ones in Herodotus, where similar phraseology

[83] Bresson 2000a: 53–4, and n. 160 dated the coin to the late fourth century contrary to Head 1886: 66–7, who argued that the head with the legend AΛE was female and that the coin dated from earlier in the fourth century. Austin 1970: 29 and Hansen 1997: 49 both followed Head. In the meantime the coins were reexamined by Le Rider 1997 who determined that the coins definitely depicted Alexander's head and therefore dated to the Hellenistic period. Bresson 2000b: 75 reiterated his claim and Möller 2000: 189 agrees.

[84] *OGIS* 120. [85] Hermeias *apud* Athenaios: 4.149d-150a.

[86] Detienne 1985 considers Hestia's presence in the Prytaneion as a sign of Naukratis' autonomy. Malkin 1987: 129–31 thinks that the Prytaneion was a building that appeared in the fourth century.

is used. One discusses the Peloponnesians' proposal to give a place to the
Ionians to settle.[87] The other offers evidence for what became usual practice
by Egyptian pharaohs, namely to grant places to mercenary soldiers in which
they could settle permanently.[88] Similar language was used by a Greek from
Priene, probably a mercenary soldier, in an inscribed dedication dating to
the second half of the seventh century, which says that Psammetichos I had
given him a golden bracelet and a polis on account of his excellence.[89] In all
these cases, what is given is a geographical location for the various groups
or persons to settle. Moreover, the verb used, ἐνοικῆσαι, is revealing: it does
not imply the foundation of a polis, but rather residency.[90]

This opinion is one that Hansen vehemently resists. Based on the Copenhagen Polis Centre's research on poleis Hansen claims that ancient sources
do not call any urban town a polis, but only those that were political
centers.[91] In the specific case of Naukratis, Hansen emphasizes the distinction Herodotus makes between the resident population of Naukratis
and the traders who did not settle there,[92] and aligns with this distinction
the two terms Herodotus employs to describe Naukratis, namely, polis and
emporion.[93] In this one instance, Herodotus may have used the word emporion in both of its senses: while it designated Naukratis, a self-governing
Greek polis dependent on the Egyptian authorities, whose main function
was trade, it also signified Naukratis' port area and the space with the
facilities for commercial exchange.

Further, a community of the citizens of Naukratis, one of the elements
essential to the definition of the Greek polis, can be attested in the use of the
city-ethnic Naukratite, on various inscriptions dating to the late fifth and
fourth centuries BC found outside of Naukratis in several places in the Greek
world.[94] Bresson, however, disputed the date of the earliest attestation of the
ethnic Naukratite, dating it to the early fourth century BC, and argued that
city-ethnics designated not a citizen member of a polis but rather simply

[87] Herodotus 9.106: δοῦναι τὴν χώρην Ἴωσι ἐνοικῆσαι.
[88] Herodotus 2.154: τοῖσι δὲ Ἴωσι καὶ τοῖσι Καρσὶ τοῖσι συγκατεργασαμένοισι αὐτῷ ὁ
Ψαμμήτιχος δίδωσι χώρους ἐνοικῆσαι ἀντίους ἀλλήλων.
[89] SEG 37, 994: Πηδῶμ μ' ἀνέθηκε|ν ὠμφίννεω : ἐξ Αἰγ|ύπτωγαγών : ῥῶι βασιλεὺς ἔδωϙ'
ὠγύπ|τιος : Ψαμμήτιχο|ς : ἀριστήϊα ψίλιό|ν τε χρυσέοϙ καὶ | πόλιν ἀρετῆς ἔ|νεκα.
[90] Bresson 2000a: 15–23; Möller 2000: 188–9 follows Bresson's argument.
[91] Hansen 1996a: 23–34, and 39–41. Hansen's analysis has shown than Herodotus uses the term
polis most often (320 times out of 469) in the sense of urban town, rather than political
community, but when other sources are considered, or even other passages in Herodotus, the
named Greek urban centers are also shown to be polities.
[92] Herodotus 2.178.   [93] Hansen 1996a: 40–1.
[94] Hansen 1996c: 184–5. For example, *IG* II² 206; *IG* II² 9984–6; *CID* 2:4, 2:10; *FD* III 1: 114, 5:2,
5:3. *Iscr. di Cos* E.D. 95; *IG* XI.4 561.

a resident.[95] Nonetheless, in an earlier study of the use of city-ethnics
Hansen persuasively concluded that whenever a toponym from which an
ethnic was derived designated an urban center, and if this urban center
was not a civic subdivision, such as a *kome* or a demos, then the toponym
almost certainly designated a polis and, consequently, the ethnic a citizen.[96]
The use of the ethnic Naukratite, therefore, should indicate a citizen of
Naukratis. In addition to the inscriptions mentioned above, there is also
an Egyptian dedication in Memphis, dated to 554 BC, by someone who
describes himself as "a man from Naukratis."[97] These Naukratite citizens
suggest that Naukratis was not just a geographical point but also a political
entity at least from the middle of the sixth century, if not before.

Since the polis of Naukratis was a Greek settlement in Egypt, a powerful
state with a centralized bureaucracy, it was dependent on the Egyptian
authorities, even if it were self-governing. The Egyptian state did exercise
its authority over the Greek settlement. In the first place, it was Amasis, the
Egyptian pharaoh, who reorganized the settlement and who granted Greeks
the right to live there. Second, the so-called Stele of Nektanebis, also known
as the Naukratite Stele, dating from 380 BC, records the taxes the Greeks of
Naukratis had to pay in the temple of the goddess Neith in Sais, under the
Pharaoh Nektanebis. The relevant part of the inscription comes after a long
encomium of the Pharaoh's bravery, just rule, and piety:[98]

[T]he tithe of the gold and of the silver and of all things which are produced in
Pr-mryt, called <Nau>kratis, on the bank of the 'Anu, and which are reckoned to
the King's Domain, to be a temple endowment of my mother Neith for all time, in
excess of what has existed formerly. And let them be converted into one portion of
an ox, one fat *ro*-goose and five measures of wine, as a continual daily offering, the
delivery of them to be at the treasury of my mother Neith; for she is the mistress of
the ocean, and it is she who bestows its bounty.

My Majesty has commanded that the temple-endowments of my mother Neith be
protected and reserved, and that everything that those of former time have done
be perpetuated, in order that what I have done may be perpetuated for those who
are yet to be during an eon of years.

And His Majesty ordered that this should be recorded upon this stele, which should
be placed in Naukratis on the bank of the 'Anu; thus would his goodness be remem-
bered to the end of eternity.

[95] Bresson 2000a: 59–60. Such a date would fall within the time when Naukratis started minting
coins.
[96] Hansen 1996c: 195.   [97] Hermitage 8499.
[98] Text translated by Gunn 1943: 58–9, minimally modified.

It is important to note that the stele characterizes Neith as the goddess who gave Egypt all that came from the sea. It is for this reason that the Greek traders importing and exporting goods by sea were expected to pay their dues at the Egyptian goddess's sanctuary.[99] By means of this politico-religious action, the Egyptian government declared its sovereignty; Naukratis and its residents were legally and politically dependent on the Egyptians. For Bresson, this suggests that Naukratis was not a polis but a dependency of the Pharaoh, like various mercenary settlements in Egypt, such as Elephantine, Daphnai, and Stratopeda.[100] However, as Hansen points out, being a Pharaonic dependency did not necessarily mean that Naukratis was not a polis similar to the Ionian poleis of Asia Minor, which, though subjugated and controlled by the Persian Empire, were still poleis.[101] Autonomy, in the sense of independence, was not an essential prerequisite for defining an urban settlement as a polis.[102]

The subordination of Naukratis to the Egyptian state is also evident in Herodotus' text, which makes it clear that the Egyptian government controlled the site: if ships arrived anywhere other than Naukratis, they had to assure the Egyptian authorities that they had not done this on purpose, and even if they could not sail because of contrary winds, they had to disembark, load their goods on barges and carry them to Naukratis.[103] The implication is that the Egyptian government wanted to control all trade that took place in its midst. This may have been what motivated Amasis to give a whole settlement to the Greeks where they could carry out their commercial operations. In this way, the Egyptian government could exercise control over trade, which also meant that it could exact taxes on imports and exports more easily than if traders could arrive anywhere and trade their goods. The Stele of Nektanebis attests that at a later period, the Egyptian Pharaohs were still exacting taxes from Naukratis.

A fifth-century inscription, dating between 475 and 454 BC, adds to the evidence concerning the collection of taxes by the Egyptian government. It is an Egyptian register of taxes that captains of ships, thirty-six of which are described as "Ionian Phaselian" ships, had to pay when they entered Egypt.[104] As will be discussed below, the term Ionian is the usual Egyptian designation of Greeks; ordinarily they did not distinguish among the different Greek groups. This register, however, specifies further that the ships

---

[99] Interestingly, Francis and Vickers 1984 argue that one of the statues Amasis gifted to the city of Lindos was actually a representation of the Egyptian deity Neith. Given the administrative role of Lindos in Naukratis, Amasis' choice of giving a statue of Neith as a gift might be significant.

[100] Bresson 2000a: 21–2.   [101] Hansen 1997: 93 and 2006a: 18.

[102] Hansen 1995 and 2000a: 19.   [103] Herodotus 2.179.   [104] Briant and Descat 1998.

were from Phaselis. The editors of the Egyptian register suggested that the taxes were exacted from the captains as soon as they entered the Kanobic branch of the Nile; then they were free to proceed to their final destination, Naukratis or Memphis, where they would unload and sell their products. At this time, Egypt was part of the Persian Empire, whose Egyptian headquarters were in Memphis. It is likely, therefore, that as Memphis became more central to the administration of Egypt, Naukratis lost its privilege as the only emporion in Egypt. The taxes that the Greeks had to pay are an example of the complementary and at the same time competitive relations between host-societies and trader communities.[105] The import of goods was beneficial for both Greeks, who profited from their sales, and Egyptians, who had access to new products and a stimulated local economy. At the same time, the presence of a foreign settlement in its land was a potential threat and had to be controlled: by paying taxes to the Egyptian government the Greek traders ensured that peaceful relations were maintained between them and the Egyptians.

Administering the emporion

In addition to detailing how the Egyptian government exercised control over trade in Naukratis, Herodotus offers some details on the internal administration of Naukratis. He states that the same nine cities that jointly founded the emporion, Chios, Teos, Phokaia, Klazomenai, Rhodes, Knidos, Halikarnassos, Phaselis, and Mytilene, were also the ones responsible for appointing the presiding officers (*prostatai*) of the emporion and, therefore, its administration.[106] Unfortunately no other information is given about the specific duties of the *prostatai* of the emporion. Here the abundant information from the emporion of Peiraieus provides comparative information that helps conceptualize the role of the Naukratite *prostatai*. Peiraieus had similar officers, the *epimeletai* (supervisors) of the emporion,[107] most likely in charge of all operations. More specialized officers, who probably ultimately reported to the supervisors in Peiraieus, were those who supervised the harbor and the ship-sheds[108] and those who collected taxes on imports.[109] There were also other officers, such as the *astynomoi* and the *agoranomoi*, who were in charge of the urban center of Peiraieus.[110] In addition to

[105] For parallels throughout different periods and areas see Curtin 1984. [106] Herodotus 2.178.
[107] Ps.-Aristotle, *Athenian Constitution* 51.4.
[108] *IG* II² 1607, 1609, 1611, 1620, 1622, 1623, 1627, 1628, 1631.
[109] Demosthenes, *Against Midias* 133 and *Against Phormio* 6.
[110] Ps.-Aristotle, *Athenian Constitution* 50, 51.1; *IG* II² 380.

furnishing the Naukratite *prostatai*, the nine poleis in charge of the emporion also administered the Hellenion, a religious establishment. Their role
was not merely commercial but also religious.

Naukratis' function as an important commercial settlement in the
Mediterranean carried on in the Classical and Hellenistic periods. Ancient
authors continue to relate Naukratis to trade: Demosthenes refers to a
Naukratite ship full of goods stolen before they could be traded;[111] Athenaios
mentions trade as an early activity in Naukratis;[112] Strabo writes that while
on a trading mission in Naukratis Sappho's brother squandered his fortune to free the courtesan Rhodopis;[113] Libanius mentions some Naukratite
traders who had their money stolen;[114] Heliodorus in two different passages speaks of Naukratite traders;[115] and finally, lexicographers also link
Naukratis to trade.[116] Besides these literary sources, two Greek inscriptions
attest to Naukratis' commercial and political ties with other parts of the
Greek world and reveal more about the administration of the emporion.
The first inscription is a Rhodian decree bought in Cairo, whose provenance
is unknown, dating from between 440 and 411 BC. It honors Damoxenos,
the *proxenos* of the city of Lindos on Rhodes, by awarding him and his
descendants tax exemptions for importing and exporting goods. It also dic-
tates the erection of the decree in the Hellenion in Egypt, which must be
the Hellenion of Naukratis:[117]

ἔδοξε τᾶι βωλᾶι κα-	1
ὶ τῶι δάμωι· Δέσπων	
ἐγραμμάτευε, Ἀρχε-	
άναξς εἶπε· Δαμόξεν-	4
ον Ἕρμωνος ἐν Αἰγύ-	
πτωι οἰκέοντα ἀγγ-	
ράψαι πρόξενον Λι-	
νδίων καὶ εὐεργέτ-	8
αν ἐν τῶι ἱαρῶι τᾶς Ἀ-	
θαναίας καὶ ἀτέλε-	
ιαν ἦμεν καὶ αὐτῶι	
καὶ ἐκγόνοις καὶ ἐ-	12
σαγωγὰν καὶ ἐξαγω-	
γὰν καὶ ἐμ πολέμωι	

---

[111] Demosthenes, *Against Timokrates* 11.   [112] Athenaios 15.675f.   [113] Strabo 17.1.33.
[114] Libanius, *Oration* 23 3.7.   [115] Heliodorus, *Ethiopica* 2.8.5.5 and 6.2.3.17.
[116] Photios s.v. Naukraria; Harpokration s.v. Naukrarika; Suda s.v. Naukraria.
[117] Pridik 1908: 19 no. 12; *SEG* 32, 1586.

καὶ ἐν ἰρήναι· ἀγγρ-
άψαι δὲ καὶ ἐν Αἰγύ-
πτωι ἐν τῶ[ι] Ἑλλανί   16
ωι Π[ο]λυ[κλ]έα Ἁλιπό-
λιος· τὸ [δ]ὲ ψάφισμα
ἀγγρά[ψ]αι ἐστάλαν   20
λιθίναν. *vac.*

The council and the people decided; Despon was the secretary, Archeanax made the motion to inscribe Damoxenos, son of Hermon, living in Egypt, as a *proxenos* and benefactor of the Lindians, in the temple of Athenaia and to grant him and his descendants exemption from import and export taxes both in war and in peace; and that Polykles, son of Halipolis, should also inscribe this in Egypt in the Hellenion; and that this decree should be inscribed on a stone stele.

There are several noteworthy points about this decree. First, the name of the man who became a *proxenos* of the Lindians, Damoxenos (a foreigner – or a guest-friend – to the demos), is appropriate not only for his future role as a *proxenos* but also for his capacity as a Greek resident in Egypt. Second, it is important to note that the Lindian *boule* describes Damoxenos as living (οἰκέοντα) in Egypt, and not in a precise town. This point recurs towards the end of the inscription with the order to inscribe this decree in Egypt, but in this instance the prescription is followed by the specification to set up the stele in the Hellenion. It is in itself significant that the Hellenion could represent all of Egypt, with no need to name Naukratis, though the Hellenion in Naukratis was the only temple with this name in this period.[118] This implies that, after Amasis' reorganization, Naukratis was the only recognized Greek trading settlement in Egypt. Finally, the right of tax exemption on imports and exports granted to Damoxenos and his descendants demonstrates that, though Damoxenos resided in Egypt, he also traveled for business. This stands in direct contrast to Herodotus' text detailing the organization of Naukratis, which seems to make a distinction

[118] There are two references to a Hellenion in Memphis. One is a third century text that records the visit of Zenon to the sanctuary to perform sacrifices: *P. Cair. Zen.* 59593.7–8; the other is a third century papyrus, a declaration of an individual's real estate assets (Mitteis and Wilcken 1912: 256 no. 221). He describes himself as a Hellenomemphitis, a common name of the Greeks living in Memphis, attested only in the Hellenistic period, and locates his house in the Hellenion. In this case, the word "Hellenion" carries its secondary meaning, signifying the name of a neighborhood, not a temple. Similarly, the Hellenion of Memphis is not attested before the Hellenistic period, and could not, therefore, be the one mentioned on the inscription (Thompson 1988: 95–7). A later reference in a papyrus of the second century AD mentions a Hellenion in Arsinoe (*Aegyptische Urkunden aus den königlichen Museen zu Berlin*, no. 133). This is the earliest reference to the Arsinoite Hellenion, a Ptolemaic foundation.

between the itinerant traders and those who wanted to reside in Egypt.[119] This observation is significant because it implies that the nine cities in charge of the administration of the emporion were not only itinerant traders but also provided part of the resident population of Naukratis. The clarification that tax exemption was granted to Damoxenos both in times of peace and war, a typical clause in proxeny decrees, might in this case have a precise function: it might refer to the opening and closing of emporia – emporia were often closed in times of war, as is discussed in the next chapter – or, alternatively, the phrase could indicate the permanence of the ties between Lindos and Damoxenos: even if Naukratis and Lindos found themselves opposed to one another politically, Damoxenos would keep his privileges.

The other Greek inscription, dating to 411–407 BC, is also a Rhodian decree, excavated from the acropolis in Lindos. It honors a man from Naukratis and his descendants with *proxenia* and the freedom to enter and leave the port anytime:

[ἔδοξε τᾶι β]ολᾶι· ἐπὶ π[ρ]-	1
[υτανίων τ]ῶν ἀμφὶ Δει[ν]-	
[ίαν.....]αν Πυθέω Αἰγ-	
[ύπτιον τ]ὸν ἐγ Ναυκράτ-	4
[ιος], ἑρμ[α]νέα, πρόξενον	
[ἤμ]εν Ρο[δ]ίων πάντων κα-	
ὶ αὐτὸν καὶ ἐκγόνους, κ-	
αὶ ἤμεν αὐτῶι καὶ ἔσπλ-	8
[ο]υ καὶ ἔκπλον καὶ αὐτῶ-	
[ι κα]ὶ ἐκγόνοις ἀσυλὶ κ-	
[αὶ ἀσ]πονδὶ καὶ πολέμο	
[καὶ εἰρήνης. *Vac.*	12

IG XII.1, 760

The council decreed under the prytaneis of Deinias that: [. . .]as, son of Pytheas, an Egyptian from Naukratis, an interpreter, and his descendants, should be a *proxenos* of all the Rhodians; he and his descendants should have the right to enter and leave the port with the privilege of inviolability and neutrality, both in peace and war.

The grants that Pytheas' son receives are very similar to those that Damoxenos was given. He and his descendants have the right to enter and leave the port with inviolability in times of peace and war. Unlike Damoxenos, Pytheas' son did not receive tax exemption, as he was a translator and not a trader. The right of *proxeny* given to the two men (and their

[119] Herodotus 2.178.

descendants) probably involved taking care of any Lindians, or, according to the second inscription, Rhodians, who were in Naukratis on business. In effect, Damoxenos and Pytheas' son were guarantors for the Lindians and Rhodians visiting Naukratis. On the one hand, they ensured that these Rhodian *xenoi* remained safe while they visited Naukratis, and on the other, they were liable before their fellow Naukratites in all affairs involving these *xenoi*.[120] From at least the fifth century onwards, therefore, the institution of *proxenia* was an official and important part of the emporion's administration. Each polis whose traders dealt with Naukratis with any frequency probably had a *proxenos* in Naukratis. Thus, in the context of an emporion, *proxenia* was another network that connected various individuals with different poleis. This institution probably also affected how Naukratis saw itself: if *proxenoi* were responsible for foreigners frequenting Naukratis vis-à-vis their own community, Naukratis must have developed a civic identity.

Another noteworthy point is that Pytheas' son, according to the above reconstruction, is described as being Egyptian.[121] Objecting that this man was a Greek and not an Egyptian, some scholars have provided an alternate supplement: "Αἰγ|[ινάταν τ]ὸν ἐγ Ναυκράτι|[ιος]" (Aiginetan from Naukratis).[122] With this reconstruction, Pytheas' son becomes an Aiginetan from Naukratis. However, even if the former restoration is correct, the designation "Egyptian" should not necessarily refer to an indigenous Egyptian as opposed to a Greek born in Egypt and perhaps therefore be considered as an Egyptian by Greeks who lived in the Greek world.

The fact that this inscription does not make Pytheas' son a *proxenos* of the Lindians, which is where the inscription was discovered, but rather a *proxenos* of the Rhodians, requires further explanation, especially since Damoxenos was made a *proxenos* of Lindos. Lindos was not one of the poleis mentioned by Herodotus as founders of the Hellenion, though elsewhere the historian mentions that Amasis had very close ties to Lindos, even giving dedications at the sanctuary of Athena Lindia.[123] Instead, Herodotus names Rhodes as one of the founding "poleis." The island of Rhodes, however, had traditionally not been considered a single entity until its three different poleis, Lindos, Kameiros, and Ialysos, formed a *synoikismos* in 408/7 BC. Yet even before this time the three Rhodian poleis were very closely affiliated with one another and were probably politically united in a

---

[120] Gauthier 1972: 27–33.   [121] Roebuck 1951: 219 n. 26; Bresson 2000a: 29–36 and 1991.
[122] Kinch 1905: 34–48; Blinkenberg 1941: no. 16; Austin 1970: 29 n. 3; Figueira 1988: 543–51.
[123] Herodotus 2.182. The Lindian Chronicle also mentions Amasis' dedications in the temple of Athena Lindia: C. 29. For a discussion of the Lindian Chronicle, see Higbie 2003: 35, 113–19.

federal state.[124] Pindar's ode to Diagoras of Rhodes from 464 BC, for example, describes the mythical common ancestry of the brothers Ialysos, Kameiros, and Lindos, the three grandsons of Helios and the nymph Rhodos, who gave their names to the Rhodian poleis.[125] This close connection is manifest also in a monetary alliance between the three poleis from the archaic period onwards.[126] Ialysos, Kameiros, and Lindos also undertook joint efforts abroad, demonstrating their capacity to take political decisions as a unit. For example, in the sixth century BC they established in their colony of Akragas a temple of Zeus Atabyrios, a cult common to the three Rhodian poleis and appropriately located in the geographical center of Rhodes.[127] Another pan-Rhodian cult before the *synoikismos* was that of Helios, which became the central cult around which the Rhodians unified.[128] Similarly, in Naukratis citizens from all three Rhodian poleis participated in the administration of the Hellenion in the shared name of Rhodes. In fact, there exists also a single dedication from the Hellenion by Teleson, who identifies himself as a Rhodian.[129] Based on the fact that the *synoikismos* of Rhodes took place in 408/7 BC, this inscription has been assigned to a period after that date. However, since the ethnic *Rhodios* is also attested on two fifth-century inscriptions,[130] and, as we have seen, the three poleis of Rhodes had undertaken joint cult foundations abroad before the *synoikismos*, this date should be reconsidered.[131] It is interesting that both *Rhodios* and *Lindios* are used as ethnics in Naukratis. At the same time as citizens from each of the individual poleis on Rhodes identified themselves as such, they also asserted their collective Rhodian identity, especially in religious actions. With its intra-Rhodian and pan-Rhodian identity, Rhodes mirrors the general patterns of self-identification observed in Naukratis, as will soon become clear.

Identifying the Greeks of Naukratis

The context of a multiethnic emporion located in a non-Greek land meant that Greeks from different poleis resided in Naukratis just as they did in Gravisca, Pistiros, and Peiraieus. Where did these Greeks come from, did they express any level of collective identity, and if so, what means did they use to do that? As in the case of Gravisca, religion emerges as the major

---

[124] Cordano 1974; Gabrielsen 2000: 180–7.   [125] Pindar, *Olympian* 7.70–7.
[126] Bresson 1993: 211–26; Babelon 1910: 1011–12.   [127] Polybius 9.27.
[128] Pindar, *Olympian* 7; Bresson 2000a: 37–8.   [129] Hogarth 1905: 117 no. 16.
[130] *IG* XII 1, 728 and 1, 977.   [131] See also Möller 2000: 171 n. 650 and Austin 1970: 62 n. 2.

vehicle through which individual Greek traders declared their civic and ethnic identities.

Herodotus' description of Naukratis is informative about the Greeks who lived there. The historian differentiates between the residents of Naukratis and the traders who did not permanently reside there when he says that Amasis gave the Greeks who came to Egypt the polis Naukratis to dwell in. To those among them who did not wish to settle there and who were sailors he gave lands on which to erect altars and sanctuaries for the gods.[132] This distinction may be artificial, as Damoxenos' case has demonstrated: this man is described both as a resident of Naukratis and as an itinerant trader who had a tax exemption on goods he imported and exported to Lindos. In fact, we can infer that the resident population of Naukratis included members of all the poleis that Herodotus mentions either as founders of the Hellenion, namely, Chios, Teos, Phokaia, Klazomenai, Rhodes, Knidos, Halikarnassos, Phaselis, and Mytilene, or as founders of the three separate sanctuaries, namely, Aigina, Samos, and Miletos. The first nine cities provided the *prostatai* of the emporion and other priests and priestesses, who presumably would have to live in Naukratis in order to manage affairs and to run the Hellenion respectively; the remaining three cities provided priests and priestesses who would have to reside in Naukratis in order to work, when needed, in their own temples.

A survey of dedicatory inscriptions in the Naukratite sanctuaries reveals that most of the groups Herodotus mentions are attested in Naukratis. There are dedications by men who proclaimed they are Chian, Teian, Phokaian, Mytilenean, Rhodian, and Klazomenean, but never part of a larger collective.[133] Knidians can be detected only through their script, used in dedicatory inscriptions.[134] No evidence from Naukratis itself corroborates a Phaselian presence, but the fifth-century Egyptian register of taxes that ship-captains had to pay mentions that some of the ships were from Phaselis.[135] It is possible that these ships would eventually dock at Naukratis, although there is a possibility that they sailed to Memphis, as mentioned above.[136] Unfortunately, the epigraphic evidence is silent as to the presence of Halikarnassians and Aiginetans, who were probably present anyway since

[132] Herodotus 2.178.

[133] Chians: Gardner 1888: 63 no. 706 pl. 21, 64 no. 757 pl. 21; Hogarth 1898–9: 55 no. 51 pl. 4 and no. 60 pl. 5. Teians: Petrie et al. 1886: 61 no. 209 pl. 32, 62 no. 700 pl. 35; Gardner 1888: 64 no. 758 pl. 21, 65 no. 779 pl. 21, 68 no. 876 pl. 20. Phokaians: Petrie et al. 1886: 62 no. 666 pl. 35, Hogarth 1905: 117 no. 39. Mytileneans: Gardner 1888: 65 nos. 788–90, 792 pl. 21. Rhodians: Hogarth 1905: 117 no. 16. Klazomeneans: Hogarth 1898–9: 55 no. 55a-b pl. 4.

[134] Möller 2000: 166–81.   [135] Briant and Descat 1998.   [136] Briant and Descat 1998: 91–2.

the former was one of the poleis that provided the *prostatai* of the emporion and the latter had its own temple there.

The material culture excavated from Naukratis, which consists mostly of pottery, matches the origin of its inhabitants.[137] Most of it is from East Greece, and recent chemical analysis has shown that some of it was manufactured in Miletos, Chios, Klazomenai, Samos, Knidos, Teos, and the region of Aeolis, including certain pieces from Mytilene.[138] In addition, a lot of painted pottery came from Athens, Corinth, Laconia, Cyprus, and to a lesser extent Etruria.[139] There are also a couple of fragments of Carian pottery, which is unique in that no other examples of this fabric exist outside of Caria. Unlike Athenian, Corinthian, and Laconian pottery, which was traded widely and is attested in all the other emporia studied here as well as in poleis and settlements throughout the Mediterranean, the Carian fabrics were not part of the pottery trade in the Aegean.[140] Their unusual presence in Naukratis might constitute evidence for Carians passing through or living in Naukratis. As far as the rest of the East Greek pottery discovered here is concerned, the fact that the provenance of the pottery found in Naukratis coincides with the origins of the founding cities does not necessarily indicate that they carried pottery from their home with them. On the contrary, pottery from each of these places was popular throughout East Greece. Even undecorated pottery fits this picture well: clay mortaria, for instance, many of which were excavated from the temple of Milesian Apollo in Naukratis, belong to a type that in the archaic period was popular in the Eastern Mediterranean, particularly in Cyprus and Ionia.[141] Thus, Naukratis was part of a region that shared a particular material culture that consisted not only of the usual wares – Athenian, Corinthian, and Laconian – but also of East Greek pottery.

This repertoire should be expanded to include locally produced Naukratite pottery. Both decorated and undecorated Greek pottery was produced by one or more Naukratite workshops.[142] The shapes and

---

[137] Unfortunately, the pottery kept from the excavations in Naukratis is not representative of the whole as Petrie kept pieces with inscriptions or decoration but only samples of other types of finds. See Schlotzhauer and Villing 2006: 53 and 56. Artifacts from Naukratis can now be searched and viewed on an online database of the British Museum.

[138] R. E. Jones 1986: 698–702; Venit 1988; Dupont and Thomas 2006; Schlotzhauer and Villing 2006: 54–5; Mommsen et al. 2006.

[139] Venit 1988. Athenian painted pottery from Naukratis is now being studied by V. Smallwood and S. Woodford. For Etruscan wares see Naso 2006.

[140] Williams and Villing 2006.   [141] Villing 2006: 37–40.

[142] Potters' quarters are mentioned in literary sources from the early third century BC (*apud* Athenaios 9.480) and are attested archaeologically (Petrie et al. 1886: 22 and pl. 41; Leonard 1997: 25–6).

decoration of the vases combine several East Greek features in unexpected ways, creating a unique Naukratite style. For example, decorative elements from Aeolian pottery are found side by side with Milesian ones on vases produced in Naukratis.[143] Other workshops in the Aegean, such as some in Chios, also created eclectic products borrowing from the visual repertoire of Athenian, Corinthian, Laconian, and other East Greek potters.[144] Some of the Naukratite pottery was used locally, as graffiti on vases produced here that record the dedication of an object in the temple of Aphrodite show.[145] Other samples were exported within Egypt and have been found at Tell Defenneh, which has been traditionally identified as the ancient site of Daphnai, and other places.[146] Interestingly, Egyptian influence on Naukratite pottery is lacking, despite the fact that the potters seem to have adopted styles from various places in the Greek world and that vases produced by Greeks in other places did exhibit Egyptian influences.[147] Naukratite pottery, therefore, must be understood both as a hybrid product, the result of permanent encounters in a multiethnic settlement, and as representing a common type of pottery popular in the whole of the East Aegean region.

The local Naukratite sculpture workshops produced similarly eclectic sculpture that has been described as mixed style because it exhibits a variety of artistic influences, such as Egyptian, Phoenician, Cypriot and Ionian. Unlike local pottery, therefore, local sculpture did incorporate Egyptianizing characteristics.[148] Examples of local Naukratite productions with Egyptian features include a female statuette wearing an Egyptian wig (Figure 9),[149] statuettes of a female nursing a child similar to representations of Isis and Horus,[150] a male statuette with an Egyptian wig and facial features executed in an Egyptian manner,[151] among many others.[152] Some of these statues and statuettes were dedicated in the local sanctuaries and bore Greek inscriptions; others were found around the town. The locally produced archaic Naukratite sculpture bears close similarities to Cypriot sculpture produced in the same period.[153] Based on this observation, scholars have argued for

[143] Schlotzhauer and Villing 2006: 62–6.   [144] Williams 2006.
[145] Schlotzhauer and Villing 2006: 64. The vase dedicated to Aphrodite is BM GR 1888.6.-1.739.
[146] Schlotzhauer and Villing 2006: 64. See also Boardman 1998: 144 and 222, and 2006.
[147] The famous Apries amphora, for instance, bears cartouches with the name of the pharaoh Apries but is clearly an East Greek product (Bailey 2006).
[148] Möller 2000: 154–61.   [149] Cambridge, Fitzwilliam Museum GR. 1. 1899.
[150] For example, Pryce 1928: B463 (Gardner 1888: 58, pl. 14 no. 7).
[151] Pryce 1928: B 440 (Gardner 1888: pl. 17 no. 2).
[152] Möller 2000: 157–9 discusses these and other statuettes.
[153] Höckmann and Kreikenbom 2001. In particular, see Hermary 2001; Fourrier 2001; Nick 2001.

Figure 9 Mixed-style female statuette with Greek features and Egyptian hairstyle from Naukratis. Probably of local Naukratite production, sixth century BC.

the presence of a Cypriot workshop in Naukratis and therefore the presence of Cypriots.[154] This sculpture type was, however, popular not just in Cyprus and Naukratis but also in East Greece, with examples found on Rhodes, in Miletos, Knidos, Samos, Chios, Phokaia, and Aigina.[155] What this means is that the "mixed-style" statues were popular throughout the

---

[154] Fourrier 2001: 46; Jenkins 2001.   [155] Fourrier 2001: 41–6.

Eastern Mediterranean.[156] There is no need, therefore, to infer the presence of Cypriots in Naukratis from the presence of this style of sculpture.[157] These statues cannot tell us anything about the ethnicity of either those who produced it or those who used it, but they do constitute evidence for long-term contacts across cultures, especially through trade, and they attest to regional preferences and trends in artistic production.

Others have argued that Cypriots resided in Naukratis based on the discovery of Cypriot pottery.[158] However, as Möller points out, the number of Cypriot examples is relatively small compared to Greek pottery, and it bears mostly Greek inscriptions, which makes it unlikely that it was used by either Greek or Phoenician Cypriots.[159] More importantly, the ethnicity of a trader carrying pottery does not necessarily coincide with the ethnicity of the group that produced it. Two inscriptions written on Attic bowls in the Cypriot syllabic script, one dating to the last quarter of the fifth century BC and the other to the fourth century BC, do suggest that Cypriots were present in Naukratis.[160] Another inscription, carved on a fourth-century statue base and written in the Greek alphabet, has also been used as supporting evidence for a Cypriot presence in Naukratis: "Σίκω[ν ἐπ]οίη|σε Κύπ[ριο]ς.| Ἀριστί[ων] Ἡρακλεῖ" (Siko[n] the Cyp[rio]t [m]ade [this]. Aristi[on] for Heracles).[161] The reconstruction "Cypriot" is interesting. Most other inscriptions in which Cypriots identified themselves, several of which have been found in Peiraieus, usually mention only the name of the specific polis the Cypriot in question came from, such as Kition, Kourion, or Paphos.[162] The only instance in which they located themselves as coming from the island of Cyprus is when they specify that they are Salaminians from Cyprus so as not to be confused with those from the Salaminian deme of Athens.[163] Based on a similar reconstruction, it has also been suggested that the trader attested on the lead inscription from Pech-Maho, discussed

[156] Cypriot goods circulated in elite circles also in the western Mediterranean from the Bronze Age onwards (Bonfante and Karageorghis 2001).

[157] Nick 2001: 65 suggests that it is also possible that the sculptors in Naukratis imitated this style of statuary or that Cypriots exported these statues to Naukratis and other places.

[158] Davis 1979 and 1980; Cassimatis 1984.

[159] Presumably because in this period Phoenician Cypriots would have used Phoenician, while Greek ones would have used the Cypriot syllabic script. See Möller 2000: 161–3 and A. W. Johnston 1982: 36.

[160] BM 1900.2–14.17; Oxford G141.29. One more inscription is a dedication by a Syracusan. It dates from the Hellenistic period, a time beyond the scope of this project: Gardner 1888: 68 no. 874, pl. 22.

[161] London, BM 1900.2–14.22.

[162] These inscriptions will be discussed in the final chapter.

[163] Only three grave stelai (*IG* II/III² 10216–10218) specify that the deceased are Salaminians from Cyprus; *IG* II/III² 10171–10215 possibly attest Salaminians from Cyprus.

in the chapter on Emporion, was a Cypriot.[164] If, indeed, these two men, Sikon and the trader in Iberia, identified themselves as Cypriots, they might have been expressing a regional Cypriot identity rather than an ethnic or civic one.

One Cypriot coin of 368–351 BC was also discovered in Naukratis. Numismatic evidence, however, does not help identify the constituent parts of the Naukratite population. In the Greek world more generally, early coins tended to be retained in the region where they had been minted, and the little evidence available suggests that early coinage was too valuable to be used in daily exchange.[165] The total number of coins from the archaic and classical periods discovered in Naukratis is about one hundred.[166] The majority of these date to the classical period. In addition to the one coin from Cyprus, fifteen of the earliest coins were found together with roughly cut lumps of silver or gashed coins and are assumed to be a silversmith's stock. The accepted opinion is that Greeks brought the silver coins with them to satisfy a demand for the metal rather than to use them as a means of exchange.[167] Of these fifteen coins, one each was minted in Cilicia, Lycia, Chios, Aigina, Cyrene, and Syracuse, and three others in Samos. The remaining six coins were Athenian tetradrachms. Another eighty Athenian tetradrachms were discovered in two hoards and were probably also used to obtain silver metal. Most of the Athenian coins date from 500 to 350 BC, at which time they were the most popular currency not only in Athens but also throughout the Greek world, implying that anyone could have carried them to Naukratis.

Civic and religious identities

An examination of the inscriptions that bear the names of the dedicators, and especially those that mention a city-ethnic, shows that, as in Gravisca, all Greeks regardless of their origin could worship at any temple they liked, but some chose to worship divinities that were particularly prominent in their poleis of origin. It is practically impossible to distinguish between the permanent and temporary residents from their dedications. Even though certain sanctuaries were located in the residential part of Naukratis and others in the trading sector, this need not imply that traders used exclusively the

---

[164] Lejeune et al. 1988. This reconstruction is odd because it would suggest that the trader identified himself with an ethnic rather than his own personal name, which was the custom.
[165] Kraay 1964.   [166] Head 1886: 64.
[167] Roebuck 1951: 237; Austin 1970: 38 and n. 2; Möller 2000: 209–10.

sanctuaries in the northern part, and settlers the sanctuaries in the southern part. Just as in Gravisca, both the traders and residents of the emporion could use all the temples. Moreover, women dedicators are attested from most of the sanctuaries in Naukratis, implying that all residents could dedicate at all sanctuaries, even those that according to Herodotus were only for traders.[168] One of the characteristics of emporia was the way in which their residents recognized and exploited the flexibility of the Greek polytheistic religion. The gods of the temples were common to all the Greeks, regardless of their polis of origin and their status as residents or visitors to Naukratis. Thus, despite the difficulty of identifying the residents vs. the itinerant traders, the evidence from all the sanctuaries of Naukratis may be considered as representative for the resident population of Naukratis.

Herodotus describes the sanctuaries of Naukratis, except for the Hellenion, in terms of their polis of origin: the Aiginetans set up a temple to Zeus, the Samians one to Hera, and the Milesians one to Apollo (Figure 10).[169] These are highly reminiscent of the colonization movements of the eighth to sixth centuries BC, during which colonists transferred cults from the metropolis to the colony, thus articulating their individual polis identity. The temple to Aiginetan Zeus has not been identified, despite two inscriptions that attest to the worship of Zeus in Naukratis.[170] The temple to Hera dating to the last quarter of the seventh century, on the other hand, has been unearthed and identified by votive inscriptions (Figure 10).[171] The majority of the pottery found in this sanctuary are the so-called Hera-cups, chemically proven to have been produced on Samos,[172] and discovered only in the temple of Hera in Naukratis and the temple of Hera on Samos, thus confirming the Samian connection of the temple in Naukratis. These cups sometimes bear the simple inscription "HPH" and in general are thought to have had been cult equipment used in ritual dining (Figure 11).[173] Similar ritual practices, therefore, were observed in both the temple of Hera on Samos and the goddess's temple in Naukratis. These cups, which preserve

---

[168] Apollo's temple: Lampyris, Petrie et al. 1886: 61 no 117 pl. 32. Aphrodite's temple: Mikis, Gardner 1888: 64 no. 745 pl. 21; Pylia, Gardner 1888: 64 no. 761 pl. 21; Philis, Gardner 1888: 65 no. 780 pl. 21; Doris, Gardner 1888: 66 no. 798 pl.21; Phyllis, Gardner 1888: 66 no. 808 pl. 21. Hellenion: Eudemia, Hogarth 1905: 117 no. 34.

[169] Herodotus 2.178.

[170] One is an archaic inscription discovered in the sanctuary of Hera, indicating perhaps a joint worship of Zeus and Hera: ἱερὸν Δ[ιὸς ἀπ]οτροπ[αίου] (sanctuary of Zeus Apotropaios) (Gardner 1888: 68 no. 14 pl. 22). The other is a graffito τ]ōι Ζενὶ τ[οῖ (To Zeus) (Petrie et al. 1886: 61 no. 122 pl. 32).

[171] Gardner 1888: 13, 60–61, 67 nos. 841–8 pl. 22.

[172] R. E. Jones 1986: 665; Mommsen et al. 2006.   [173] Kron 1984.

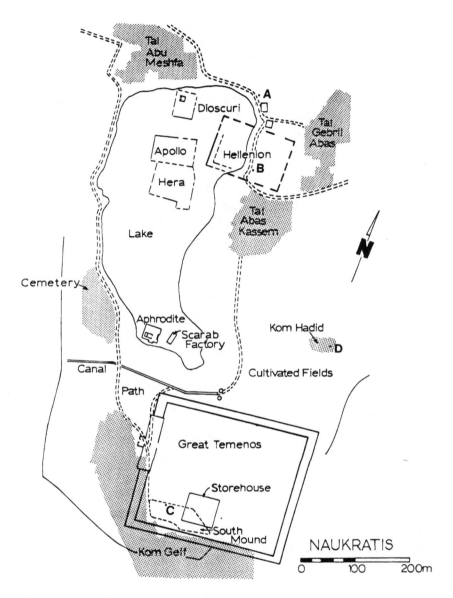

Figure 10 Plan of the excavated parts of Naukratis. Reproduced from Coulson et al. 1982: 92.

the religious traditions of the polis that founded this temple, proclaim a Samian identity.

In the chapter on Gravisca the dedications of the itinerant trader Hyblesios were briefly discussed. The rarity of this man's name, common only on

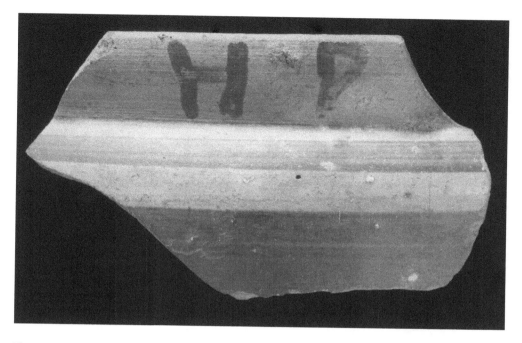

Figure 11 Hera-cup from the sanctuary of Hera in Naukratis, sixth century BC.

Samos, found on dedications in both the temple of Hera in Naukratis and the temple of Hera in Gravisca around the same time (*c.* 550 BC), suggest that he was one and the same person. His choice of divinity to worship also suggests that he used the temples of Hera as a way to identify himself as a Samian.

The temple of Apollo dating to 570–560 BC[174] has yielded several archaic inscriptions, which are dedications specifically to Apollo of Miletos.[175] The dedications to Milesian Apollo are the only ones in Naukratis that refer to a divinity with a city-ethnic, just as Apollo was the only deity with a city-ethnic (Aiginetan) in Gravisca. These dedications were not all made by Milesians; on the contrary, Chians and Teians, identified by city-ethnics, and Knidians, identified from the script, gave offerings in this temple.[176] The names of other dedicators from the temple of Apollo, which are either preserved

---

[174] Gjerstad 1934 and 1959; Bresson 2000a: 25 n. 52.

[175] Petrie et al. 1886: 60 no. 2 pl. 32, 61 nos. 99 and 110 pl. 32: ὁ δεῖνα ἀνέθ]ηκε τῶι Ἀπόλλωνι τῶι [Μ]ιλησί(ωι) (So and so dedicated me to Milesian Apollo); Petrie et al. 1886: 61 nos. 218–19 and 233–4 pl. 33: Ἀπόλλωνός ἐ[μ]ι Μιλησί[ο] (I belong to Milesian Apollo); Petrie et al. 1886: 62 nos. 237 and 341 pl. 33: τὠπόλλωνος τοῦ Μ[ιλη]σίου (of Milesian Apollo).

[176] Teians: Petrie et al. 1886: 61 no. 209 pl. 32; Gardner 1888: 68 no. 876 pl. 20; Chians: Hogarth 1898–9: 55 no. 51; Knidians: Petrie et al. 1886: 62 no. 237 pl. 33.

Figure 12 Chian bowl from Naukratis with an inscribed dedication by Sostratos to Aphrodite, *c.* 620–600 BC.

or can be securely reconstructed, were mostly inscribed in an East Ionian script, which Bernand identified as possibly Chian.[177] Möller suggests that some details of the scripts used in the dedications in Apollo's sanctuary might also point to Aiginetans.[178] In the previous chapter we saw that some scholars identified a certain Sostratos who gave offerings to the temple of Aphrodite in Naukratis as an Aiginetan, because they claimed that he was related to the Aiginetan Sostratos who gave the votive anchor dedication in Gravisca. However, as I mentioned in that discussion, the Sostratos who dedicated in Aphrodite's temple in Naukratis was probably a Chian in view of the dialect he used (Figure 12). The inscribed mortaria dedicated to Apollo excavated from this sanctuary were probably imported from Cyprus and while neither the dedications nor the provenance of the bowls reveals

---

[177] Fraser and Matthews 1987–2005: I, s.v. Polemarchos, Lampyris, Polyarkides, Phanes, Charidion, Sleues, Klepsias, Karophnis.
[178] Möller 2000: 174–5.

anything about the civic identity of the dedicators, it is important to note that this cultic instrument, probably used for ritual dining, was common in other sanctuaries in the East Greek world, as well as domestic contexts in the same region.[179] The epigraphic evidence from the temple of Apollo, therefore, shows that Chians, Teians, Knidians, and possibly Aiginetans used this particular sanctuary. This suggests that Greeks, regardless of their origin, could worship the god, even though he was specifically identified as being Milesian.

Herodotus does not mention two other sanctuaries in Naukratis. The first of these was dedicated to the Dioskouroi, probably dating from sometime in the sixth century BC, known only from a few dedicatory inscriptions Δ]ιοσφούροισι [ὁ δεῖνα ἀν]έθηκεν, Διοσφού[ροις], neither of which reveals any particular affiliation with a specific polis since they do not bear the dedicator's city-ethnic.[180]

The second is the temple of Aphrodite, the oldest temple of the settlement, which also claims no polis identity.[181] In contrast to the temple of the Dioskouroi, however, it has been one of the most fruitful sanctuaries, yielding abundant inscriptions, pottery, and statuettes. In fact, the distinguishing characteristic of this temple is the lack of uniformity exhibited by the finds: statues of athletes, armed men, flute-players, hunters, draped female figures holding flowers, animals, or birds, lamps, naked female figures reclining on cushions, and seated kourotrophos statuettes holding children.[182] The kourotrophos figurines are reminiscent of the female statuettes discovered in Aphrodite's sanctuary in Gravisca, and those discovered in Aphrodite's sanctuaries throughout the Greek world.[183] As I have argued, these typically feminine dedications were part of what became a common material culture popular throughout the Mediterranean world. The finds from this sanctuary, moreover, exhibit East Greek, Cypriot, Phoenician, and Egyptian influences, reflecting both the multiethnic population of the emporion and the East Greek regional artistic preferences discussed above.[184]

The archaic dedicatory inscriptions from Aphrodite's sanctuary in Naukratis show that the goddess received offerings from dedicators from

---

[179] Villing 2006. In Cyprus, however, most of these mortaria were excavated from funerary contexts.

[180] Petrie et al. 1886: 62 nos. 655 and 675–682 pl. 35; Gardner 1888: 67 nos. 833–37 and 839 pl. 52.

[181] The preponderance of Chian pottery excavated from the sanctuary might indicate a Chian origin of the cult. See Austin 1970: 25 and Möller 2000: 104, 108–9, and 195.

[182] Gardner 1888: 55–9.   [183] Gardner 1888: no. 7 pl. 14 and no. 7 pl. 15.

[184] One limestone statue (Pryce 1928: B451 = Gardner 1888: no. 5 pl. 13), for example, has an Egyptian stance with a straight back and one foot forward, wears a Greek chiton that looks like an Egyptian loincloth, a Cypriot cap on his head, and bears a Greek inscription.

a variety of backgrounds, such as Chians, Teians, and Mytileneans.[185] It is important to note that Aphrodite in Naukratis was worshipped under several epithets – *pandemos*, *hiere* – unlike the deities venerated in the other sanctuaries.[186] The goddess may not have been worshipped under a single title or for a unique role, but the fact that Greeks who identified themselves as originating from different places felt the freedom to worship Aphrodite under various epithets and for a variety of reasons shows that the sanctuary had a cosmopolitan character. As discussed in the previous chapter, sanctuaries in emporia or other coastal trading posts often provided open access to worshippers. The sanctuary of Aphrodite in Naukratis, as Scholtz argues, was common to all, an apt translation of the epithet *pandemos*, under which Aphrodite was worshipped in Naukratis.[187]

Dedications to Aphrodite Pandemos are attested in Naukratis twice from the goddess's temple and once from the Hellenion.[188] All three inscriptions date from the late archaic period and can be counted among some of the earliest attestations for this epithet. Although the epithet might indicate that Aphrodite was a goddess common to all, allowing any individual to participate in the goddess's worship, there is another level on which the word *pandemos* could operate. This epithet has been much discussed in the context of Aphrodite's function in providing civic harmony and unity, especially in Athens.[189] This role would be much needed in a multiethnic emporion located in a non-Greek land, where Greeks from many poleis came together, cooperated in trade, ran the emporion, administered the temples, and even formed a self-governing polis, albeit one dependent on Egyptian authorities.[190] In fact, it is only in Aphrodite's temple that a cohesive Naukratite identity is ever expressed in the dedication –]ου[– Ἀφροδί]τηι : τῆι ἐ(ν) Ναυκράτι (to Aphrodite who is in Naukratis), which firmly localizes the goddess and her worship.[191]

Aphrodite, a goddess common to all the Greeks of Naukratis and a civic goddess, was also always a goddess of sex, as the dedications of female nude

---

[185] Chian: Hogarth 1898–9: 55 no. 60; Gardner 1888: 63 no. 706 pl. 21, 64 no. 757 pl. 21; Jeffery 1961: 343 no. 43. Teians: Petrie et al. 1886: 62 no. 700 pl. 35, Gardner 1888: 64 no. 758 pl. 21, 65 no. 779 pl. 21. Mytilenean: Gardner 1888: 65 nos. 788–90 pl. 21.

[186] Gardner 1888: 64 no. 753 pl. 21 (holy Aphrodite); 66 no. 818, 821 pl. 21 (Pandemos); Hogarth 1898–9: 56 no. 107 (Pandemos).

[187] Scholtz 2002/2003: 234–9.

[188] Gardner 1888: 66 nos. 818 and 821 (London BM GR 1888.6–1.211 and 1888.6–1.212) are from the temple of Aphrodite. Hogarth 1898–9: 56 no. 107 (London BM GR 1900.2.-14.6) is from the precinct of the Hellenion.

[189] Rosenzweig 2004.

[190] For a similar argument see Höckmann and Möller 2006: 16–17.

[191] Gardner 1888: 64 no. 768 pl. 21.

figures and kourotrophic statuettes in her temple show. That Naukratis was known for its courtesans was a common literary trope from Sappho, who wrote about the Thracian courtesan Rhodopis who seduced her brother, to Herodotus, who named Archedike as being among the beautiful courtesans of this emporion, and later sources, such as Athenaios, who discusses both Rhodopis and Archedike.[192] Literary trope or not, Naukratite prostitutes in all likelihood used the sanctuary dedicated to Aphrodite. Several women who gave inscribed offerings at Aphrodite's temple have been interpreted as prostitutes, but, in fact, there is little evidence to prove this.[193] One of these dedications, made by Doris, has been restored as being a *philtron*, a love potion.[194] Even so, given that most women who used love potions, if the restoration of *philtron* is correct, were wives and not courtesans or prostitutes, Doris need not have been a prostitute.[195] On the contrary, another dedication from the sanctuary of Aphrodite, by Iunx, might in fact indicate a prostitute or courtesan, given that that the name represents magic spells used by prostitutes and courtesans.[196] Aphrodite, therefore, was certainly worshipped in Naukratis for her best-known role as a goddess of sex.

At the same time, just as in Gravisca, Aphrodite's temple in Naukratis was the first built, probably because of Aphrodite's connection with the sea and her role as a patron of navigation and protector of sailors and traders.[197] The location of Aphrodite's sanctuary on the Kanobic branch of the Nile might actually have been the original landing site for ships.[198] Ship-sheds adjacent to and associated with sanctuaries of Aphrodite are attested also at the unusual sanctuary of Aphrodite Pandamos and Pontia at Kos, where Aphrodite had a double cult, identical twin temples, and one priestess serving both cults; she was venerated by manumitted slaves, women who got married, and sailors (including traders, fishermen, and the navy), among others.[199] More specifically, the story of the trader Heros-tratos, discussed in the previous chapter on Gravisca, explicitly connects

---

[192] Sappho fr. 138 (ed. Campbell); Herodotus 2.135; Athenaios 13.596d.
[193] Mikis, Gardner 1888: 64 no. 745 pl. 21; Pylia, Gardner 1888: 64 no. 761 pl. 21; Philis, Gardner 1888: 65 no. 780 pl. 21; Doris, Gardner 1888: 66 no. 798 pl. 21; Phyllis, Gardner 1888: 66 no. 808 pl. 21.
[194] Gardner 1888: 66 no. 798 pl. 21.
[195] Faraone 1999: 26–8. Prostitutes and courtesans used other devices to induce spells.
[196] Gardner 1888: 63 no. 712. For *iugges* see Faraone 1993 and 1999: 28.
[197] Scholtz 2002/2003: 239 also thinks she was worshipped for this reason in Naukratis. For Aphrodite's role in seafaring see Pirenne-Delforge 1994: 233–437, Romero Recio 2000, and Demetriou 2010b.
[198] Möller 2000: 118; Scholtz 2002/2003: 239.
[199] *Iscr. di Cos* E.D. 178, b. 105 mentions the ship-sheds (Parker 2002; Parker and Obbink 2000).

Aphrodite with Naukratis and with saving sailors. Herostratos was on his way to Naukratis when he stopped and bought a statuette of Aphrodite from the goddess' temple in Paphos, on Cyprus. Aphrodite's statuette miraculously sprouted myrtle branches that soothed the sailors' seasickness and calmed the weather, thereby saving the crew. Herostratos promptly dedicated the statuette in Aphrodite's temple in Naukratis, which he also called "Aphrodite's polis," as thanks for the goddess's help on his sailing trip.[200] Other offerings at Aphrodite's temple may have been gifts dedicated upon arrival, presumably for the goddess' protection.[201]

Aphrodite in Naukratis, like Aphrodite in Gravisca, was a goddess who afforded cohesion and unity, at least to the Greek population of the emporion. All the Naukratite inhabitants and traders recognized that they had this goddess in common, and they worshipped her for her role as a patron of navigation, a guardian of the civic harmony of the emporion and the polis, as well as a deity of sex. Despite the wide differences in cults and ritual practices of different regions, in the temple of Aphrodite in Naukratis Greeks were able to worship the goddess in whatever manner they were accustomed to. Without doubt, this was true for all the deities worshipped in Naukratis, as is evidenced by the dedications of Greeks from different poleis in all the temples. Therefore, even though Zeus's temple was specifically connected to Aigina, Hera's temple to Samos, and Apollo's temple to Miletos, these deities could be used to express both an individual polis identity and also a collective Greek identity. The flexibility of Greek religion, especially as it was articulated in emporia abroad, was important in the recognition of religion as a characteristic common to all Greeks. As such, religion in emporia was formative in the coalescence of new collective identities, whether civic, religious, or even Hellenic, as the next section demonstrates.

From civic identity to Hellenicity

The religious forces bringing Greeks from a variety of backgrounds together are manifest also in the temple Herodotus calls the greatest, most famous, and most frequented, whose name was significantly Hellenion (Figure 13). This sanctuary was originally identified as being at the site of what Petrie

---

[200] Polycharmos *apud* Athenaios 15.675f-676c.

[201] Scholtz 2002/2003: 239 includes as evidence two dedications: Gardner 1888: 66 no. 795, if it is correctly restored as an offering by Kaikos "having arrived in Naukratis" (εἰ]ς Nα(ύ)κρατιν [ἀφικόμεν]ος); and, Gardner 1888: 63 no. 717, because it may have been dedicated by the same Kaikos based on the handwriting.

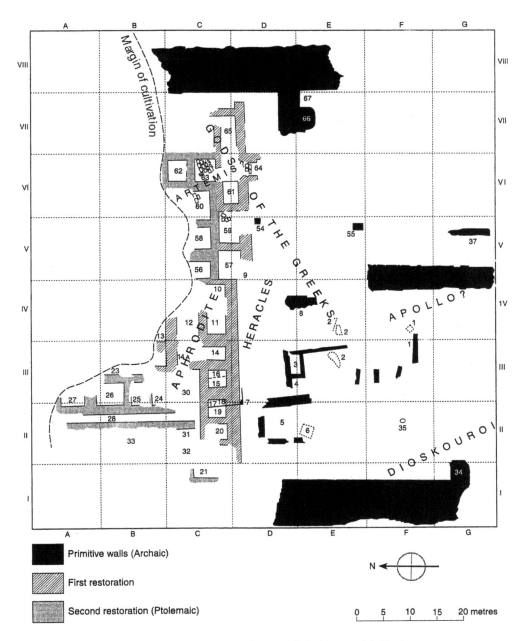

Figure 13 Detailed plan of the Hellenion in Naukratis with find-spots of dedications to Greek divinities. Reproduced from Möller 2000: 295.

called the "Great Temenos," south of the temple of Aphrodite.[202] Hogarth, one of the original excavators of Naukratis, questioned this identification since the "Great Temenos" yielded material that was Ptolemaic but not of an earlier date.[203] Coulson and Leonard's more recent excavations have only provided support for Hogarth's view, since they found nothing but Ptolemaic material from the "Great Temenos."[204] Hogarth also excavated a building in the northern part of the site, near the temple of Milesian Apollo, Samian Hera, and Aphrodite, which he identified as the Hellenion, based on a series of fragmentary dedications found within the sanctuary that can be restored to θεοῖσι τοῖς Ελλήνων (to the gods of the Greeks) or θεῶν τῶν Ἑλλήνων (of the gods of the Greeks).[205] Dedications to individual gods like Aphrodite, Artemis, Heracles, Apollo, the Dioskouroi, and Poseidon, were also discovered in this sanctuary.[206] The earliest structures of the Hellenion date to the sixth century, *c.* 570 BC, and the pottery finds date from the sixth century to the Ptolemaic period.[207] This area is the one now accepted as being the Hellenion.[208]

The formula "to the gods of the Greeks" is not attested epigraphically anywhere else in the Greek world. It is paralleled only by two passages in Herodotus, as the original excavators of Naukratis observed.[209] In the first passage Aristagoras, the tyrant of Miletos, beseeches Kleomenes, the king of Sparta, by the Greek gods (πρὸς θεῶν τῶν Ἑλληνίων) to save the Ionians who are his blood-kin (ὁμαίμονας) from slavery.[210] The second is a passionate speech on the dangers of tyranny given to the Spartans by Sokles, a Corinthian envoy. At the very end, Sokles entreats the Spartans in the name of the Greek gods (θεοὺς τοὺς Ἑλληνίους) not to establish tyranny in the poleis.[211] These speeches identify the Greek gods, and in Aristagoras' case, blood, as the link between Ionians and Spartans. There is one difference between the two passages and the Hellenion inscriptions. In Herodotus' text "Greek" is an adjective that assigns an ethnicity to the gods, whereas in the Hellenion inscriptions "Greek" is a noun that signifies the collective

[202] Petrie et al. 1886: 23–4.   [203] Hogarth 1905: 110–11.
[204] Leonard 1997: 30. Muhs 1994 also argues that the "Great Temenos" was not the Hellenion but an Egyptian-style temple of the Ptolemaic period.
[205] Hogarth 1898–9: 28–39 and 53–5 nos. 18, 64, 71–81, 95, 106 and 1905: 116 nos. 1–4.
[206] Aphrodite: Hogarth 1898–9: 28, 46, 54, 60, 86–8, 91, 93 107 and 1905: 117 nos. 9–16; Artemis: Hogarth 1905: 117 no. 8; Heracles: Hogarth 1898–9: 53–5 nos. 3 and 63; Apollo: Hogarth 1898–9: 30 no. 52; Dioskouroi: Hogarth 1898–9: 30 and Bernand 1970: 697–700 nos. 546, 557–8, 560, 567, 571, 580; Poseidon: Hogarth 1898–9: 55 no. 62.
[207] Hogarth 1898–9: 30–1; Möller 2000: 105–8; Höckmann and Möller 2006: 12–13.
[208] This identification remains controversial for Bowden 1996: 24–5.
[209] Hogarth 1898–9: 44–5, 55–6.   [210] Herodotus 5.49.   [211] Herodotus 5.92.

group of Greek people.[212] Some of the earliest expressions of Hellenicity in the whole of the Greek world, therefore, can be seen in both the name of the sanctuary and the dedications found in it.

Just as in the other sanctuaries in Naukratis, Mytileneans and Rhodians are attested as dedicators in the Hellenion.[213] The two vases with inscriptions in the Cypriot syllabic script, mentioned above, were also discovered in the sanctuary of the Hellenion (between spots 7 and 9 in Figure 13), near the dedications to Heracles and the base for Heracles' statue sculpted by Sikon, perhaps a Cypriot. In Naukratis Greeks from different places not only used all the sanctuaries, even those that were founded by specific poleis, but they also founded jointly a sanctuary common to all of them, where they worshipped both individual Greek gods and collectively "the gods of the Greeks." Malkin asks how the gods of the Greeks were worshipped in the Hellenion and whose sacred calendar they followed, since *nomima* differed not only according to the sub-Hellenic groups, but also locally.[214] As we have seen, this is not a problem just for the Hellenion, but also for the other sanctuaries in Naukratis that were used by all Greeks, as well as in the case of the cult of the Ephesian Artemis in Massalia, Emporion, and the other cities along the Phokaian network described in the first chapter. Further, all Greeks are attested as dedicators in all sanctuaries in Gravisca, and the same might have been the case in Pistiros, as well. I proposed in the previous chapter that the multiethnic context of emporia brought to light the flexibility of Greek religion, which was exploited by Greeks from different places in order to mediate among themselves. The exclusivity of cult that ordinarily determined who had and who did not have the right to perform sacrifices in specific temples seems to disappear at emporia. Perhaps we should imagine that there were representatives in every temple who could mediate on behalf of foreigners, so that they could perform sacrifices.[215] Gauthier has proposed that the *proxenoi* at Delphi and Olympia had the function of facilitating visits of foreigners by performing sacrifices on their

---

[212] Zeus may have received the cult epithet Hellenios in Aigina (scholia to Aristophanes, *Knights* 1253). The evidence, however, is late. Pindar, *Nemean* 5.9–11 also refers to Zeus Hellenios and Euripides, *Hippolytus* 1121 refers to Athena Hellania. These examples are similar to the passages in Herodotus just quoted: they use the word Hellenios/a (Greek) as an adjective to describe Zeus and Athena. They do not define the Greeks as a collective as do the dedicatory inscriptions from the Hellenion.

[213] Teleson who identifies himself as being from Rhodes gave an offering to Aphrodite in the Hellenion (Oxford, Ashmolean Museum G 141.13). Hogarth 1898–9: 38 mentions a base for a statuette of Aphrodite dedicated by Deinomachos from Mytilene, but this base has disappeared.

[214] Malkin 2003b: 95.   [215] Detienne and Vernant 1989: 4.

behalf.[216] What the sanctuaries of Delphi, Olympia, and emporia have in common is that by their very nature they were all, in one sense, pan-Hellenic centers. Perhaps one of the roles of the *proxenoi* in Naukratis was to sacrifice at the temples on traders' behalf, bypassing the problem of exclusivity of cult.

The Hellenion in Naukratis is a unique example from the sixth century of the expression of a Hellenic identity through the recognition of a common, polytheistic religion. What was different about Naukratis that led to the explicit naming of a temple in honor of the gods of the Greeks? For Hall, Naukratis represents one of the first examples of the formation of an "aggregative" identity: an Ionian identity was expressed simply by founding the temples to Milesian Apollo and Samian Hera next to one another (Figure 10). Later the intra-Hellenic ethnic groups living in Naukratis, Ionians, Dorians and Aeolians, came to recognize their similarities and common descent and expressed their common identity by founding the Hellenion.[217] Hall's proposal is not convincing. First, the sanctuaries Herodotus mentions dedicated to the individual deities were not in fact all earlier than the Hellenion; only the temple to Hera dates from the late seventh century, as stated above. The temple to Aphrodite was the first built on site and does not necessarily have a sub-ethnic affiliation, but Hall does not take it into account since he only considers the temples Herodotus mentions. Second, the Greeks of Naukratis themselves never indicated their sub-Hellenic group – Dorian, Ionian or Aeolian. Third, and perhaps more importantly, it is only Herodotus who divides the participating poleis into their sub-Hellenic ethnic groups. Four Ionian and four Dorian poleis along with one Aeolian polis were the founding members of the sanctuary. Only by counting Rhodes as a single entity rather than three different poleis is this convenient symmetry achieved,[218] by which the number of Dorian poleis is equal to the number of Ionian ones. The Aeolians are represented by only one polis, albeit the most powerful one, Mytilene. Bresson argues that, on the one hand, this reflects a need for equilibrium between the Ionian and Dorian components;

---

[216] Gauthier 1972: 45–7.

[217] J. Hall 1997: 49–50. The same assumption that the three temples of Samian Hera, Milesian Apollo, and Aiginetan Zeus were older than the Hellenion is implicit in Malkin 2003b: 94, who argues that the Hellenion was a new expression of Hellenic identity (see below).

[218] Herodotus is fond of such symmetries. When describing the poleis in Asia Minor, Herodotus states that there were twelve Ionian ones. The number was consciously limited to twelve because this was also the number of Achaean poleis in the Peloponnese that drove out the Ionians (1.145). Similarly, when Herodotus writes about the Aeolian poleis, he focuses on the fact that there are twelve of them in mainland Asia Minor (1.149). Only later does he add the Aeolian poleis located on the islands off the coast of Asia Minor (1.151).

on the other hand, the Aeolians would have the power to side with one group or the other, should either the Dorian or Ionian poleis act in accordance to their ethnic interests.[219] The balance between the three groups, and especially between the Dorians and Ionians, is one that Herodotus subtly emphasizes.

This is, I would argue, because Herodotus is writing a history of the Persian Wars, when the two groups cooperated to fight against a common enemy, and because he is writing at the beginning of the Peloponnesian War, when the two groups found themselves in opposition to one another. In fact, tensions between the Ionian Athenians and the Dorian Spartans are explicit throughout the *Histories*, foreshadowing the events of the Peloponnesian War. In this context, the Hellenion serves as an example of cooperation and equality between the Ionians and Dorians. The rhetoric in various speeches in the *Histories* focuses on what the Ionians and Dorians, and all the other Greeks, have in common in an effort to unite them in their fight against the Persians. To a certain extent, in overcoming their differences by undertaking joint efforts, such as the foundation of the Hellenion and the administration of the emporion in Naukratis, the Ionians, Dorians, and Aeolians of Asia Minor become an example to all Greeks. In fact, the Hellenion represents the one and only case in the whole of the *Histories* in which the Ionians, Dorians, and Aeolians are said to undertake any common endeavor. There are only two other instances in which Herodotus mentions all three groups together: in Book 1 they represent the Greeks subjugated by the Lydian king Croesus and in Book 7 those conquered by the Persians.[220] In both cases the Ionians, Dorians, and Aeolians of Asia Minor were distinct sub-Hellenic groups who shared the luckless fate of being under foreign control. It is this fate and their common fight against the Persians that ultimately brought the three groups closer together. For Herodotus, the Hellenion acquires special importance as one of the first documented situations where Greeks of different origins defined themselves as Greek in the face of a strong foreign population.

Malkin sees Naukratis as one the earliest expressions of a pan-Hellenic identity, perceived predominantly as antithetical to that of the Egyptians.[221] He argues that the Greeks of Naukratis internalized the pan-Hellenic perception of themselves held by the Egyptians, and consequently expressed a collective Greek identity, especially through the Hellenion.[222] As he points

[219] Bresson 2000a: 40. [220] Herodotus 1.6; 7.9.
[221] Malkin 2001: 9. Höckmann and Möller 2006: 17–18 understand the creation of the Hellenion in the same way.
[222] Malkin 2003b.

out, the Egyptians had always seen the Greeks as a collective entity.[223] For instance, Psammetichos I (664–610 BC), who had used foreign mercenaries in his armies, rewarded the Ionian and the Carian contingents of his army with places to live:

τοῖσι δὲ Ἴωσι καὶ τοῖσι Καρσὶ τοῖσι συγκατεργασαμένοισι αὐτῷ ὁ Ψαμμήτιχος δίδωσι χώρους ἐνοικῆσαι ἀντίους ἀλλήλων, τοῦ Νείλου τὸ μέσον ἔχοντος, τοῖσι οὐνόματα ἐτέθη Στρατόπεδα. (Herodotus 2.154)

Psammetichos gave to the Ionians and Carians who worked with him places opposite each other to settle in on either side of the Nile, whose names were Stratopeda.

The name of the settlements, Stratopeda, literally means Encampments, reflecting the profession of these settlers. Herodotus adds that Psammetichos I also placed some Egyptian children in their hands so that they would learn the Greek language.[224] Stratopeda displayed a grouping along ethnic lines: one settlement housed Carians, the other Ionians, and the fact that the Pharaoh allowed Egyptian children to live there implies that Egyptians did not originally make up part of the population. The Egyptian government followed the same practice with mercenary soldiers from other origins. The Phoenician soldiers from Tyre, for example, resided in the "Tyrian camp,"[225] and Jewish soldiers were settled in Elephantine.[226] These settlements were enclaves within Egyptian territory that never became fully independent: Amasis moved the inhabitants of Stratopeda to Memphis, in order to have a guard closer to him.[227]

It is interesting that Herodotus describes the Greek population of the settlement as "Ionian." He might have adopted this term from the Egyptians, who called the Greeks with collective names, namely, Wjnn, Yawanîn, Weyenîn, all of which derive from "Ionian."[228] This practice was not only common in Egypt; Assyrian, Hebrew and Persian records also call Greeks "Yawan," "Yaunā," and variations of these, irrespective of their ethnic or polis affiliations.[229] This designation confirms that the Egyptian government did not distinguish among Greek groups.

Another piece of evidence that provides strong parallels to the settlement of the Ionians and Carians in Egypt is the Stele of Amasis.[230] This inscription

---

[223] Malkin 2003b: 92–4.
[224] Herodotus 2.154: καὶ δὴ καὶ παῖδας παρέβαλε αὐτοῖσι Αἰγυπτίους τὴν Ἑλλάδα ἐκδιδάσκεσθαι.
[225] Herodotus 2.112.   [226] Porten 1984.   [227] Herodotus 2.154.
[228] Thompson 1988: 96.   [229] Sancisi-Weerdenburg 2001: 323; Helm 1980.
[230] Daressy 1900. The translation below is by Leahy 1988.

records retroactively the battles fought between the Pharaoh Amasis and his predecessor Apries when the latter rebelled against the former. The text documents the use of Greek mercenaries in these rebellions and expresses dislike of the Greeks, whose loyalty probably went to whoever paid the most:

His majesty [Amasis] was in the palace, deliberating the affairs of the land, when one came to say to him: "Apries has [left]. He [leads] the vessels that [have departed]. Greeks (*H'w-nbw*) without number traverse the northland. It is as if they have no master to govern them. He [Apries] has summoned them and they have accepted. The king had assigned them a residence in the Pehu An. They infest all of Egypt. They have reached Sekhet-Mafek: everything that is in your waters [=territory] runs away from them.

According to the text of this inscription, the Egyptians did not distinguish between the different Greek ethnic groups but rather called them all by the collective name "H'w-nbw,"[231] since the Pharaoh assigned one and the same residence to all Greeks, regardless of their origin. The text is tantalizing because it locates the residence given to the Greeks in the Pehu An, the district in which Naukratis lay, which the Stele of Nektanebis, quoted above, also mentions. If the residence this inscription refers to is Naukratis, some of the inhabitants of Naukratis may have originally been mercenary soldiers who fought against Amasis. Indeed, this may explain why Herodotus emphasizes that it was after Amasis became a philhellene that he granted the Greeks the right to reside in Naukratis. Perhaps after securing his position he gave back to the Greeks the privilege of living legally in Egypt again.

Malkin adduces further evidence from Greek mercenary soldiers to show that the Egyptians grouped all Greeks together.[232] Some Greeks employed in the mercenary armies of Psammetichos II (595–589 BC) scratched graffiti on the leg of a colossal statue of Rameses II in Abu Simbel, in Nubia, when they went there on an expedition in 591 BC. The longest of the graffiti mentions that the Egyptian army was divided in two groups, one consisting of Egyptians, and the other consisting of foreigners grouped together and characterized as "foreign speakers":

βασιλέος ἐλθόντος ἐς Ἐλεφαντίναν Ψαματίχο,
ταῦτα ἔγραψαν τοὶ σὺν Ψαμματίχοι τõι Θεοκλõς

---

[231]   Leahy 1988: 190 gives the reasons why *h'w-nbw* is coterminous with "Greeks."
[232]   Malkin 2003b: 92.

ἔπλεον, ἦλθον δὲ Κέρκιος κατύπερθε, υἷς ὁ ποταμὸς
ἀνίη· ἀλογλόσος δ' ἦχε Ποτασιμτο, Αἰγυπτίος δὲ Ἄμασις·
ἔγραφε δ' ἀμὲ Ἄρχον Ἀμοιβίχο καὶ Πέλεφος Ουδάμο.

ML 7a

When King Psammetichos came to Elephantine, those who sailed with Psammetichos, son of Theokles, wrote this; and they came above Kerkis as far as the river
allowed; and Potasimto had command of those of foreign speech and Amasis of
the Egyptians; and Archon the son of Amoibichos wrote us and Pelekos the son of
Eudamos.

Language emerges as the distinctive characteristic that determined the
separation of the Egyptian soldiers from others. Potasimto is also called
"General of the Greeks" on a sarcophagus that bears his name.[233] However,
the contingent of the *alloglossoi* is not made up only of Greeks. On the
same spot where the Greek soldiers scratched their graffiti, Carians and
Phoenicians also defaced the statue with their own graffiti.[234] Although the
linguistic separation of Egyptians and non-Egyptian speakers surely served
to group the Greeks together, it also placed them together with other groups,
unlike the situation of the settlements, where ethnic groups were separated.
It is also important to note that this graffito implies that Greeks called their
hosts by their collective name, Egyptian: Amasis was the commander of
the "Egyptian" forces. Herodotus uses the same term *alloglossos* to describe
the first foreigners, Ionians and Carians, settled in Egypt at Stratopeda.[235]
Here the historian reflects the importance granted to language by the
Egyptians in defining collective identities, as he does in a later passage
when he says that the Egyptians call all those who speak other languages
barbarians.[236]

While the Egyptian pharaohs so clearly considered the Greek soldiers as
a collective, the Greeks themselves did not exhibit a similar cohesiveness.
The inscriptions scratched on the leg of the statue of Rameses II by Greek
mercenaries demonstrate this clearly since each of the soldiers only identifies himself with a city-ethnic, such as Teian, Ialysian, and Kolophonian.[237]

---

[233] Rowe 1938: 169 and 189.   [234] Bernand and Masson 1957.

[235] Herodotus 2.154: πρῶτοι γὰρ οὗτοι ἐν Αἰγύπτῳ ἀλλόγλωσσοι κατοικίσθησαν. In relation
to this, it is interesting to note that the same passage records that Psammetichos I sent
Egyptian children to Stratopeda so that they learn the Greek language.

[236] Herodotus 2.158: βαρβάρους δὲ πάντας οἱ Αἰγύπτιοι καλέουσι τοὺς μὴ σφίσι ὁμογλώσσους.

[237] *ML* 7b, c, f, g: Ἐλεσίβιος ὁ Τήιος (Helesibios the Teian), Τήλεφός μ' ἔγραφε ho Ἰαλύσιος
(Telephos the Ialysian wrote me), Πάβις ὁ Ϙολοφόνιος | σὺν Ψαμματᾶ" (Pabis the
Kolophonian is with Psammetichos), Ἀναχσανορ ε[.....] hλο Ἰαλύσιος hόκα βασιλ|εὺς

Whereas the Egyptian army distinguished Egyptians and foreigners in terms of language, the Greeks of this latter group distinguished among themselves according to their place of origin, and exhibited their civic identity, just as they did in Emporion, Naukratis, Gravisca, Pistiros, Peiraieus, and elsewhere.

Conclusion

Naukratis seems to follow in the tradition of foreign settlements in Egypt. According to Herodotus, an Egyptian pharaoh granted the space to the Greek settlers and traders just as previous pharaohs had settled Greeks, Carians, Jews, and Phoenicians in separate enclaves. Further, like his predecessors, Amasis did not distinguish among the different Greeks but rather grouped them all together in Naukratis. It was the strength of the Egyptian collective identity and the Egyptian perception of the Greeks as a single collective entity that led the Greeks to recognize their commonalities and express their Hellenic identity. Nonetheless, the foundation of a temple in honor of the gods of the Greeks, called the Hellenion, is without doubt the result of a combination of two factors. On the one hand, the Greeks in Naukratis faced a group with a strong collective identity of their own, which did not distinguish among different Greek groups. Moreover, grouped together in the Greek settlements granted to them by the Egyptians, and set apart from the Egyptians in the mercenary armies because of linguistic differences, the Greeks of Egypt, and in particular Naukratis, were forced to recognize their similarities. The Greeks of Naukratis had extra impetus to see themselves as Hellenes, because this is how the Egyptians viewed them. This is probably the reason that an explicitly Hellenic identity was actively expressed through the Hellenion. On the other hand, the formation of a collective identity, even a Hellenic one, was characteristic of multicultural emporia, where Greeks acknowledged their similarities in their recognition of all their deities as something they had in common. Thus, while the Greeks of Naukratis always considered themselves as individuals from specific poleis, as is shown by the various dedications in the temples of Naukratis and the temples of Samian Hera, Milesian Apollo, and Aiginetan Zeus, they also realized they had language, religion, and customs

---

ἤλασε τὸν στρατὸν τὸ πρᾶτον [- - - - -] Ψαμάτιχος (Anaxanor the Ialysian m[arched] when the king Psammetichos drove the army [. . .]).

in common. The temple of Aphrodite in Gravisca and Naukratis certainly became implicitly emblematic of a Hellenic identity. Similarly, the temple of Ephesian Artemis acquired a pan-Ionian, albeit not pan-Hellenic, aspect in all the Phokaian colonies. In Naukratis, however, the Greeks took a step further and expressed their common Hellenic identity most spectacularly with the foundation of a common temple dedicated to the gods of the Greeks, the Hellenion.

4 | Pistiros

In 1990 archaeologists discovered an inscription near the modern village of Vetren in Bulgaria that records privileges that Thracian dynasts granted the resident traders and the Greeks living in an emporion called Pistiros and reiterated rights given to them by a certain Kotys (Figure 14).[1] The reference to Kotys has been taken to indicate Kotys I who ruled the Odrysian kingdom from 383/2 to 360/59 BC, and has been used to date the inscription to sometime shortly after 360/59 BC when Kotys I was assassinated. The Vetren inscription is a unique document whose detailed legislation reveals how a host population dealt with foreign traders living in its midst, how an emporion located in a non-Greek land was organized legally, and how different ethnic groups interacted with one another in day-to-day life; there is nothing like it from any other emporion in the Greek world, not even Peiraieus. It is of singular importance for the study of mediation and the construction of identity in multiethnic settlements in the Mediterranean because it is the only document available that offers an official, government version of a non-Greek state's dealings with foreigners living in an emporion it controlled. Recorded on this inscription are the rights of Greek traders in relation both to other Greek traders and to the Thracian natives and rulers; the rights of the Thracian authorities in relation to resident Greeks in Thrace; and economic provisions that describe the routes used and the inviolability granted to itinerant traders and those residing in Pistiros. These legal stipulations illuminate how the host society sought to regulate through religion and law its interaction with the Greeks of Pistiros and the internal affairs of this diverse community – for, as in Gravisca, Naukratis, and Peiraieus, the Greek traders of Pistiros came from different poleis.

The relationship between Thrace and its neighbors, from the Bronze Age to the Roman period, including the Mycenaeans, Illyrians, Macedonians, Scythians, Greeks, and, subsequently, Romans, has been the subject of many works.[2] In the archaic period, contacts between Thrace and the rest of the Mediterranean increased. The establishment of Greek colonies in

---

[1] Velkov and Domaradzka 1994.

[2] For example: Gindin 1982; Best and de Vries 1989; Fol 2002; Veligianni-Terzi 2004; Bouzek and Domaradzka 2005 with references to older works.

Figure 14 The Vetren inscription, *c.* 359 BC.

different regions of Thrace, including the lower Strymon Valley and the rest of the North Aegean coast, the Chersonese, Propontis, and the Black Sea coast, started from as early as the seventh century, in keeping with the pan-Mediterranean movement to found new settlements.[3] Phoenicians were not absent from expeditions in these regions in the same period. According to the literary tradition they were the first to discover the gold mines of Mt. Pangaion, and there is archaeological evidence that may indicate that they were permanently present on the island of Thasos before the Parian Greeks settled there.[4] This island may actually have been the home of Thracians before either the Phoenicians or the Greeks arrived.[5] Later interactions between Thracians and their Aegean neighbors are well known. The early permanent contacts between Thrace and the Greek world, in particular, developed by the fifth and fourth centuries BC into shifting political alliances with different Greek city-states, with Athens, Sparta, and Thasos emerging as the three main Greek actors with economic and political interests who exercised influence and control in the region. By the middle of the fourth century BC, the Macedonians also became involved in this political landscape, and Philip II waged campaigns in Thrace soon after he took power in Macedonia in 359 BC. These campaigns, aimed at securing his position in Macedonia and controlling the natural resources of Thrace, such as the gold mines of Mt. Pangaion, eventually led to the capture of Greek poleis in Thrace allied to Athens. Athens lost the revenues it had been receiving from the gold mines and from that point onward Athens and Macedon were pitted against each other as they fought over control and influence in North Aegean Thrace. Philip II established the colony Philippopolis, modern Plovdiv in Bulgaria, to secure control of the region, a policy followed by Alexander when he founded a colony called Alexandropolis in Thrace. The presence of Greeks, Phoenicians, and, eventually, Macedonians in Thrace, and their colonies redefined the ethnic make-up and had significant ramifications for the history and culture of the region.

The emphasis until recently had been placed on the Greek and Macedonian dealings with Thrace, but this has been remedied by several new works that deal with the Thracian point of view.[6] At the same time that the

---

[3] Skarlatidou 1984; Isaac 1986.

[4] Pliny, *Natural History* 7.56 and Strabo 14.5.28 say that Phoenicians discovered the gold mines. For the presence of Phoenicians on Thasos see Herodotus 2.44 and 6.47, Pouilloux 1954: 21, Bergquist 1973, and Graham 1978: 88–92.

[5] For Thasos as a Thracian site see Markov 1978 and Owen 2000 and 2003.

[6] For the Greek or Macedonian perspectives: Lazarides 1971; Youroukova 1982; Isaac 1986; Pébarthe 1999; Veligianni-Terzi 2004. For the Thracian perspective: Archibald 1998; Domaradzki et al. 2000; Theodossiev 2000a.

Thracians have become a popular research subject Thracian history, religion, and archaeology have become accessible to a wider scholarly audience.[7]
From these works it has emerged that, like the Greeks, the Thracians were
divided into several sub-ethnic groups, some of which are recorded in Greek
sources, and that it was not until the Odrysian dynasty that large parts of
Thrace were unified under a single rule.[8] Further, Thracian religion, like
that of most of the other Mediterranean populations, was polytheistic.[9]
With the growing interest in colonial encounters, studies on the effects
of Greek colonization in Thrace have appeared. These deal mostly with
the popularity of Greek imports, the adoption of the Greek language,
and the influence of Greek art and architecture in Thrace.[10] Some of the
newest scholarship on Thrace discusses the creation of a hybrid material
culture that developed in specific places with mixed populations, such as
Samothrace,[11] and hybrid religious practices resulting from extensive contacts with the Greeks.[12] Cross-cultural influences, however, were not unidi-
rectional. Greeks adopted the worship of Thracian divinities, such as when
Athens incorporated the cult of Bendis into official Athenian religion, an
issue that will be discussed in the next chapter. Moreover, several mythological figures popular among Greeks were Thracian, such as Orpheus, Boreas,
and King Lykourgos. Just as Iberia and Etruria were incorporated into Greek
mythology through Heracles and Odysseus, so Thrace became part of Greek
myths.

The close contacts that Thrace had with rest of the Mediterranean world
are evident also in the significant migration waves that took Thracians to
several places in the Mediterranean, where they had lasting influence. One
Thracian abroad has already been encountered in the person of Rhodopis,

[7] The following list is not exhaustive; I cite only some of the classic works on Thrace and the
Thracians in addition to the most recent scholarship and exhibition catalogues on the subject:
Mihailov 1972; Fol and Marazov 1977; Danov 1977; Vlahov 1982; Fol 1983a; Poulter 1983;
Archibald 1998; Marazov 1998; Theodossiev 2000b; Fol et al. 2004; Fol and Fol 2005.

[8] Archilochus fr. 5 (ed. M. L. West) refers to the Saians; Herodotus 7.110 mentions the Paitoi,
Kikones, Bistones, Sapaioi, Dersaioi, Edonoi, and Satrai. Herodotus 5.3 also says that the
Thracians were the most numerous ethnic group and would have ruled the world had it not
been for their political fragmentation. Archibald 1998 and Veligianni-Terzi 2004 discuss the
social and political history of the Odrysian kingdom.

[9] Fol and Marazov 1977: 17–36; Vlahov 1982; Najdenova 1983. In typical fashion Herodotus 5.7
mentions three divinities that the Thracians worshipped but translates them into Greek when
he says that they worship Ares, Dionysus, and Artemis. The ancient historian might have
equated the Thracian goddess Bendis with Artemis, whose worship and cult-practices are
known from Athens and discussed in the next chapter.

[10] Archibald 1983; Bouzek and Ondřejova 1987 and 1988; Loukopoulou 1989; Bouzek 2001b and
2004; Domaradzka 2007c.

[11] Ilieva 2009.   [12] Bouzek 1999b.

the Thracian courtesan whose Mediterranean connections are impressive. According to Herodotus, Rhodopis was first the slave of a Samian called Iadmon, and subsequently of another Samian, Xanthes, who took her to Egypt. Another man from Mytilene, Sappho's brother, Charaxos, a trader who had traveled to Naukratis on business, freed her so that she could practice her profession, and Rhodopis stayed in Naukratis, where she worked as a courtesan. It was the fact that Charaxos spent money on the Thracian courtesan that prompted Sappho to write a poem about her brother's folly in wasting his money to free a Thracian slave, and a courtesan into the bargain.[13] In Naukratis, Rhodopis acquired such a large fortune that she set up a memorial to herself at Delphi, one of the most important pan-Hellenic centers of the Greek world, using one tenth of her property.[14] Rhodopis, having traveled from Thrace to Samos and from there to a Greek multiethnic commercial settlement in Egypt, was freed by a Mytilenean trader whose sister's work was part of the pan-Hellenic poetic repertoire, became rich and showed off her wealth at the pan-Hellenic sanctuary of Delphi, where Greeks and non-Greeks set up monuments for the rest of the Greek world (and beyond) to see and admire.[15]

Other famous connections involving Thracians abroad include (a) Kimon's mother Hegesipyle, the daughter of the Thracian king Oloros, married to the Athenian general Miltiades, and (b) possibly also the mother of another Athenian general, Themistokles.[16] Epigraphic evidence also attests to the presence of Thracians in Samothrace, Athens, Egypt, and other places in the Greek world, especially as mercenary soldiers.[17] The Thracian presence in Athens was probably the strongest in the whole of the Mediterranean world; consequently, many works deal with either the presence of Thracians in Athens or Thrace in the Athenian imagination.[18] Herodotus' account of Rhodopis, which is so obviously negative, contains one of the most common elements of the Athenian stereotype of Thracians: she was a slave,

---

[13] Sappho fr. 138 (ed. Cambell).   [14] Herodotus 2.134–5.

[15] Kurke 1999: 220–7 discusses Herodotus' presentation of Rhodopis and Keesling 2006: 61–3 discusses Rhodopis' dedication at Delphi. Strabo 17.1.33–4 recounts a different story about Rhodopis, one which Herodotus had tried to dispel. In Strabo's story, an eagle snatched Rhodopis' sandal when she was bathing, carried it to Memphis, and dropped it on the king's lap. The king was intrigued, sent out messengers to find the sandal's owner, and eventually married Rhodopis, who then became an Egyptian queen and was buried in a pyramid that she built herself. Diodorus Siculus 1.64 preserves a slightly different tradition that it was the administrators of different nomes that built the pyramid for Rhodopis and not herself.

[16] Plutarch, *Life of Kimon* 4.1–2. Themistokles' mother was either Thracian or Carian, according to Plutarch, *Life of Themistokles* 1.

[17] Fraser 1993; Fol 1971.   [18] Fol 1983b; Shapiro 1983; Bäbler 1998; Tsiafaki 1998 and 2000.

just as many Thracians in Athens were.[19] Thracians were also horsemen, fierce warriors, famous musicians, bore tattoos, and wore a specific Thracian costume, which consisted of a cap (*alopekis*) made of animal pelt, a coat (*zeira*), and fawn-skin boots (*embades*).[20] Yet, just as Egyptian stereotypes of Greeks, and more generally, other foreigners living in Egypt, do not necessarily match up with the treatment that Greeks and other non-Egyptians received on a daily basis in Egypt, so too Athenian stereotypes of Thracians have to be reconciled with the actual interactions between Greeks and Thracians, both in Thrace and in Athens. The latter is a subject discussed in the next chapter. The Vetren inscription, discussed in this chapter, reveals many details about the legal consequences of administering a multiethnic settlement from the Thracian perspective.

The Vetren inscription

The Vetren inscription, which mentions an emporion called Pistiros, is so called because it was discovered about 2 km north of the modern village of Vetren, Bulgaria. More specifically, it was excavated from a Roman station known as *Bona Mansio*, but traces of mortar found on the stone suggest that it had been brought there from another site and reused as building material. A fifth-century BC settlement in Adjiyska Vodenitza near Vetren was quickly identified as the Pistiros mentioned on the inscription, earning Pistiros the honor of being the only named site called an emporion in ancient sources that was located inland and not on the coast.[21] The identification of the settlement at Adjiyska Vodenitza as the Greek emporion Pistiros, however, is problematic, as several scholars have noted.[22] Although the finds from this site include a surprising number of Greek imports when compared to other inland Thracian sites, the majority of the pottery discovered here

---

[19] Literary and epigraphic sources suggest that Thrace was a major source of slaves: Herodotus 5.6; Aristophanes, *Women at the Thesmophoria* 280; Scholia to Plato, *Laches* 187b; Pliny, *Natural History* 35.70; ML 240–7 (Velkov 1967: 70–80).

[20] Literary descriptions of Thracian stereotypes and costume exist in Herodotus 5.3–8 and 7.75, Thucydides 2.97, 4.109, and 2.96, Strabo 1.3.17, and Euripides, *Hekuba* 1153. These typically Thracian characteristics are depicted in Athenian art, especially in vase-painting (Tsiafakis 2000: 367–86).

[21] Domaradzki 1993: 40 and 1996; Velkov and Domaradzka 1994: 1; Kolarova 1996; V. Chankowski and Fouache 2000; Bouzek 2001a; Archibald 2002b: 311–12; Veligianni-Terzi 2004: 318; Hansen 2006a: 20–4. Bouzek et al. 2010: 11–16 with plates offers the most recent and comprehensive description of this settlement.

[22] Bravo and A. S. Chankowski 1999: 279–87; Tsetskhladze 2000: 233–9; Demetriou 2010a.

was locally produced,[23] the variety of the published amphora stamps,[24] Greek graffiti, and Greek inscriptions[25] is rather limited, coins are mostly Thracian,[26] and the altars discovered thus far are all Thracian.[27] Over 70 percent of the imported amphora stamps are from Thasos, and the rest originate mostly from the North Aegean and Black Sea areas.[28] Similarly, the Greek coins discovered from this site are mostly from the Chersonese, Thasos, and Maroneia.[29] All this shows that Vetren was well-connected within the North-Aegean region, but not necessarily a Greek emporion of such importance that Thracian dynasts needed to legislate about it. Correlated with the absence of evidence for a significant Greek presence in Pistiros is the suggestion that what little trade took place in the inland site of Vetren probably involved river transport, which was more expensive than sea transport.[30] While the settlement at Vetren may have had a minor role in trade – hence the amphora stamps, Greek imports, and Greek graffiti – it is unlikely that it was Pistiros, an emporion. Moreover, the settlement at Adjiyska Vodenitza, with its Greek-style fortification system and monumental architecture, could be considered more similar to the Thracian sites of Vani, Seuthopolis, and Kabyle, and Scythian Neapolis, than to Greek emporia.[31]

---

[23] Archibald 1996; Jurina 1996; Bouzek 2001b, 2002 and 2007; Archibald 2002a; Boháč 2002; Grmela 2007.

[24] The most recent count in Tušlová et al. 2010 was seventy-seven. Earlier discussions of amphora stamps can be found in Titz 2002: 233–4 and Bouzek et al. 2007: 133–46.

[25] About 250 individual pieces of Greek graffiti have been discovered and only 7 inscriptions: Domaradzka 1996, 1999: 347–8 and 352–8, 2002a, 2007a, and 2007b; Domaradzki 1993: 55–7; A. S. Chankowski in Bravo and A. S. Chankowski 1999: 296–9; Bouzek and Domaradzka 2007: 747.

[26] Bouzek 2001b: 95 of the 162 coins found are Thracian and 11 are local imitations of coins from Thasos. There are also several hundred Macedonian coins, which I have not included in the numbers I have presented here.

[27] Lazov 1996.

[28] Tušlová et al. 2010. Similar trends can be seen in the provenance of amphora fragments published from this site.

[29] Of the fifty-six Greek coins that have been published, twenty-four are from the Chersonese, seven from Thasos, and nine from Maroneia. The rest are from cities in the general North Aegean region: two are from Messambria, two from Ainos, one from Damastion, four from Parion, five from Kypsela, one from Kardia, and one from Semyle.

[30] Bouzek 1996b and 1999a: 189–92.

[31] Tsetskhladze 2000: 233–9. The archaeology of Odrysian residences, however, remains elusive, and comparing these sites to Adjiyska Vodenitza is not without problems. Bouzek and Domaradzka 2002: 391 and 2010: 236 argue that the fortifications of Adjiyska Vodenitza are different from those at Vani and that a palace structure has not been discovered yet. The fortifications have not survived well (Bouzek and Musil 2002: 103–5), and arguments based on the evidence of the walls cannot be sustained. A nearby chamber tomb may belong to an Odrysian dynast; hence it is likely that Adjiyska Vodenitza was an Odrysian residence (Archibald 1998: 295 and Bouzek et al. 2007: pl. 58).

The literary sources that mention a site called Pistiros considered together with a linguistic analysis of the toponym suggest that the emporion Pistiros should be identified with a polis called Pistyros, which Herodotus characterizes as a polis on the North Aegean coast in his description of Xerxes' march.[32] After the discovery of the Vetren inscription, scholars have tried to argue that Pistyros was not located on the coast but rather at Adjiyska Vodenitza, contrary to what Herodotus says.[33] These arguments remain unfounded in view of the archaeological evidence from Pistiros just described. Moreover, a provisional identification of Herodotus' Pistyros does exist; before the discovery of the Vetren inscription it had been identified with a site on the Thasian *peraia*.[34] The find spot of the inscription in Adjiyska Vodenitza, which is the main reason the site has been identified as Pistiros, can be explained differently. Since the inscription records a multilateral treaty between three Thracian dynasts, as I argue below, it is possible that a copy of the text was published or kept here, especially so if this place was a dynastic residence.[35] Pistiros, which was one and the same as Pistyros,[36] should, therefore, be located on the North Aegean coast across from the island of Thasos. Such a location would make Pistiros a coastal emporion, dependent on the Thracian authorities, and part of a trade network that spanned the North Aegean coast of Thrace and reached all the way to the Propontis. It is regrettable that the original identification of the site on the Thasian *peraia* as Pistiros remains only provisional.[37] The archaeological evidence from the emporion of Pistiros, therefore, cannot be considered in this chapter. The content of the Vetren inscription, however, more than makes up for this circumstance because it provides unparalleled information about the interethnic relations of Greeks and Thracians at this emporion.

[32] Herodotus 7.109–10. Bravo and A. S. Chankowski 1999: 281; Velkova 1986: 133; Detschew 1976: 370; Lazova 1996: 217–19; Jannaris 1897: 47–8; Yordanov 2002: 331–3. Demetriou 2010a reviews all the possible identifications of the site and the scholarly literature on the subject of Pistiros' location and supports the original identification of Pistiros as a site on the North Aegean coast across from Thasos.

[33] Salviat 1999: 267–71. For a different identification of Adjiyska Vodenitza see Boshnakov 1999.

[34] Koukouli-Chrysanthaki 1972: 529; Lazarides 1971; Isaac 1986: 12–13 and 70. Bouzek and Domaradzka 2010: 237 reprint Bouzek and Domaradzka 2009 and maintain that the inscription refers to the settlement at Vetren because it was found there.

[35] Demetriou 2010a: 90.

[36] The variation can be accounted for by the interchange of ypsilon and iota in the medieval manuscript tradition, by which time the two had converged in pronunciation; cf. Browning 1983: 56–7.

[37] In fact, the location of several cities that should be on the Thracian coast between the Nestos and Hebros rivers remains uncertain. See Psoma et al. 2008, Loukopoulou and Psoma 2008, Zahrnt 2008, and Saba in press.

The text of the Vetren inscription is as follows:[38]

[– *ca* 20 –] ΙΚΙ
[– *ca* 12 –] ΔΕΝΝΥ..Η εἰ δὲ..
[. . . . ὀμνύτ]ω τὸν Διόνυσογ καὶ
[. . . .] ὀφειλέτω· ὅ τι ἂν δέ τις τῶν
[ἐμπ]οριτέων ἐπικαλῆι ὁ ἕτερος τ-
[ῶι ἑ]τέρωι κρίνεσθαι αὐτοὺς ἐπὶ τ-
[οῖς] συγγενέσι καὶ ὅσα ὀφείλετα[ι]
τοῖς ἐμπορίταις παρὰ τοῖς Θραιξ-
[ί]ν, τούτων χρεῶν ἀποκοπὰς μὴ
ποιεῖγ· γῆγ καὶ βοσκὴν ὅσην ἔχουσ-
ιν ἐμπορῖται, ταῦτα μὴ ἀφαιρεῖ-
[σθ]αι· ἐπαυλιστὰς μὴ πέμπειν το-
[ῖς] ἐμπορίταις· φρουρὴμ μηδεμίαν
εἰς Πίστιρον καταστῆσαι μήτε α-
[ὀτ]ὸμ μήτε ἄλλωι ἐπιτρέπειν·
[ὁμ]ήρους Πιστιρηνῶμ μὴ λαμ-
[βάν]ειμ μηδὲ ἄλλωι ἐπιτρέπειν·
[τὰ] τῶν ἐμπορίτέωμ μὴ [ἀ]φαιρεῖ-
[σθ]αι μήτε αὀτὸμ μήτ[ε το]ὺς ἑ-
[αυτ]οῦ· τέλεα κατὰ τὰς ὁδοὺς
μὴ πρήσσειν, ὅσα εἰς Μαρώνεια[ν]
[εἰσ]άγεται ἐκ Πιστίρου ἢ ἐκ τῶν ἐ-
[μ]πορίων ἢ 'γ Μαρωνείης εἰς Πίστ-
[ιρ]ον ἢ τὰ ἐμπόρια Βελανα Πρασε-
[.ω]ν· τοὺς ἐμπορίτας τὰς ΑΠΑΖ-
[–2–3–] καὶ ἀνοίγειγ καὶ κλείειν· ἅμα
[καθ]άπερ καὶ ἐπὶ Κότυος· ἄνδρα Μ-
[αρω]νίτην οὐ δήσω οὐδὲ ἀποκτ-
[ενέ]ω οὐδὲ ἀφαιρήσομαι χρήμα-
[τα] οὔτε ζῶντος οὔτε ἀποθανόν-
[τος] οὔτε αὐτὸς οὔτε τῶν ἐμῶν
[οὐ]δείς· οὐδὲ Ἀπολλωνιητέων, οὐδ-
[ὲ Θ]ασίων, ὅσοι ἐμ Πιστίρωι εἰσί[ν],
[οὔ]τε ἀποκτενέω οὐδένα, οὔτε
[δήσω] οὔτε ἀφαιρήσομαι χρήμα-

4

8

12

16

20

24

28

32

[38] Velkov and Domaradzka 1994; Avram 1997–8; V. Chankowski and Domaradzka 1999. Following J. E. Johnston 1998: I have restored α|[ὐτ]ὸμ to α|[ὀτ]ὸμ (line 15) based on αὀτὸμ in line 19.

[τα οὔ]τε ζῶντος οὔτε ἀποθανό-   36
[ντος οὔτε] αὐτὸς οὔτε τῶν ἐμῶν
[οὐδεὶς· εἰ δέ τις] τῶν οἰκητόρων
[– ca 14–16 –]τῶν οὗ ὁ ἐμπορ-
[– ca 14–16 –]ον εἰσὶν ΑΙΜ-   40
[– ca 14–16 –]ν, ἐὰμ μὴ ΑΜ-
[– ca 14–16 –τ]ις ἀδικῆι τὸ
[ν δεῖνα *vel* ὺς δεῖνας] τε ΕΨΩΑΛΛΑ
[ἀναδο- *vel* ἀποδο]χεὺς τὴν ἐπ-   44
[– ca 5–6 – δι᾽ ἑκάστ]ου ἐνιαυτοῦ
[–] Α.

Let it be sworn by Dionysus and let him pledge[the following]. Whatever claim any of the *emporitai* bring against one another, they are to be judged by their *syngeneis*; there will be no cancellation of debts on however much is owed by the Thracians to the *emporitai*; however much arable land and pasture the *emporitai* have will not be taken away; he will not send *epaulistai* to the *emporitai*; he will neither establish a garrison in Pistiros himself nor will he allow another to do so; he will not seize hostages from among the Pistirenoi or allow another to do so; neither he, nor his own, will seize the possessions of the *emporitai*; dues will not be levied along the routes on however much is brought to Maroneia from Pistiros or from the emporia, or from Maroneia to Pistiros or to the Belana emporia of the Prasenoi; the *emporitai* are to open and close their [–], just as in the time of Kotys. Neither I, nor any of my own, will take a Maroneian man captive, or kill him, or take away his property, dead or alive. Neither I, nor any of my own, will kill, take captive, or seize the property, dead or alive, of any of the Apollonians or Thasians who are in Pistiros. If any of the settlers . . .

Although the first editors of the inscription did not propose an exact date for it, they suggested that the text itself provides a *terminus post quem* with the mention of Kotys in line 27. These scholars identified Kotys as King Kotys I of Thrace and dated the decree to sometime shortly after his assassination in 360/59 BC.[39] Tsetskhladze reports that more recently scholars have cast doubts on this dating of the inscription, which could be early Hellenistic, but no publication discussing such a date has appeared yet.[40] Down-dating the inscription does not, however, take into consideration the mid-fourth century form of the letters and the historical context of this period.[41] If one contextualizes the provisions of the inscription within the political events

[39] Velkov and Domaradzka 1994.   [40] Tsetskhladze 2000: 240 n. 2.
[41] Archibald 2000–1: 267 and n. 5.

of Thrace during this period, it becomes apparent that a date of 359 BC better fits the situation that the inscription describes.

According to Demosthenes, the years immediately after Kotys' assassination were characterized by political turmoil while his three successors – Kersobleptes (Kotys' son), Amadokos II, and Berisades – fought for the throne of the Odrysian kingdom. Athens finally intervened and forced Kotys' successors to divide the rule of Thrace among them and to restore some land to Athens.[42] An inscription from 357 BC suggests that by this time the tripartite division of the Odrysian kingdom among the successors had already taken place: one of the provisions in this text indicates that Greek poleis in Thrace had to pay taxes to Kersobleptes or Amadokos II or Berisades, depending on whose jurisdiction they fell under.[43] Just as Athens hurried to ensure that the Greek poleis in Thrace did not suffer unnecessarily from the transfer of power from Kotys to his successors and the latter's squabbles, the Thracian authorities and the resident traders of Pistiros, both of whom benefited from the commercial operations there, were anxious to ensure the smooth running of the emporion under the new leadership. This resulted in the reiteration of some privileges the traders and Greeks living in Pistiros had under Kotys – "ἅμα [καθ]άπερ καὶ ἐπὶ Κότυος" (lines 26–7), suggesting that the Kotys in question is Kotys I.

Like the date, the authorship of the text is also disputed. Most scholars agree that Kotys enacted some of the laws and one or all of his successors passed the rest. An alternative proposal is that the island of Thasos and not the Thracian dynasts created the legislation on the inscription.[44] The argument is based on the fact that the political fragmentation after Kotys' death meant that none of the successors wielded enough authority to control their territory and to draw up an agreement administering all the various sites mentioned in the inscription – Pistiros, Maroneia, Thasos, Apollonia, and several emporia, called Belana, possibly located on the Melas Gulf.[45] There is no need, however, to suppose that only a single ruler could enforce these laws. The inscription of 357 BC mentioned above, recording a multilateral treaty that details the taxes all the Greek poleis in Thrace had to pay to Berisades, Amadokos II, or Kersobleptes, provides a parallel situation, in which Kotys' three successors participated in an agreement collectively rather than individually.[46] Similarly, the safeguards of the Vetren

---

[42] Demosthenes, *Against Aristokrates* 8 and 170.　　[43] *IG* II² 126.

[44] J. E. Johnston 1998: 43–66.

[45] J. E. Johnston, 1998: 31–43. Chapters I and II deal with the identification of various named and unnamed emporia: 10–30. See also the discussion below.

[46] *IG* II² 126.

inscription probably bound all three of the successors, as well as the Greeks and traders living in Pistiros. Further, internal evidence from the inscription does point to the Thracian authorities and not to Thasos as the author of the text. Most of the guarantees in the Vetren inscription are put in place in order to protect various Greeks, like Thasians, Apollonians, and Maroneians (lines 27–36); to ensure that any outstanding debts the Thracians owed to the resident traders, who were not Thracian, would be paid (lines 7–9); to guarantee that no taxes would be levied on specific trade routes (lines 20–7); and to protect the personal safety and possessions of the resident traders (lines 9–12 and 15–20). As I will argue shortly, these concessions granted to the Greeks, as well as the ability to send military servicemen (ἐπαυλιστάς) and a garrison (φρουρήμ) to Pistiros, lay only within the power of the Thracian rulers. The Thracian rulers, therefore, are the most likely candidates as the source of authority and hence as the authors of the inscription.

Several scholars have proposed that a specific, single author commissioned the text. Some have argued that Amadokos II, one of three successors to Kotys' kingdom, commissioned this inscription some time after Kotys' death and before Philip of Macedon's incursion into Thrace in 357/6[47] while others think it was Kersobleptes, Kotys' son and the strongest of the three successors, who reiterated Kotys' grants to the resident traders soon after the king's death.[48] Yet others have assumed that the reference to the legal statutes effective under Kotys (lines 26–7) implies that the three Odrysian successors of Kotys acted as a single authority in commissioning this document.[49] There are several indications, however, that the inscription actually records a multilateral agreement, binding for all three of Kotys' successors. For instance, the provisions on the inscription dealing with taxes levied on roads (lines 20–27) running from Pistiros or from the emporia located on the Melas Gulf, which, as I show later, should be the same as the Belana emporia, to Maroneia, and from Maroneia to Pistiros or to the Belana emporia, describe routes that spanned the territories of all three successors: Maroneia was under the control of Amadokos II, the Belana emporia were under Kersobleptes, and Pistiros was within Berisades' jurisdiction.[50] Perhaps equally telling is a phrase that repeats

---

[47] Von Bredow 1997: 111–13, followed by Hansen 2006a: 20. A. S. Chankowski proposed the same in Bravo and A. S. Chankowski 1999: 308–9. Domaradzka 2002b: 340 suggests that one could reconstruct Amadokos' name in line 41.

[48] Salviat 1999: 259.

[49] Domaradzki 1993: 41–2; Bresson 1993: 226; Velkov and Domaradzka 1994: *passim*; Avram 1997–8: 41; Bravo and A. S. Chankowski 1999: 284–6, 305–9; Picard 1999: 339–40; Archibald 2000–1: 266–7.

[50] The production of coins shows the extent of the territories of each of the three successors: coins of Kersobleptes bear mint marks identified with Kypsela, a city on the Hebros river in

in the inscription, which may reflect a multilateral agreement among the Thracian dynasts (lines 14–16, 17, 19–20). The phrase is "μήτε α[ὁτ]ὁμ μήτε ἄλλωι ἐπιτρέπειν" (neither he, nor will he allow another [to do so]). Each of the Thracian dynasts, therefore, agreed to grant certain privileges to the resident traders and Greeks of Pistiros, not to violate these, and not to allow his fellow dynasts to do so.[51]

The inscription recording the dues Greek settlements had to pay the three successors also shows that the Odrysian dynasts did dominate their territory, contrary to the objection that neither Kotys nor his successors had power over their lands. Having to pay taxes to a foreign authority is strong evidence that these poleis, and therefore perhaps also Pistiros, were subordinate to the Thracian kings. They nonetheless enjoyed some political autonomy, much like the Greek poleis controlled by the Persians in Asia Minor and the emporia of Naukratis and Gravisca. In any case, the taxes the poleis in Thrace had to pay to the Thracian kings is evidence that the three successors, whether independently or collectively, exercised some territorial control over the Thracian coast. It is important to remember that this was the context in which the Vetren inscription was produced, since the text describes the types of interactions the Greek resident traders had with their Thracian hosts.

A passage from ps.-Aristotle, also quoted by the editors of the Vetren inscription, provides further evidence that the Thracian dynasts controlled their territories:[52]

Ἰφικράτης Ἀθηναῖος, Κότυος συναγαγόντος στρατιώτας, ἐπόρισεν αὐτῷ χρήματα τρόπον τοιοῦτον. ἐκέλευσε τῶν ἀνθρώπων ὧν ἦρχε προστάξαι κατασπεῖραι αὐτῷ γῆν τριῶν μεδίμνων. τούτου δὲ πραχθέντος συνελέγη σίτου πολὺ πλῆθος. καταγαγὼν οὖν ἐπὶ τὰ ἐμπόρια ἀπέδοτο, καὶ εὐπόρησε χρημάτων. (Ps.-Aristotle, *Economics* 1351a18–24.)

When Kotys was gathering soldiers, Iphikrates the Athenian provided him with money in the following way: he urged him to order the men he ruled to sow

Eastern Thrace, while Amadokos II minted coins that imitated coinage from Maroneia and ruled central Thrace. Although no coins of Berisades have been discovered, his successor Ketriporis probably ruled over western Thrace and minted coins modeled after Thasian ones (Youroukova 1976: 19–20).

[51] Bravo and A. S. Chankowski 1999: 303–5 have offered an alternative explanation for this phrase. They argue that the phrase has a parallel in Thucydides 2.97. This passage describes the taxes paid to the Odrysian kingdom by Greek and non-Greek cities, and it specifies that taxes are due not only to the Thracian dynast of the time (Seuthes) but also to high dignitaries and other members of the Odrysian nobility (καὶ οὐ μόνον αὐτῷ, ἀλλὰ καὶ τοῖς παραδυναστεύουσί τε καὶ γενναίοις Ὀδρυσῶν).

[52] Velkov and Domaradzka 1994: 10. The editors proposed that Kotys had granted land to some Greek *emporitai* and that he was responsible for supervising the agricultural production. J. E. Johnston 1998: 44 rightly notes that the text does not make this explicit.

three *medimnoi* of land for him. When this was done, a great amount of grain was collected. Then, taking it down to the coast to the emporia, he sold it and earned money.

Although the implication of this passage is that levying tithes was not something Kotys was accustomed to do, it nonetheless shows that he had control over a certain territory since he could force the people he ruled to turn their harvest over to him. Kotys subsequently took the harvest and sold it in some coastal emporia. Johnston located the emporia in this passage in the Chersonese, in view of the fact that Kotys had a strong influence in this area.[53] She then identified these emporia with Deris, Kobrys, and Kypasis, which she also equated with the ἐμπόρια Βέλανα Πρασέ[νων] (lines 24–5) mentioned on the Vetren inscription.[54] While ps.-Aristotle does not specify whether Kotys had power over these emporia, other evidence suggests that he did. According to Demosthenes, Kersobleptes, who ruled basically over the same territory as his father, did control several emporia located in this very region:

οὐκ ἔστιν ὅπως ποτὲ Κερσοβλέπτης αἱρήσεται Χερρόνησον ἀποστερεῖν ἐπιχειρῶν ἐχθρὸς ὑμῖν εἶναι· οὐδὲ γὰρ εἰ λάβοι καὶ κατάσχοι, λυσιτελήσειν αὐτῷ. ἐκ μὲν γ᾽ ἐκείνης οὐκ ἔστιν ὑπὲρ τριάκοντα τάλανθ᾽ ἡ πρόσοδος μὴ πολεμουμένης, εἰ πολεμήσεται δε, οὐδέν ἕν. ἐκ δὲ τῶν ἐμπορίων, ἃ τότ᾽ ἂν κλεισθείη, πλεῖν ἢ διακόσια τάλαντά ἐσθ᾽ ἡ πρόσοδος. (Demosthenes, *Against Aristokrates* 110)

It is inconceivable that Kersobleptes would ever deliberately attempt to be your enemy by trying to rob you of the Chersonese, because, even if he should take it and hold it, it will be of no use to him. Indeed, the revenue from that land, when it is not at war, is no more than thirty talents and when it is at war, not a single talent. On the other hand, the revenues from his emporia, which would be closed, are more than two hundred talents.

These coastal emporia must have been the same ones ps.-Aristotle mentions, namely Deris and Kobrys on the Melas Gulf,[55] given ps.-Skylax's connection of Deris and Kobrys with the Greek polis Kardia in the Chersonese that served as a base of operations (ὁρμητήριον) for Kersobleptes.[56] Although ps.-Aristotle does not indicate whether Kotys controlled the emporia, in all likelihood he had the same powers as his son, Kersobleptes. One of Kotys'

[53] J. E. Johnston 1998: 46.
[54] J. E. Johnston 1998: 24–30 argues that based on the common consonant shift between *b* and *m* Belana must be a regional adjective that describes the area in the Melas Gulf. She also identifies Deris, Kobrys, and Kypasis with the Belana emporia (45).
[55] J. E. Johnston 1998: 46.   [56] Ps.-Skylax, 67; Demosthenes, *Against Aristokrates* 181–2.

successors, therefore, must have controlled the Belana emporia mentioned on the inscription.

The inscription itself provides another example of Thracian territorial control when the Thracian authorities promise not to send *epaulistai* to the *emporitai* and neither to establish a garrison in Pistiros nor allow another to do so (lines 12–15): ἐπαυλιστὰς μὴ πέμπειν το|[ῖς] ἐμπορίταις· φρουρὴμ μηδεμίαν | εἰς Πίστιρον καταστῆσαι μήτε α|[ὸτ]ὸμ μήτε ἄλλωι ἐπιτρέπειν. While these lines do not necessarily imply that it is the Thracian kings who sent the *epaulistai* and the garrison, the meaning and use of the word *epaulistai* does suggest that they were specifically Thracian servicemen. There is also evidence to show that Thracian dynasts occasionally did set up garrisons in Greek poleis in Thrace.

The word ἐπαυλισταί occurs only on the Vetren inscription. The editors thought it described the inhabitants of an ἔπαυλις, which they understood as an unfortified place.[57] They argued that the word is linked etymologically to the root *αὐλ, designating a stable or a house. Various ancient authors, most notably Diodorus Siculus, used the word in this sense to indicate a house, stable, and a Roman villa where production of goods took place.[58] Avram, who examined the use of other words from the same root, has proposed the more likely interpretation of ἔπαυλις or ἐπαύλιον as a fortified site, thereby identifying ἐπαυλισταί as Thracian military servicemen who patrolled territories for a king.[59] Words related to ἐπαυλισταί almost always occur in relation to Thrace. The scholia to Apollonios of Rhodes explain ἐπαύλεις as Thracian homes that the Lemnians besieged.[60] Aeschylus says that the Acheloan cities on the Strymonian sea are next to the Thracian *epauleis*.[61] From these attestations it is not clear whether the word in question refers to fortified or unfortified places, although the context in both cases is military. Thucydides employs the verb ἐπαυλίζομαι for the encampment of military units,[62] and Polybius and some inscriptions use the word *epaulion* more specifically to designate a fortified site.[63] Hesychios also glosses ἔπαυλις as

---

[57] Velkov and Domaradzka 1994: 11.

[58] Bejor 1991: 266–8 discusses Diodorus Siculus' use of the word.

[59] Avram 1997–8: 43–4; Bravo and A. S. Chankowski 1999: 276 also attribute a military context to the word ἐπαυλισταί. V. Chankowski and Domaradzka 1999: 250 accepted this meaning.

[60] Scholia to Apollonios of Rhodes (ed. Wendel) on line 800: ἐπαύλους· τὰς οἰκίας τῶν Θρᾳκῶν ἐπόρθουν οἱ Λήμνιοι.

[61] Aeschylus, *Persians* 869–70: οἶαι Στρυμονίου πελάγους Ἀχελαΐδες εἰσὶ πάροικοι Θρηικίων ἐπαύλων.

[62] Thucydides 3.5 and 4.134.

[63] Polybius 4.4.1 and 16.15.5; *OGIS* 765 (line 13); Welles 1966: no. 3 (line 98); L. Robert 1970: 588–9; *IG* XIV 1284.

a stable for oxen, building, court, or military encampment.[64] One inscription from Paros records some hostile actions taken by Thracians against the Parians and Naxians, who, eventually, with the help of Athena, managed to defeat the Thracian *epaulia*, presumably fortified settlements.[65] The military connotations of the word would also better explain Aeschylus' text, probably inspired by the tragedian's participation in a military expedition against Thrace when he served in the Athenian army as a hoplite. The Thracian ἐπαύλεις he saw were worthy of note because they were military sites. Since the word *epaulistai* is connected specifically with Thracian fortified sites, it provides further evidence that it was the Thracian dynasts, and not Greek authorities, who had the power to send soldiers to places within their territories.

A passage from ps.-Aristotle, quoted also by Velkov and Domaradzka, demonstrates that Kotys had the additional power of setting up garrisons around Greek communities in Thrace:[66]

Κότυς Θρᾷξ παρὰ Πειρινθίων ἐδανείζετο χρήματα εἰς τὸ τοὺς στρατιώτας συναγαγεῖν. οἱ Πειρίνθιοι οὐκ ἐδίδοσαν αὐτῷ. ἠξίωσε οὖν αὐτοὺς ἄνδρας γε τῶν πολιτῶν φρουροὺς δοῦναι εἰς χωρία τινά, ἵνα τοῖς ἐκεῖ στρατιώταις νῦν φρουροῦσι σχῇ ἀποχρήσασθαι. οἱ δὲ τοῦτο ταχέως ἐποίησαν οἰόμενοι τῶν χωρίων κύριοι ἔσεσθαι. ὁ δὲ Κότυς τοὺς ἀποσταλέντας εἰς φυλακὴν ποιήσας τὰ χρήματα αὐτοὺς ἐκέλευσεν ἀποστείλαντας, ἃ ἐδανείζετο παρ' αὐτῶν, κομίσασθαι.

Ps.-Aristotle, *Economics* 1351a 24–32

Kotys the Thracian was borrowing money from the Peirinthians in order to collect soldiers. The Peirinthians did not give it to him. Therefore, he asked them to provide some men of the citizen body to serve as guards in certain fortified places, in order that he might use the soldiers who were now guarding these places. The Peirinthians did this quickly, thinking that they would become masters of these fortified places. Kotys, however, placed those who were sent under guard and ordered that they be sent back only when they brought money he wished to borrow from them.

This passage provides at least one instance when Kotys installed a garrison near a Greek polis, in this case Peirinthos. This is strong evidence that the ἐπαυλισταί and the φρουρή, mentioned in the Vetren inscription, were both Thracian institutions, further supporting the argument that the authors of the inscription were Thracian dynasts.

All the evidence considered so far, namely, the inscription recording the taxes Greek poleis on the North Aegean coast had to pay the three

---

[64] Hesychios s.v. ἔπαυλις: μάνδρα βοῶν· ἢ οἴκημα· ἢ αὐλή· ἢ στρατοπεδεία.
[65] *IG* XII, 5 445.   [66] Velkov and Domaradzka 1994: 10 and 12.

Thracian dynasts, the passage in ps.-Aristotle showing that Kotys collected the harvest produced by people he ruled, the passage in Demosthenes demonstrating Kersobleptes had revenues from certain emporia probably located on the Melas Gulf, the word *epaulistai*, connected with *epaulai*, often used for Thracian fortified sites, and the Thracian dynasts' power to set up garrisons near Greek communities, points strongly to the following conclusion. There is no need to look for an author other than the Thracian authorities, such as the island of Thasos, for the laws detailed on this inscription. Moreover, it is not necessary to assume that a single king ruled a unified Thrace in order to account for the legislation recorded on the Vetren inscription. Rather, the three Thracian dynasts in their totality exercised control over a large territory in Thrace that encompassed all the places mentioned on the Vetren inscription – Pistiros, Maroneia, and the Belana emporia – that describe a North Aegean trading network. As Greek coastal poleis in Thrace, these settlements represented the frontier between Thrace and various Greek colonies. The goal of the Thracian authorities in commissioning the Vetren text, therefore, was to delineate their relations with the resident Greek traders of Pistiros.[67] More specifically, as the host of several Greek trading communities, the Thracian authorities granted specific rights to traders so that they could operate within a tightly controlled environment. At the same time, these rights ensured that the Greek traders could continue their operations without any threat to their personal safety and possessions and with limited autonomy in their settlement. In Pistiros, a Greek settlement under Thracian control, Greeks from different poleis encountered one another and collectively dealt with the Thracians. Once again, the cross-cultural context provided by emporia necessitated the development of some forms of mediation among the different groups, and led to the formation, or expression, of different levels of collective identities. The inscription reveals how the Thracian hosts and the resident Greeks were each changed by their interactions.

Mediating Greco-Thracian relations

The Vetren text begins with an invocation to the god Dionysus (line 3): [. . . ὀμνύτ]ω τὸν Διόνυσογ. The reconstructed text suggests that the inscription actually records an oath sworn by the Thracian rulers. This

---

[67] Archibald 2000–1: 267 considers the text as a royal edict rather than a multilateral treaty between the community of Pistiros and the three Thracian dynasts. In fact, as the beneficiaries of the oath, the Greeks of Pistiros must have had some role in the production of the text.

might be expected, as it would be beneath a king to make an agreement with an entity of lesser status, such as Pistiros. Indeed, the inscription dating to 357/6 BC that records taxes the Greek cities of Thrace had to pay Kotys' successors also contains an oath.[68] In that case, the Greek cities of the Chersonese were said to be free and autonomous while they swore to be allies to both Athens and the three successors.

Dionysus is particularly appropriate as the deity by whom the Thracian kings and the Greek traders swear this oath because both groups worshipped him. Dionysus' veneration is well attested on Thasos, where he was the most prominent divinity along with Heracles,[69] and in the Thasian colonies in the *peraia*, such as Galepsos.[70] Other Greek cities in Thrace, like Maroneia, also venerated Dionysus.[71]

The common perception that Thracians worshipped Dionysus originates in Greek literary sources. Herodotus, for example, in his usual attempts to translate foreign divinities into Greek ones, says that the Thracians worshipped only Ares, Dionysus, and Artemis[72] and that the Thracian group Satrai had a temple dedicated to Dionysus.[73] Other Greek authors equated the cult of Sabazios, widely spread in Thrace,[74] with that of Dionysus by saying that the Thracians call Dionysus *Sabazios* and his priests *Saboi*.[75] Carried away by these ancient comments, scholars have even claimed that the worship of Dionysus first began in Thrace, whence it spread to Greece.[76] Others have questioned this opinion, since little evidence on Thracian cults survives.[77] Nonetheless, archaeological and epigraphic sources attest to the god's worship in Thrace. Early in the third century, the Thracian queen Berenike and her sons swore an oath to deliver a certain Epimenes from the temple of the Samothracian gods, to a man called Spartokos.[78] This inscription provides another instance in which Thracian rulers swear an oath, rather than drawing up an agreement with their subjects. This oath

[68] *IG* II² 126, line 17.   [69] Daux 1968: 816; Pouilloux 1954: 216–19, 344–50.

[70] Bon 1936: 172–4 discusses coins depicting Dionysus.

[71] Maroneian coins dating from the second half of the fifth century to the early fourth century depict vine-stock, grape-clusters, a thyrsus, and a vine growing out of Selinus' head. After 400 BC they depict the head of a young Dionysus. See May 1965: 27–8; A. B. West 1929: 10, 74, 116; Youroukova 1976: 14–15.

[72] Herodotus 5.7.   [73] Herodotus 7.111.   [74] Tacheva-Hitova 1983: 162–89.

[75] Scholia to Aristophanes, *Wasps* 9: Σαβάζιον δὲ τὸν Διόνυσον οἱ Θρᾷκες καλοῦσι, καὶ Σαβοὺς τοὺς ἱεροὺς αὐτοῦ. Diodorus Siculus 4.4.1 also claims that some Thracians used the name Sabazios for Dionysus.

[76] Dragan 1976: 142; Todorov 1987: 19–34.

[77] Archibald 1999. Nonetheless, representations of satyrs, who typically belong within the Dionysian circle, do exist from Thracian sites (Bouzek and Domaradzka 2010).

[78] *IGBulg* III.2, 1731.

was to be inscribed and set up in the temple of Dionysus in Seuthopolis, showing that Thracians worshipped this god.[79] Thus, as a divinity that both Thracians and Greeks recognized, Dionysus acted as a trans-cultural mediator between two different ethnic groups: Thracians and Greeks alike accepted him as a guarantor of the provisions of the Vetren text.

Mediating Greek affairs

The next few lines of the inscription regulate affairs among the *emporitai*, providing that whatever accusations any of the *emporitai* bring against one another were to be judged by the *syngeneis* (lines 4–7): ὅ τι ἂν δέ τις τῶν | [ἐμπ]οριτέων ἐπικαλῆι ὁ ἕτερος τ|[ῶι ἑ]τέρωι κρίνεσθαι αὐτοὺς ἐπὶ τ|[οῖς] συγγενέσι. Such regulations were vital for the smooth functioning of a trading settlement, especially when the population was heterogeneous, as in the case of Gravisca, Naukratis, and Peiraieus. According to the inscription, the *emporitai* of Pistiros were Apollonians, Thasians, and perhaps also Maroneians (lines 28–29 and 32–33).

Picard contended that the verb ἐπικαλέω was used specifically for demanding monetary restitution.[80] He also found a parallel between the provision on the Vetren text and a passage in ps.-Demosthenes in which ἐπικαλέω was used in a trial brought against a dead man whose heir inherited his position as a defendent in the trial (κληρονόμος). Similarly, should a trial be brought against a dead trader, his *syngeneis* (relatives) would replace him.[81] A closer look at the Vetren text reveals that the verb κρίνεσθαι should be taken together with the preposition ἐπί, which always means "to be judged by someone." The *syngeneis*, therefore, were not judged; they adjudicated these disputes.

The editors translated *syngeneis* as relatives.[82] Others proposed that they were from the same city as the *emporitai* involved in the disputes,[83] or that they were Ionians since the resident traders of Pistiros were all Ionians.[84] Avram offered "congénères" (congeners), the Latin cognate of συγγενέσι, as a more appropriate translation.[85] He argued that men were often forbidden from regulating the internal affairs of a foreign community located in their land and that the community itself adjudicated any trials that concerned its members only. Johnston proposed a similar reading for these lines: any disputes among the resident traders of Pistiros were to be judged in

[79] Elvers 1994.   [80] Picard 1999: 333.
[81] Demosthenes, *Against Kallippos* 17; Picard 1999: 334.   [82] Velkov and Domaradzka 1994: 4.
[83] Bravo and A. S. Chankowski 1999: 288.   [84] Salviat 1999: 262.   [85] Avram 1997–8: 39–40.

Pistiros by its inhabitants and, more specifically, by fellow merchants.[86] As several passages in Demosthenes suggest, Athens may have followed a similar practice, whereby arbitrators for the commercial courts were chosen from among other merchants.[87]

Although these interpretations are possible, I argue that the word *syngeneia* does not necessarily refer to an actual familial relationship among the traders, or to their classification as a group according to their profession, but rather to inter-poleis relations. *Syngeneia* was a term often used to describe relationships between poleis, especially in diplomatic documents of the Hellenistic period. Curty and Elwyn have both argued that the term was used only when there were grounds for claiming that the two poleis in question were related, either through a common mythological ancestry or through a mother-city/daughter-colony relation.[88] More recently, Lücke challenged these views, offering instead a more flexible definition that does not require real or fictitious claims to common descent between poleis but rather simply familiarity, correlation, or community between two political entities.[89] Poleis were often described as *syngeneis* in decrees that recognized *asylia* or *proxeny*, inaugurated games between cities, and, significantly for the discussion here, expressed gratitude to foreign judges.

Plutarch and Polybius both mention the employment of foreign judges.[90] The custom of inviting foreign judges was common even in earlier periods: there are several hundred diplomatic documents from the Hellenistic period, honoring foreign judges who arbitrated disputes.[91] In fact, more than twenty of these inscriptions called the poleis from which the judges came "*syngeneis* poleis."[92] Even more to the point, several sovereigns used foreign judges to officiate over affairs in other poleis.[93] For instance, Antigonos sent a tribunal from Magnesia to Kyme;[94] Philokles, king of Sidon, sent judges from Halikarnassos, Myndos, and Miletos to Samos;[95]

---

[86] J. E. Johnston 1998: 54–5 and n. 159.
[87] Demosthenes, *Against Lakritos* 43 and 46: these passages imply that the men judging the *emporikai dikai* are conversant with commercial matters. In *Against Dionysodoros* 16 Demosthenes suggests that the arbitrators were chosen from those commercially active in the Peiraieus and in *Against Zenothemis* 10 he expects the judges to recognize a group of men from Peiraieus, thereby implying that the judges were familiar with the port. See also E. Cohen 1973: 93–5.
[88] Curty 1995: xiii-xiv; Elwyn 1991.   [89] Lücke 2000: 26–7.
[90] Plutarch, *On Affection of Offspring* 1; Polybius 28.7.10.
[91] Daux 1970 and 1975; Helly 1971; Biscardi 1972; L. Robert 1989; Gauthier 1993, 1994, and 1999; Crowther 1993, 1994, 1995, 1997, and 1999; Ager 1997; Hamon 1999.
[92] For example, Curty 1995: nos. 19, 51, 57, 68, 77.
[93] The list here is not exhaustive: *OGIS* 44; *Tit. Calymnii* 17; *IG* XII 5, 1065; *SEG* 14, 543; *IG* XI 4, 1052; *SEG* 19, 569; *IPriene* 24; *SEG* 1, 363; *SIG*³, 426; Crowther 1993; Gauthier 1994.
[94] *OGIS* 7.   [95] *SEG* 1, 363.

Antiochos Soter sent a judge from Teos to Bargylia in Caria.[96] These foreign judges were an easy way for foreign royals to adjudicate affairs in subjugated cities without violating the cities' autonomy since it was other Greeks who would judge trials and not foreign sovereigns. The Vetren text suggests that the Thracian dynasts followed this practice of delegating the right to judge disputes among the Greek traders to official judges from *syngeneis* poleis. The *syngeneis* of the Vetren text, therefore, were probably official judges from Pistiros' *syngeneis* poleis. The institution of foreign judges must have been particularly useful for communities such as Pistiros whose ethnic make-up was not homogeneous. On the one hand, the deployment of foreign judges was a compromise that mediated between the two ethnic groups, in this case the Thracian rulers and the subject Greeks. On the other hand, since Greek traders living in emporia often came from different poleis, an institution like that of the foreign judges could act as a regulator of interactions among Greeks. While the Thracians seemed to have identified the Greeks as a collective by calling on other Greeks to help solve the disputes, they also recognized the multiplicity of civic identities among the Greeks living in Pistiros. At the same time, therefore, that they defined the Greeks as a collective they also treated them as a multicultural collective. Just as in the case of Naukratis, the Greeks of Pistiros might also have internalized the Thracian perspective and expressed a Greek identity vis-à-vis the Thracian authorities on whom they were dependent, while also maintaining their civic identities vis-à-vis other Greeks.

Thracian guarantees to Pistiros and its residents

While this first provision deals exclusively with the affairs of the *emporitai* themselves, the next one addresses the relations between the *emporitai* and the Thracians (lines 7–10): ὅσα ὀφείλετα[ι] | τοῖς ἐμπορίταις παρὰ τοῖς Θραιξ|[ί]ν, τούτων χρεῶν ἀποκοπὰς μὴ | ποιεῖγ· (there will be no cancellation of debts on however much is owed by the Thracians to the *emporitai*). Scholars have debated whether Thracians owed the *emporitai* or vice versa. The editors thought the *emporitai* owed the Thracians and translated the text accordingly: "and with respect to such things as are owed by the *emporitai* at [*sic*] the Thracians, no cancellation of debts is to be made."[97] In the translation of this passage into French for publication, Lefèvre preserved this meaning ("et en ce qui concerne les dettes des emporitains envers les

---

[96] *SIG*³ 426. [97] Velkov and Domaradzka 1996: 207.

Thraces, qu'il n'y ait aucune annulation de ces dettes"),[98] while noting that the preposition παρά could also indicate that the Thracians owed debts to the *emporitai*.[99] Avram provided another example in which the preposition παρά was used to introduce the debtor,[100] and argued that this provision should be read in the context of the whole inscription, which records only concessions the Thracians made to the Greeks rather than the other way round.[101] Domaradzka has since accepted the reading that Thracians had debts they owed to the *emporitai*, and that these debts were not cancelled.[102]

The use of the ethnic *Thracians* (Θραιξίν), rather than the specific intra-Thracian group, probably reflects Greek perceptions rather than Thracian ones. Although Greeks knew several Thracian groups – Saians, Paitoi, Kikones, Bistones, Sapaioi, Dersaioi, Edonoi, Satrai, etc.[103] – it seems that in the particular case of Pistiros, the Greeks did not distinguish among the Thracian groups, perhaps because they were under the dominion of a single ruler. Similarly, Egyptians did not differentiate among Greeks, even though they came from a variety of poleis, lumping them together in Naukratis and other settlements, such as Stratopeda. The parallel between Naukratis and Pistiros may be drawn further. As I suggested in the previous chapter, the traders of Naukratis internalized the way the Egyptians perceived them as Greeks and expressed this perception in the foundation of a temple dedicated to the gods of the Hellenes, the Hellenion. In Pistiros, it is the Thracian dynasts who assumed Greek perceptions calling themselves Thracians, while distinguishing among the Greek *emporitai*, who are subdivided into Maroneians, Apollonians, and Thasians. This should not be surprising given that the oath on the inscription had to be comprehensible to the Greeks. In many ways it was tailored for Greeks: it was written in Greek; the measures put in place protected Greek traders; finally, the name of the divinity by whom the oath is sworn was Greek. The adoption of a group's perceptions, especially in the context of emporia, which facilitated interactions among different ethnic groups, is a sign of inter-ethnic mediation. Such adoptions must have been vital both in creating a mutually intelligible world for all parties involved and in expressing collective identities.

One of the difficulties in establishing trading settlements in a foreign land was to ensure legal protection not only for the personal safety of the

---

[98] Velkov and Domaradzka 1994: 4.
[99] Translator's note in Velkov and Domaradzka 1994: 4.
[100] *IScM* I no. 9, line 5–6: ὀφειλομ[ένου α]ὐτῶι πα[ρ]ὰ τῆι πόλει δαν[είου πα]τρικοῦ (an ancestral debt owed to them by the polis).
[101] Avram 1997–8: 39.   [102] V. Chankowski and Domaradzka 1999: 250.
[103] Archilochus fr. 5 (ed. M. L. West); Herodotus 7.110.

residents and the integrity of their possessions, but also for the safety of the
trading settlement itself.[104] The next few provisions of the text guarantee
such rights to the traders and the town of Pistiros. The first one protects
the traders' property by assuring that however much arable land and pasture
the *emporitai* have will not be taken away (lines 10–12): γῆγ καὶ βοσκὴν
ὅσην ἔχουσ|ιν ἐμπορῖται, ταθτα μὴ ἀφαιρεῖ|[σθ]αι. Since the Thracian king
Kotys, and probably his successors, had the power to exact tithes from his
subjects,[105] as mentioned above, it was necessary that the Greeks living in this
emporion had legal guarantees for their property rights. This concession to
the resident traders suggests that the *emporitai* not only resided in Pistiros
but also owned land and animals (βοσκή). In turn, this implies that the
residents of Pistiros were self-sufficient in terms of their food production,
suggesting that Pistiros enjoyed some degree of autonomy.[106]

The next two concessions grant autonomy not only to the *emporitai* but
also to the polity of Pistiros by guaranteeing that none of the Thracian
dynasts would send any *epaulistai* to the *emporitai*, would not establish a
garrison in Pistiros, or allow another to do so (lines 12–15): ἐπαυλιστὰς μὴ
πέμπειν το|[ῖς] ἐμπορίταις· φρουρὴμ μηδεμίαν | εἰς Πίστιρον καταστῆσαι
μήτε α|[ὸτ]ὸμ μήτε ἄλλωι ἐπιτρέπειν. The case of Peirinthos, discussed
above, demonstrated that Thracian rulers had the power to post garrisons
in Greek poleis.[107] Moreover, the *epaulistai*, as I have argued, were Thracian
soldiers. By promising not to station any garrison in Pistiros and not to send
any soldiers to the *emporitai*, the Thracian rulers in effect granted extra-
territoriality and some independence to Pistiros and the resident traders.

The Thracian dynasts also offered personal guarantees to the resident
traders and inhabitants of Pistiros by promising not to seize hostages from
among the Pistirenoi or allow another to do so (lines 16–17): [ὁμ]ήρους
Πιστιρηνῶμ μὴ λαμ|[βάν]ειμ μηδὲ ἄλλωι ἐπιτρέπειν. *Pistirenoi* is probably
the city-ethnic derived from Pistiros.[108] The city-ethnic strongly suggests
that the entity of Pistiros had a political character and that it was considered
as a polis, even if it was under the dominion of the Odrysian dynasty.
The fragmentary nature of the inscription renders the reading of these
lines somewhat tentative. Bravo helped the editors reconstruct some of
the missing letters at the most crucial points. More specifically, Bravo first

---

[104] In some societies trading settlements paid protection costs to the host country, both directly
and in the form of taxes: Curtin 1984: 41–5.
[105] Ps.-Aristotle, *Economics* 1351a18–24.
[106] For a much earlier parallel, see Stein 2002: 50–51, 55, 58.
[107] Ps.-Aristotle, *Economics* 1351a24–32.
[108] Stephanos of Byzantion s.v. Pistiros mentions another city-ethnic derived from Pistiros,
namely, Pistirites.

suggested the reading ἀλλ[άσσ]ειμ (to alter) instead of λαμ[βάν]ειμ to the editors, which led them to propose that the first word on line 16 was [κλ]ήρους: "he will not alter the plots of the Pistirenoi or allow another to do so."[109] Upon reexamining the stone Bravo noticed that the first three letters of the verb (line 16) are clearly ΛΑΜ and consequently restored it to λαμ[βάν]ειμ. He then changed [κλ]ήρους to [όμ]ήρους.[110] The Thracian rulers, therefore, promise not to take any hostages from Pistiros, an action that lay within their powers, as ps.-Aristotle shows when he narrates how Kotys took hostages from Peirinthos in time of war.[111] With this concession, Kotys' successors in effect guaranteed inviolability to the community of Pistiros.

The next clause is fragmentary (lines 18–20): [τὰ] τῶν ἐμπορίτέωμ μὴ [ἀ]φαιρεῖ|[σθ]αι μήτε αὐτὸμ μήτ[ε το]ὺς ἑ|[αυτ]οῦ (neither he, nor his own, will seize the possessions of the *emporitai*). Loukopoulou suggested the alternative reconstruction of [γῆν] instead of [τὰ] (neither he, nor his own, will seize the land of the *emporitai*).[112] However, this alternative reading would lead to a repetition almost word for word of lines 10–12 (γῆν καὶ βοσκὴν ὅσην ἔχουσιν ἐμπορίται, ταῦτα μὴ ἀφαιρεῖσθαι). There is no point in guaranteeing the same right of land inalienability twice. Moreover, τά is not too vague as Loukopoulou claims, but rather simply indicates that it was the possessions of the *emporitai* that had to be protected.

These guarantees recognize both the political identity of the settlement as a whole and the professional identity of the traders in particular. On the one hand, granting independence to the community of Pistiros through the pledge of neither taking any hostages nor stationing a garrison in the city ensured that the city was autonomous. On the other hand, giving autonomy to the *emporitai* by the promise not to send any soldiers to them enabled the resident traders to continue their commercial operations uninhibited. The repeated assurances that the author of the inscription would not allow anyone else to send *epaulistai* or a garrison to the Greeks suggests that the settlement was in a contested area. Perhaps the three successors who fought among themselves for control of the Odrysian kingdom also quarreled over Pistiros. After all, as an emporion, Pistiros must have been a lucrative possession. By granting a certain degree of autonomy to Pistiros, the Thracian dynasts did not relinquish all the profits they stood to make

---

[109] Velkov and Domaradzka 1994: 4, n. 4.
[110] Bravo and A. S. Chankowski 1999: 277. Domaradzka accepted this restitution in V. Chankowski and Domaradzka 1999: 248 and 250, as did Loukopoulou 1999: 360.
[111] Ps.-Aristotle, *Economics* 1351a 24–32.   [112] Loukopoulou 1999: 360.

from this emporion. Even if Pistiros had the freedom to conduct its commercial affairs as it wished, the Thracian authorities still had to gain from it, probably from exacting various forms of import, export, or sales taxes, as I discuss next.

Facilitating commerce

So far, the concessions address issues of administering justice among the *emporitai*, securing independence for both the resident traders and the other inhabitants of Pistiros vis-à-vis the Thracian authorities, and guaranteeing the property rights of the *emporitai*.[113] The next provisions concern the mechanisms that enabled commercial exchanges (lines 20–7): τέλεα κατὰ τὰς ὁδοὺς | μὴ πρήσσειν, ὅσα εἰς Μαρώνεια[ν] | [εἰσ]άγεται ἐκ Πιστίρου ἢ ἐκ τῶν ἐ|[μ]πορίων ἢ 'γ Μαρωνείης εἰς Πίστ||ιρ]ον ἢ τὰ ἐμπόρια Βελανα Πρασε||[.ω]ν· τοὺς ἐμπορίτας τὰς ΑΠΑΞ||[–2–3–] καὶ ἀνοίγειν καὶ κλείειν· ἅμα | [καθ]άπερ καὶ ἐπὶ Κότυος· (dues will not be levied along the roads on however much is brought to Maroneia from Pistiros or from the emporia, or from Maroneia to Pistiros or to the Belana emporia of the Prasenoi; the *emporitai* are to open and close their [?], just as in the time of Kotys).

These clauses have been emended and punctuated variously, by many scholars. Before discussing the proposed readings, it is important to note that these clauses describe coastal routes and to identify the various emporia named here. First, the word ὁδός is often used to describe traveling or journeying not only by land but also by sea. Second, Pistiros and Maroneia both lay on the North Aegean coast.[114] What about the other named and unnamed emporia mentioned in the text? Although the former are more difficult to locate because there is no other attestation of the words Belana or Prasenoi, the ethnic the editors reconstructed for Πρασε[.ω]ν, scholars have put forth several propositions. The editors of the inscription suggested that the word Prasenoi must be related to the Prasias Lake in the Belasitsa Mountains, mentioned by Herodotus, and that, therefore, the emporia of the Prasenoi must be located near there.[115] This identification is hard to maintain since transporting merchandise on mountain roads would be extremely difficult and costly. Bravo has argued that Prase[..]n is not a

---

[113] This section is reproduced by permission of *L'Antiquité classique* from Demetriou 2010a: 85–9.
[114] For Pistiros see Bravo and A. S. Chankowski 1999 and Demetriou 2010a. For the location of Maroneia see Saba in press.
[115] Velkov and Domaradzka, 1994: 12; Boshnakov 1999: 325; Salviat 1999: 265–6.

genitive plural noun but an accusative one, and hence that the text refers to two emporia, Belana, and Prase[..]n, which he did not attempt to locate.[116] Loukopoulou went so far as to deny that *Belana* is a toponym, arguing instead that the text should be reconstructed as the verb ἀναπράσ[σει]ν (retail dealing), and that the letters ΒΕΛ were a scribal error.[117]

The best resolution of this clause is that put forth by Johnston: she argues that *Belana* is a Thracian gloss of the Greek *Melana* and thus locates these emporia on the Melas Gulf.[118] This is an ingenious argument based on the common consonant mutation in Thracian from an *m* to a *b*. The word *Belana*, therefore, would be a regional adjective that describes the Melas Gulf, an area at the crossroads of ancient trade routes, accessible through the coastal routes of North Aegean Thrace, that connected Thrace, the Black Sea, the Aegean, and the Asian continent. Not only does Johnston place the Belana emporia of the Prasenoi in this area, she also proceeds to identify them with specific sites known as emporia in antiquity, namely, Kobrys, Kypasis, and Deris.[119] This identification has the merit of keeping the routes described in the inscription along the North Aegean coast, a simpler and more plausible solution than any other proposed thus far.

The nameless emporia should also be identified as the Belana emporia. The clause describes a route that ran from Pistiros all the way to the Melas Gulf. More specifically, one road ran west from Maroneia to Pistiros, and the other ran east from Maroneia to the Belana emporia. Everything that was imported from Pistiros to Maroneia and exported from Maroneia to Pistiros was tax exempt, as was everything exported from Maroneia to the Belana emporia, and imported from the nameless emporia to Maroneia. The nameless emporia must surely be the Belana emporia.

Lines 20–27, quoted above, are particularly hard to interpret, and none of the readings that have been proposed provides an entirely satisfactory solution. The first edition of the inscription gave a French translation of this passage, which does not follow the Greek text: "qu'on ne perçoive pas des taxes sur les routes menant de Pistiros ou des emporia à Maronée, de Maronée à Pistiros ou aux emporia de Belana de Prasenoi; que les emporitains ouvrent et ferment les chariots; comme du temps de Kotys, [que soit en usage le serment]."[120] Avram rightly criticized this translation, which mistranslates εἰσάγεται as "menant" and makes ὁδούς rather than ὅσα the object of this verb.[121] Perhaps the problem lies in the fact that the editors of the inscription wrote their paper in English, which was later

---

[116] Bravo and A. S. Chankowski 1999: 277.   [117] Loukopoulou 1999: 361.
[118] J. E. Johnston 1998: 24–30.   [119] Ps.-Skylax 67.
[120] Velkov and Domaradzka 1994: 5.   [121] Avram 1997–8: 40–1.

translated into French. The English translation the editors gave is certainly a lot closer to the Greek despite its awkward grammar, though Avram claims that it is not much better: "No dues shall be levied on the goods which are imported to Maroneia from Pistiros or from the emporia, or from Maroneia to Pistiros and the emporia Belana of the Prasenoi. The *emporitai* the wagons to open and close. At the same time valid is as in Kotys' time [*sic*]."[122] Avram instead followed the editors who reconstructed ΑΠΑΞ[−] to ἁμάξ[ας][123] and punctuated this passage differently at two separate places, resulting in an alternate interpretation: he changed the comma in line 21 to a semicolon and removed the semicolon in line 26. His reconstruction and translation reads: τέλεα κατὰ τὰς ὁδοὺς | μὴ πρήσσειν· ὅσα εἰς Μαρώνεια[ν] | [εἰσ]άγεται ἐκ Πιστίρου ἢ ἐκ τῶν ἐ|[μ]πορίων ἢ γ Μαρωνείης εἰς Πίστ|[ιρ]ον ἢ τὰ ἐμπόρια Βελανα Πρασε|[νω]ν· τοὺς ἐμπορίτας τὰς ἁμάξ|[ας] καὶ ἀνοίγειν καὶ κλείειν ἅμα | [καθ]άπερ καὶ ἐπὶ Κοτυος· (dues along the roads will not be exacted; the *emporitai* may open and close their [wagons], just as in the time of Kotys, on whatever is imported to Maroneia from Pistiros or the emporia, from Maroneia to Pistiros or to the Belana emporia of the Prasenoi).[124] There are a few problems with this reading of lines 20–27. First, the removal of the semicolon after κλείειν is unjustified since punctuation marks before ἅμα and after Κότυος are visible on the inscription.[125] The punctuation marks indicate that this phrase introduces the oath that follows line 27 and not that it concludes the section that precedes it, as Avram's reconstruction suggests. Further, the change of the comma after πρήσσειν to a semicolon results in the creation of two distinct provisions: that all taxes on all roads are abolished and that the traders are allowed to open and close their

---

[122] Velkov and Domaradzka 1996: 207.

[123] Velkov and Domaradzka 1994: 4 explain that the emendation ἁμαξας rather than ΑΠΑΞ[−] was proposed by M. Hatzopoulos. The very first appearance of the text (Domaradzka in Domaradzki 1993: 56) had ἁμάξ- instead of ΑΠΑΞ despite the fact that the letter on the inscription is clearly a π. See also Domaradzka 2002b: 342, who maintains that ἁπαξ[−] was a mistake made by the stone cutter. This emendation is discussed below.

[124] Avram 1997–8: 40–1.

[125] Domaradzka in the appendix to Domaradzki 1993: 57 states that there are punctuation marks before ἅμα and after Κότυς in lines 26–7, a claim that she makes again in Velkov and Domaradzka 1994: 4. However, already in the same paper, Lefèvre, who translated the passage from English to French, asked whether a different punctuation might be better. What is at stake here is whether the phrase ἅμα καθάπερ καὶ ἐπὶ Κότυος concludes the preceding section of the inscription or whether it introduces the oath that follows. Velkov and Domaradzka 1994: 5 attached it to the oath that follows the phrase, whereas Gauthier 1995, 432 saw it as a conclusion of the provisions that precede it. Bravo in Bravo and A. S. Chankowski 1999: 277–8 notes that the word ἅμα should indicate that at the same time as the successors of Kotys granted the *emporitai* and the Greeks of Pistiros the various privileges recorded on the inscription up to this point (line 27), they also reiterated the provisions included in the oath following line 27, which had originally been granted by Kotys I.

wagons on the specified routes to and from Maroneia, Pistiros, and the other emporia. Abolishing all taxes on all roads is an unusual grant, given that usually authorities controlling emporia benefited most concretely from taxes on imports and exports, and the emendation of ΑΠΑΞ to ἀμάξας is a questionable one, as I argue next. For these reasons it is better to follow the punctuation visible on the inscription.

Part of the problem in understanding this passage is the widely accepted emendation of ΑΠΑΞ[..] to ἀμάξας.[126] Loukopoulou, noting that the inland site identified as Pistiros lies on the river Hebros and thus that transport was by water, doubted that merchandise was ever transported on wagons. She also questioned whether the right of opening and closing wagons for inspection was important enough to be recorded on the inscription. She proposed, instead, the following reconstruction, which contains three different rights granted to the traders (and not two, as do most other readings of these clauses): τέλεα κατὰ τὰς ὁδοὺς | μὴ πρήσσειν, ὅσα εἰς Μαρώνεια[ν] | [εἰσ]άγεται ἐκ Πιστίρου ἢ ἐκ τῶν ἐ|[μ]πορίων ἢ 'γ Μαρωνείης εἰς Πίστ|[ιρ]ον ἢ τὰ ἐμπόρια (Βελ) αναπράσ||[σει]ν τοὺς ἐμπορίτας (τας) ἀπαξ[άπ|αν] καὶ ἀνοίγειν καὶ κλείειν ἅμα, | [καθ]άπερ καὶ ἐπὶ Κότυος.[127] This reading, for Loukopoulou, implies that dues should not be exacted on the specified roads, that the traders have the right to protest against taxes that they thought they paid unduly, and that the opening and closing of markets should follow the regulations instituted under Kotys. This would be a very condensed way of rendering the various grants that Loukopoulou wishes to see in these clauses. Moreover, as I have noted above, this restoration is unsatisfactory since it ignores the three letters "ΒΕΛ." It also disregards the punctuation before ἅμα visible on the inscription, assumes that the scribe duplicated erroneously the last three letters of the word ἐμπορίτας, and that, contrary to what the editors claim, there are not two, but four letters missing on the stone.[128]

Still, there is a twofold merit in contesting the reading ἀμάξας, even though I cannot offer a satisfactory reading of the letters on the stone (ΑΠΑΞ[–]). First, there is no parallel in Greek texts or documents for opening and closing wagons. There are, however, several instances of closing emporia.[129] Demosthenes, for example, mentions some emporia on the

[126] Hatzopoulos suggested this emendation (Velkov and Domaradzka 1994: 4 n. 5).
[127] Loukopoulou 1999: 361–3.
[128] Velkov and Domaradzka 1994: 4 claim that there are only two letters missing at the beginning of line 26 but no letters missing at the end of line 25.
[129] See also Loukopoulou 1999: 362 n. 14 who claims that there are instances of opening emporia, but this is not attested anywhere in the extant Greek literature or inscriptions.

Chersonese that lay within the jurisdiction of Kersobleptes. These emporia would normally bring in the significant revenue of more than two hundred talents.[130] Demosthenes uses this expression elsewhere when he says that the Athenians would close Philip's emporia if he marched against Attica.[131] Lysias also refers to closing emporia in a list of terrible things that happen to Athenians in wartime, such as the loss of ships in the Black Sea, the capture of ships by Spartans, and the breaking of a truce.[132] In all three instances the emporia close in time of war. Even though there are no attestations of opening (ἀνοίγω) emporia, it seems more likely that the inscription refers to opening and closing emporia rather than opening and closing wagons. Second, as I have argued, these were all coastal routes and transport was carried out by boats, rather than by any other means, and certainly not by wagons. The provision, therefore, probably controlled the timing of selling rather than the goods sold.

The itinerant traders of the inscription were given tremendous freedom to carry out their commercial operations along the route that ran from Pistiros on the North Aegean coast through Maroneia to the Belana emporia on the Melas Gulf. Even more impressive is the fact that each of these sites was technically in territory controlled by a different successor, as discussed above. The grant of tax exemption, therefore, should be interpreted as a multilateral agreement, binding for all three of Kotys' successors. Each of the Thracian dynasts agreed to allow traders to travel along the North Aegean coast, crossing frontiers while they did so, without having to pay taxes on any of these roads in any of the successors' territories. The same is true for the concession that allowed the *emporitai* to open and close emporia. The *emporitai* were in control of the commercial operations and were not subject to taxation by the Thracians on these specific roads.

"Just as in the time of Kotys": oaths of the Thracian dynasts

The language of the inscription changes at this point. While all the provisions discussed so far use an accusative and infinitive construction, the rest of the text is in the first person. This change signifies that the

---

[130] Demosthenes, *Against Aristokrates* 110: ἐκ δὲ τῶν ἐμπορίων, ἃ τότ' ἂν κλεισθείη, πλεῖν ἢ διακόσια τάλαντά ἐσθ' ἡ πρόσοδος.

[131] Demosthenes, *On the False Embassy* 153: εἰ μὴ τὰ δίκαια ποιοίη, κλείσειν τὰ ἐμπόρια.

[132] Lysias, *Against the Corn Dealers* 14: ἢ τὰς ναῦς διεφθάρθαι τὰς ἐν τῷ Πόντῳ, ἢ ὑπὸ Λακεδαιμονίων ἐκπλεούσας συνειλῆφθαι, ἢ τὰ ἐμπόρια κεκλῆσθαι.

inscription preserves two different texts: the first is an agreement between the new Thracian dynasts and the Greek *emporitai*, and the second is a separate oath introduced by the phrase "just as in the time of Kotys."[133] The change in language mirrors a change in the content of the last two provisions. Whereas the concessions granted by the accusative and infinitive construction concern Pistiros as a community and the *emporitai* as a group of professionals, the next part, written in first person, is a personal promise not to harm or strip of his property any person, further described as a Maroneian, Thasian, or Apollonian living in Pistiros (lines 27–38): ἄνδρα Μ|[αρω]νίτην οὐ δήσω οὐδὲ ἀποκτ|[ενέ]ω οὐδὲ ἀφαιρήσομαι χρήμα|[τα] οὔτε ζῶντος οὔτε ἀποθανόν|[τος] οὔτε αὐτὸς οὔτε τῶν ἐμῶν | [οὐ]δείς· οὐδὲ Ἀπολλωνιητέων, οὐδ|[ὲ Θ]ασίων, ὅσοι ἐμ Πιστίρωι εἰσί[ν], | [οὔ]τε ἀποκτενέω οὐδένα, οὔτε | [δήσω] οὔτε ἀφαιρήσομαι χρήμα|[τα οὔ]τε ζῶντος οὔτε ἀποθανό|[ντος οὔτε] αὐτὸς οὔτε τῶν ἐμῶν [οὐδεὶς]. These provisions guarantee personal inviolability and security of property for persons from Maroneia, Apollonia, and Thasos. The almost verbatim repetition in these two clauses has led some scholars to assume that Maroneians also resided in Pistiros.[134] However, as others have responded, the text does not anywhere describe Maroneians as residents of Pistiros.[135] In fact, this part of the inscription might be an agreement between the two Thracian dynasts who controlled the territories in which Maroneia and Pistiros were located, with the ultimate purpose of enabling commercial operations. Thus, Amadokos II might be the person who swore the first part of the oath (lines 27–32), while Berisades swore the second half of this oath (lines 32–8).

Even if no Maroneians were present in Pistiros, it is clear from the second part of the oath, that Thasians and Apollonians were resident traders in Pistiros. The Apollonians are difficult to identify more precisely since there were forty-three cities named Apollonia in antiquity.[136] The editors of the inscription identified it plausibly with a coastal site between the Nestos and Strymon Rivers,[137] within the geographical range described in the Vetren text. The specification that the Thracian dynast should guarantee the inviolability of the Thasians and Apollonians living in Pistiros leads to the question of whether there were other Greeks, from other poleis, living

---

[133] Bravo and A. S. Chankowski 1999: 278.
[134] Velkov and Domaradzka 1994: 10; Hansen 2006a: 22.
[135] Avram 1997–8: 41 n.10; Salviat 1999: 260–1; Bravo and A. S. Chankowski 1999: 284; Loukopoulou 1999: 363.
[136] Shachar 2000: 4 admits that he may have included duplicates in his count.
[137] Strabo 7.31.3; Velkov and Domaradzka 1994: 12.

there. Were these privileges given only to these specific Greeks but not to others? Or were these poleis the only ones that furnished Pistiros' population? Unfortunately, in the absence of any other evidence, either epigraphic or archaeological, no clear answer can be given to these questions. In any case, it is important to note again that the Thracian rulers were able to distinguish among the Greek groups inhabiting Pistiros, possibly a reflection of Greek perceptions.

Maroneia, lying at the center of the duty-free trade routes, found its way into the first clause of these guarantees of personal inviolability and inalienability of property. The provisions of the Vetren text, therefore, privilege Maroneia in addition to Pistiros. It may have been the city's special relationship with the Odrysian kings in the fourth century that elicited such attention. Before then, Homer described how Maroneia, then called Ismaros, famous for its riches and excellent wine, fell prey to Greeks who plundered it during their return homeward.[138] Archilochus also mentions the Ismarian wine: ἐν δορὶ μέν μοι μᾶζα μεμαγμένη, ἐν δορὶ δ' οἶνος Ἰσ-μαρικός· πίνω δ' ἐν δορὶ κεκλιμένος.[139] Although Maroneia was known for its resources at this early period, when it started minting its own coins, in the sixth century, it did so at a slower pace than other Greek cities in Thrace like Dikaia and Abdera, but it gradually gained speed.[140] The sharp increase in coin production in the last third of the fifth century, combined with an increase in the tribute Maroneia paid to Athens from 436/5 to 433/2 BC, suggests that Maroneia at this time enjoyed a period of prosperity[141] that coincided with the rise of the Odrysian dynasts in Thrace. Indeed, the city seems to have had good relations with these Thracian rulers: two Odrysian kings, Metokos – who may be the same as Amadokos II – and Teres, either minted their coins at Maroneia or adopted Maroneian coin-types.[142] This relationship between Maroneia and the Odrysian dynasts may have contributed to the city's privileged position in the text.

There are nine more lines on the stone, but only a few letters can be read in each one, since the left side of the inscription breaks off after the grants of personal inviolability and inalienability of property. At the end of line 39 the letters ἔμπορ- can be read, which perhaps stand for either ἔμπορος, ἐμπορίτης, or ἐμποριάρχης as has been proposed.[143] Line 42 ends with ἀδικῆι τὸ-, indicating that the text continued with more provisions of legal recourse for a party, perhaps the *emporitai*.

---

[138] Homer, *Odyssey* 9.40.   [139] Archilochus fr. 2 (ed. M. L. West).
[140] May 1965: 29–30.   [141] A. B. West 1929: 56–8; May 1968: 151 n. 3.
[142] A. B. West 1929: 125–37; Youroukova 1976: 8, 15–16.
[143] Velkov and Domaradzka 1994: 12.

A last point of interest is the end of line 38: "[εἰ δέ τις] τῶν οἰκητόρων" (if anyone of the settlers). Hansen understood the word οἰκήτορες in contrast to the word ἐμπορῖται, on the assumption that the οἰκήτορες were indigenous Thracians and living alongside the resident Greek traders.[144] There is no reason, however, for this presumption. On the contrary, there is evidence to suggest that the οἰκήτορες were Greek. The word indicates more than just the inhabitants of a place; it often describes settlers sent with the intention of residing somewhere. Thucydides and Herodotus, for example, both use this term to describe groups of people who settle in foreign lands. Herodotus says that King Sostratos left a part of his army behind at the River Phasis as settlers,[145] and Thucydides often talks about cities sending settlers to conquered lands.[146] It is also clear that οἰκήτορες are not founders: Thucydides says that the Athenians first sent colonists (ἔποικοι) to Aigina, shortly followed by settlers (οἰκήτορες).[147] Indeed, in all the examples given here, the meaning of the word οἰκήτωρ approximates the Latin *colonus*, a veteran who settled in conquered cities. The οἰκήτορες of Pistiros, therefore, were not Thracians but rather Greek settlers. Since this concession follows one guaranteeing the personal safety of Maroneians and the resident traders of Pistiros, it may have granted similar rights to the settlers (οἰκήτορες) against any who might harm them, as the verb ἀδικῆι (line 42) suggests.

In sum, the Thracians left the administration of justice among the *emporitai* to the Greeks, promised autonomy to the community of Pistiros, granted tax exemptions to facilitate trade, and also conceded personal inviolability to the residents of Pistiros and of Maroneia. This must have had two effects. On the one hand, it guaranteed that Pistiros and Maroneia continued to function both as poleis and emporia since their populations and property were left intact. On the other hand, the Thasians, Apollonians, and Maroneians who traveled for trade, perhaps on the routes specified in previous provisions, were protected. It is also interesting to note that the Thracians guarantee the inalienability of the property of Maroneians, Thasians, and Apollonians, whether they are dead or alive. Since the *emporitai* were resident traders, it is likely that they had their families living with them and that their children were the legal heirs of their property. Or, perhaps traders' property was inheritable by other traders. Unfortunately, no laws from

---

[144] Hansen 1997: 90–1.   [145] Herodotus 2.103.
[146] Thucydides 1.103: the Athenians send ten thousand to settle at a place then called Ennea Hodoi, later Amphipolis; 3.92: the Lacedaemonians send out inhabitants of Sparta and its perioikoi to settle in Heraklea in Trachis; 4.49: The Akarnanians send settlers to Anaktorion.
[147] Thucydides 2.27.

other emporia survive regarding the inheritance rights of traders abroad to clarify these concessions. What is clear is that the concessions described in the Vetren text are meant to be permanent: they protected the traders in the past, are reiterated in the present, and will be in effect for future generations.

Conclusion

The fortuitous discovery of the Vetren inscription has shed light on the relations between two different ethnic groups, Greeks and Thracians, in the late classical period, and more particularly on how a state regulated a multiethnic population. In 359 BC, when King Kotys I was assassinated, the Odrysian kingdom of Thrace fell into disarray. Kotys' three successors fought over control of the kingdom and eventually, with Athens' help, divided the territory into three different parts: Kersobleptes ruled over eastern Thrace, Amadokos II controlled central Thrace, and Berisades, about whom almost nothing is known, had power over western Thrace. This tripartite division had significant implications for the Greeks living and trading in Thrace: the degree of autonomy of Greek cities had to be clarified; the rights of traders and other inhabitants of the communities were renegotiated; finally, commercial operations carried out by the Greeks had to be facilitated. This was the context in which the Vetren inscription was produced. It attempted to organize the Greek community of Pistiros vis-à-vis the Thracians, to regulate Greek commercial activities in Thrace, and to administer affairs within the diverse community of Pistiros.

The Vetren text describes a coastal trading network from Pistiros in western Thrace all the way to the Melas Gulf in eastern Thrace. Tax exemption on specific trade routes that ran back and forth from Pistiros to Maroneia and from Maroneia to emporia on the Melas Gulf, and the right of Greek traders to open and close markets whenever they wished, are the two provisions on the inscription that facilitate trade directly. These settlements were located in territories contested by the three Thracian rulers, while their location on the coast made them part of the frontier between Greek settlements and Thrace as a whole. The legislation on the Vetren text, therefore, in effect mediated not only among Kotys' three successors but also between the two ethnic groups, Greeks and Thracians. Thus, the Thracian rulers collectively made several guarantees to the Greeks of Pistiros, preserving the community and granting it a certain degree of political autonomy: Thracian debts owed to the Greeks would not be cancelled; the traders' land, pasture, and other possessions would not be confiscated; soldiers would not be sent to the traders nor a garrison to Pistiros; hostages would not be taken from among the residents.

The Vetren text also reveals that unlike the Egyptians, who did not distinguish among the different Greek groups, Thracians differentiated among the Greeks of Pistiros according to their polis of origin. Thus the rulers granted several personal guarantees not only to the Pistirenoi, but also to the Thasians and Apollonians who lived in Pistiros, mentioning them by name: Thracians would not take captive, kill, or seize the property of members of these groups. The diverse community of Pistiros may also partly explain the fact that foreign judges were invited to adjudicate the traders' affairs. Trials may have been problematic in a mixed population, where each group followed the laws of their mother-city. Moreover, barbarian kings often exploited foreign judges to administer the affairs of a Greek city. The custom of using foreign judges, therefore, was yet another mechanism that mediated both among the different Greek groups, but also between Greeks and Thracians.

Religion also played a role in creating a mutually comprehensible world for Thracians and Greeks. In Gravisca and Naukratis the different Greek groups realized that they all worshipped more or less the same divinities; it was the customs and rituals associated with specific local cults that differed. In Naukratis the acknowledgment of the gods as something they had in common was finally expressed in the dedication of a temple to the gods of the Greeks. The polytheistic frame of mind allowed the Greeks to recognize both the pan-Hellenic nature of certain gods, and to identify their own gods with divinities worshiped by other ethnic groups. Dionysus, by whose name the Thracian rulers swore the Vetren oath, was recognized by all the Thracians and all the Greeks of Pistiros and Maroneia, whatever their origin. Thus, Dionysus was a suitable deity to act as a guarantor of an oath that involved all these groups.

In Pistiros, a multiethnic emporion situated in a non-Greek land, the close encounters among different Greek groups and between Greeks and Thracians also led to the expression of several levels of collective identities: Greeks identified in terms of their polis of origin in relation to other Greeks, they had a strong political identity as Pistirenoi vis-à-vis the other Greek communities in the Thasian *peraia*, and they probably also saw themselves as Greeks when encountering Thracians; the Thracians, on the other hand, adopted Greek perceptions of themselves and thus distinguished among the various Greeks groups and even called themselves Thracians, rather than specifying their intra-Thracian group.

The Vetren text is significant in that it is a unique source from an emporion that details both the inner workings of trade across cultural borders and also the legal mechanisms a host society used to manage and control foreign communities in its lands. More than religion, therefore, in the commercial settlement of Pistiros, law emerges as the main vehicle used to mediate among different Greeks, between Greeks and Thracians, and even among the three Thracian ruling houses.

5 | Peiraieus

This journey around the Mediterranean has taken us through Emporion to Gravisca, from there to Naukratis, and to Pistiros. It is now time to reach the final destination, the famous emporion of Attica. Unlike the four case-studies examined thus far, Peiraieus was not a Greek emporion abroad. Instead, founded in the early fifth century, Peiraieus was an emporion located on the Greek mainland, near what was becoming at that time the center of the Greek world, Athens. There are more literary references to Peiraieus than to all other Greek emporia in the Mediterranean combined. Consequently, and because of its proximity to Athens, there are many studies of the harbor's archaeology, its relationship with Athens, and its role in the ancient economy. Peiraieus continues to be the subject of excavations to this day, and its topography is constantly being revised.

When Peiraieus was founded, at the very beginning of the fifth century, Athens was arguably one of the most important poleis of the Greek world, and it would go on to be the most important in terms of the lasting influence it has had in subsequent history. Yet it had not participated in the expeditions of the eighth to the sixth centuries BC as had other Greek, Phoenician, and Etruscan city-states. Despite the fact that Athens was a latecomer in the colonization movements of the archaic period, it was never isolated from the rest of the Mediterranean. Athens expanded its influence in the mid-sixth century, especially in Thrace, but also in the Aegean circle more generally.[1] In the fifth century, when Athens was the hegemon in the Aegean, it established klerouchies throughout the area. As is well known, these were not new independent and autonomous city-states as were the colonies established during the earlier colonizing expeditions undertaken by the rest of the Greek world; instead, they were effectively part of Athenian territory,

---

[1] Miltiades, the son of Kypselos, settled together with other Athenians in the Thracian Chersonese around 555 BC (Herodotus 6.34–7). It was here that Miltiades the younger, the nephew of Miltiades son of Kypselos, in 516 BC met and married the Thracian Hegesipyle, with whom he fathered Kimon (Herodotus 6.39). In the same period, Peisistratos and his sons cultivated relationships with other tyrants in the Aegean, such as Lygdamis the tyrant of Naxos, Polykrates the tyrant of Samos, etc. (Herodotus 1.61–4; 5.94; Polyainos 1.23).

and their inhabitants remained Athenian citizens.[2] It was not until the fifth century that Athens started establishing colonies that were independent poleis, though they were subordinate to the Athenian hegemony of the period, such as Amphipolis on the northern coast of Thrace.[3]

Athens' absence from the establishment of new poleis in the eighth and seventh centuries did not prevent Athenian culture from being exported to the rest of the Mediterranean world, however. The popularity of Athenian figured vases in Etruria, for instance, and the presence of Athenian vases in Iberia, Egypt, and Thrace has been touched on in the previous chapters.[4] In addition, the success of Athenian currency was exceptional to the point that in the classical period demand for Athenian coinage was the highest in the Mediterranean: 78 percent of Athenian coin hoards have been discovered outside Attica, a fact suggesting a wide distribution and use of Athenian silver.[5] Olive oil was another Athenian product exported in the characteristic "SOS" amphorae, which are attested throughout the Mediterranean world and the Black Sea coast.[6] Overall, it seems that Athenian exports were part of a common Mediterranean material culture and enjoyed the same popularity as Egyptian faience, Etruscan bucchero-ware, and Laconian and Corinthian pottery, among other products. Moreover, just as these items were imitated by local workshops, so Athenian figured vases, to take one example, were imitated in Etruria, Iberia, South Italy, etc.[7]

Athenian products and practices, in their turn, exhibit influences from other Greek and Near Eastern traditions. Many have argued that in the archaic period Athenian elites emulated their counterparts in the Near East, adopting both Eastern customs, such as the symposium, and Eastern dress or accessories.[8] At the same time, Athenian vases were heavily influenced by Near Eastern techniques and representations and imitated Corinthian prototypes.[9] Athens, therefore, was never isolated from its Mediterranean context, even though it did not send out official expeditions to establish poleis either in the western or the eastern Mediterranean as did other Greek

---

[2] Brunt 1966 and Cawkwell 1992 discuss the difference between early colonization and Athenian colonization. For Athenian klerouchies see Salomon 1997; Moreno 2009.
[3] Thucydides 4.102 narrates the foundation of Amphipolis.
[4] For Athenian vases in: Etruria, see Shapiro 2000 and Osborne 2001; Naukratis, see Venit 1988; Iberia, see Shefton 1982; Domínguez and Sánchez 2001; Thrace, see Archibald 1996 and 2002a. For the trade in Athenian vases in the archaic and classical periods, more generally, see Boardman 1979, A. W. Johnston 1991, Osborne 1996. Gill 1991 and 1994 argues that vases were space fillers on ships that accompanied other commodities being traded.
[5] Ober 2008: 48–52.   [6] A. W. Johnston and R. E. Jones 1978; A. W. Johnston 1979: 48–50.
[7] Etruria: Martelli 1987: 9–64; Turfa 2005: 40. Iberia: Pages del Pozo 1984; Domínguez 1999a: 314. South Italy: Denoyelle 2008.
[8] Miller 2004.   [9] Hurwit 1985: 218–22; Ebbinghaus 2008.

poleis. Athens of the archaic period, however, was not as diverse in its population as it was from the fifth century onward, after Peiraieus was founded and Athens became one of the most powerful poleis, one of the richest economic centers, and the cultural capital of the Mediterranean.

It is this moment that provides the historical context for the final chapter, which focuses on Peiraieus, a port that constitutes an important counterpart to the Greek emporia examined in previous chapters. First, as a manifestation of a polis' conscious decision to found an emporion, Peiraieus provides a final opportunity to examine the relationship between the political status of an emporion and its function. Second, Peiraieus enables an examination of how the Athenian polis dealt legally with its multiethnic population, complementing the previous chapter, which discussed how Thracian dynasts dealt with multiethnic city-states in Thracian territory. Third, as a Greek emporion on mainland Greece, Peiraieus reveals that non-Athenians and non-Greeks living in a Greek polis, either as metics or as *xenoi*, employed a common Mediterranean culture to mediate among themselves and Athenians and to negotiate and maintain their identity, as did the Greeks living in emporia in Egypt, Etruria, Iberia, or Thrace. Finally, it reveals how Athenian culture changed because of the multicultural nature of Peiraieus.

An Attic deme and emporion

Peiraieus had always been one of the Athenian demes.[10] It was not until Themistokles was a magistrate, however, that it became officially the port of Athens. The date of the fortification of Peiraieus is traditionally taken to be 493/2 BC, when Themistokles held the archonship.[11] Fornara has disputed this precise date, claiming that the construction of the fortifications began some time in the first twenty years of the fifth century when Themistokles held an annual magistracy other than the archonship.[12] Thucydides describes the development of the harbor and Themistokles' role in the whole process:

ἔπεισε δὲ καὶ τοῦ Πειραιῶς τὰ λοιπὰ ὁ Θεμιστοκλῆς οἰκοδομεῖν (ὑπῆρκτο δ' αὐτοῦ πρότερον ἐπὶ τῆς ἐκείνου ἀρχῆς ἧς κατ' ἐνιαυτὸν Ἀθηναίοις ἦρξε) νομίζων τό τε χωρίον καλὸν εἶναι, λιμένας ἔχον τρεῖς αὐτοφυεῖς, καὶ αὐτοὺς ναυτικοὺς γεγενημέ-νους μέγα προφέρειν ἐς τὸ κτήσασθαι δύναμιν (τῆς γὰρ δὴ θαλάσσης πρῶτος ἐτόλμησεν εἰπεῖν ὡς ἀνθεκτέα ἐστί), καὶ τὴν ἀρχὴν εὐθὺς ξυγκατεσκεύαζεν. καὶ

---

[10] Traill 1975; Garland 2001: 14 and 59.   [11] See for example Garland 2001: 15.
[12] Fornara 1971. I follow his suggestion in translating the passage.

ᾠκοδόμησαν τῇ ἐκείνου γνώμῃ τὸ πάχος τοῦ τείχους ὅπερ νῦν ἔτι δῆλόν ἐστι
περὶ τὸν Πειραιᾶ· δύο γὰρ ἅμαξαι ἐναντίαι ἀλλήλαις τοὺς λίθους ἐπῆγον. ἐντὸς
δὲ οὔτε χάλιξ οὔτε πηλὸς ἦν, ἀλλὰ ξυνῳκοδομημένοι μεγάλοι λίθοι καὶ ἐντομῇ
ἐγγώνιοι, σιδήρῳ πρὸς ἀλλήλους τὰ ἔξωθεν καὶ μολύβδῳ δεδεμένοι. τὸ δὲ ὕψος
ἥμισυ μάλιστα ἐτελέσθη οὗ διενοεῖτο. ἐβούλετο γὰρ τῷ μεγέθει καὶ τῷ πάχει
ἀφιστάναι τὰς τῶν πολεμίων ἐπιβουλάς, ἀνθρώπων τε ἐνόμιζεν ὀλίγων καὶ τῶν
ἀχρειοτάτων ἀρκέσειν τὴν φυλακήν, τοὺς δ' ἄλλους ἐς τὰς ναῦς ἐσβήσεσθαι. ταῖς
γὰρ ναυσὶ μάλιστα προσέκειτο, ἰδών, ὡς ἐμοὶ δοκεῖ, τῆς βασιλέως στρατιᾶς τὴν
κατὰ θάλασσαν ἔφοδον εὐπορωτέραν τῆς κατὰ γῆν οὖσαν· τόν τε Πειραιᾶ ὠφε-
λιμώτερον ἐνόμιζε τῆς ἄνω πόλεως, καὶ πολλάκις τοῖς Ἀθηναίοις παρῄνει, ἢν ἄρα
ποτὲ κατὰ γῆν βιασθῶσι, καταβάντας ἐς αὐτὸν ταῖς ναυσὶ πρὸς ἅπαντας ἀνθίσ-
τασθαι. Ἀθηναῖοι μὲν οὖν οὕτως ἐτειχίσθησαν καὶ τἆλλα κατεσκευάζοντο εὐθὺς
μετὰ τὴν Μήδων ἀναχώρησιν. (Thucydides 1.93)

Themistokles persuaded the Athenians to fortify also the rest of Peiraieus (the project
had been initiated earlier in the magistracy he held yearly). He believed the location
was good because it has three natural harbors, and he thought that becoming a
naval people would help the Athenians greatly in acquiring power. Indeed, he was
the first who dared suggest that the Athenians should attach themselves to the
sea and thus helped directly in establishing their empire. The Athenians built the
thickness of the walls according to his opinion, as can be seen even now around
Peiraieus. Two wagons opposite each other brought the stones. Between the walls
there was neither rubble nor mud, but great stones, cut square, and fitted together,
bound to each other on the outside with iron and lead. Only about half the height
that he intended was finished. For, he wanted to fend off the enemy's attacks by
the walls' size and thickness. He also thought that a few men, of the ones most
unfit for war, would be adequate to guard them, and the rest would be on board
the fleet. He attached particular importance to the navy because, as it seems to me,
he recognized that a naval offensive would be easier for the Persian king to launch
than a military offensive. He believed that Peiraieus was more useful than the upper
polis and urged frequently the Athenians to go down to Peiraieus if ever they were
hard-pressed on land in order to resist all their enemies with their fleet. In this way,
therefore, the Athenians completed the wall and constructed their other buildings
immediately after the Persian retreat.

The conscious act of turning Peiraieus into the harbor of Athens was often
presented in ancient sources as a foundation. Themistokles may not have
consulted the oracle at Delphi in order to receive sanction for this reinven-
tion of Peiraieus, but he was credited with being the founder of the harbor.
Much like other founders of colonies, Themistokles was later honored as
such when his monument, usually called the tomb of Themistokles, was

erected in Peiraieus and afterwards became the site of cultic activity.[13] Originally, Themistokles' tomb in Peiraieus must have acted as a reminder of the great might of the Athenian navy, but by the fourth century Peiraieus had developed into the indispensable emporion that provided Athens with grain, and the comic poet Plato mocked Themistokles' tomb that now oversaw commercial activities:

ὁ σὸς δὲ τύμβος ἐν καλῷ κεχωσμένος
τοῖς ἐμπόροις πρόσρησις ἔσται πανταχοῦ,
τούς τ᾽ ἐκπλέοντας εἰσπλέοντάς τ᾽ ὄψεται,
χὠπόταν ἅμιλλ᾽ ᾖ τῶν νεῶν θεάσεται.

Plato fr. 183 (ed. Kassel and Austin)

Your tomb is heaped at a good place
It is the welcome for merchants from everywhere
It will behold those sailing out and those sailing in
And it will watch whenever there is a boat race.

The Athenian rhetoric of the foundation of Peiraieus did not stop with the work of its founder.[14] The reorganization of the port's layout, purportedly by Hippodamos of Miletos, also presented Peiraieus as a new colony.[15] Just as Greek colonies of the archaic period, or modern cities like Washington, D.C., had to plan their layouts virtually at the moment of foundation, so Peiraieus received a makeover when it was founded as the port of Athens (Figure 15). Its topography is not easily discernible, but what is clear from the *horoi* discovered in Peiraieus is that the city was divided into sectors, each sector was divided into a rectilinear street system, and several sectors were reserved for public use (political, commercial, and religious).[16] For example, two of the boundary stones read: ἄχρι τες hοδο τεσδε τὸ ἄστυ τεῖδε νενέμεται (Here, up to this street, the *asty* has been planned);[17] ἄχρι τεσδε τεσ hοδο τεῖδε he Μονιχίας ἐστι νέμησις (Here, up to this street, is the plan of Mounychia).[18] The choice of the word νέμησις is interesting because it is also the word that Hesychios and Photios use in the title of their entry on Hippodamos, "Ἱπποδάμου νέμησις."[19] This word supports the ancient sources' suggestion that Hippodamos was the architect of the new Peiraieus.[20] The tradition that survived concerning Peiraieus, therefore,

---

[13] Pausanias 1.1.2; Plutarch, *Life of Themistokles* 32.5. The *oikistes* of a colony could be elevated to the status of a hero and receive a cult, especially at the site of his tomb (Malkin 1987: 204–40). This is what happened to Battos in Cyrene (Pindar, *Pythian* 5.124–5).
[14] Von Reden 1995a: 26–7.   [15] Aristotle, *Politics* 2.1267b.   [16] Hill 1932.   [17] *IG* I² 893.
[18] *IG* I² 894.   [19] Hesychios s.v. Ἱπποδάμου νέμησις; Photios s.v. Ἱπποδάμου νέμησις.
[20] Aristotle, *Politics* 2.1267b; Hesychios s.v. Ἱπποδάμου νέμησις; Strabo 14.2.9.

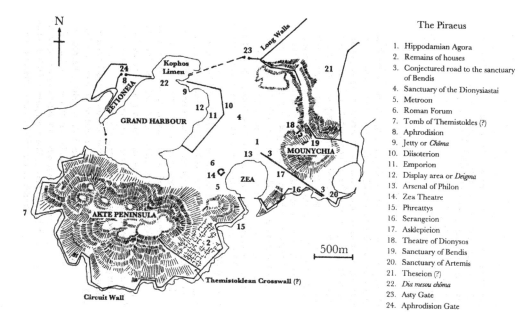

Figure 15 Plan of the port of Peiraieus. Reproduced from Garland 2001: 8.

was that Peiraieus was planned like all other colonies, although it was clearly not a colony but rather an Athenian deme.

Although nominally Peiraieus was an Athenian deme, it actually had a more complex administrative system than other demes. First of all, there was an agora marked by *horoi*, supervised by a set of five *agoranomoi*, who were different from the five *agoranomoi* responsible for the agora in Athens.[21] There were also a *bouleuterion* and a *strategeion* in Peiraieus, attested in an inscription of the third century.[22] The inscription actually refers to the "old *bouleuterion*" and the "old *strategeion*" (ἀρχαῖον βουλευτήριον; στρατήγιον τὸ ἀρχαῖον) implying that by the third century BC these two buildings no longer had the same function. The presence of most of the public buildings, like the agora and the *strategeion* can be explained in terms of the commercial function of the former and the military function of the latter. Likewise it is possible that the *bouleuterion* hosted the Athenian *boule* whenever some of the topics discussed related to Peiraieus. The earliest attested instance when the *boule* met in Peiraieus was in 426/5 BC when they discussed the importation of grain.[23] The Athenian *ekklesia* also met

---

[21] *IG* I² 896; ps.-Aristotle, *Athenian Constitution* 51.1.   [22] *IG* II² 1035.
[23] See Garland 2001: 82. The *boule* met again in Peiraieus in 325/4 BC, when they supervised a naval expedition.

in Peiraieus. Demosthenes, for example, mentions that in 347/6 BC the assembly met in Peiraieus, when a matter concerning the dockyards was the subject of debate.[24] In the third century, several inscriptions attest that the Athenian *ekklesia* often met in Peiraieus for the last meeting of the prytany, either at the theater of Dionysus or Mounychia (Figure 15).[25]

In addition to these public buildings, there existed also at least one, and possibly two courts in Peiraieus. The first court in Phreatto, near one of the three natural ports of Peiraieus, Zea, was the location where a specific kind of homicide trial took place (Figure 15). Anyone who was exiled for committing an unintentional homicide, not reconciled with his accusers, who was accused of a second, willful, murder, had to be tried in Phreatto. Phreatto was a place near the sea, so that the accused, who could not step on land, could be tried while he was in a boat.[26] Several bronze ballots inscribed with "ψῆφος δημοσία" (public vote) discovered in Peiraieus probably attest to the presence of a second court that perhaps housed the *emporikai dikai* (commercial trials).[27] Since this type of trial was introduced with the single aim of expediting procedures that involved *emporoi*, it is possible that the court trying such trials was located in Peiraieus.

The political infrastructure in Peiraieus was not limited to the buildings just discussed and the institutions that they represented. There were also administrative offices and officials in charge of the administration of Peiraieus *qua* urban center and *qua* commercial port, chosen by lot from the Athenian citizen body.[28] For instance, five *astynomoi* took care of the streets and public buildings of Peiraieus while another five operated in Athens at least until 320 BC, when some of their duties were transferred to the *agoranomoi*.[29] The presence of the extra *astynomoi* in Peiraieus was probably necessitated because Peiraieus was one of the most densely populated demes. In addition to the *astynomoi*, several offices in charge of commercial functions were also duplicated: there were five *agoranomoi* in Athens and another five in Peiraieus;[30] five *metronomoi* in Peiraieus and five in Athens responsible for weights and measures;[31] five *sitophylakes* apiece for Athens and Peiraieus in charge of enforcing the various laws and regulations

---

[24] Demosthenes, *On the False Embassy* 60 and 125.

[25] *IG* II² 785, 849, 850, 890, 978, 910, 946, 971, 974, *IDélos* 1505, Dow 1937: nos. 38 and 79; Meritt 1936: 422 no. 15 and 429 no. 17; Pritchett 1941: 280 no. 75. For a discussion of these inscriptions, see McDonald 1943: 51–6.

[26] Demosthenes, *Against Aristokrates* 77–8.   [27] Boegehold 1976.

[28] Ps.-Aristotle, *Athenian Constitution* 50.

[29] Ps.-Aristotle, *Athenian Constitution* 50, 51.1. *IG* II² 380 records the transference of some duties from the *astynomoi* to the *agoranomoi*: Vatin 1976.

[30] Ps.-Aristotle, *Athenian Constitution* 51.1.   [31] Ps.-Aristotle, *Athenian Constitution* 51.2.

regarding the import and export of grain;[32] one *dokimastes* each in Athens and Peiraieus who tested silver currency to see whether coins were counterfeit or not.[33]

Because of the eventual development of the commercial port, several offices were specific to Peiraieus, introduced to ensure the smooth running of the emporion, like the ἐπιμεληταὶ τοῦ ἐμπορίου (supervisors of the emporion), who probably had similar duties to the Naukratite *prostatai* of the emporion.[34] Conversely, the νεωροί (dockyard officials),[35] or as they were later known ἐπιμεληταὶ τῶν νεωρίων (supervisors of the docks),[36] were in charge of equipping the naval fleet and recording all such transactions. In the second century BC there was also a harbor supervisor known as ἐπιμελητὴς τοῦ λιμένος.[37] Other officers were in charge of collecting dues, like the *pentekostologoi*, responsible for exacting the 2 percent tax on all imports arriving in Peiraieus.[38]

The duplication of public buildings and offices witnessed in Peiraieus is reminiscent of the transference of *nomima* – elements of the constitution such as the names and numbers of magistracies and the sacred calendar – from the mother-city to the colony. This should not imply that Peiraieus was a colony, despite the fact that in some ways it was presented as such. Rather, the presence of these offices was necessitated by the growth and development of the emporion and the need to administer it. Further, as mentioned above, all the officers were elected by lot from among the Athenian citizens. In fact, Athens seems to have been extremely interested in controlling this particular deme, perhaps more than the others: while other demes were responsible for electing their own officer in charge of the deme (*demarch*), Peiraieus was not granted this right. Instead, the *demarch* of Peiraieus was elected in Athens.[39] Even the fact that the Athenian assembly and council sometimes met in Peiraieus may have served the double role of, on the one hand, privileging Peiraieus over the other demes and, on the other, implicitly showing that Peiraieus was an integral part of Athens. The port and the urban town, although geographically distinct, were politically part of the Athenian polis.

---

[32] Lysias, *Against the Corn Dealers*; ps.-Aristotle, *Athenian Constitution* 51.3. Gauthier 1981 discusses the functions of the *sitophylakes*.

[33] *Agora Inventory I* 7180 (Pls. 25–7). For an analysis of the currency law of 375/4 BC, see Stroud 1974.

[34] Ps.-Aristotle, *Athenian Constitution* 51.4; *SEG* 26, 72.

[35] *IG* I² 73 (ἐπιμε]λόμενοι τοῦ νεωρίου); *IG* II² 1 (νεωροί).

[36] *IG* II² 1607, 1609, 1611, 1622, 1623, 1627, 1628, 1631.   [37] *IG* II² 1012, 1013, 2336.

[38] Demosthenes, *Against Midias* 133 and *Against Phormio* 34.6.

[39] Ps.-Aristotle, *Athenian Constitution* 54.8.

In some ways, Peiraieus represents the inverse situation of all the other emporia discussed so far. Naukratis, Gravisca, and Pistiros were poleis that were dependent on foreign powers: the Egyptian authorities in the first case, the Etruscan city of Tarquinia in the second, and the Thracian dynasts in the last. In contrast, Emporion was an autonomous polis. These four settlements were emporia from their very foundation. Peiraieus, however, was first an Athenian deme before it was developed as an emporion. The commercial functions that it acquired came to it long after Athens had been established as a political center. Yet, what is common to all five emporia was that they had some degree of autonomy. Although dependent on the Egyptian government, Greeks administered Naukratis; Emporion was independent; the Thracian authorities guaranteed some independence and autonomy for Pistiros; the Greeks organized all trade activities in Gravisca, even though they were a minority living among an Etruscan majority; and, finally, Peiraieus had the infrastructure necessary to run all commercial operations independently, though it was Athens that provided the officers in charge. The partial or full political autonomy that these emporia had was one of the most important characteristics that enabled them to conduct commercial operations and serve their function of facilitating trade.

A Greek multiethnic emporion

The foundation of Peiraieus in the fifth century BC as the port of Athens was one of the most important landmarks in Athenian history. By "attaching themselves to the sea,"[40] the Athenians opened their polis to the outside world in two major ways: on the one hand, the port of Peiraieus allowed Athens to become the greatest naval, and consequently, hegemonic power in the Greek world; on the other hand, the port led to the establishment of one of the most famous and cosmopolitan emporia of the ancient world, resulting in the influx of foreign people and culture. Before the fifth century, Athens had used the bay of Phaleron as its port[41] but was not known as a seafaring nation. For instance, at the very beginning of his history of the Peloponnesian War, Thucydides narrates that King Minos of Crete was the first to organize a navy,[42] the Corinthians developed the first triremes,[43] and Corinth and Korkyra fought the first naval battle.[44] Athens is conspicuous by its absence in this early history of naval developments and only appears in

---

[40] Thucydides 1.93: τῆς γὰρ δὴ θαλάσσης πρῶτος ἐτόλμησεν εἰπεῖν ὡς ἀνθεκτέα ἐστί.
[41] Homer, *Iliad* 2.552; Herodotus 6.116.
[42] Thucydides 1.4.   [43] Thucydides 1.13.   [44] Thucydides 1.13.

the picture during the war between Athens and Aigina, when Themistokles realized the great need for a navy.[45] In contrast, several monuments in Athens that commemorated the city's ancient seafaring, such as an altar dedicated to Phaleros, the eponymous hero who sailed with Jason on his trip to Kolchis and gave his name to the port,[46] proclaimed that Athens was a seafaring nation of old to veil the fact that in the archaic period Athens did not participate in seafaring in a major way.

Thucydides may point out the obvious fact that Athens was not one of the first poleis to build ships or to engage in seafaring, but his aim in doing this is to paint in the starkest terms the transition from an agrarian Athens to an Athens that had conquered the seas.[47] The reason for doing this may be, as von Reden argues, that Thucydides considered shipbuilding and seafaring as one of the human victories over nature. In von Reden's analysis, Thucydides viewed the turn towards the sea and, therefore, exchange as a step in the political evolution of constitutions: first there were monarchies, which were replaced by tyrannies as Hellas grew stronger and the importance of acquiring money became evident; in turn, this led to more prosperity and a reorientation towards the sea that facilitated exchange and produced more money. The superiority of Athens, then, lay in her eventual orientation towards the sea, the triumph of human strength over nature exemplified by shipbuilding and navigation and the extensive trade and exchange that took place in the emporion of Peiraieus.[48]

It was precisely these economic activities that attracted traders from elsewhere in the Mediterranean world to come to Peiraieus and seek their fortunes, turning the port of Peiraieus into the cosmopolitan emporion that provides the multiethnic context for the study of the negotiation of identity. The population of Peiraieus was made up by the demesmen of Peiraieus, Athenian citizens registered in other demes, metics, *xenoi*, and slaves. The proportion of each of these population segments is not easy to discern because of spotty evidence. Nonetheless it is indicative that out of the 240 funerary inscriptions of Athenian citizens discovered in Peiraieus only 8 belonged to demesmen of Peiraieus. The rest are obviously Athenian citizens registered in other demes but who had resided in Peiraieus, drawn to the emporion because of all the economic attractions that it offered.[49] In

---

[45] Thucydides 1.14.

[46] Pausanias 1.1.4 describes these monuments as being very old. Menestheus and his fleet also sailed from this ancient port on their way to Troy: Pausanias 1.1.2.

[47] I disagree with Thein 1999 who argues that Thucydides rejected the sea in favor of the land and autochthony.

[48] Von Reden 1995b: 127–31.   [49] Garland 2001: 60.

fact, Athenian citizens participated in all activities related to foreign commerce. In forensic speeches, for instance, alongside fourteen metic *emporoi* and *naukleroi* who are discussed below, appear fifteen citizens.[50] Athenians present in Peiraieus, however, were not only traders; they were also bankers. Bankers' tables were set up both in the Athenian agora and in Peiraieus.[51] Although only one Athenian citizen is attested as a banker in ancient sources, others no doubt also existed.[52] The *emporikai dikai* that took place in Peiraieus also needed jurors and witnesses, who would, therefore, also have frequented Peiraieus. The dockyards provided another place of business for various professional Athenians, such as the citizens holding *trierarchies*,[53] hoplites patrolling the two promontories of Peiraieus, Akte and Mounychia,[54] and the navy training here. To these residents and visitors of Peiraieus we must add prostitutes[55] and heralds.[56]

As a commercial port, Peiraieus was also a magnet for foreigners, both non-Greeks and non-Athenian Greeks, who, like the Athenian residents of Peiraieus, came here to take advantage of the opportunities afforded to them by the emporion. Of course, foreigners besides *emporoi*, such as slaves, manumitted slaves, craftsmen, political refugees, intellectuals, etc., were also living in Peiraieus. Many of the traders who had entered Athens through Peiraieus probably became permanent residents (metics), but others remained simply temporary visitors (*xenoi*). Of the 366 metics whose deme affiliation is known, 69 named Peiraieus as their deme, a rather high number.[57] When literary sources, mostly forensic speeches, mention specific traders, they do not always state the exact status of the trader in question. Thus, of all the *emporoi* and *naukleroi* who appear in the forensic

[50] Andokides: Lysias, *Against Andokides* 19 and 49; Androkles: Demosthenes, *Against Lakritos* 10 and 49; Archeneus: Lysias, *Against Eratosthenes* 16; Diodotus: Lysias, *Against Diogeiton* 4 and 32; Philippos: Demosthenes, *Against Timokrates* 138; Hyblesios: Demosthenes, *Against Lakritos* 33; Leokrates: Lycurgus, *Against Leokrates* 55; Megaklides: Demosthenes, *Against Kallippos* 20; Miko: Demosthenes, *Against Theokrines* 6–10; Nikippos: Demosthenes, *Olynthiac I* 17; Nikoboulos: Demosthenes, *Against Pantainetos* 6, 46, and 54; Timosthenes: Demosthenes, *Against Timotheos* 31; Thrasyllos: Demosthenes, *Against Lakritos* 20; Two anonymous citizens: Demosthenes, *Against Phormio* 50 and *P. Oxy.* 2538.
[51] Demosthenes, *Against Timotheos* 6 and *Against Lakritos* 8; Polyainos 6.2.2.
[52] Demosthenes, *For Phormio* 50 and *Against Dionysodoros* 63.
[53] Lysias, *Defense Against the Charge of Taking Bribes* 1–4 and *Against Diogeiton* 26–7.
[54] Ps.- Aristotle, *Athenian Constitution* 42.3.
[55] Aeschines, *Against Timarchos* 40.   [56] Demosthenes, *Against Leochares* 4.
[57] Whitehead 1986: 83–4. There is one inscription (414/13 BC) that refers to a metic from Peiraieus: *IG* I² 329. Other lists of metics appear in the building accounts of the Erechtheion (*IG* I² 373–4) and fifth-century casualty lists (Pope 1935: 75–80). In these lists the formula οἰκῶν/οἰκοῦσα (residing) is taken to describe metics.

speeches, fifteen are clearly citizens and fourteen are either metics or *xenoi*. Three *emporoi* can be securely identified as metics;[58] a few other *emporoi* and *naukleroi* were probably metics, but this is only a conjecture.[59] The rest were most likely *xenoi*, although in one case there is no indication at all to suggest whether the trader in question, Protos, was a metic or a *xenos*.[60] The metic traders and ship-owners were probably residents in Peiraieus since it would be more convenient for them to live near their place of business, and those merchants who were *xenoi* no doubt frequented Peiraieus.[61]

When the speeches ascribe any kind of affiliation to the foreign traders, whether metics or *xenoi*, they mention their polis of origin, just as is the case of the other emporia studied here: resident traders always expressed their continued membership in the polis they came from when defining themselves. Epigraphic evidence from Athens and Peiraieus attests to the fact that it was not just the writers of the forensic speeches that characterized metics in terms of their civic association, but also the metics themselves used this method of identification. For example, Attic grave stelai from Peiraieus honoring metics, most of which date to the fourth century BC, mention the deceased's polis of origin. The most commonly represented region was the Aegean, but a high proportion of metics came from poleis in the Peloponnese, central Greece, Thessaly, Thrace, Propontis and the Hellespont, the Black Sea coast, Asia Minor, and Cyprus, while fewer originated from Macedon, Phoenicia, Syria, Egypt, Libya, and Sicily, among others.[62]

The arrival of these non-Athenians contributed to making Peiraieus a multicultural society that may have challenged the Athenian concept of

[58] Demosthenes, *Against Phormio* 38–9 makes it clear that Chrysippos and his brother had lived in Athens for several years. Isokrates, *Trapezitikos* 4 speaks of Sopaios' son. Isager and Hansen 1975: 72 think that Sopaios' son was a *naukleros*. However it is clear from the text that Sopaios was a *naukleros* who loaded the ship with grain, gave his son money, and sent him on a trading expedition. Sopaios' son was probably an *emporos*.

[59] Apollodoros and Artemon of Phaselis (*emporoi*): Demosthenes, *Against Lakritos* 10, 20, and 49; Phormio (*emporos*): Demosthenes, *Against Phormio* 6–9, 13, and 50; Lyko of Herakleia (*emporos*): Demosthenes, *Against Kallippos* 3–9; Pyro of Pherai (*emporos* or *naukleros*): Isokrates, *Trapezitikos* 20; Parmeniskos (*naukleros*): Demosthenes, *Against Dionysodoros* 5 and 7.

[60] Apatourios of Byzantion (*naukleros*): Demosthenes, *Against Apatourios* 6 and 26; Hegestratos of Massalia (*naukleros*): Demosthenes, *Against Zenothemis* 4 and 8; Theodoros of Phoenicia (*emporos*): Demosthenes, *Against Phormio* 6–8, 22, 26, and 40; Zenothemis of Massalia (*emporos*): Demosthenes, *Against Zenothemis* 4–5, and 15; Protos (*emporos*): Demosthenes, *Against Zenothemis* 8, 14, 18, 25, and 29.

[61] Hegestratos of Massalia: Demosthenes, *Against Zenothemis* 11; Theodoros of Phoenicia: Demosthenes, *Against Phormio* 6. *Xenoi* arriving in Peiraieus are mentioned in Demosthenes, *Against Polykles* 6. See also Reed 2003.

[62] *IG* II/III^2 7882–10530. See also Isager and Hansen 1975: 217–19 and Garland 2001: 64–5.

citizenship.[63] For this reason, Athens introduced measures at different periods delineating the rights of Athenian metics and *xenoi*. Since these have been dealt with elsewhere,[64] in the next sections I summarize briefly the legal status of metics and *xenoi*. Some of these were traders residing or working in Peiraieus, and thus relevant for the discussion here. Then I turn to epigraphic evidence that is specific to *emporoi* and *naukleroi*, because these men clearly entered Athens through Peiraieus. Even though it is unclear whether they were residents or *xenoi*, some of them were granted the right to buy land and therefore either became metics with special privileges or, at the very least, acquired more rights than other *xenoi* vis-à-vis Athenian citizens. A careful examination of these traders' status, especially the ones who became landed property owners by vote of the Athenian polis, reveals the attitudes of the Athenian citizenry towards the incoming traders and the ways in which they attempted to manage and regulate interactions with the non-Greeks and non-Athenian Greeks living in Peiraieus.

Metics were immigrants, who had some privileges but not full citizenship; that was restricted to persons born to Athenian citizen parents. Since the majority of metics lived in Peiraieus, it is important to inquire what being a metic involved, especially with respect to metics' rights and duties in finance, military service, law, and public life more generally.[65] Such an investigation shows how the Athenian polis attempted to delimit the rights of resident traders in a fairly precise way in order both to control their presence in the polis, and at the same time to protect them, thereby allowing them to continue performing their profession, which ultimately benefited Athens. The relationship between resident traders in Peiraieus and the Athenian authorities, therefore, is reminiscent of the ways in which the Thracian authorities delineated the rights of resident traders in Pistiros and Egyptian pharaohs controlled Naukratis.

Information about metics first comes from fifth-century tragic and comic poets. These texts seem to imply that metics were permanently established in Athens, were considered as part of the Athenian community, and as such also had to obey Athenian laws.[66] Other sources, mainly forensic speeches but also inscriptions, are more informative about what the metic status entailed. First, *xenoi* who stayed in the Athenian polis for longer than an unknown specified amount of time had to enlist in an Athenian deme. This they did

---

[63] It has been suggested, for example, that Pericles' laws restricting citizenship to those of Athenian parentage on both the female and the male side, was a result of the increase of metics and *xenoi* in Athens. See Garland 2001: 61.

[64] For example: Whitehead 1977; Gauthier 1972: 107–56 and 1988; Levy 1988.

[65] Whitehead 1986: 69–108 and references.   [66] Gauthier 1972: 111–12.

with the help of a patron (*prostates*), who acted as a guarantor for the metic vis-à-vis the Athenian community.[67] The relationship between the metic and the *prostates* was a permanent one until about 350 BC, when the role of the *prostates* declined.[68] In this sense, the role of the *prostates* was similar to that of a *proxenos*, described in the chapter on Naukratis: both individuals were responsible for incorporating foreigners into the community and also guarantors for them in any affairs that they were involved in. For instance, metics received different treatment from citizens before the law. In all *dikai* except for murder trials (*dikai phonou*) in which the metic was a defendant, the plaintiff could take him to the *polemarch*, and the *prostates* would have to attest to the fact that the defendant was indeed a metic. Then the plaintiff would demand bail, something that was not always necessary for citizens.[69] In this way, the legal procedure ensured that the metic would not abscond before the trial took place.[70] This difference probably stemmed from the fact that since metics did not own land they were more mobile than citizens. The evidence available for murder trials is restricted to cases of metic plaintiffs and victims, and it suggests that homicides of metics were punished more lightly than homicides of citizens.[71] As far as *graphai* (indictments) go, metics had recourse to the law practically on the same footing as citizens except that there were some restrictions when submitting certain kinds of *graphai*.[72] There were also procedural differences: metics might have had to appear before the *boule* in advance of their trial.[73] It seems that overall the value of a metic's life before the law was not as high as that of a citizen. The highest penalty for a citizen's murder did not apply to murders of metics and the law allowed the torture of metics as witnesses in trials.[74] The picture that emerges is one of careful treatment of foreign immigrants in order to make their stay in Athens worthwhile, while considering them legally unequal to citizens.

Metics also had to pay a personal tax called the *metoikion*. Thus, Hesychios' reductive definition of the *metoikos* as one who paid the *metoikia*[75] is on a basic level accurate. In addition, they probably had to pay another tax,

---

[67] Gauthier 1972: 126–36.

[68] Gauthier 1972: 133–5. This might be due to the introduction of *emporikai dikai*, which gave to all foreigners, both metics and *xenoi*, easy access to the Athenian legal system.

[69] Gauthier 1972: 134 and 136–41.   [70] Whitehead 1977: 92–3.

[71] Demosthenes, *Against Euergos and Mnesiboulos* 68–73. Gauthier 1972: 141–4.

[72] For the ways in which metics and citizens differed in *graphai*, see Whitehead 1977: 94–6 and references.

[73] Lysias, *Against the Corn Dealers*; Isokrates, *Trapezitikos* 42–3.

[74] Lysias *Against Simon* 33 and *Against Agoratos* 54; Thucydides 8.92.

[75] Hesychios s.v. *metoikos*.

called the *xenika tele* (foreigners' tax) if they wanted to do business in the agora.[76] Citizens obviously did not have to pay this particular tax, but both citizens and metics were responsible for the *eisphora* (taxes on an individual's capital) and liturgies.[77] There was always a chance that Athens could reward metics with *isoteleia*, the right to pay the same taxes as the citizens, if the metic performed some service to the city.[78] Xenophon considered these revenues from metics so significant that he advocated offering more privileges to metics, who would then increase the city's income with their *eisphorai* and liturgies.[79] Metics also participated in the Athenian military during the Peloponnesian War and afterwards, both in the navy and the hoplite army.[80] In fact, one of the ways that Xenophon suggested to attract more metics was to admit them into the cavalry so that their loyalty to the polis would be strengthened.[81]

Metics were not allowed to hold office[82] or own landed property or houses unless they were given exemption.[83] This exemption, known as *enktesis*, is known from decrees honoring foreigners. Some of these specifically honored traders and ship-owners who had entered Athens through their activities in Peiraieus and thus will be discussed in detail below. The formula in these cases is καὶ γῆς καὶ οἰκίας ἔγκτησιν εἶναι αὐτοῖς (they have the right of *enktesis* of land and house).[84] This right is given not only to metics but also to foreigners who were not legal residents. More often than not, this was a grant decreed to *proxenoi* who had rendered some service to Athens.[85] Of course, the right of *enktesis* effectively made these foreigners residents of Athens. *Enktesis* was also one of the privileges that Xenophon advocated giving to those metics "deemed worthy of the right," since there were empty building plots within the walls of Athens.[86] Overall, therefore, metics were expected to contribute to and participate in public life but did so in the form of paying taxes.

[76] Demosthenes, *Against Euboulides* 31.
[77] Lysias, *Against Eratosthenes* 61 mentions that Lysias and Polemarchos were subject both to *eisphorai* and also to *choregeia* (one of the liturgies). Only citizens, however, held the liturgy of the *trierarchia*, since it involved holding an office and metics could not hold offices.
[78] Whitehead 1977: 11–13. *IG* II/III² 7862–81 are grave stelai of *isoteleis*, who describe themselves as such. Metics, on the other hand, do not advertise their metic status.
[79] Xenophon, *Ways and Means* 2.1.
[80] Thucydides 2.31; 3.16; 4.90; Xenophon, *Ways and Means* 2.2–3; *IG* II² 715.
[81] Xenophon, *Ways and Means* 2.5. Earlier in the treatise, however, Xenophon advocated an abolition of hoplite service for metics (2.2–3). Whitehead 1977: 128 suggested that cavalry service was more prestigious because only those who could afford a horse could participate. In other words, Xenophon wanted to privilege wealthier metics because his goal was to attract them and their assets to the polis.
[82] Aristotle, *Politics* 1275a.   [83] Pečírka 1966.   [84] *IG* II² 342, 343, and 360.
[85] See the chronological table in Pečírca 1966: 152–9.   [86] Xenophon, *Ways and Means* 2.6.

As far as religion is concerned, metics were often given the right to practice their own cults; as a corollary of the fact that most metics resided in Peiraieus, most of these foreign cults, discussed in more detail below, were established in Peiraieus. Metics were also incorporated partially in Athenian rituals but could not perform sacrifices in cults that were exclusive, such as those organized by tribes, phratries, *gene*, or sometimes the polis as a whole. Exceptions to the rule did exist, however. For instance, the Scambonid Law of about 460 BC did grant limited participation to metics in one of the ceremonial sacrifices of their deme, in honor of the hero Leos.[87] Similarly the regulations for the Hephaistia of 421/20 BC granted three animals for metics to sacrifice, while citizens sacrificed more than a hundred animals.[88] At the Panathenaia, however, only Athenians are mentioned as performers of sacrifices, which suggests that metics were excluded from these rites.[89] Still, metics did participate in other parts of the ceremony: men performed festival liturgies such as the *skaphephoria*, and women participated in the *hydriaphoria* and *skiadephoria*.[90]

With respect to participation in the religious life of the emporion, therefore, the evidence from Peiraieus reveals more than the evidence from the other emporia studied here. I have argued that in Gravisca and Naukratis, the two emporia that are most informative about religious practices, anyone who resided in or visited the emporion could use any sanctuary (s)he wanted. I have also proposed that there was a general lack of exclusivity of cult, and that foreigners perhaps could participate in sacrifices with the mediation of a *proxenos*. In Peiraieus (and Athens), however, grants were given to metics delineating their exact rights in the performance of sacrifices and other festival rites. Thus, although evidence has not survived for all Athenian festivals, it seems clear that there were some instances in which metics were allowed to sacrifice together with the citizen body and others in which they participated under different capacities but could not sacrifice. It is difficult to assess whether private dedications given in sanctuaries were given by metics or by *xenoi*, since the dedicators identified themselves only with city-ethnics.[91] But overall it seems that they also could use sanctuaries, at least to give offerings to deities.

The limited legal, religious, and personal rights that Athens gave to its metics, in effect mediated between citizens and resident foreigners. Just as in Pistiros, where the Thracian authorities guaranteed personal inviolability,

---

[87] *IG* I² 188.   [88] *IG* I² 84.   [89] *IG* II² 334: regulations of 335/4 BC mention only Athenians.

[90] Photios s.v. μετοίκων λειτουργίαι; σκαφηφορεῖν; Dinarchos *apud* Harpokration s.v. σκαφηφόροι; Photios and Hesychios s.v. ὑδριαφόροι; Claudius Aelianus s.v. σκιαδηφορεῖν.

[91] *IG* II² 3822–4022.

property inalienability, and some kind of legal system for the Greek resident traders, so in Athens the Athenian demos attempted to regulate the interactions between itself and its resident population. Although not all metics were traders, the principle was the same: the Athenian demos provided rewards to foreigners in order to make their stay in Athens worthwhile and to facilitate their presence there so that they could engage in their activities, which ultimately benefited Athens.

Although *xenoi* did not have the same status as metics, they, too, were catered for by the Athenian demos. The term *xenos* had various meanings. Here, I use it to designate specifically foreigners who were in Athens, perhaps even living there for a short period that did not exceed the allocated amount of time before a foreigner had to find himself a *prostates* and enlist in an Athenian deme as a metic. In other words, the foreigners considered here are those who might be called *parepidemountes* (those present in the town), who had reason to be in Athens or Peiraieus, most commonly because of their profession. At least in the fourth century BC, it seems that a *xenos* could stay in Athens without becoming a metic only if he became *isoteles* – fiscally equal to citizens – or a *proxenos* – a privilege that usually came with additional rights, such as exemption from the *metoikion, isoteleia,* etc.[92] In extreme cases, a *xenos* might also be rewarded with the right to remain in Athens beyond the specified time without, however, having to pay the *metoikion* or other taxes that metics had to pay.[93] Such an example will be discussed below.

Like metics, *xenoi* had a sponsor when they were present in Athens, a *proxenos*, who was responsible for protecting the foreigner and perhaps attesting to his status if he were brought before Athenian officers.[94] Several restrictions applied to both metics and *xenoi*. For instance, members of either group could not participate in any of the government offices or in priesthoods. Moreover, the two groups were treated differently than citizens in court since both metics and *xenoi* had to be taken to the *polemarch* and since their deaths were not punished with the highest penalty. *Xenoi*, however, had distinct advantages in two areas: they did not have to pay any of the taxes that metics paid except for the *xenika tele*, if they wanted to conduct business in the agora. They also did not have to perform military service, whereas metics were liable. In addition, *xenoi* could receive the same privileges of *isoteleia* and *enktesis* as metics.[95] When it came to law, metics had better resources until a fourth-century reform introduced *emporikai dikai*, which granted

---

[92] Whitehead 1977: 10–16. Grants of *isoteleia* to *proxenoi*: *IG* II² 83, *IG* II² 288. Grants of *enktesis* to *proxenoi*: see the chronological table in Pečírka 1966: 152–9.
[93] *IG* II² 141.   [94] Gauthier 1972: 17–61, especially 57–61.
[95] *IG* II² 141, 283, 342, 363, 398, 400, 401, 407–9, 903, and Schweigert 1940: 332–3: no. 29. All these inscriptions are discussed below.

foreign traders better access to the legal system. It is interesting to note that before the introduction of commercial trials, Xenophon had already realized that if their trials were expedited, foreigners would come to Athens more frequently.[96] In religious life, too, metics were granted more privileges than *xenoi*. As we saw above, metics could participate to a limited degree not only in their own cults but also in some of the more exclusively Athenian rituals. In contrast, *xenoi* did not have this privilege, although they could presumably participate in a cult of their homeland if that happened to exist in Athens and perhaps in Athenian cults through the mediation of *proxenoi*.

The two groups, metics and *xenoi*, had to be treated differently because ultimately their presence and function in Athens was different. As residents of Athens, metic traders needed fuller recourse to the law, while *xenoi* traders needed quick resolution of their trials. Hence the varying access to the law granted to the two groups and the introduction of the *emporikai dikai*. Similarly, metics had wider participation in Athenian cults than *xenoi*, but they were also liable to be drafted into the military and they had to pay more kinds of taxes. Permanent residency came with a price. By clearly defining the rights of each group, Athens achieved a balance between including and excluding its metics and *xenoi* in polis life in order to ensure that these members continued to perform their function and render their services to Athens. When we consider that most of these metics and *xenoi* were traders, as is suggested both by the existence of the *xenika tele*, taxes that were particular to commercial transactions in the agora, and the introduction of the *emporikai dikai* (commercial trials), the control of foreign presence in Athens seems similar to the situation in other emporia, such as Pistiros and Naukratis. The reason ultimately is the complementary and competitive relationship between host-society and trader community. Athens benefited from the presence of foreign traders (and other professionals). In order to ensure that they could continue their operations uninhibited they had to grant them certain privileges. At the same time, foreigners had to pay for this protection provided by the Athenian demos. This they did through their payment of several taxes, contributions to the public life of Athens, and by accepting their definitive exclusion from the citizen body.

Rewarding resident traders

One of the ways in which Athens rewarded metics and *xenoi* was by granting honors in return to individuals who had rendered some service.[97] These

---

[96] Xenophon, *Ways and Means* 3.3.
[97] For a recent treatment of honors given to non-Athenians by Athens see Engen 2010.

honors were recorded on inscriptions and thus are excellent sources for analyzing Athenian attitudes towards foreign traders, even though it is not always clear whether these *emporoi* or *naukleroi*, the recipients of the honors, were metics or *xenoi*. The discussion here is limited to those inscriptions that involve *emporoi* or *naukleroi*, who clearly came to Athens because of the commercial port in Peiraieus.

The earliest of these inscriptions, dating to the 360s BC, is in honor of an individual, Straton, the king of Sidon (Figure 16).[98] Even though the fragmentary text of the inscription does not specify why he was honored, it seems clear from the first surviving lines that Straton must have helped an Athenian embassy on its way to the Persian King, Artaxerxes. For this service rendered to the Athenians, Straton, king of the Sidonians, was granted hereditary *proxenia*, an honor that will be discussed in more detail below, as well as assistance from the Athenians if he should ever need it. After various prescriptions about inscribing the grant of *proxenia* on a stele, the second part of the inscription states that the *boule* would explore the possibility of exchanging *symbola* with the king of the Sidonians, so that Athens and Sidon could communicate with each other securely. While this unique clause seems unrelated to the personal grant that Straton received, it does pertain to the help that Straton gave to the Athenian embassy on its way to the King. The decade of the 360s saw several revolts against the Persian king, including the great satraps' revolt, which the Sidonians joined in 362 BC. It is possible that the Athenians were trying to secure diplomatic relations with the Sidonians in case they needed to support each other against the Persians.[99] The third part of the inscription is a rider that records a proposal put forth by Menexenos, which grants Sidonian traders in Athens certain rights. Straton's diplomatic functions, therefore, did not only include political mediation between Athens and the Persian King. In his capacity as king of the Sidonians, he negotiated an extra privilege on behalf of Sidonian traders who visited Athens:

Μενέξενος εἶπεν· τὰ μὲν ἄλλα καθάπερ Κηφισόδοτος· ὁπόσοι δ᾽ ἂν Σιδω-
νίων οἰκ(ῶ)ντες ἐς Σιδῶνι καὶ πολιτευόμενοι ἐπιδημῶσιν κατ᾽ ἐμπορ-
ίαν Ἀθήνησι, μὴ ἐξεῖναι αὐτο(ὺ)ς μετ-

---

[98] The date of this inscription has been debated. Culasso Gastaldi 2004: 104–23 persuasively shows that it is impossible to date the inscription with precision and argues for a date in the 360s. See also Moysey 1976.

[99] Moysey 1976; Culasso Gastaldi 2004: 109–12 and 118–23.

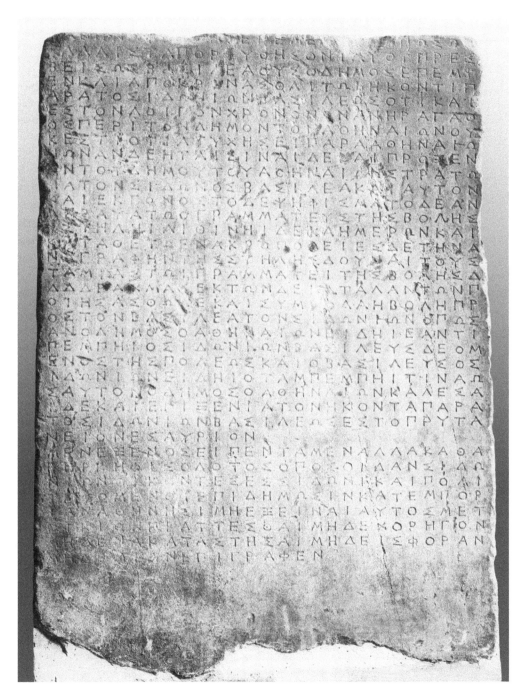

Figure 16 Stele recording honors awarded by Athens to Straton, king of the Sidonians, and to Sidonian traders in Athens (*IG* II^2 141), *c.* 360 BC.

οἴκιον πράττεσθαι μηδὲ χορηγὸν
μηδένα καταστῆσαι μηδ᾽ ἐσφορὰν
μηδεμίαν ἐπιγράφεν.   *IG* II² 141

Menexenos proposed the following; the rest is according to Kephisodotos. However many Sidonians, who live in and are citizens of Sidon, visit Athens on commercial business, no *metoikion* will be exacted from them, nor are they to be appointed to any *choregeia* or registered for any *eisphora*.

The implication is that these Sidonian *emporoi* would ordinarily have to become metics and pay taxes if they stayed in Athens, even though, as the text makes explicit, they were not only residents but also citizens (*politeuomenoi*) of Sidon. According to the text of this decree, the Sidonian merchants were given the right to remain in Athens for longer than the specified period without becoming metics and without paying metic taxes. It is not clear whether the merchants would reside in Peiraieus, although that is the most likely option since they are specifically described as being present in Athens for the purpose of commerce. This measure resembles in its goals the legislation enacted by the Thracian authorities in order to facilitate trade activities that the Greek resident traders of Pistiros performed in Thrace. On the one hand, it allowed traders to continue their commercial operations without significant restrictions, while retaining their citizen rights in their hometown of Sidon. Their primary affiliation, therefore, was a civic one. On the other hand, the Athenian polis benefited from the presence of the traders, because they either imported vital food supplies or paid taxes, such as the *xenika tele*.

The presence of Sidonian traders in Athens and Peiraieus is attested in inscriptions from the fourth to the first centuries BC.[100] One inscription is a third-century bilingual funerary inscription set up in Peiraieus by the son of the Sidonian priest of the god Nergal for his sister. The Greek part of the inscription reads: Ἀσεπτ Ἐσυμσελήμου Σιδωνία (Asept, daughter of Esumselem, a Sidonian).[101] The Phoenician text continues: "[This is that] which Yathan-bel, son of Eshmun-shillem, chief-priest of the god Nergal set up for me."[102] Although this inscription dates to the post-classical period and is thus beyond the scope of this project, it provides information on two generations of Sidonians who appear to have lived in Peiraieus and is thus significant evidence for families of immigrants in this emporion. Bilingual

---

[100] *IG* II/III² 10265a-86 are all funerary inscriptions belonging to people who identify themselves as Sidonians.
[101] *IG* II² 10271.   [102] Cooke 1903: no. 35.

inscriptions such as this also disclose perceptions of identity. For instance, the Greek text explains to the Greek passerby that the grave-stele belonged to a woman, described specifically as Sidonian. Since the Phoenician text is meant for other Phoenicians, it was essential for the person who set it up to explain his family affiliation, especially because he came from an important family: his father was a priest in a Phoenician cult in honor of Nergal. Two different levels of collective identity become apparent. To the Greeks the deceased is described as Sidonian, whereas vis-à-vis her own community, it was important to mention her family ties.

This family, which even in the second generation characterizes itself as Sidonian, may not have come to Peiraieus because of trade. Since the father was a priest, it is likely that he emigrated to Peiraieus in order to work at the sanctuary of Nergal. The presence of the sanctuary, however, may have been necessitated because of the community of Sidonian traders who were permanently present in Peiraieus. There is another bilingual inscription that supports this conjecture, though the text, again, is of a later date.[103] This text, found in Peiraieus, records the honors given to a Sidonian, the president of a corporation in charge of a temple probably dedicated to Baal, because he performed well his duties as the person in charge of the building of the temple court. Again, if we compare the extremely brief Greek inscription at the end of the much longer Phoenician text, we can see that the two texts fulfill different goals. The Greek text reads: τὸ κοινὸν τῶν Σιδωνίων | Διοπείθην Σιδώνιον (the *koinon* of the Sidonians, for Diopeithes the Sidonian). A Greek who read this inscription would immediately know that the *koinon* of the Sidonians present in Peiraieus was the party that decided to honor Diopeithes, who was also a Sidonian. The name Diopeithes is a Greek translation of the Phoenician name of the person honored, called Shama-baal in the Phoenician text.[104] Shama-baal means "Baal listens" and it is translated as Diopeithes, "he who obeys Zeus." This is a good example of the ease with which Mediterranean groups recognized their own divinities in each others' gods: for the Phoenicians residing in Peiraieus, the Phoenician Baal was the same as Zeus. In order to make the summary of the text intelligible to Greeks, therefore, the Phoenicians translated the name of the honoree into Greek.

---

[103] *IG* II² 2946 is usually dated to 96/5 BC. Some scholars, however, have noted that the Greek text is dated palaeographically to the third century and have thus argued that the inscription could be of an earlier date. See, for example, Garland 2001: 231. Teixidor 1980: 457 points out that the Phoenician script might also date to the third century BC. Dating only according to lettering, however, is not secure.

[104] Cooke 1903: 96 no. 33 (line 2).

The Phoenician text is the product of cross-cultural influences. It seems that the Sidonian community residing in Peiraieus (and Athens) adopted language used in Athenian decrees to express their decision. This part of the inscription follows closely the pattern of Athenian honorific decrees, even though it is written in Phoenician: the *koinon* of the Sidonians decrees in assembly (just as the Athenian assembly would have done) to give the honorand a golden crown (a typical Athenian award) and to inscribe this intention on a stele in the temple (just as the Athenian assembly often published its decisions in temples). The *koinon* of the Sidonians seems to have adopted the practices of the Athenian polis in their group decision-making.[105] Garland suggested that the adoption of typically Athenian formulaic phrases was a way for the Athenians to liaise with their foreign communities.[106] This, however, would imply that the Athenians forced the Sidonians to use these phrases in the Phoenician part of the inscription, which was clearly meant for Phoenicians, rather than anyone else, to read. In fact, after describing the reasons for the reward and the actual awards this man is given, the Phoenician text ends by explaining the reasons for erecting this stele: "Thereby the Sidonians shall know that the corporation knows how to requite men who have done a service before the corporation."[107] Clearly, the text written in Phoenician is intended for a Phoenician audience, whether from Sidon or not. In addition to recording whatever honors Shama-baal received, the emphasis in the last few lines of the inscription is on what the *koinon* of the Sidonians could do for its members. It is an advertisement for this particular organization of Sidonians in Peiraieus. Garland's hypothesis is more apt when it comes to the Greek text of the inscription, except that it is the Sidonians who attempt to liaise with the Athenian community, by adopting a style similar to that of the Athenians, and not the other way round.

The phrase "*koinon* of the Sidonians" might actually refer to an association of Sidonian traders in Athens, as Ameling suggests.[108] Although no traders are mentioned in this inscription, contemporary and near-contemporary parallels from Delos and Rhodes make explicit that *koina* were associations of traders, and not other groups of professionals, abroad. For instance, one inscription from Delos records the opinion of the *koinon* of the Poseidoniastes of Berytos who were traders, ship-owners, and forwarding agents on Delos,[109] and another mentions the *koinon* of traders,

---

[105] Cooke 1903: 95 no. 33 suggested that the text might be a translation of an Athenian decree.
[106] Garland 2001: 109.   [107] Teixidor 1980: 454.   [108] Ameling 1990.
[109] *IDélos* 1520: γνώμη τοῦ ἐν Δήλῳ κοινοῦ Βηρυτίων Ποσειδωνιαστῶν ἐμπόρων καὶ ναυκλήρων καὶ ἐγδοχέων.

ship-owners, and forwarding agents from Berytos on Delos.[110] These
inscriptions date from sometime before the middle of the second century BC. *Koina* of traders were common for other groups besides Phoenicians in this period. From Delos, again, there is evidence for a *koinon* of
Syrians[111] and other *koina* of Syrians are attested in Syme[112] and Malaka.[113]
These associations were social clubs with a strong religious character – the
Sidonians in Athens, the Poseidoniastes of Delos, the Adoniastes on Syme,
the Herakleistes on Delos etc. – that acted as foci for foreign communities of traders.[114] It is interesting to note that the names of the *koina*,
Herakleistes, Poseidoniastes, derive from Greek rather than Phoenician
deities. Perhaps these names were simply translations, just as the name
of the Sidonian honored by the *koinon* of the Sidonians, Shama-baal, was
translated into Greek as Diopeithes. Although these *koina* are attested from
the fourth century onwards, they resemble the earlier situation in the archaic
and classical period of foreign communities of traders rallying around specific sanctuaries, albeit with no supervising association. Thus, for example,
the Samian Hyblesios gave offerings to Hera in Gravisca and Naukratis, the
Aiginetan Sostratos gave dedications to the Aiginetan Apollo in Gravisca, the
Greeks of Naukratis, who came from different poleis, founded a common
temple – the Hellenion – expressing their collective identity as Hellenes, and
the Phokaians rallied around the cult of Ephesian Artemis. The Sidonian
traders in Peiraieus retained their language and their cults, as evidenced
by the bilingual inscriptions. And even though they did not have social
clubs in the classical period to organize their presence in Peiraieus, their
king Straton negotiated for them the right to remain in Peiraieus without
enlisting as metics and therefore without having to pay the *metoikion*, thus
facilitating their stay and execution of their trade activities in Peiraieus.

A similar method of granting partial rewards while still limiting participation in Athenian civic life is attested on another series of inscriptions
honoring foreign traders and ship-owners who by virtue of their profession
can be placed in Peiraieus; these date between 336 and 319 BC, with the
exception of one that is much later (176 BC). The honorary inscriptions in

---

[110] Dürrbach 1977: 118. For other parallels, see *IDélos* 1772–4 and 1776–82, and Dürrbach, *Choix*
119: τὸ κοινὸν Βηρυτίων τῶν ἐν Δήλῳ ἐμπόρων καὶ ναυκλήρων καὶ ἐγδοχέων. Tyrians also
had a *koinon* on Delos: *IDélos* 1519.

[111] Siebert 1968: 360: τὸ κοινὸν τῶν θιασιτῶ[ν] τῶν Σύρων.

[112] *IG* XII 3,6: κοινὸν Ἀδ[ω]νιασ[τᾶν Ἀφροδισιαστᾶν] Ἀσκλαπιαστᾶν Σύρων.

[113] *IG* XIV 2540.

[114] Vélissaropoulos 1980: 101–24, Baslez 1988, and Trümper 2006 have more detailed studies of
these groups. Kloppenborg and Ascough 2011 discuss associations in Attica, central Greece,
Thrace, and Macedonia.

question are not uniform in their formulation or the honors that they grant, despite various similarities. Yet there is one significant respect in which they are all the same: the reason for the honors. All decrees honor *emporoi* and *naukleroi* because they supplied Athens with grain, usually at a time of *spanositia*, shortage of grain.[115] Only two of these inscriptions provide extra reasons in addition to supplying grain, suggesting that the honorees in this case may have been ship-owners rather than traders. In one instance, the honoree both brought grain from Egypt and also ransomed some Athenians in Sicily and brought them back to Athens at his own expense.[116] Another man saved many Athenians who participated in the sea-battle of the Hellespont in 323/2 BC and brought them supplies, and also sent grain from the Hellespont to Athens because of the *spanositia*.[117]

Often, in addition to recording the specific event or even the specific low price at which the traders or ship-owners sold the grain, these inscriptions use several formulaic phrases to characterize the benefactors' actions. The most common are: ἀρετῆς ἕνεκα καὶ εὐνοίας τῆς εἰς τὸν δῆμον τὸν Ἀθηναίων (on account of his excellence and his goodwill towards the Athenian people);[118] εὐνοίας ἕνεκα καὶ φιλοτιμίας (on account of his excellence and zeal);[119] πρὸς τὸν δῆμον ἀποδέδεικται τὴν εὔνοιαν ἣν ἔχων (he demonstrated the favor he has towards the people);[120] ποιεῖ ὅ τι δύναται ἀγαθόν (he does whatever good he is able to [for the Athenians]);[121] or combinations of these phrases.[122] Although formulaic, these phrases at least demonstrate that the Athenian polis viewed these acts as benefactions to the whole community.

As might be expected, the decrees usually identify these individual *emporoi* or *naukleroi* with a city-ethnic, although some inscriptions are so fragmentary that they do not allow even a reconstruction of the name of these traders. Two different decrees honor Salaminians, probably from Salamis on Cyprus;[123] another honors a father and son from

---

[115] One decree explicitly honors an *emporos*: *IG* II² 360. Three others honor both *emporoi* and *naukleroi*: *IG* II² 343, 409, and 416. The remaining decrees do not mention the profession of the honoree, but since they honor men for bringing grain with their ships and selling it to the Athenians, usually at a cheap price, by implication they were also *emporoi* or *naukleroi*: *IG* II² 283, 342, 363, 398, 400, 401, 407–409, 903, and Schweigert 1940: 332–3: no. 29.

[116] *IG* II² 283.   [117] *IG* II² 398.   [118] *IG* II² 342 and 343.   [119] *IG* II² 360.

[120] *IG* II² 283; *IG* II² 416 uses a similar phraseology: τἆλλα ἐνδείκνυται τῶι ἀεὶ παραγιγνομένωι Ἀθηναίων εὔνοιαν (and he exhibited favor towards the Athenians in everything else that had happened).

[121] *IG* II² 400 and 401.   [122] *IG* II² 398, 407, and 408; Schweigert 1940: 332–3: no. 29.

[123] *IG* II² 283 and 360. Scholars have assumed that the traders are from the Cypriot Salamis: Whitehead 1977: 161; Pečírka 1966: 71 n. 1. Salaminians attested on grave stelai were also from Cyprus: *IG* II/III² 10171–215. Only three grave stelai (*IG* II/III² 10216–18) specify that the deceased are Salaminians from Cyprus.

Tyre;[124] one honoree was a certain Apollonides from Sidon;[125] another was probably from Chios;[126] yet another from Kyzikos;[127] one was probably a Milesian who brought grain from Cyprus;[128] two decrees honor men from Herakleia, but no specification is given as to which Herakleia they were from;[129] another honors an *emporos* from Kos;[130] a few other inscriptions cannot be reconstructed so as to yield either the name or the provenance of the honoree.[131]

The rewards that these men received vary slightly. Almost all of them received golden crowns[132] but one received just a στέφανος θαλλοῦ, probably an olive wreath.[133] A few of these inscriptions unfortunately break off before they give an indication of the honors bestowed.[134] More importantly, some men received more prestigious honors that amounted to residency in Athens, or at the very least, permanent ties with the Athenian civic body. Apollonides from Sidon, Herakleides from Salamis, and the two Tyrians were all made *proxenoi* and *euergetai* of the Athenians, and they were given the right of *enktesis*. The formulation of the three decrees is basically the same: εἶναι δὲ αὐτοὺς προξένους καὶ εὐεργέτας τοῦ δήμου τοῦ Ἀθηναίων αὐτοὺς καὶ ἐκγόνους αὐτῶν καὶ γῆς καὶ οἰκίας ἔγκτησιν εἶναι αὐτοῖς κατὰ τὸν νόμον ([they decided that] they would be *proxenoi* and *euergetai* of the Athenian demos, both they themselves and their descendants; they would also have *enktesis* of land and a house, according to the law).[135]

While the former category, namely, bestowing on each of these traders and ship-owners the titles of *proxenos* and *euergetes*, is mainly honorific, they did come with additional benefits. First of all, it is important to note that this honor was permanent because it was hereditary. Moreover, Whitehead proposed that the privileges given to *proxenoi* by Athens increased during the course of the fifth and fourth centuries, so that even if at first *proxenoi* were likely to remain in their own cities, by the fourth century they were residing in Athens and were given extra incentives, such as exemption from the *metoikion* or even *isoteleia*.[136] More recently, Culasso Gastaldi has noted that many of the individuals honored with *proxenia* in Athens were traders or ship-owners who were mobile and thus could reside in Athens to better serve their interests.[137] Thus, even though the phrases describing the rewards that these foreign traders received were formulaic, they carried a certain weight

---

[124] *IG* II² 342. [125] *IG* II² 343. [126] *IG* II² 400. [127] *IG* II² 401. [128] *IG* II² 407.
[129] Schweigert 1940: 332–3: no. 29; *IG* II² 408 honors two Herakleiots. [130] *IG* II² 416.
[131] *IG* II² 363 and 398. [132] *IG* II² 342, 343, 360, 401, 407, and 408. [133] *IG* II² 283.
[134] Schweigert 1940: 332–3: no. 29; *IG* II² 363, 398, 400, 409, 416, and 903.
[135] *IG* II² 342, 343, and 360. The only difference is that the inscription quoted above is in the plural because it honors two men; the other two honor only one man and are therefore in the singular.
[136] Whitehead 1977: 13–14. [137] Culasso Gastaldi 2004: 28–30.

in terms of the actual rights and privileges. Athens always considered traders indispensable; they were even more so when there was a shortage of grain. This is the context in which these inscriptions were produced, and which provides the rationale behind these important rewards, already seen in other emporia such as Naukratis and Pistiros.

The grants of *proxenia* are reminiscent of the honors given by the island of Rhodes to the two residents of Naukratis, discussed in Chapter 3. One of these inscriptions, dating to 440–411 BC, records the honors given to a man appropriately named Damoxenos (foreigner to the deme), who is described as living in Egypt.[138] The mention of the Hellenion later on in the inscription suggests that this man's residence was probably Naukratis. Damoxenos was named *proxenos* and *euergetes* of the Lindians and was also given tax exemption on imports and exports for himself and his descendants both in times of war and peace. The other inscription, slightly later (411–407 BC), gave Pytheas' son, a resident in Egypt from Naukratis, and his descendants, the title of *proxenos* of all Rhodians.[139] Pytheas' son and his descendants were also given the right to sail in and out of Rhodes both in times of war and peace. Although these two inscriptions are not Attic, they fit into Whitehead's scheme. Their earlier date may explain the fact that the inscriptions explicitly mention that these two men were residents of Naukratis and not Rhodes, where they were given the title *proxenoi*. The Rhodian inscriptions also gave the men they honored tax exemption on imports and exports and the right to sail to and from Rhodes at any time. This implies that they were probably *emporoi* or *naukleroi*, the same professions as those of the honorees of the Attic inscriptions, and that even though their official residence was Naukratis, they were mobile, as were the traders who received the Athenian rewards. The grant of tax exemption on the specific route from Naukratis to Rhodes, even if it was restricted to specific individuals, is similar to the legislation that the Thracian authorities enacted that made several trade routes from Maroneia to Pistiros and from Pistiros to the Belana emporia tax exempt. The recipients of the Athenian honors, however, do not receive tax exemption either on their imports or exports, although their status as *proxenoi* implied that they received some relief on their residency taxes. In any case, the Attic and Rhodian inscriptions suggest that Athens and Rhodes had similar ways of rewarding their foreign traders: both poleis often granted the status of *proxenos* to them. If each polis whose traders dealt with a given emporion probably had a *proxenos* there, then *proxenia* should be understood as another network that connected various poleis with each other across the Mediterranean.

---

[138] Pridik 1908: 19 no. 12; *SEG* 32, 1586.   [139] *IG* XII.1, 760.

In addition to the honorific title of *proxenos* and the privileges that came with it, the Athenian inscriptions granted the right of *enktesis* to the honored foreign traders and ship-owners. The formula in these cases is καὶ γῆς καὶ οἰκίας ἔγκτησιν εἶναι αὐτοῖς κατὰ τὸν νόμον (they have the right of *enktesis* of land and house, according to the law).[140] Pečírka, who has investigated the development of the formula for the grant of *enktesis*, argued that the attached κατὰ τὸν νόμον is a phrase that often appeared in such grants especially from the last third of the fourth century and the first third of the third century BC, a period that covers the dates of the inscriptions in question.[141] Even though the implication of this phrase is unclear, the meaning of καὶ γῆς καὶ οἰκίας ἔγκτησιν (*enktesis* of land and house) is transparent: the grant of *enktesis* gave foreigners the right to own land and a house in a foreign polis. The foreign traders who came to Peiraieus and supplied Athens with grain were essential to the welfare of the city and thus received this most precious of rights. Of course, the right of *enktesis* effectively rendered these foreign traders residents of Athens. Moreover, although the phrasing in the inscription suggests that it was only the grant of *proxenia* that was inheritable, it would only make sense to assume that once one became an owner of landed property and a home, these assets could be bequeathed to one's own relatives and descendants.

Herakleides of Salamis is the only foreign trader who receives the two extra rewards of enlisting in the army and paying the *eisphorai* together with the Athenians.[142] He probably came from Salamis of Cyprus, and though some scholars have claimed he was a Phoenician, there is no reason to suppose this since Salamis was a Greek city on Cyprus.[143] Although these awards may seem like burdens, they brought Herakleides closer to being an Athenian citizen. The reason that this trader received more honors than others is that he saved the Athenian polis not once, but several times. At one point (330/29 BC) he, first of all the *emporoi*, sailed into Peiraieus and sold barley below the market price.[144] Later, in 328/7 BC, he contributed money towards the purchase of grain. The most recent awards, given in 325/4 BC, state explicitly that previous decrees concerning Herakleides should also

[140] *IG* II² 342, 343, and 360.   [141] Pečírka 1966: 143.

[142] *IG* II² 360: στρατεύεσθαι αὐτοὺς τὰς στρατείας καὶ εἰσφέρειν τὰς εἰσφορὰς μετὰ Ἀθηναίων.

[143] Culasso Gastaldi 2004: 180–1 suggests that the name Herakleides was a translation of a Phoenician name, Abdelmelqart, which means Melqart's servant. Melqart was a Phoenician deity often recognized as Heracles in antiquity (Malkin 2005a). However, there is no evidence to support the idea that Herakleides from Salamis was a Phoenician. The majority of Phoenicians from Cyprus who lived in Athens were from Kition, as bilingual funerary inscriptions discovered in Peiraieus suggest. These inscriptions are discussed below.

[144] Selling products below the market place is recorded in one other decree (*IG* II² 903) and in Demosthenes, *Against Phormio* 38–9.

be inscribed on this same stone. Herakleides had proven himself to be a conscientious benefactor of Athens on several occasions, and Athens in return honored him first with a golden crown, then with the status of *proxenos* and *euergetes*, together with the right of land ownership, as well as with the attendant obligations of participation in the army and liability to taxes that Athenians paid.[145]

From the more general exposition of the metic and *xenos* status, and the specific information on the treatment of individual traders and ship-owners, one can infer the Athenian attitudes towards these groups. Athens defined metics and *xenoi* in the same way the latter defined themselves, that is, in terms of their city-state of origin, as grave stelai, honorific inscriptions, and forensic speeches show. Further, the presence of these non-Athenian traders, both Greek and foreign, required Athens to put an elaborate mechanism in place in order to incorporate partly, yet without recognizing as citizens, these residents or transients who supplied Athens with grain and participated in its commercial operations. Thus, metics and *xenoi* were not legally equal to citizens, they had to pay taxes in order to remain present in Athens, and they could not participate fully in religious festivals organized by the polis. The exclusivity of citizenship must have been most obvious in instances when foreigners were juxtaposed with citizens, such as during sacrifices in the deme to which they belonged, during the Panathenaia, or when members of the two groups met each other in the courts as legal adversaries. Nevertheless, both metics and *xenoi* were eligible for rewards that in effect led to their further inclusion in the Athenian polis. The individual rewards that traders and ship-owners received, for example, were not only monetary – the gold crowns given to them – but also established permanent ties between Athens and the honorees. Grants of *proxenia*, *euergesia*, and *enktesis*, given in return for acts of generosity foreigners performed that benefited the whole polis, all lifted some of the limitations imposed on foreign traders and their families. Athens had to walk the tightrope of mediating between itself and its foreign residents and regulating their presence in Athens. The foreigners also attempted to have smooth relations with the Athenians, as the Sidonian bilingual inscription suggests, so that they could continue their profitable commercial activities without unnecessary interruptions. In addition to the grave stelai and inscriptions set up by Sidonians, there is another group of

---

[145] Two other traders who claimed to have helped Athens three times were Chrysippos and his brother. Demosthenes, *Against Phormio* 38–9 says that once they imported grain and sold it at a low price, another time they gave a monetary gift to Athens with which to buy grain, and finally they also gave a monetary gift to Athens when Alexander entered Thebes in 335 BC. These are similar benefactions to those of Herakleides.

Athenian decrees that offers a glimpse into other ways in which foreigners in Peiraieus expressed their collective identity and mediated between themselves and the Athenian community. This epigraphic corpus, which records the right given to foreigners in Peiraieus to dedicate temples to their own deities, is the subject of the final section.

Foreign cults in Athens

The existence of foreign cults in Peiraieus has already been alluded to in previous sections: the epigraphically attested priest of Nergal and the inscription recording honors given to Shama-baal for supervising the building of a court at the temple of Baal, attest to two Phoenician deities – Nergal and Baal – worshipped in Peiraieus, at least from the third century BC onwards. There is, however, evidence for the worship of other foreign divinities from the fifth and fourth centuries BC.[146] The worship of foreign divinities in Peiraieus has usually been ascribed to Athens' political and economic policies.[147] Although that may have been part of the motivation for either acknowledging these foreign cults, adopting them as official Athenian cults, or simply allowing them to exist privately, I argue that the right given to foreigners to worship their own divinities resembled in its scope the rights given to individual traders: it was a way to mediate relations with the foreign population of Peiraieus, while at the same time regulating their involvement in the Athenian community in other ways. This was also what happened in Naukratis when the Egyptian Pharaoh Amasis granted the Greek traders sites where they could worship their divinities. There all the various Greeks came together and founded a common temple, the Hellenion. In Peiraieus, however, such a collective effort never came about, no doubt because the foreigners living there did not have much in common with one another. Rather individual cults emerged that were common to specific ethnic or civic groups.

In total, Garland counts seventeen foreign cults in Peiraieus, while Simms mentions only six.[148] As von Reden has pointed out, six of the cults on Garland's list date to the post-classical period, which is beyond the scope of this project (Artemis Nana, Baal, Men, Nergal, Serapis, and Zeus Labraundos); another three are not only attested in Peiraieus but also in other parts of the Greek world and thus cannot be considered as particular to Peiraieus or

---

[146] Garland 2001: 109.   [147] Von Reden 1995a: 31. Simms 1985: 284–6.
[148] Simms 1985. The six cults overlap with the list of Garland 2001: 109 (Bendis, Mother of Gods, Sabazios, Ammon, Isis, Aphrodite).

even as foreign (Mother of Gods, Sabazios, Kabyroi); the cult of Aphrodite
Euploia is not uniquely Carian, as Garland supposed, but rather, as we saw in
the chapter on Gravisca, Aphrodite was worshipped as Euploia ubiquitously
in the Greek world; and, finally, there is the double entry of Ammon and
Zeus Ammon, which in any case was not a cult particular to foreigners.[149]
This leaves only three of Garland's list of seventeen foreign cults, those of
Aphrodite, Isis, and Bendis.[150]

It is important to note that these three cults are attested on inscriptions
that record grants of *enktesis*. The right of *enktesis* did not belong only to
individuals; it was also a right parallel to that given by Amasis to the Greeks
of Naukratis, granted to groups of foreigners so that they could own land on
which to establish their temples.[151] This effectively meant that the temples
were built on private land and, therefore, were not recognized by Athens as
official cults of the city. Rather, they were merely publicly acknowledged.
One such grant was given to the Kitian *emporoi* from Cyprus (Figure 17).
The inscribed text records that an entity called δῆμος τῶν Κιτιείων, perhaps
something akin to the *koinon* of the Sidonians discussed above, approached
the Athenian assembly and asked to be allowed to establish a sanctuary
dedicated to Aphrodite. The text goes on to say that the Athenian demos
considered this request and then decided that the Kitians had lawfully
(ἔννομα) asked for the right of *enktesis*, so that they could own a piece of land
on which to found their sanctuary. In 333/2 BC, therefore, Athens granted
the right of *enktesis* to them, according to lines 33–45 of the inscription:

περὶ ὧν οἱ ἔμποροι οἱ Κ-
ιτιεῖς ἔδοξαν ἔννομα ἱκ-
ετεύειν αἰτοῦντες τὸν δ-
ῆμον χωρίου ἔνκτησιν ἐν
ὧι ἱδρύσονται ἱερόν Ἀφρ-
οδίτης, δεδόχθαι τῶι δήμ-
ωι δοῦναι τοῖς ἐμπόροις
τῶν Κιτιέων ἔνκτησι[ν] χ[ω]-
ρίου ἐν ὧι ἱδρύσονται τὸ

---

[149] Von Reden 1995a: 31. The worship of the Phoenician deities Nergal and Baal was discussed briefly above. Some of the post-classical cults in Athens were common throughout the Greek world, such as that of Serapis and Zeus Ammon (or Ammon *tout court*).

[150] If Greek metics in Peiraieus introduced other cults, they are not known. Otherwise, Greek metics may have simply used Athenian sanctuaries for their cults (some of these instances have been discussed above in the general exposition of metics).

[151] It was also granted to groups of political exiles, but since this is outside the scope of this study, these inscriptions will not be discussed: *IG* II² 237 and 545.

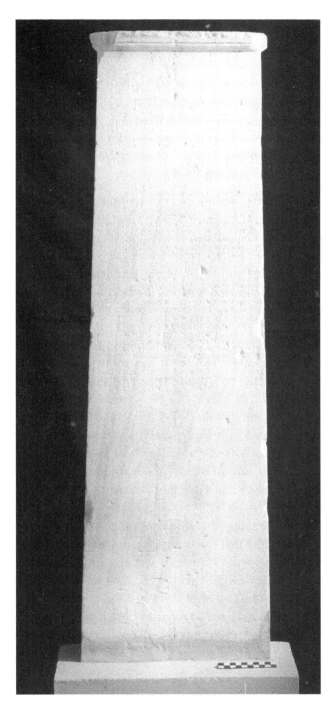

Figure 17 Stele recording an Athenian grant of permission to the Kitians of Cyprus to set up a sanctuary of Aphrodite in Athens (*IG* II² 337), 333/2 BC.

ἱερὸν τῆς Ἀφροδίτης καθ-
άπερ καὶ οἱ Ἀιγύπτιοι τὸ
τῆς Ἴσιδος ἱερὸν ἵδρυντ-
αι   *IG* II² 337

Since they decided that the Kitians were making a lawful request in demanding that the demos grant them the right to own (*enktesis*) land on which to establish a sanctuary of Aphrodite, it was resolved by the demos to grant the *emporoi* from Kition the right to own land (*enktesis*) on which to establish the sanctuary of Aphrodite, just as the Egyptians founded one for Isis.

This inscription, discovered in Peiraieus, is in fact the only secure evidence that attests to the worship of Isis in Athens.[152] The Kitians cited the Egyptian example as a precedent for the Athenian demos donating the right of *enktesis* to groups of foreigners who wanted to erect a temple in honor of one of their gods. It is not clear whether the Egyptians in question were traders or not. Nonetheless if the parallel worked for the Kitians, it is reasonable to assume that other foreigners, whether metics or not, could ask for and obtain the right to worship their own divinities. Religion, as I have argued, was one of the most common ways in which different groups mediated among themselves. The action of giving the right to foreigners to worship their own divinities was itself an act of mediation. Further, the various religious associations, such as the Sidonian *koinon* and perhaps the demos of the Kitians in Peiraieus, and also jointly founded temples like the Hellenion, probably had the social function of bringing citizens together when they were in a foreign land. Religion was also a vehicle through which groups expressed their identity when in foreign lands. Thus, it is not surprising that the Egyptians, Phoenicians, and Kitians living in Peiraieus would wish to continue to venerate their own deities.

Garland calls the cult of Aphrodite "the cult of Aphrodite Ourania" based on some supplementary evidence that could suggest this was the title under which the goddess was worshipped.[153] Three dedications, dating from the middle of the fourth century BC, approximately the time when the sanctuary was founded, were also discovered in Peiraieus: Ἀριστοκλέα Κιτιὰς Ἀφροδίτηι Οὐρανίαι εὐξαμένη ἀνέθηκεν (Aristoklea from Kition, fulfilling a vow, dedicated this to Aphrodite Ourania);[154] "Ἀφροδίτηι Καλλίστιον

[152] A statue found in Peiraieus is a representation either of Isis or one of her priestesses: Dunand 1973: 8.
[153] Garland 2001: 112–13. Kloppenborg and Ascough 2011: 26–32 follow this suggestion.
[154] *IG* II² 4636. The second inscription, *IG* II² 4637, is fragmentary but can be reconstructed because it was found in exactly the same location as *IG* II² 4636: [——Ἀφροδ]ίτηι [Οὐρανίαι

Ὀνησάνδρου Πειραιέως, ἐπὶ ἱερέως Κίκωνος" (Kallistion of Onesandros of Peiraieus [dedicated this] to Aphrodite when Kikon was the priest.)[155] There is another dedication to Aphrodite, excavated in Peiraieus, but it is of much later date and thus will not be considered here.[156] It was the inscription to Aphrodite Ourania that led Garland to specify that the cult introduced by the Kitians was dedicated to Aphrodite Ourania. Although his identification might be correct, it is also possible that traders worshipped Aphrodite for various roles, and therefore under various names, as they did in Gravisca and Naukratis. It is also noteworthy that the names of the dedicators on the two inscriptions quoted are female. The first one in particular, who identifies herself as a woman from Kition, suggests that women metics or *xenoi* – family members of traders or other professionals, slaves, prostitutes, or priestesses in charge of temples – were present in Peiraieus.

There is also the question of whether these Kitians were Greeks or Phoenicians. Kition, on Cyprus, was one of the largest Phoenician colonies. Given the usual association of Aphrodite Ourania with Phoenicia, already present in Herodotus, some scholars have assumed that the Kitians in Peiraieus were Phoenician.[157] A few grave stelai from Peiraieus of men who state they are from Kition suggests this could be the case.[158] Four of the six inscriptions are bilingual.[159] The Greek text states the name of the dedicator and his city-ethnic; the Phoenician text is usually a simple translation, or else it gives the family affiliation as well. Contrariwise, the dedications offered to Aphrodite by women, quoted above, were only in Greek. The comparative evidence for the Sidonian *koinon* and the Sidonian funerary inscriptions shows that the Sidonians in Peiraieus retained their language and worshipped their own deities. The discrepancy in the practices of the two groups of Phoenicians might be due to centuries of cohabitation with Greeks in Kition. Bilingualism may have been more common in Kition, or cross-cultural interactions for a long period of time may have made it easier for Phoenician Kitians to use Greek in their inscriptions than for other Phoenician groups that had not been living next to Greeks.

Two other decrees are concerned with the worship of Aphrodite in Peiraieus. One stele bears three decrees, dating to 302, 301, and 300 BC, which record the honors that the *thiasotai* of Aphrodite bestowed on their

---

εὐξαμεν- ὑ]πὲρ τοῦ [υἱοῦ? —]ίου (To Aphrodite Ourania, in fulfillment of a vow, on behalf of . . .).

[155] *IG* II² 4586.
[156] *IG* II² 1337 dates to 95/4 BC and attests to the worship of the Syrian Aphrodite.
[157] Herodotus 1.105; Raptou 1999: 160.   [158] *IG* II/III² 9031–6.
[159] *IG* II/III² 9031, 9033, 9034, and 9035.

epimeletes, who supervised a procession during the Adonia, the festival in honor of Adonis.[160] A *thiasos* was originally an association that belonged to a phratry, but by the fourth century it had come to designate a cult association similar to a *koinon*.[161] In fact, one of the inscriptions from Delos that honors the Herakleistes from Tyre uses the two terms interchangeably.[162] Although the decree does not name the polis of origin of the *thiasotai* who decided to honor the supervisor of the festival, it is likely that they were metics (or *xenoi*), especially given the parallels between a *thiasos* and a *koinon*. Another inscription from Peiraieus dating to the middle of the third century BC records a decree that honored the *epimeletes* of the Adonia and some sacrifices that took place in honor of Aphrodite.[163] The group that granted these honors is explicitly identified as a group of Salaminians, probably from Cyprus.[164]

Of the three decrees that attest to the worship of Aphrodite in Peiraieus, only the one that involves the Kitians may be securely identified as a cult that metics introduced in Peiraieus, even though similar bodies of non-Athenian traders who were at some point granted the right to worship Aphrodite produced the other two inscriptions. In any case, it is clear that the Kitians, whether Phoenicians or not, regarded Aphrodite (or probably Astarte, if they were Phoenicians) as a special deity. That they asked to build a sanctuary for her as opposed to any other god is important. First, since Aphrodite was a goddess of the Greek pantheon, the Kitian request must have been easy to fulfill for the Athenians. Second, Aphrodite and Astarte were both prominent deities in Kition, and Aphrodite was of special importance throughout the other Cypriot poleis.[165] Choosing her as a goddess to worship was an expression of their collective identity as Kitians, and possibly also as Cypriots. This last observation suggests the possibility that the Salaminians and Kitians worshipped Aphrodite in the same temple.

The grant of *enktesis* for the specific purpose of building a temple given to the Kitian merchants was not the earliest. About a hundred years earlier, sometime shortly before 429/8 BC, the Thracians in Athens were granted *enktesis* and the right to worship their goddess Bendis in Peiraieus. This is

---

[160] *IG* II^2 1261.   [161] Vélissaropoulos 1980: 95.

[162] *IDélos* 1219 (lines 12, 35, and 40 call the association *koinon*; line 26 calls it a *thiasos*; and lines 4, 6, 8, 19, 24, 28, and 31–2 call it a *synodos*).

[163] *IG* II^2 1290.

[164] Other Cypriots present in Peiraieus are attested from grave stelai. One was a woman from Kourion (*IG* II/III^2 9084), another a woman from Soloi (*IG* II/III^2 10376), and three others were women from Paphos (*IG* II/III^2 10048–50). One man was from Soloi; *IG* II/III^2 10382 (Σόλιος ἀπὸ Κύπρου).

[165] Pirenne-Delforge 1994: 309–70; Ulbrich 2008.

known indirectly because a later decree, dating to 261/0 BC, mentions that in an earlier period Athens had given this right to Thracians:

ἐπειδὴ τοῦ δήμου τοῦ Ἀθηναίων δεδωκότος τοῖς Θραιξὶ μ-
όνοις τῶν ἄλλων ἔθνων τὴν ἔγκτησιν καὶ τὴν ἵδρυσιν τοῦ
ἱεροῦ κατὰ τὴν μ[α]ντείαν τὴν ἐγ Δωδώνης καὶ τὴν πονπὴν π-
ένπειν ἀπὸ τῆς ἑστίας τῆς ἐκκ τοῦ πρυτανείου . . .

IG II² 1283, lines 4–7

Since the Athenian *demos* has granted only to the Thracians of all the other *ethne* both the right of *enktesis* for the foundation of a sanctuary, according to the oracle from Dodona, and the right to hold a procession from the sacred hearth of the prytaneion . . .

The grant to own land and establish a sanctuary dedicated to Bendis was the first such grant the Athenian demos gave to any of its resident aliens, as the inscription records.[166] The grant of *enktesis* and right to build a temple given to the Egyptians and, subsequently, the Kitian merchants perhaps should suggest that such awards had become common practice by the fourth century BC. The Thracians who received this grant in the fifth century BC may or may not have been *emporoi*; the relevant inscriptions are silent on this point. Nonetheless, the cult was established in Peiraieus and contributes to our understanding of how Athens regulated its interactions with resident aliens and how different ethnic groups expressed their own identity.

Although *enktesis* and the right to establish a sanctuary to Bendis was originally given as a private grant to the Thracian residents of Athens, by the last quarter of the fifth century, the worship of this Thracian goddess was adopted as Athenian state religion. This is evident from various inscriptions, spanning from the fifth to the third centuries BC, which attest to the fact that the festival of Bendis was part of the official Athenian religious calendar. For instance, the earliest secure attestation for an Athenian cult of Bendis is in the treasury accounts of the Other Gods, dating to 429/8 BC.[167] The original grant of *enktesis*, therefore, must have been given to the Thracians at some point before this date. Regulations regarding the public worship of

---

[166] Notwithstanding the fact that this inscription does not anywhere mention the name of the divinity worshipped, scholars are fairly secure in their identification of the goddess as Bendis. Not only is the cult of Bendis the only Thracian cult attested in Peiraieus, but also the details of the procession from the prytaneion to Peiraieus correspond to those attested in other inscriptions concerning Bendis' worship, discussed below.

[167] IG I³ 383. Accounts from 334–30 BC (IG II² 1496) also record earnings from the sale of sacrificial hides.

---

the goddess were enacted in another Athenian decree passed in 413/12 BC that legislated both the conditions of appointment of the priest or priestess, who was to be chosen from all the Athenians, and details of the sacrifices.[168] By 404 BC, according to Xenophon, a Bendideion had been established on the promontory of Mounychia.[169] A later inscription of 337/6 defined the worship of the goddess even further.[170] The decree details the honors that Athenian citizen *orgeones* of Bendis gave to their *hieropoioi*. Two other inscriptions also refer to the Athenian citizen *orgeones*, who honor their *epimeletai*.[171] Yet another inscription of the fourth century is a sacred law that records the fee that citizen-members paid for the sacrifice. It also indicates that membership in these *orgeones* was hereditary and details the sacrificial rituals that had to be followed.[172]

Orgeones were religious associations, much like the *koina* and *thiasoi* that emerged in Peiraieus, Delos, Rhodes, and elsewhere, discussed above.[173] All of the *orgeones* mentioned thus far were Athenian, and indeed all *orgeones* known from the classical period were Athenian.[174] However, further inscriptions regarding Bendis' cult in Athens complicate the picture because they suggest that in addition to the citizen *orgeones* there may have also been Thracian *orgeones* participating in the Athenian festival for Bendis. For example, two contemporary decrees, one of which is the one quoted above that refers to the first grant of *enktesis* to the Thracian residents of Athens, mention that the celebration of the festival would take place on the eighth day of a given month, whereas an inscription that mentions only Athenian citizens records that the celebration would take place on the second day of the month.[175] Moreover, the same two inscriptions that mention the eighth day of the month, also suggest that the honorees would receive oak wreaths, whereas inscriptions that mention Athenian *orgeones* award olive wreaths.[176] These distinctions have led scholars to conclude that there were

---

[168] *SEG* 10, 64. Ferguson 1949 and Bingen 1959 discuss this inscription, which has survived in three fragments.

[169] Xenophon, *Hellenika* 2.4.10–11.   [170] *IG* II² 1255 (337/6 BC).

[171] *IG* II² 1324 (late fourth/early third century BC) and *IG* II² 1256 (329/8 BC). They probably refer to Athenian *orgeones* because they gave olive wreaths to the honorees. See the discussion in the next paragraph.

[172] *IG* II² 1361.

[173] Ferguson 1944 and 1949; N. F. Jones 1999: 249–67; Kloppenborg and Ascough 2011: 1–13.

[174] Kearns 1989: 73–7; Lambert 1993: 74–7; Mikalson 1998: 141; Kloppenborg and Ascough 2011: 5.

[175] *IG* II² 1283 and 1284 say that the *orgeones* met on the eighth day of the month, whereas *IG* II² 1361 names the second day of the month as the day the *orgeones* would meet.

[176] *IG* II² 1324 (late fourth/early third century BC) and *IG* II² 1256. The former specifically mentions the olive wreaths in the text of the inscription, while the latter has engraved olive wreaths on the stele. *IG* II² 1283 and 1284 both state that the wreath given to those honored is

two different sets of *orgeones* in Peiraieus: one was made up of Athenian citizens and the other of Thracians.[177] This is certainly supported by the beginning of Plato's *Republic*, where Socrates describes the events of the festival of Bendis during which there was one procession of Athenian citizens and another of Thracians.[178] Internal evidence from *IG* II² 1283 also suggests that there existed a Thracian procession. The inscription records that the Thracian *orgeones* wished to comply with an earlier law, perhaps as early as the original grant of *enktesis* given to the Thracians, that ordered them to send their procession from the hearth in the prytaneion in Athens to Peiraieus. The new legislation of 261/0 BC, recorded on the same inscription, outlines the procedures for the joint celebration of the procession by *orgeones* in Peiraieus and the *asty* and the reception of the *orgeones* in Peiraieus, suggesting that perhaps there were Thracian *orgeones* both in Athens and in Peiraieus.[179] The *orgeones* in the *asty* were also given reciprocal membership rights with those of Peiraieus, thus bringing the two groups of Thracians together in this festival.

How were these Thracians and Athenians supposed to worship this Thracian goddess in Athens? Here we face a similar question to that asked in relation to the worship of the Ephesian Artemis in Massalia and Emporion. In Bendis' case, however, we have some further information. The same inscription from 261/0 BC, after detailing regulations on how the procession from the *asty* should be received once it has arrived in Peiraieus, adds provisions about the method of worship of the goddess:

... ὅ[πως ἂν τούτ]-
ων γινομένων καὶ ὁμονοοῦντος παντὸς τοῦ ἔθ[νους αἵ τ]-
ε θυσίαι γίνωνται τοῖς θεοῖς καὶ τὰ ἄλλα ὅσα πρ[οσήκει]
κατά τε τὰ πάτρια τῶν Θραικῶν καὶ τοὺς τῆς πόλ[εως νόμου]-
ς καὶ ἔχει καλῶς καὶ εὐσεβῶς παντὶ τῶι ἔθν[ει τὰ πρὸς τοὺ]-
ς θεούς...   *IG* II² 1283, lines 22–27

In order that when these things are done and the whole *ethnos* is in agreement the sacrifices to the gods and everything else that is appropriate may be performed according to the ancestral customs of the Thracians and the laws of the polis. And everything that concerns the gods should proceed well and piously for the whole *ethnos*.

---

made out of oak leaves. A third inscription that records the honors given to their *epimeletai* and other officers, *IG* II² 1317, dating from the end of the third century, might also refer to Thracian *orgeones*.
[177] Ferguson 1944: 98–101; N. F. Jones 1999: 256–62; Kloppenborg and Ascough 2011: 24.
[178] Plato, *Republic* 1.327a.   [179] N. F. Jones 1999: 257–9.

These few lines are the only evidence that exists delineating precisely how foreign cults maintained their festival rites and the extent to which foreigners had to change their practices because they lived abroad. The rites performed in honor of Bendis had to follow both the ancestral habits of the Thracians and also Athenian laws, in addition to being acceptable to the whole Thracian *ethnos* present in Athens and Peiraieus. Here, the delicate balance that had to be kept in order for all parties involved to be satisfied is obvious. The Thracians were allowed to maintain all their customs as they did in their homeland, but only to the extent that they did not violate any Athenian laws. This also implies that the citizen *orgeones* had to venerate the goddess according to the Thracian customs. Here is an example of reciprocal relations between Athenians and Thracians, which no doubt led to bringing together the two groups for the single purpose of worshipping Bendis, a goddess who acted, therefore, as a mediator between them.

The worship of Bendis in Athens is substantially different from other foreign cults that were never adopted by Athens as official and probably had little or no participation by citizens.[180] Already in the late fifth century, as we have seen, Bendis' cult had been incorporated into the official Athenian cults, and both citizens and Thracians participated in the festival held annually in honor of this goddess. Bendis' worship was also different in that both citizens and Thracians had equal participation, unlike other official Athenian cults that allowed only limited contributions by foreigners, whether metics or *xenoi*. It has already been recognized that the official adoption of Bendis' veneration in the late fifth century may ultimately have had a political motive. The cult was perhaps adopted in order to confirm an alliance between Athens and King Sitalkes, a Thracian dynast, at the beginning of the Peloponnesian War.[181] Even if this was so, I argue that granting *enktesis* to the Thracian residents was part and parcel of the mediation among Athenians and Thracians, one of the most represented groups in the metic and slave population of Athens.[182] Of the whole pantheon of Thracian gods, Bendis was a particularly appropriate goddess to choose because she was similar to the Greek goddess Artemis.[183] The usual translatability of

---

[180] The cult of Zeus Ammon mentioned earlier also became an official Athenian cult, in the third century BC.

[181] Nilsson 1960; Simms 1985: 49–50; Von Reden 1995a: 31; Montepaone 1990.

[182] N. F. Jones 1999: 261 proposes that the Athenian demos intervened in the activities of the citizen *orgeones* in order to counteract social segregation between Athenian citizens and Thracian metics. I would add that since many of the Thracians present in Athens were slaves, such a policy would have the effect of appeasing Thracian slaves by equating them with citizens in the festivals of the goddess.

[183] In fact, Greek lexicographers often define Bendis as the Thracian Artemis (Hesychios s.v. Bendis).

deities among Mediterranean cultures would have made it easier to accept Bendis in Athens. In this context, it may be significant that Bendis' cult-site was near the temple of Artemis Mounychia in Peiraieus.[184] Various artistic representations of Bendis on vases and reliefs also demonstrate that she was portrayed in visually similar ways to Artemis.[185] Finally, the adoption of a Thracian cult as part of the Athenian state religion is a clear example of how the extensive cross-cultural interactions facilitated in multiethnic emporia affected the host-community – in this case, Athens – which adopted a foreign god as her own.

It is interesting to note, as Garland does, that all the foreign religious activity in Peiraieus was conducted in the Greek language, with the single exception of the bilingual Phoenician cults discussed earlier in this chapter. Garland interpreted this uniformity as evidence that the Athenian community used cult associations to liaise with its foreign community.[186] The example of the Sidonians, however, shows that it was also possible to maintain and use the original language of the group to produce and publicize long texts (as opposed to the short Greek description attached to the Phoenician text). The use of the Greek language in official documents produced by foreigners may have been a way for them to relate to the Athenian community, the non-Athenian Greeks present in Peiraieus, and other foreigners living there. It is likely that the non-Greek inhabitants of Peiraieus did not all speak the same language, but rather used Greek as a lingua franca in their commercial transactions, and perhaps also in their day-to-day life. The same was true in Iberia, where the commercial transactions recorded on the lead letters from Emporion and Pech-Maho, were inscribed in Greek despite the fact that the parties involved in the transaction were Greek and Iberian.

Conclusion

The foundation of the port of Peiraieus brought with it incredible commercial growth, eventually resulting in the creation of the cosmopolitan emporion of Peiraieus, frequented by non-Athenian Greeks and non-Greeks

---

[184] Xenophon, *Hellenika* 2.4.11: τὴν ὁδὸν ἥ φέρει πρός τε τὸ ἱερὸν τῆς Μουνιχίας Ἀρτέμιδος καὶ τὸ Βενδίδειον (the road that brings one to the sanctuary of Artemis Mounychia and the Bendideion). Garland 1992: 113.

[185] Reliefs from Peiraieus: BM 2155, Copenhagen Glypt. 462 C; Vases: Mus. Teatro Romano 52, Tübingen, Univ. S/10 1347. The latter vase, dating from the end of the fifth century, represents Themis and Bendis together. The pairing of the two goddesses might indicate the official introduction of Bendis' worship in Peiraieus (and Athens). See Nilsson 1955: I 834 and Shapiro 1993: 225.

[186] Garland 2001: 109.

alike. As such, Peiraieus provides a foil against which to compare the situations encountered in previous chapters. The evidence from Peiraieus suggests that the same complementary yet sometimes competitive relationship, witnessed also in Pistiros and Naukratis, existed between Athens and its foreign residents and visitors. For Athens, foreign traders were an indispensable part of the polis. Athens had to make residency in Athens attractive to these groups, even if it never fully incorporated them into the citizenry.

Legal measures were introduced that delineated the rights of foreign residents and visitors, most of whom probably resided in Peiraieus. Metics and *xenoi* remained excluded from the citizenry, could not own land, continued to identify themselves in terms of their native civic identity, and paid for their residency in Athens in taxes. In return they were granted limited participation in the civic life of the polis: they had recourse to Athenian law, although not always on an equal footing with citizens, and metics could take part only in some festivals and only rarely sacrifice in exclusive cults. When individual traders, whether metics or *xenoi*, benefited the whole Athenian community by selling their grain for a minimum price fixed by the Athenian state, giving money to Athens to buy grain, or simply importing grain from other areas in times of *sitospania*, Athens gave special privileges to these men, which increased their participation in the Athenian civic body by giving them the right to own land and a house, exempting them from taxes that traders had to pay, and granting them honorific titles and crowns. At the most extreme, Athens allowed metics to participate in military service and gave them *isoteleia*. The latter grant eliminated the foreign taxes immigrants had to pay, but it meant that they had to pay the same taxes as citizens, for which they were not liable before. Inclusion in the citizenry also entailed more obligations and responsibilities, but foreigners must have considered it a privilege.

As is clear from the epigraphic evidence and the forensic speeches studied here, in addition to never fully including its foreigners as citizens, Athens always distinguished among them in terms of their polis of origin. The foreigners themselves also proclaimed their civic identity in grave stelai and honorific inscriptions. The willingness of Athens to grant foreigners the right to worship their own deities is another example of the elaborate mechanism that both accommodated and excluded foreigners. By the fourth century, social groups crystallized around specific cults in Peiraieus, as they did also in emporia throughout the Greek world. In Athens there were the *koinon* of the Sidonians, the *orgeones* of the Thracian cult of Bendis, the *thiasotai* of Aphrodite, the demos of the Kitians, who set up a sanctuary to Aphrodite, and a group of Egyptians who established a sanctuary dedicated to the Egyptian goddess Isis. These associations acted as nuclei that organized foreign cults and expressed collective identities centered around ethnic or civic groups.

Finally, by translating Bendis into Artemis, or Zeus into Baal, the multiethnic population of Athens could communicate with each other. The translatability of polytheistic religious systems throughout the Mediterranean made the acceptance of foreign cults in Peiraieus easier than it would have been otherwise. These examples in particular demonstrate the more general conclusion that Mediterranean groups had the ability to transcend religious boundaries while retaining distinctive features in the specific customs of each cult.

Conclusion

Trade was one of many activities that connected the Mediterranean basin, bringing a degree of geographical and cultural unity to the region. Contacts among the different groups inhabiting the Mediterranean lands began in the Bronze Age and continued uninterrupted, albeit not always with the same intensity. By the end of the seventh century BC, Greeks, Etruscans, and Phoenicians, among many other groups, shared a maritime perspective, a city-state culture, polytheistic religions that were easily translatable from one to another, and a common material culture, which included Attic vases and coins, Egyptian faience, Etruscan bucchero-ware, Corinthian vases, and Cypriot sculptures, among other products.

It was precisely the existence of a common Mediterranean culture that facilitated contact among different groups in multiethnic settlements, such as emporia. The cross-cultural exchanges examined in each of the five emporia considered in this book, namely, Emporion in Iberia, Gravisca in Etruria, Naukratis in Egypt, Pistiros in Thrace, and Peiraieus in Attica, reveal not only how host societies and foreign residents mediated their interactions but also how different groups constructed distinct identities. The interactions among different Greek groups and between Greeks and non-Greeks that took place in such settlements were not static, monolithic or unilateral, but rather dynamic, multifaceted, and creative. Any group could appropriate myths, artistic styles and techniques, objects, gods, political institutions, and legal systems in order to mediate among themselves by constructing a new, common, and mutually comprehensible world, in which all groups present could participate. Moreover, the close encounters experienced by the various groups that came together in these commercial settlements also led to the creation of new identities.

Administrating multiethnic settlements

The investigation of the five different emporia discussed in this book shows that in order to facilitate commerce in multiethnic emporia, several sophisticated political, administrative, and judicial mechanisms were put in place. First, it is important to remember that with the exception of Peiraieus, which was an Athenian deme, the other emporia considered here were independent, self-governing Greek poleis located in non-Greek lands. These settlements had to have some degree of autonomy to carry out their commercial operations. Thus, the Egyptian government granted specific areas in which the Greek traders could set up an emporion in Naukratis and left the administration to the *prostatai* of the emporion. Similarly the Thracian authorities granted limited autonomy to the community of Pistiros by guaranteeing that no hostages would be taken from among the citizens and the resident traders, and no military force would be sent to the polis. Likewise, the information from Gravisca suggests that although the Greek traders were probably a minority living among an Etruscan majority, they were in charge of all trade activities. Peiraieus had its own administrators (*epimeletai*) of the emporion along with other officials, chosen by lot from among Athenian citizens. Finally, Emporion was an independent polis that had complete control over its commercial operations, even after it included the Iberian Indiketans in the Greek polis. At that point, both parties adopted a mixed constitution, which led to the creation of a new common social order achieved by the two-way adoption of specific traits, in this case, *nomima*, political customs that organized the public life of a polis.

The administrative language of emporia depended on the situation of both the host society and the trader community. Overall, it seems that the dominant party used its own language in official contexts, whereas individuals usually used their mother tongue. When the Thracian authorities published legislation that had been passed regarding the Greeks living in Thrace, they did so in Greek, a language adopted by Thracians of that period, but when the Egyptians did the same for the Greeks living in Naukratis, they inscribed the stele in Egyptian. Greek seems to have been the language of trade when both Greek and Iberian parties were involved in particular commercial transactions, as the lead letters from Emporion and Pech-Maho show. There also exist commercial letters written in Iberian, but since the language has not been deciphered yet, it is not possible to say who was involved in the transactions these letters recorded. In Athens, the main language used officially when dealing with foreigners was Greek. For example, the city itself honored its foreigners by setting up inscriptions that recorded the awards granted to them in Greek. Similarly, the Sidonians who set up an inscription to honor one of their own inscribed it in both Greek and Phoenician. The Greek text followed some of the conventions that Athenian decrees used, by naming both the deciding body and the honoree.

Individual Sidonians, Phoenician Kitians, and others, however, set up bilingual inscriptions in public but for unofficial purposes, such as funerary monuments.

Relations between host-societies and trader communities were both complementary and competitive. Host-societies recognized that trade was beneficial to the local economy, increased the variety of goods available, and could bring in significant revenues. The latter were usually through taxes. Taxes on imports and exports were a form of income for host-societies. So, for instance, in Peiraieus there was a specific office of the *pentekostologoi* who exacted the 2 percent import tax, and any foreigner who conducted business in the agora had to pay the *xenika tele* (foreigners' taxes). In Naukratis, too, the Greek traders paid import and export taxes to the Egyptian government, which also strictly controlled the entry of traders into the country, allowing them to enter only through Naukratis and no other port. In other cases, taxes were lifted on specific trade routes in order to allow traders to conduct commerce more easily, as when the Thracian authorities made the North Aegean trade routes from Pistiros to the Melas Gulf tax exempt, or when Rhodes granted free passage as a reward to specific traders traveling from Naukratis to different poleis on Rhodes. Traders were probably happy to pay these taxes because they were a way to ensure the smooth running of their operations and their personal safety. In a sense, therefore, taxes, and even the political subordination that often accompanied them, constituted protection costs that the resident traders had to pay.

The multiethnic nature of emporia necessitated the elaboration of legislation in the host-society that dealt with foreigners living in its midst. In Pistiros, the Thracian dynasts delineated the rights of Greek traders vis-à-vis Thracians. They granted Greeks living in Thrace personal inviolability, inalienability of property and possessions, safety for their community from the Thracian military, and the guarantee that Thracian debts owed to Greek traders would not be absolved. The evidence from Peiraieus, too, demonstrates the detailed legislation enacted in order to deal with non-Athenians, whether Greek or not, who lived in Athens. Foreign traders fell into two legally defined categories, those who resided permanently in Athens, metics, and those who visited for a short period, *xenoi*. The rights and liabilities of these non-Athenians were clear: members of neither category could own land or a house, and they had restricted access to the law. Metics had to pay the *metoikion*, residency tax, and, like citizens, they paid income taxes (*eisphora*), performed liturgies, and were even liable to Athenian military service. *Xenoi* were liable to pay fewer taxes since they were not permanent residents of the city, but they also had a more limited access to the

Athenian legal system than metics. At the same time, Athens could at any point award its foreign traders special privileges when they performed services benefiting the Athenian community, such as the grant of *isoteleia*, equality in taxation, the right to own land and a home (*enktesis*), and honorary titles, such as *proxenos* or *euergetes* (benefactor). While laws regulated the presence of foreigners, they also mediated with them by making it worthwhile for foreign traders to reside in an emporion.

The legal systems of host societies catered to the multiethnic populations of emporia. The most obvious example is the use of foreign judges to arbitrate disputes in emporia; the practice was introduced in Pistiros and used frequently also by Hellenistic rulers. Foreign judges were usually appointed from a *syngenes* polis – a polis that had formal ties to the one that requested arbitrators. The institution of foreign judges must have been particularly useful in the context of multiethnic emporia such as Pistiros because they could settle disputes between parties that followed different laws. At the same time, the fact that the Thracian dynasts requested these men indicates that using external Greek judges was a convenient method for foreign sovereigns to arbitrate cases without imposing Thracian justice on residents of Greek poleis under their dominion. Although different in nature, the introduction of the *emporikai dikai* in fourth-century Peiraieus also ensured that traders would have quick access to a legal system, at least to the extent that it dealt with trade activities.

Cosmopolitan religion: creating a middle ground

The political, commercial, and legal administration of emporia organized and facilitated trade at the same time as it regulated the presence of foreigners living in emporia and mediated their interactions. The religious practices in the five emporia studied in this book show that religion played a central role in reaching accommodation. The translatability of pantheons among Mediterranean cultures allowed Greeks and whichever local population they encountered to recognize similarities between their respective gods, who acted as mediators between groups, facilitating their coexistence. Recognizing that certain Greek divinities were part of their common heritage was also instrumental in facilitating interactions among different Greek groups that came together in emporia.

In Gravisca, for example, Aphrodite and her Etruscan analogue, Turan, acted as trans-cultural mediators between Greeks and Etruscans living there and thus facilitated their coexistence. Greeks and Etruscans alike could use the predominantly Greek sanctuaries to worship both goddesses, and after the Greek abandonment of Gravisca, the Etruscans appropriated the sanctuaries and continued to worship their own divinities there. Similarly, Dionysus played a similar mediating role among the Greeks of Pistiros and also between the Greeks and Thracians in Pistiros. As a god venerated by all the parties involved, including Thasians and Apollonians who lived in Pistiros, Maroneians, the citizens of Pistiros themselves, and the Thracian dynasts, Dionysus could act as the guarantor of the provisions of the Vetren text, which applied to all of these groups. It is for this reason that the Thracian authorities swore an oath in the god's name. The introduction of the cult of Bendis in Peiraieus and its adoption as an official Athenian cult was the result of a similar process of accommodation. The fact that both citizen and Thracian *orgeones* worshipped the Thracian goddess in Athens suggests that the Thracian *metics* and the Athenian state attempted to relate to one another through the common worship of Bendis. In a different fashion, the Greeks of Naukratis had to pay taxes in the temple of the Egyptian goddess Neith, identified as a goddess of the sea and trade.

At the same time as religion was a way for different ethnic groups to liaise with one another, it offered the opportunity for different Greek groups to do the same. In Emporion, for instance, the Phokaian-Massaliote Greeks venerated the goddess Artemis, whom they had borrowed from the Ephesian Greeks. In Pistiros, the Thasian and Apollonian Greeks who lived there, as well as the citizens of Pistiros, had the worship of Dionysus in common. Aphrodite mediated among the different Greek groups residing in Gravisca. Having been brought together in one settlement, Greeks who came from different poleis acknowledged that they had in common the worship of this goddess. The ways in which they practiced Aphrodite's cult in their home poleis may have been different, but there were several ways in which Aphrodite's worship was common to them all: Aphrodite's role as a patron of navigation and as a goddess of sex, for example, was common throughout the Greek world. The Greeks of Naukratis also used religion to facilitate interactions among themselves. They shared a common temple, called the Hellenion, in which they worshipped individual heroes or divinities that they acknowledged having in common, such as Heracles, the Dioskouroi, Artemis, Aphrodite, Poseidon, and Apollo, as well as the gods of the Greeks collectively. Recognizing that these deities were part of their common heritage was instrumental in facilitating interactions among all the Greeks.

What is also common in temples in emporia is that access to them was not restricted. All the Greeks frequenting and residing in Naukratis and

Gravisca, for example, could give offerings in any temple, as the surviving dedicatory inscriptions show. This was true not only of the Hellenion in Naukratis, whose name suggests that it was a temple common to all the Greeks, but also of temples founded by specific poleis, such as the temple dedicated to Hera founded by Samians and the temple of Apollo founded by Milesians in Naukratis, and temples dedicated to individual divinities, like the temples of Aphrodite, Apollo, and Hera in Gravisca, or Aphrodite in Naukratis. Moreover, the divinities venerated were not worshipped for a single role or in a particular manner. In fact, the norm in emporia was to bypass the usual exclusivity of cult that characterized Greek religion by allowing any Greek, regardless of his origin, to worship at any sanctuary and to venerate whichever of the god's many functions he wanted. Thus Greeks who came from all over the Greek world worshipped Aphrodite in both Gravisca and Naukratis for her role as a protector of sailors, guardian of civic order, and goddess of sex, in the same temple.

Cults in multiethnic settlements, therefore, were flexible and offered open access to all who visited. The evidence from Naukratis, Emporion, and Peiraieus presented in this book demonstrates how these cosmopolitan religious practices could have been performed. The rituals in honor of the Thracian goddess Bendis in Peiraieus, for example, were required by law to follow the Thracian customary rites but only to the extent that these obeyed Athenian laws. In Emporion and other Greek sites in Iberia, both Greeks and Iberians had to perform the appropriate rites for Artemis of Ephesos in Greek. Finally, the institution of *proxenia* might have also had a religious aspect. *Proxenoi* were intermediaries between their own community and the foreigners for whom they were responsible. They acted as guarantors of the foreigner in question, being liable for him vis-à-vis both the foreigner's and also the *proxenos'* polis. I have also suggested that in emporia *proxenoi* may have had a similar role to the *proxenoi* at Delphi and Olympia, namely, the function of performing sacrifices on behalf of the foreigner. In this way, a foreigner was incorporated, if only temporarily, into the community and thus surmounted restrictions that otherwise existed on participating in specific cults.

Religion, political institutions, and legal systems were all to a significant degree trans-cultural phenomena. They may have had characteristics that were specific to a polis, a region, or a particular group, but they also had structural similarities that allowed them to function as part of a Mediterranean *koine*. Dynamic processes of co-optation, mediation, and adaptability used religion, politics, and law, to create a middle ground that facilitated interactions among groups.

Negotiating identities

The extensive relations among groups of different backgrounds throughout the Mediterranean, especially as they played out in multiethnic emporia, had profound effects both on host-societies and trader communities. With the creation of new, common worlds, new collective identities were also articulated. One of the findings of this work is that the primary form of Greek self-identification was based on civic identity, both in the archaic and classical periods. None of the individuals studied here ever used their sub-Hellenic group ascriptions to identify themselves. It is only in the mid-fifth century, in the context of the Peloponnesian War, that the terms Ionian and Dorian became more salient and when myths concerning these groups appear and proliferate in our sources. Thus Herodotus describes the poleis that founded Naukratis as Ionian, Dorian, or Aeolian and not the actual Greeks who lived there. The Greeks living in and visiting Naukratis, Peiraieus, and Emporion, only used their city-ethnics to identify themselves. The Greeks of Pistiros, if the text of the inscription that differentiates among Greeks according to their polis is any indication, expressed this level of collective identity as well. The Phoenicians of Peiraieus also defined themselves in terms of their polis of origin. With the exception of Egypt, which did not distinguish among Greek poleis but grouped Greeks together, the other host-societies also adopted this identification for their resident traders. Athens, for example, distinguished among its foreigners according to their polis of origin as did the Thracian dynasts on the Vetren text. Polis-identity was universally the primary self-identification.

It was not only individuals who used their polis of origin to define themselves. Communities also proclaimed their civic identity. For example, *nomima*, the political customs specific to a polis, represented the collective identity of a political community. They were especially important for colonies, which had to define themselves vis-à-vis their metropoleis, other colonies, and the local populations with which they came in contact. With this in mind, Strabo's comment that in Emporion the Phokaian Greeks and the Indiketan Iberians retained their own *nomima* until they finally came together in a common constitution is significant for the civic identity of Emporion.

A second result of the investigation on the negotiation of identity in the ancient Mediterranean is that religion, a mediator among groups, was also used to express and maintain civic identities. When the provenance of dedicators is related to the choice of divinity that was worshipped, it emerges that traders from specific cities tended to give dedications to deities prominent in their polis of origin, so that they had a certain affinity for divinities that represented their poleis. Thus, Samian traders gave dedications in both Gravisca and Naukratis in Hera's temple, and an Aiginetan gave dedications specifically to Aiginetan Apollo. Similarly, temples founded in emporia were sometimes established by specific poleis, as the temple dedicated to Hera founded by Samos, the one to Apollo established by Miletos, and the one to Zeus founded by Aigina. Although all the Greeks of Naukratis used these temples, the act of their foundation by a polis expressed a civic identity, as did the similar process of the transference of cult from mother-city to colony.

Koina are another example of the formative role of religion in the context of communities living in foreign lands. *Koina*, like *thiasoi*, were social associations with a religious focus, explicitly defined as originating from specific political communities. Since they could take decisions in running their own affairs and honoring members, as the bilingual inscription that honored Diopeithes/Shama-baal suggests, they probably acted on behalf of the specific communities that they represented. They functioned as foci for their members, facilitating their presence in a foreign land by offering them a network of other fellow citizens and the possibility of worshipping at a sanctuary with which they were familiar and which perhaps was important in their polis of origin. These religious associations are mostly attested for Phoenician trader communities in Greek emporia on Delos, Rhodes, and Peiraieus, although the demos of the Kitians in Peiraieus, whether Greeks or Phoenicians, might have had similar functions as the *koina*. It is interesting to note that these associations were explicitly defined as originating from specific political communities in Phoenicia, such as Sidon, Tyre, and Berytos. *Koina* brought communities of citizens together by emphasizing both the civic and religious identities of groups.

The Kitian traders' request to the Athenian *boule* for permission to build a temple to Aphrodite demonstrates one more way in which religion was used to construct and express collective identity in emporia abroad. The Kitians considered the worship of Aphrodite as central to their polis religion, and therefore to their identity as citizens of Kition in Cyprus. The case of the Phokaians in the western Mediterranean is particularly interesting because they constructed their civic identity by co-opting a cult that was prominent in another Greek polis. The cult of Ephesian Artemis that had protected and saved so many different communities in Asia Minor from their Persian overlords was especially suitable for the Phokaians to take with them to their western colonies in view of the circumstances under which they left Phokaia: theirs was a forced migration to Massalia and other Phokaian foundations in southern France, Corsica, and Iberia. When they found themselves under Persian threat, it was natural to seek help from the Ephesian Artemis, who from that point on became a symbol of Phokaian identity. The flexibility of Greek religion allowed the Phokaian Greeks to appropriate this goddess as their own.

A third conclusion is that new levels of collective identity, larger than civic identity, developed in emporia, such as regional and ethnic identities. Certain gods acquired a particular importance for the inhabitants of certain regions and became popular in all the areas served by specific trade networks. All the Phokaian colonies in the west, for example, worshipped the Ephesian Artemis, and in the Phokaian trade network that ran from southern France to northern Iberia, the Ephesian Artemis acquired special prominence. The recognition of the worship of Ephesian Artemis as something all western Phokaian colonies had in common, probably resulted in the development of a regional identity. At the other end of the Mediterranean, the Ephesian Artemis had become a symbol of a regional Ionian identity, because she had saved not only Ephesos and Phokaia, but also Magnesia and Teos. Similarly, the trade network on the North Aegean coast that ran from Pistiros to Maroneia and to the Belana emporia also resulted in the development of a regional identity, perhaps exemplified by the choice of Dionysus as a divinity who could represent all the Greeks and Thracians involved.

Sometimes religion transcended civic and regional identity and was one of the means used to express ethnic identities, both Greek and non-Greek. For instance, all the Thracian *metics* residing in Peiraieus, irrespective of their sub-Thracian group, were granted the right to worship the Thracian goddess Bendis. The city of Athens treated the Thracians as an ethnic group when they regulated the festival of Bendis in Athens. It was perhaps the fact that Thracians made up a large percentage of the *metics*, and certainly slaves, who resided in Athens, that led Athens to view them as a collective entity. Recognizing that all Greek traders had some gods in common was also instrumental in the articulation of a Hellenic identity. This was true of all Greek gods and should explain why all Greeks were able to worship at all sanctuaries in Gravisca and Naukratis, and no doubt elsewhere. The acknowledgment that Greek religion was one of their shared similarities was a catalyst in the formation of a Hellenic identity. In the one clear instance of an expression of Hellenicity in the archaic period, the foundation of the Hellenion in Naukratis, it seems that a Hellenic identity emerged when Greeks, in a process of negotiation of identity, internalized the outsiders' perception that individuals who came from specific poleis were, in fact, all Greeks. Being treated by others as a collective group often led Greeks and non-Greek ethnic groups to adopt these larger identities, once they recognized the similarities they shared.

Epilogue

The Mediterranean was an interconnected region consisting of distinct, smaller parts – the various cultures that inhabited it – tied together by a city-state culture, polytheistic religious systems, a common material culture, and a common maritime perspective. Citizens of different poleis all around the Mediterranean basin who came together in multiethnic emporia used these common Mediterranean structures to mediate among themselves. The Mediterranean perspective that informs this work demonstrates that the construction of identity in emporia exploited cultural phenomena like law, political institutions, and religion, rather than the invention of mythical genealogies or claims to a common territory. This was true as much of the Greeks living in emporia situated in non-Greek lands as it was of non-Greeks living in the Greek emporion of Peiraieus, and by extension in the Mediterranean world in general.

Bibliography

Abad Casal, L. and J. A. Soler Díaz (eds.) (2007) *Arte ibérico en la España Mediterránea: Actas del Congreso, Alicante, 24–27 de octubre de 2005*. Alicante.

Abulafia, D. (ed.) (2003) *The Mediterranean in History*. Los Angeles.

Adamesteanu, D. (1971) "L'attività archeologica in Basilicata," in *La Magna Grecia e Roma nell' età arcaica. Atti dell'VIII convegno di studi sulla Magna Grecia, 1968*. Naples: 163–77.

Adroher, A. M., E. Pons i Brun, J. Ruiz de Arbulo (1993) "El yacimiento de Mas Castellar de Pontós y el comercio del cereal ibérico en la zona de Emporion y Rhode (ss. IV-II a.C.)," *AEA* 66: 31–70.

Aegyptische Urkunden aus den königlichen Museen zu Berlin. Griechische Urkunden. (1895) Berlin.

Ager, S. L. (1997) "Foreign Judges and Δικαιοδοσία: A Rhodian Fragment," *ZPE* 117: 123–5.

Alcock, S. and R. Osborne (eds.) (1994) *Placing the Gods: Sanctuaries and Sacred Space in Ancient Greece*. Oxford.

Almagro, M. (1953–5) *Las necrópolis de Ampurias*. 2 vols. Barcelona.

Almagro Basch, M. (1952) *Las inscripciones ampuritanas; griegas, ibéricas y latinas*. Barcelona.

(1966) *Ampurias: Guide to the Excavations and Museum*. Barcelona.

Almagro-Gorbea, M. (1982) "La 'colonizacíon' focense en la Península Ibérica. Estado actual de la cuestión," *PP* 204–8: 432–44.

(1983) "Colonizzazione e acculturazione nella penisola iberica," in *Modes de contacts et processus de transformation dans les sociétés anciennes*. Pisa and Rome: 429–61.

(1995) "From Hillforts to *Oppida* in 'Celtic' Iberia," in *Social Complexity and the Development of Towns in Iberia from the Copper Age to the Second Century AD*, ed. B. Cunliffe and S. Keay. Oxford: 175–207.

Aloni, A. (1982) "Osservazioni sul rapporto tra schiavitú, commercio e prostituzione sacra nel mondo archaico," *Index* 11: 257–63.

Amantini, L. S. (1984) "Ancora sulla prostituzione sacra a Locri Epizefirii," *MGR* 9: 39–62.

Ameling, W. (1990) "ΚΟΙΝΟΝ ΤΩΝ ΣΙΔΩΝΙΩΝ," *ZPE* 81: 189–99.

Amorós, J. V. (1933) *Les Dracmes empuritanes. In Junia de Museus. Cabinet Numismàtic de Catalunya*. ser. A, no. 2. Barcelona.

Ampolo, C. and T. Caruso (1990–1) "I Greci e gli altri nel Mediterraneo occidentale. Le iscrizioni greca ed etrusca di Pech-Maho: circolazione di beni, di uomini, di istituti," *Opus* 9–10: 28–57.

Ancient Greek and Related Pottery: Proceedings of the 2nd International Vase Symposium, Amsterdam 1984. (1984) Amsterdam.

Anderson, B. (1991) *Imagined Communities: Reflections on the Origins and Spread of Nationalism*, 2nd edn. London and New York.

Antonaccio, C. (2001) "Ethnicity and Colonization," in *Ancient Perceptions of Greek Ethnicity*, ed. I. Malkin. Washington, D.C.: 113–58.

(2003) "Hybridity and the Cultures Within Greek Culture," in *The Cultures Within Ancient Greek Culture*, ed. C. Dougherty and L. Kurke. Cambridge: 57–74.

(2009) "(Re)Defining Ethnicity: Culture, Material Culture, and Identity," in *Material Culture and Social Identities in the Ancient World.*, ed. S. Hales and T. Hodos. Cambridge: 32–53.

Aquilué, X., P. Castanyer, M. Santos, J. Tremoleda (2000) *Empúries.* Tarragona.

(2002) "Nuevos datos acerca del habitat arcaico de la Palaia Polis de Emporion," *Pallas* 58: 301–27.

Aranegui-Gascó, C., J.-P. Mohen, P. Rouillard, M. J. Sánchez, and P. Eluère (eds.) (1997) *Les Ibères.* Barcelona.

Arcelin, P., M. Bats, D. Garcia, G. Marchand, and M. Schwaller (eds.) (1995) *Sur les pas des Grecs en Occident.* Études Massaliètes 4. Aix-en-Provence.

Archibald, Z. H. (1983) "Greek Imports. Some Aspects of the Hellenic Impact on Thrace," in *Ancient Bulgaria. Papers Presented to the International Symposium on the Ancient History and Archaeology of Bulgaria, University of Nottingham, 1981*, vol. 1, ed. A. G. Poulter. Nottingham: 304–21.

(1996) "Imported Athenian figured pottery (1988–91)," in *Pistiros I: Excavations and Studies*, ed. J. Bouzek, M. Domaradzki, and Z. H. Archibald. Prague: 77–88.

(1998) *The Odrysian Kingdom of Thrace. Orpheus Unmasked.* Oxford.

(1999) "Thracian Cult – From Practice to Belief," in *Ancient Greeks West and East*, ed. G. Tsetskhladze. Leiden: 427–69.

(2000–1) "The Odrysian River Port Near Vetren, Bulgaria, and the Pistiros Inscription," in *TAΛANTA Proceedings of the Dutch Archaeological and Historical Society* 32–3: 253–75.

(2002a) "Attic Figured Pottery from Adjiyska Vodenitsa, Vetren, 1989–95, with pls. 36–37," in *Pistiros II: Excavations and Studies*, ed. J. Bouzek, L. Domaradzka, and Z. H. Archibald. Prague: 131–48.

(2002b) "A River Port and Emporion in Central Bulgaria: An Interim Report on the British Project at Vetren," *ABSA* 97: 309–51.

Arruda, A. M. (2009) "Phoenician Colonization on the Atlantic Coast of the Iberian Peninsula," in *Colonial Encounters in Ancient Iberia. Phoenician, Greek, and Indigenous Relations*, ed. M. Dietler and C. López-Ruiz. Chicago: 113–30.

Artzu, M. (1994) "Incense, Camels, and Collared Rim Jars: Desert Trade Routes and Maritime Outlets in the Second Millenium," *OJA* 13.2: 121–47.

Αρχαία Μακεδονία V. Ανακοινώσεις κατά το πέμπτο διεθνές συμπόσιο. Θεσσαλονίκη, 10–15 Οκτωβρίου, 1989. Vol. 2. (1993) Thessaloniki.

Αρχαία Μακεδονία VI. Ανακοινώσεις κατά το έκτο διεθνές συμπόσιο. Θεσσαλονίκη, 15–19 Οκτωβρίου, 1996. Vol. 1. (1999) Thessaloniki.

Assmann, H. and D. Frankfurter (2004) "Egypt," in *Religions of the Ancient World: A Guide*, ed. S. Iles Johnston. Cambridge, MA: 155–64.

Aubet, M. E. (1971) *Los marfiles orientalizantes de Praeneste*. Barcelona.

(2001) *The Phoenicians in the West. Politics, Colonies, and Trade*. Transl. M. Turton. 2nd edn. Cambridge.

Austin, M. M. (1970) *Greece and Egypt in the Archaic Age*. PCPS Supplement 2. Cambridge.

(2004) "From Syria to the Pillars of Herakles," in *An Inventory of Archaic and Classical Poleis: An Investigation Conducted by the Copenhagen Polis Centre for the Danish National Research Foundation*, ed. M. H. Hansen and T. H. Nielsen. Oxford: 1233–49.

Austin, C. and G. Bastianini (eds.) (2002) *Posidippi Pellaei quae supersunt omnia*. Milan.

Avram, A. (1997–8) "Notes sur l'inscription de *l'emporion* de Pistiros en Thrace," *Il Mar Nero* 3: 37–46.

Babelon, E. (1910) *Traité des monnaies grecques et romaines*. II.2. Paris.

Bäbler, B. (1998) *Fleissige Thrakerinnen und wehrhafte Skythen: Nichtgriechen im klassischen Athen und ihre archäologische Hinterlassenschaft*. Stuttgart.

Badian. E. (ed.) (1966) *Ancient Society and Institutions. Studies Presented to Victor Ehrenberg on his 75th Birthday*. Oxford.

Bailey, D. (2006) "The Apries-Amphora: Another Cartouche," in *Naukratis: Greek Diversity in Egypt. Studies on East Greek Pottery and Exchange in the Eastern Mediterranean*, ed. A. Villing and U. Schlotzhauer. London: 155–8.

Baines, J. (1996) "Contextualizing Egyptian Representations of Society and Ethnicity," in *The Study of the Ancient Near East in the 21st Century*, ed. J. S. Cooper and G. M. Schwartz. Winona Lake, IN: 339–84.

Balmuth, M. S., A. Gilman, and L. Prados-Torreira (eds.) (1997) *Encounters and Transformations: The Archaeology of Iberia in Transition*. Sheffield.

Barth F. (ed.) (1969) *Ethnic Groups and Boundaries: the Social Organization of Culture Difference*. Boston.

Baslez, M-F. (1988) "Les Communautés d'orientaux dans la cité grecque: formes de sociabilité et modèles associatifs," in *L'Étranger dans le monde grec*, ed. R. Lonis. Nancy: 139–58.

Bats, M. (1982) "Commerce et politique massaliète aux IVe. et IIIe. siècles av. J. C. Essai d'interprètation du faciès céramique d'Olbia de Provence (Hyères, Var)," *PP* 204–8: 256–68.

(ed.) (1990) *Les Amphores de Marseille grecque: chronologie et diffusion (VIe-Ier s. av. J-C.).* Lattes.

(1992) "Marseille, les colonies massaliètes et les relais indigènes dans le long du littoral méditerranéen gaulois (VIe-Ier s. av. J-C.)," in *Marseille grecque et la Gaule,* ed. M. Bat, G. Bertucchi, G. Congès, and H. Tréziny. Études Massaliètes 3. Aix-en-Provence: 263–78.

(1998) "Marseille archaïque: Étrusques et Phocéens en Méditerranée nord-occidentale," *MEFRA* 110: 609–33.

Bats, M., G. Bertucchi, G. Congès, and H. Tréziny (eds.) (1992) *Marseille grecque et la Gaule.* Études Massaliètes 3. Aix-en-Provence.

Bats, M., M. Leguilloux, F. Brien-Poitevin (1995) "La Tour d'angle sud-est d'Olbia de Provence et son dépotoir (v. 225–150 av. J.-C)," in *Sur les pas des Grecs en Occident,* ed. P. Arcelin, M. Bats, D. Garcia, G. Marchand, and M. Schwaller. Études Massaliètes 4. Aix-en-Provence: 371–92.

Beard, M. and J. Henderson (1997) "With This Body I Thee Worship: Sacred Prostitution in Antiquity," *Gender & History* 9: 480–503.

Beckby, H. (ed.) (1965–7) *Anthologia Graeca.* 4 vols. 2nd edn. Munich.

Bejor, G. (1991) "Spunti diodorei e problematiche dell' archeologia siciliana," in *Mito, storia, tradizione: Diodoro Siculo e la storiografia classica. Atti del Convegno internazionale Catania-Agira 7–8 dicembre 1984,* ed. E. Galvagno and C. Molè Ventura. Catania: 255–69.

Belarte, M. C. (2009) "Colonial Contacts and Protohistoric Indigenous Urbanism on the Mediterranean Coast of the Iberian Peninsula," in *Colonial Encounters in Ancient Iberia: Phoenicians, Greeks, and Indigenous Relations,* ed. M. Dietler and C. López-Ruiz. Chicago: 91–112.

Belén Deamos, M. (2009) "Phoenicians in Tartessos," in *Colonial Encounters in Ancient Iberia: Phoenician, Greek, and Indigenous Relations,* ed. M. Dietlier and C. López-Ruiz. Chicago: 193–228.

Benoit, J. (1985) "L'Étude des cadastres antiques: à propos d'Olbia de Provence," *Documents d'archéologie méridionale* 8: 25–48.

Bergquist, B. (1973) *Herakles on Thasos. The Archaeological, Literary, and Epigraphic Evidence for his Sanctuary, Status, and Cult Reconsidered.* Uppsala.

Bernal, M. (1987) *Black Athena: The Afroasiatic Roots of Classical Civilization.* Vol. 1. *The Fabrication of Ancient Greece 1785–1985.* New Brunswick, NJ.

(1991) *Black Athena: The Afroasiatic Roots of Classical Civilization.* Vol. 2. *The Archaeological and Documentary Evidence.* New Brunswick, NJ.

Bernand, A. (1970) *Le Delta égyptien d'après les texts grecs.* I.2. Cairo.

Bernand, A. and A. Aly (1959) *Abou-Simbel: Inscriptions grecques, cariennes et sémitiques des statues de la façade.* Cairo.

Bernand, A. and M. Masson (1957) "Les Inscriptions grecques d'Abou-Simbel," *REG*: 1–20.

Bernardini, P. (2002) "I bronzi sardi di Cavalupo di Vulci e i rapporti tra la Sardegna e l'area tirrenica nei secoli IX-VI a.C. Una rilettura," in *Etruria e Sardegna centro-settentrionale tra l'età del bronzo finale e l'archaismo. Atti del XXI convegno di studi etruschi ed italici,* ed. O. Paoletti. Pisa and Rome.

Best, J. G. P. and N. M. W. de Vries (eds.) (1989) *Thracians and Mycenaeans: Proceedings of the Fourth International Congress.* Leiden.

Bhabha, H. (1994) *The Location of Culture.* London and New York.

Bietak, M. (ed.) (2001) *Archaische griechische Tempel und Altägypten.* Vienna.

Bingen, J. (1959) "Le Décret *SEG* X 64 (le Pirée, 413/2)," *Revue belge de philologie et d'histoire* 37: 31–44.

Biscardi, A. (1972) "L'Institution des juges étrangers ('xenokritai') dans le monde gréco-romain," *Revue internationale des droits de l'antiquité* 19: 515–16.

Bissing, F. W. von (1941) *Zeit und Herkunft der in Cerveteri gefundenen Gefässe aus ägyptischer Fayence und glasiertem Ton.* Munich.

  (1949) "Forschungen zur Geschichte und kulturellen Bedeutung der griechischen Kolonie Naukratis in Ägypten," *F&F* 25: 1–2.

  (1951) "Naukratis," *BSAA* 39: 33–82.

Blech, M. (1996) "Terracotas arcaicas de la Península Ibérica," in *Formes archaïques et arts ibériques – Formas arcaicas y arte ibérico,* ed. R. Olmos and P. Rouillard. Collection de la Casa de Velázquez 59. Madrid: 111–28.

Blinkenberg, C. (1941) *Lindos. Fouilles de l'acropole 1902–1914. Inscriptions. Vol. 2.* In *Lindos. Fouilles et Recherches 1902–1914,* ed. C. Blinkenberg and K. F. Kinch. Berlin.

Boardman, J. (1967) *Excavations in Chios, 1952–1955: Greek Emporio.* London.

  (1979) "The Athenian Pottery Trade. The Classical Period," *Expedition* 21: 33–9.

  (1988) "Dates and Doubts," *AA:* 423–5.

  (1990) "Al-Mina and History," *OJA* 9: 169–90.

  (1998) *Early Greek Vase Painting.* London.

  (2006) "The Study of East Greek Pottery," in *Naukratis: Greek Diversity in Egypt. Studies on East Greek Pottery and Exchange in the Eastern Mediterranean,* ed. A. Villing and U. Schlotzhauer. London: 49–52.

Boegehold, A. L. (1976) "Ten distinctive ballots: the law court in Zea," *CSCA* 9: 1–19.

Boháč, L. (2002) "Lamps from Pistiros II (1995–1998)," in *Pistiros II: Excavations and Studies,* ed. J. Bouzek, L. Domaradzka, and Z. H. Archibald. Prague: 183–7.

Boldrini, S. (1994) *Le ceramiche ioniche.* Gravisca: scavi nel santuario greco. Vol. 4. Bari.

Bon, A. M. (1936) "Monnaie inédite de Galepsos," *BCH* 60: 172–4.

Bon, A. and H. Seyrig (1929) "Le Sanctuaire de Poseidon à Thasos," *BCH* 53: 317–50.

Bonfante, G. and L. Bonfante (2002) *The Etruscan Language. An Introduction.* Revised edn. [1983]. Lancaster.

Bonfante, L. and V. Karageorghis (eds.) (2001) *Italy and Cyprus in Antiquity: 1500–450 B.C. Proceedings of an International Symposium Held at the Italian Academy for Advanced Studies in America, Columbia University. November 16–18 2000.* Nicosia.

Bonnet, C. (1996) *Astarté. Dossier documentaire et perspectives historiques.* Rome.

Bonnet C. and A. Motte (eds.) (1999) *Les Syncrétismes religieux dans le monde méditerranéen antique.* Brussels.

Bonnet C. and V. Pirenne-Delforge (1999) "Deux déesses en interaction: Astarté et Aphrodite dans le monde égéen," in *Les syncrétismes religieux dans le monde méditerranéen antique,* ed. C. Bonnet and A. Motte. Brussels: 248–73.

Borelli, F. and M. C. Targia (2004) *The Etruscans: Art, Architecture, and History.* Transl. T. M. Hartmann. Los Angeles.

Bosch-Gimpera, P. (1977) "Cronologia e historia de Emporion," in *Homenaje a Garcia Bellido II.* Madrid: 37–57.

Boshnakov, K. (1999) "Identification archéologique et historique de l'*emporion* de Pistiros en Thrace," *BCH* 123: 319–29.

Bouloumié, B. (1987) "Le Rôle des Etrusques dans la diffusion des produits étrusques et grecs en milieu préceltique et celtique," in *Hallstatt-Studien: Tübinger Kolloquium zur westeuropäischen Hallstatt-Zeit,* ed. F. Fischer, B. Bouloumié, and C. Lagrand. Weinheim: 20–43.

Bourdieu, P. (1977) *Outline of a Theory of Practice.* Transl. R. Nice. Cambridge.

Bouzek, J. M. (1996a) "The Position of the Pistiros Fortification in the Development of the Ancient Poliorcetics and Stonecutting Techniques," in *Pistiros I: Excavations and Studies,* ed. J. Bouzek, M. Domaradzki, and Z. H. Archibald. Prague: 43–6.

(1996b) "Pistiros as a River Harbor: Sea and River Transport in Antiquity and its Costs," in *Pistiros I: Excavations and Studies,* ed. J. Bouzek, M. Domaradzki, and Z. H. Archibald. Prague: 221–2.

(1999a) "Pistiros and the South: Land and River Connections," in Αρχαία Μακεδονία VI. Ανακοινώσεις κατά το έκτο διεθνές συμπόσιο. Θεσσαλονίκη, 15–19 Οκτωβρίου, 1996. Vol. 1. 1999. Thessaloniki: 189–96.

(1999b) "'Syncretism' and the Transmission of Religious Ideas between the Greeks and their Neighbours in the Black Sea Area," in *Réligions du Pont-Euxin. Actes du VIIIe symposium de Vanie (Colchide), 1999,* ed. O. Lordkipanidze and P. Lévêque. Transl. A. Fraysse and É. Geny. Paris: 11–16.

(2001a) "Pistiros," *RA* 1: 196–202.

(2001b) "Le Trésor de Pistiros, imitations thraces des monnaies grecques et les premières monnaies des Celtes," *Studia Hercynia* 5: 41–3.

(2002) "The North Greek Wheel-Made Glazed Pottery in Pistiros, Part I: Classification and Possible Sources, with Colour Pls. A-F," in *Pistiros II: Excavations and Studies,* ed. J. Bouzek, L. Domaradzka, and Z. H. Archibald. Prague: 149–82.

(2004) "Les Vases grecs et la poterie des Thraces," *Il Mar Nero* 6: 37–46.

(2007) "The Development of Local Pottery at Pistiros: Preliminary Sketch of its Chronology," in *Pistiros III: Excavations and Studies*, ed. J. Bouzek, L. Domaradzka, and Z. H. Archibald. Prague: 205–20.

Bouzek, J. and L. Domaradzka (2002) "More than 300 Talents from the Emporia for Kersobleptes (With Reference to Demosthenes, *Against Aristocrates* 110)," in *Thrace and the Aegean. Proceedings of the Eighth International Congress of Thracology*, ed. A. Fol. Vol. 1. Sofia: 391–8.

(eds.) (2005) *The Culture of Thracians and their Neighbors. Proceedings of the International Symposium in Memory of Prof. Mieczyslaw Domaradzki, with a Round Table "Archaeological Map of Bulgaria."* BAR International Series 1350. Oxford.

(2007) "Pistiros and North Aegean Greek Cities," in Αρχαία Μακεδονία VII. Ανακοινώσεις κατά το έβδομο διεθνές συμπόσιο Θεσσαλονίκη, 14–18 Οκτωβρίου 2002. Thessaloniki: 745–58.

(2009) "Pistiros: Facts and Opinions," *Eirene* 45: 147–54.

(2010) "Dionysus at Pistiros," in *Pistiros IV: Excavations and Studies*, ed. J. Bouzek, L. Domaradzka, and Z. H. Archibald. Prague: 233–4.

Bouzek, K. and J. Musil (2002) "Adžijska Vodenica II, 1994–1998: Excavation Report by the Czech Mission, with Pls. 9–31 and Colour Pls. A-H," in *Pistiros II: Excavations and Studies*, ed. J. Bouzek, L. Domaradzka, and Z. H. Archibald. Prague: 37–110.

Bouzek, J., M. Domaradzki, and Z. H. Archibald (eds.) (1996) *Pistiros I: Excavations and Studies*. Prague.

Bouzek, J., L. Domaradzka, and Z. H. Archibald (eds.) (2002) *Pistiros II: Excavations and Studies*. Prague.

(eds.) (2007) *Pistiros III: Excavations and Studies*. Prague.

(eds.) (2010) *Pistiros IV: Excavations and Studies*. Prague.

Bouzek, J. and I. Ondřejova (1987) "Some Notes on the Relations of the Thracian, Macedonian, Iranian, and Scythian Arts in the Fourth Century BC," *Eirene* 24: 67–93.

(1988) "Sindos – Trebenishte – Duvanli. Interrelations between Thrace, Macedonia, and Greece in the 6th and 5th centuries BC," *MedArch* 1: 84–94.

Bouzek, J., S. Rückl. P. Titz, and C. Tsotshev (2007) "Trade Amphorae," in *Pistiros III: Excavations and Studies*, ed. J. Bouzek, L. Domaradzka, and Z. H. Archibald. Prague: 133–86.

Bowden, H. (1996) "The Greek Settlement and Sanctuaries at Naukratis: Herodotus and Archaeology," in *More Studies in the Ancient Greek Polis*, ed. M. H. Hansen and K. Raaflaub. Stuttgart: 17–37.

Braccesi, L. (1968) "La menzione di Naucrati in Aesch. *Prom.* 813–5," *RFIC* 96: 28–32.

Braisch, M. and O. von Winkelmann (eds.) (1982) *Festschrift für Johannes Hubschmid zum 65. Geburtstag. Beiträge zur allgemeinen, indogermanischen und romanischen Sprachwissenschaft*. Bern.

Braudel, F. (1949) *La Méditerranée et la monde méditerranéen à l'époque de Philippe II.* 3 vols. Paris.

Bravo, B. (1974) "Une lettre sur plomb de Berezan. Colonisation et modes de contact dans le Pont," *DHA* 1: 110–87.

Bravo, B. and A. S. Chankowski (1999) "Cités et emporia dans le commerce avec les barbares à la lumière du document dit à tort 'inscription de Pistiros,'" *BCH* 123: 275–317.

Bredow, I. von (1997) "Das Emporion Pistiros in Thrakien," *OTerr* 3: 109–20.

Bresciani, E. (1997) "Foreigners," in *The Egyptians*, ed. S. Donadoni. Chicago: 221–54.

Bresson, A. (1991) "Le Fils de Pythéas, Égyptien de Naucratis," in *Mélanges Étienne Bernard*, ed. Nicole Fick and Jean-Claude Carrière. Paris: 37–42.

(1993) "Les Cités grecques et leurs emporia," in *L'Emporion*, ed. A. Bresson and P. Rouillard. Paris: 163–226.

(2000a) "Rhodes, l' Hellénion et le statut de Naucratis," in *La Cité marchande.* Paris: 15–63.

(2000b) "Retour à Naucratis," in *La Cité marchande.* Paris: 64–84.

(2000c) *La Cité marchande.* Paris.

(2002) "Quatre *emporia* antiques: Abul, La Picola, Elizavetovskoie, Naucratis." *REA* 104: 475–505.

Bresson, A. and P. Rouillard (eds.) (1993) *L'Emporion.* Paris.

Brewer, D. J. and E. Teeter (1999) *Egypt and the Egyptians.* Reprint 2003. Cambridge.

Briant, P. and R. Descat (1998) "Un register douanier de la satrapie d'Égypte à l'époque achéménide," in *Le Commerce en Égypte ancienne*, ed. N. Grimal and B. Menu. Cairo: 59–104.

Browning, R. (1983) *Medieval and Modern Greek.* 2nd edn. Cambridge.

Brunaux, J.-L. (ed.) (1991) *Les Sanctuaires celtiques et leurs rapports avec le monde méditerranéen. Actes du colloque de St-Riquier (8 au 11 novembre 1990).* Paris.

Bruneau, P. (1970) *Recherches sur les cultes de Délos à l'époque hellénistique et à l'époque impériale.* Paris.

Brunel, J. (1948) "Marseille et les fugitives de Phocée," *REA* 50: 1–26.

Brunet, M. (ed.) (1999) *Territoires des cités grecques.* BCH Supplement 34. Paris.

Bruni, S. (2009) *Le ceramiche corinzie ed etrusco-corinzie.* Gravisca. Scavi del santuario greco. Vol. 2. Bari.

Bruni, S. and M. J. Conde. (1991) "Presencia ibérica en Etruria y el mundo itálico a través de los hallazgos cerámicos de los ss. III-I a.C," in *La presencia de material etrusco en el ámbito de la colonización arcaica de la Península Ibérica*, ed. J. Remesal and O. Musso. Barcelona: 543–75.

Brunt, P. A. (1966) "Athenian Settlements Abroad in the Fifth Century B.C," in *Ancient Society and Institutions. Studies Presented to Victor Ehrenberg on his 75th Birthday*, ed. E. Badian. Oxford: 71–92.

Budin, S. L. (2008) *The Myth of Sacred Prostitution in Antiquity.* Cambridge.

Burkert, W. (1992) *The Orientalizing Revolution: Near Eastern Influence on Greek Culture in the Early Archaic Age.* Cambridge, MA.

Burnett, R. B. (1975) "A Provisional Catalogue of and Commentary on Egyptian and Egyptianizing Artifacts Found on Greek Sites," Ph.D. Dissertation, University of Pennsylvania.

Burstein, S. M. (1995) *Graeco-Africa: Studies in the History of Greek Relations with Egypt and Nubia.* New Rochelle, NY.

Buxó, R. (2009) "Botanical and Archaeological Dimensions of the Colonial Encounter," in *Colonial Encounters in Ancient Iberia. Phoenician, Greek, and Indigenous Relations,* ed. M. Dietler and C. López-Ruiz. Chicago: 155–68.

Buxton, R. (ed.) (2000) *Oxford Readings in Greek Religion.* Oxford.

Cabrera Bonet, P. (1996) "Emporion y el comercio griego arcaico en el nordeste de la Península Ibérica," in *Formes archaïques et arts ibériques – Formas arcaicas y arte ibérico,* ed. R. Olmos and P. Rouillard. Collection de la Casa de Velázquez 59. Madrid: 43–54.

Cabrera Bonet, P. and C. Sanchez Fernandez (eds.) (1988) *Οι αρχαίοι Έλληνες στην Ισπανία: στα ίχνη του Ηρακλή.* Exhibition Catalogue. Madrid.

Calame, C. (1989) "Entre rapports de parenté et relations civiques: Aphrodite l'hétaïre au banquet politique des hétaïroi," in *Aux sources de la puissance: sociabilité et parenté,* ed. F. Thelamon. Rouen.

Calligas, P. (1971) "An inscribed lead plaque from Korkyra," *BSA* 66: 79–84.

Camp, J. McK. II (2000) "Walls and the Polis," in *Polis & Politics: Studies in Ancient Greek History,* ed. P. Flensted-Jensen, T. H. Nielsen, L. Rubinstein. Copenhagen: 41–57.

Campbell, D. A. (ed.) (2002) *Sappho and Alcaeus.* Cambridge, MA.

Campo, M. (1992) "Inicios de la amonedación en la Península Ibérica: los griegos en Emporion y Rhode," in *Griegos en Occidente,* ed. F. Chaves. Seville: 195–209.

Camporeale, G. (ed.) (1981) *L'Etruria mineraria: Atti del XII Covegno di Studi Etruschi e Italici, Firenze 1979.* Florence.

  (ed.) (2004) *The Etruscans Outside Etruria.* Transl. T. M. Hartmann. Los Angeles.

Caratelli, G. P. (ed.) (1996) *The Western Greeks.* London.

Carpentier, J. and F. Lebrun (1998) *Histoire de la Méditerranée.* Paris.

Cartledge, P. (1993) *The Greeks: A Portrait of Self and Other.* Oxford.

Casevitz, M. (1993) "*Emporion.* Emplois classiques et histoire du mot," in *L'Emporion,* ed. A. Bresson and P. Rouillard. Paris: 9–22.

Cassimatis, H. (1984) "Des Chypriotes chez les Pharaons," *CCEC* 1: 33–8.

Castellano i Arolas, M. (2007) "Datos para una reconstrucción de los hechos contenidos en el plomo griego de Pech Maho," *Dike* 10: 137–54.

Cawkwell, G. L. (1992) "Early Colonisation," *CQ* 42: 289–303.

Celestino Pérez, S. (ed.) (1995) *Arqueología del vino. Los orígenes del vino en Occidente.* Jerez de la Frontera.

(2009) "Precolonization and Colonization in the Interior of Tartessos," in *Colonial Encounters in Ancient Iberia: Phoenician, Greek, and Indigenous Relations*, ed. M. Dietler and C. López-Ruiz. Chicago: 229–51.

Cesnola, L. P. di (1885) *A Descriptive Atlas of the Cesnola Collection of Cypriote Antiquities in the Metropolitan Museum of Art. New York.* Vol. 1. Boston.

Chadwick, J. (1990) "The Pech-Maho Lead," *ZPE* 82: 161–6.

Chankowski, V. and É. Fouache (2000) "Pistiros (Bulgarie)," *BCH* 124: 643–54.

Chankowski, V. and L. Domaradzka (1999) "Réédition de l'inscription de Pistiros et problèmes d'interprétation," *BCH* 123: 246–58.

Chapa Brunet, T. (1982) "Influences de la colonisation phocéenne sur la sculpture ibérique," *PP* 204–8: 374–92.

Chapman, R. (1995) "Urbanism in Copper and Bronze Age Iberia?," in *Social Complexity and the Development of Towns in Iberia from the Copper Age to the Second Century AD*, ed. B. Cunliffe and S. Keay. Oxford: 29–46.

Chaves, F. (ed.) (1992) *Griegos en Occidente.* Seville.

Childs, W. A. P. (1993) "Herodotos, Archaic Chronology, and the Temple of Apollo at Delphi," *JDAI* 108: 399–441.

Clavel-Lévêque, M. (1983a) "Cadastres, centuriations et problèmes d'occupation du sol," in *Cadastres et espace rural: approches et réalités antiques: table ronde de Besançon, mai 1980*, ed. M. Clavel-Lévêque. Paris: 207–58.

(ed.) (1983b) *Cadastres et espace rural: approches et réalités antiques: table ronde de Besançon, mai 1980.* Paris.

(1999) "Le Territoire d'Agde grecque: histoire et structures," in *Territoires des cités grecques*, ed. M. Brunet. BCH Supplement 34. Paris: 177–97.

Cohen, B. (ed.) (2000) *Not the Classical Ideal: Athens and the Construction of the Other in Greek Art.* Leiden.

Cohen, E. E. (1973) *Ancient Maritime Courts.* Princeton.

Cole, S. G. (1994) "Demeter in the Ancient Greek City and its Countryside," in *Placing the Gods: Sanctuaries and Sacred Space in Ancient Greece*, ed. S. E. Alcock and R. Osborne. Oxford: 199–216.

Coleman, J. E. and C. A. Walz (eds.) (1997) *Greeks and Barbarians. Essays on the Interactions between Greeks and non-Greeks in Antiquity and the Consequences of Eurocentrism.* Bethesda, MD.

Colivicchi, F. (2004) *I materiali minori.* Gravisca: scavi nel santuario greco. Vol. 16. Bari.

Colonna, G. (1967) "Rivista di epigrafia etrusca," *SE* 35: 547.

(1984–85) "Novità sui culti di Pyrgi," *RPAA* 57: 57–88.

(1985) *Santuari d'Etruria.* Milan.

(1988) "L'iscrizione etrusca del piombo di Linguadoca," *Scienze dell'Antichità* 2: 547–55.

Comella, A. (1978) *Il materiale votivo tardo di Gravisca.* Rome.

(1981) "Tipologia e diffusione dei complessi votivi in Italia in epoca medio-e-tardo-repubblicana. Contributo alla storia dell'artigianato antico," *MEFRA* 93: 717–803.

Compernolle, R. van (1976) "Le tradizioni sulla fondazione e sulla storica arcaica di Locri Epizefiri e la propaganda politica alla fine del V e nel IV secolo av. Cr.," *ASNP* 6: 329–400.

Conzelmann, H. (1967) "Korinth und die Mädchen der Aphrodite. Zur Religions-geschichte der Stadt Korinth," *Nachrichten von der Akademie der Wissenschaften in Göttingen* 8: 246–61.

Cook, R. M. (1937) "Amasis and the Greeks in Egypt," *JHS* 57: 227–37.

(1989) "The Francis-Vickers Chronology," *JHS* 109: 164–70.

Cooke, G. A. (1903) *A Text-book of North-Semitic Inscriptions.* Oxford.

Cooper, J. S. and G. M. Schwartz (eds.) (1996) *The Study of the Ancient Near East in the 21st Century.* Winona Lake, IN.

Cordano, F. (1974) "Ῥόδος prima del sinecismo e Ῥόδιοι fondatori di colonie," *PP* 156: 179–82.

Cornell, T. J. (1991) "Rome: The History of an Anachronism," in *City-States in Classical Antiquity and Medieval Italy*, ed. A. Mohlo, K. Raaflaub, and J. Emlen. Stuttgart: 53–69.

(1995) *The Beginnings of Rome. Italy and Rome from the Bronze Age to the Punic Wars (c.1000–246 BC).* London.

(2000) "The City-States in Latium," in *A Comparative Study of Thirty City-State Cultures*, ed. M. H. Hansen. Copenhagen: 209–28.

Coulson, W. D. E. (1996) *Ancient Naukratis: Volume II. Part I: The Survey at Naukratis.* Exeter.

Coulson, W. D. E., A. Leonard Jr., and N. Wilkie (1982) "Three Seasons of Excava-tions and Survey at Naukratis and Environs," *JARCE* 19: 73–109.

Counillon, P. (1993) "L'*Emporion* des géographes grecs," in *L'Emporion*, ed. A. Bresson and P. Rouillard. Paris: 47–57.

Cristofani, M. (1983) *Gli Etruschi del mare.* Milan.

Cristofani, M., P. Moscati, G. Nardi, and M. Pandolfini (eds.) (1985) *Il commercio etrusco arcaico. Atti dell'incontro di studio, 5–7 dicembre, 1983.* Rome.

Croissant, F. and P. Rouillard (1996) "Le Problème de l'art 'gréco-ibère': état de la question," in *Formes archaïques et arts ibériques*, ed. R. Olmos and P. Rouillard. Madrid: 55–66.

Crowther, C. V. (1993) "Foreign Judges in Seleucid Cities," *JAC* 8: 40–77.

(1994) "Foreign Courts on Kalymna in the Third Century B.C.," *JAC* 9: 33–55.

(1995) "Iasos in the Second Century BCE III: Foreign Judges from Priene," *BICS* 40: 91–138.

(1997) "Inscriptions from the Sparta and Larissa Museums," *ABSA* 92: 345–58.

(1999) "Aus der Arbeit der 'Inscriptiones Graecae.' IV. Koan Decrees for Foreign Judges," *Chiron* 29: 251–319.

Culasso Gastaldi, E. (2004) *Le prossenie ateniesi del IV secolo a.C. Gli onorati asiatici.* Alessandria.

Cunliffe, B. and S. Keay (eds.) (1995) *Social Complexity and the Development of Towns in Iberia: From the Copper Age to the Second Century AD.* Oxford.

Curtin, P. D. (1984) *Cross-Cultural Trade in World History.* Cambridge.

Curty, O. (1995) *Les Parentés legendaires entre cités grecques.* Geneva.

D'Agostino, B. (1999) "Euboean Colonisation in the Gulf of Naples," in *Ancient Greeks West and East,* ed. G. Tsetskhladze. Leiden 207–27.

Danov, C. M. (1977) "Thracian Culture from the Close of the Ninth to the Outset of the Third Century BC," *QS* 3.6: 117–28.

Daressy, G. (1900) "Stèle de l'an III d'Amasis," *RT* 22: 1–9.

Daux, G. (1968) "Chronique de fouilles et découvertes archéologiques en Grèce en 1967," *BCH* 92: 712–1135.

  (1970) "Deux fragments de décrets à Siphnos," *Klio* 52: 67–72.

  (1975) "Note sur un décret thessalien pour des juges étrangers," *ZPE* 16: 37–8.

Davis, W. M. (1979) "Ancient Naukratis and the Cypriotes in Egypt," *GM* 35: 13–23.

  (1980) "The Cypriotes in Naukratis," *GM* 41: 7–19.

De Angelis, F. (2002) "Trade and Agriculture at Megara Hyblaia," *OJA* 21(3): 299–310.

De Angelis, F. and B. Garstad (2006) "Euhemerus in Context," *CA* 25: 211–42.

De Cazanove, O. (1991) "Ex-voto de l'Italie républicaine: sur quelques aspects de leur mise au rebut," in *Les Sanctuaires celtiques et leurs rapports avec le monde méditerranéen. Actes du colloque de St-Riquier (8 au 11 novembre 1990),* ed. J.-L. Brunaux. Paris: 203–14.

De Grummond, N. T. and E. Simon (eds.) (2006) *The Religion of the Etruscans.* Austin.

De Hoz, J. (1979) "Escrittura e influencia clásica en los pueblos prerromanos de la Península." *AEA* 52: 227–50.

  (1993) "La lengua y la escritura ibéricas, y las lenguas de los íberos," in *Lengua y cultura en la Hispania prerromana: Actas del V coloquio sobre lenguas y culturas prerromanas de la Península Ibérica,* ed. J. Untermann and F. Villas. Salamanca: 635–66.

  (1998) "Western Greek Epigraphy and Graeco-Iberian Writing," in *Οι αρχαίοι Έλληνες στην Ισπανία· στα ίχνη του Ηρακλή.* Exhibition Catalogue. Madrid: 503–10.

  (1999) "Los negocios del señor Heronoiyos. Un documento mercantile, jonio clásico temprano, del sur de Francia," in *Desde los poemas homéricos hasta la prosa griega del siglo IV d.C.,* ed. J. A. López Férez. Madrid: 61–90.

  (2004) "The Greek Man in the Iberian Street: Non-Colonial Greek Identity in Spain and Southern France," in *Greek Identity in the Western Mediterranean,* ed. K. Lomas. Leiden: 411–27.

De Polignac, F. (1995) *Cults, Territory, and the Origins of the Greek City-State.* Transl. J. Lloyd. Chicago.

(1997) "Héra, le navire et la demeure: offrandes, divinité et société en Grèce archaïque," in *Héra. Images, espaces, cultes. Actes du Colloque International de Lille (1993)*. Naples: 113–22.

De Salvia, F. (1983) "La problematica della reazione culturale egea all'influenza della civiltà egizia durante l'età arcaica," *Orientalia* 52: 201–14.

De Simone, C. (2009) "La nuova iscrizione tirsenica di Efestia," *Tripodes* 11: 3–58.

Delgado y Hernández, A. (1876) *Nuevo método de clasificación de las Medallas Autónomas de España III*. Madrid.

Demand. N. (2004) "Models in Greek History and the Question of the Origins of the Polis," *AHB* 18: 61–86.

Demetriou, D. (2010a) "Pistiros and a North Aegean Trade Route," *AC* 79: 77–93.

(2010b) "τῆς πάσης ναυτιλίης φύλαξ: Aphrodite and the Sea," *Kernos* 23: 67–89.

(2011) "What is an Emporion? A Reassessment," *Historia* 60.3: 255–72.

Denoyelle, M. (2008) "Athenian Vases in Special Techniques in Magna Graecia and Sicily, and their Influence on Local Production," in *Papers on Special Techniques in Athenian Vases: Proceedings of a Symposium Held in Connection with the Exhibition "The Colors of Clay: Special Techniques in Athenian Vases,"* at the Getty Villa, June 15–17, 2006, ed. K. Lapatin. Los Angeles: 207–14.

Derks, R. and N. Roymans (eds.) (2009) *Ethnic Constructs in Antiquity. The Role of Power and Tradition*. Amsterdam.

Deonna, W. (1938) *Exploration archéologique de Délos. XVIII*. Paris.

Descat, R. (1993) "La Loi de Solon sur l'interdiction d'exporter les produits attiques," in *L'Emporion*, ed. A. Bresson and P. Rouillard. Paris: 145–61.

Detienne, M. (1974) "La Corneille de mer," in *Les Ruses de l'intelligence: La Métis des Grecs*, ed. M. Detienne and J.-P. Vernant. Paris: 203–43.

(1985) "La Cité et son autonomie. Autour d'Hestia," *QS* 11: 67–72.

Detienne, M. and Vernant, J.-P. (1989) *The Cuisine of Sacrifice among the Greeks*. Transl. P. Wissing. Chicago.

(eds.) (1974) *Les Ruses de l'intelligence: La Métis des Grecs*. Paris.

Detschew, D. (1976) *Die Thrakischen Sprachreste*. 2nd edn. [1956] Vienna.

Dietler, M. (1990) "Driven by drink: The Role of Drinking in the Political Economy and the Case of Early Iron Age France," *Journal of Anthropological Archaeology* 9: 352–406.

(2009) "Colonial Encounters in Iberia and the Western Mediterranean," in *Colonial Encounters in Ancient Iberia: Phoenician, Greek, and Indigenous Relations*, ed. M. Dietler and C. López-Ruiz. Chicago: 3–48.

Dietler, M. and C. López-Ruiz (eds.) (2009) *Colonial Encounters in Ancient Iberia: Phoenician, Greek, and Indigenous Relations*. Chicago.

Doescœdres, J.-P. (ed.) (1990) *Greek Colonists and Native Populations*. Oxford.

Domaradzka, L. (1996) "Graffiti," in *Pistiros I: Excavations and Studies*, ed. J. Bouzek, M. Domaradzki, and Z. H. Archibald. Prague: 89–96.

(1999) "Monuments épigraphiques de Pistiros," *BCH* 123: 347–58.

(2002a) "Catalogue of Graffiti Discovered During the Excvations at Pistiros-Vetren 1988–1998. Part One: Graffiti on Imported Fine Pottery, with Pls. 44–50," in *Pistiros II: Excavations and Studies*, ed. J. Bouzek, L. Domaradzka, and Z. H. Archibald. Prague: 209–28.

(2002b) "Addenda ad Pistiros I: The Pistiros-Vetren Inscription," in *Pistiros II: Excavations and Studies*, ed. J. Bouzek, L. Domaradzka, and Z. H. Archibald. Prague: 339–42.

(2007a) "Catalogue of Graffiti Discovered in Pistiros –Vetren 1988–2004." Part Two: Graffiti on Pottery Used in the Household," in *Pistiros III: Excavations and Studies*, ed. J. Bouzek, L. Domaradzka, and Z. H. Archibald. Prague: 221–35.

(2007b) "ADDENDA I: Newly Discovered Graffiti on Black-Figured, Red-Figured, and Black-Glazed Attic Pottery," in *Pistiros III: Excavations and Studies*, ed. J. Bouzek, L. Domaradzka, and Z. H. Archibald. Prague: 283–5.

(2007c) "The Extent and Use of Greek Language and Literacy in Thrace During the Classical and Early Hellenistic Times (Based on Epigraphic Evidence)," *Eirene* 43: 69–81.

Domaradzki, M. (1993) "Pistiros - Centre commercial et politique dans la valée de Maritza (Thrace)," *Archeologia* (Warsaw) 44: 35–57.

(1996) "An Interim Report on Archaeological Investigations at Vetren – Pistiros, 1988–94," in *Pistiros I: Excavations and Studies*, ed. J. Bouzek, M. Doramardzki, and Z. H. Archibald. Prague: 13–34.

Domaradzki, M., L. Domaradzka, J. Bouzek, and J. Rostropowicz (eds.) (2000) *Pistiros et Thasos: structures économiques dans la péninsule balkanique aux VIIe-IIe siècles avant J.-C.* Opole.

Domínguez, A. J. (1986) "La ciudad griega de Emporion y su organización politica," *AEA* 59: 3–12.

(1995) "Del simposio griego a los bárbaros bebedores: El vino en Iberia y su imagen en los autores antiguos," in *Arqueología del vino. Los orígenes del vino en Occidente*, ed. S. Celestino. Jerez de la Frontera: 21–72.

(1999a) "Hellenisation in Iberia?: The Reception of Greek Products and Influences by the Iberians," in *Ancient Greeks West and East*, ed. G. R. Tsetskhladze. Leiden: 301–29.

(1999b) "Ephesos and Greek Colonization," in *100 Jahre österreichische Forschungen in Ephesos. Akten des Symposions Wien 1995*, ed. H. Friesinger and F. Krinzinger. Vienna: 75–80.

(2001) "La religión en el emporion," *Gerión* 19: 221–57.

(2002) "Greeks in Iberia: Colonialism without Colonization," in *The Archaeology of Colonialism*, ed. C. L. Lyons and J. K. Papadopoulos. Los Angeles: 65–95.

(2004a) "Greek Identity in the Phocaean Colonies," in *Greek Identity in the Western Mediterranean*, ed. K. Lomas. Leiden: 429–56.

(2004b) "Spain and France (Including Corsica)," in *An Inventory of Archaic and Classical Poleis: An Investigation Conducted by the Copenhagen Polis Centre for the Danish National Research Foundation*, ed. M. H. Hansen and T. H. Nielsen. Oxford: 157–71.

Domínguez A. J. and C. Sánchez (2001) *Greek Pottery from the Iberian Peninsula: Archaic and Classical Periods*. Leiden.

Dommelen, P. van (1997) "Colonial constructs: Colonialism and Archaeology in the Mediterranean," *World Archaeology* 28: 305–23.

Dougherty, C. (2003) "The Aristonothos Krater. Competing Stories of Conflict and Collaboration," in *The Cultures Within Ancient Greek Culture. Contact, Conflict, Collaboration*, ed. C. Dougherty and L. Kurke. Cambridge: 35–56.

Dougherty, C. and L. Kurke (eds.) (2003) *The Cultures Within Ancient Greek Culture. Contact, Conflict, Collaboration*. Cambridge.

Dow, S. (1937) *Prytaneis. A Study of the Inscriptions Honoring the Athenian Councillors*. Hesperia Supplement 1. Athens.

Dragan, J. C. (1976) *We, the Thracians and our Multimillenary History*. Milan.

Drews, R. (1981) "The Coming of the City to Central Italy," *AJAH* 6: 133–65.

Drijvers, J. W. (1999) "Strabo 17.1.18 (801C): Inaros, the Milesians and Naucratis," *Mnemosyne* 52: 16–22.

Duchêne, H. (1993) "Délos, réalités portuaires et *emporion*," in *L'Emporion*, ed. A. Bresson and P. Rouillard. Paris: 113–25.

Dueck. D. (2000) *Strabo of Amasia: A Greek Man of Letters in Augustan Rome*. London & New York.

Dunand, F. (1973) *Le Culte d'Isis dans le basin oriental de la Méditerranée*. Vol. 2. *Le Culte d'Isis en Grèce*. Leiden.

Duplouy, A. (2006) *Le Prestige des élites. Recherches sur les modes de reconnaissance sociale en Grèce entre les Xe et Ve siècles avant J.–C.* Paris.

Dupont, P. and A. Thomas (2006) "Naukratis: les importations grecques orientales archaiques. Classification et determination d'origine en laboratoire," in *Naukratis: Greek Diversity in Egypt. Studies on East Greek Pottery and Exchange in the Eastern Mediterranean*, ed. A. Villing and U. Schlotzhauer. London: 77–84.

Dürrbach, F. (1977) *Choix d'inscriptions de Délos*. Chicago.

Ebbinghaus, S. (2008) "Of Rams, Women, and Orientals: A Brief History of Attic Plastic Vases," in *Papers on Special Techniques in Athenian Vases: Proceedings of a Symposium Held in Connection with the Exhibition "The Colors of Clay: Special Techniques in Athenian Vases," at the Getty Villa, June 15–17, 2006*, ed. K. Lapatin. Los Angeles: 145–60.

Effentere, H. van and J. Vélissaropoulos (1991) "Une affaire d'affrètement à propos du 'plomb de Pech-Maho,'" *RD* 62: 217–25.

Ehrhardt, N. (1985) "Bemerkungen zu den Weihgraffiti aus Graviscae," *ZPE* 60: 139–43.

Elvers, K.-L. (1994) "Der 'Eid der Berenike und ihre Söhne,'" *Chiron* 24: 241–66.

Elwyn, S. F. (1991) "The Use of Kinship Terminology in Hellenistic Diplomatic Documents: An Epigraphical Study," Ph.D. Dissertation, University of Pennsylvania.

Engen, D. T. (2010) *Honor and Profit: Athenian Trade Policy and the Economy and Society of Greece.* Ann Arbor, MI.

Espagne, M., M. Geyer, M. Middell (eds.) (2010) *European History in an Interconnected World: An Introduction to Transnational History.* Basingstoke.

Étienne, R. (1993) "L'*Emporion* chez Strabon: les *emporia* straboniens: inventaire, hiérarchies et mécanisms commerciaux," in *L'Emporion,* ed. A. Bresson and P. Rouillard. Paris: 23–34.

Fabre, D. (2004a) *Le Destin maritime de l'Égypte ancienne.* London.

(2004b) *Seafaring in Ancient Egypt.* London.

(2007) "Recherches sur l'organisation du commerce maritime dans l'Égypte ancienne. L'Apport de l'anthropologie: enjeux et questionnements," *Proceedings of the Ninth International Congress of Egyptologists.* Grenoble: 677–94.

Fantalkin, A. (2001) "Low Chronology and Greek Protogeometric and Geometric Pottery in the Southern Levant," *Levant* 33: 117–25.

In press. "Naukratis as a Contact Zone: Revealing the Lydian Connection," in *Kulturkontakte in antiken Welten. Vom Denkmodell zur Fallstudie. Proceedings des internationalen Kolloquiums aus Anlass des 60. Geburtstages von Christoph Ulf, Innsbruck, 26.–30. Jänner 2009,* Innsbruck, ed. R. Rollinger and K. Schnegg. Colloquia Antiqua. Leuven.

Faraguna, M. (2002) "Commercio, scrittura, pratiche giuridiche. Recenti studi sull''emporía' greca," *Dike* 5: 237–54.

Faraone, C. (1993) "The Wheel, the Whip, and Other Implements of Torture: Erotic Magic in Pindar *Pythian* 4.213–19," *CJ* 89: 1–19.

(1999) *Ancient Greek Love Magic.* Cambridge, MA.

Faraone, C. and L. K. McClure (2006) *Prostitutes and Courtesans in the Ancient World.* Madison.

Ferguson, W. S. (1944) "The Attic Orgeones," *HTR* 37: 61–140.

(1949) "Orgeonika," *Hesperia Supplement* 8: 130–63.

Fick, N. and J.-C. Carrière (eds.) (1991) *Mélanges Étienne Bernard.* Paris.

Figueira, T. J. (1984) "Karl Polanyi and Ancient Greek Trade: The Port of Trade," *AW* 10: 15–30.

(1988) "Four Notes on the Aiginetans in Exile," *Athenaeum* 66: 523–51.

Fiorini, L. (2005) *Topografia generale e storia del santuario: Analisi dei contesti e delle stratigrafie.* Gravisca: scavi nel santuario greco. Vol. 1.1. Bari.

Fischer, F., B. Bouloumié, and C. Lagrand (eds.) (1987) *Hallstatt-Studien: Tübinger Kolloquium zur westeuropäischen Hallstatt-Zeit.* Weinheim.

Fisher, N. and H. van Wees (1998) *Archaic Greece: New Approaches and New Evidence.* London.

Flensted-Jensen, P., T. H. Nielsen, L. Rubinstein (eds.) (2000) *Polis and Politics: Studies in Ancient Greek History.* Copenhagen.

Fol, A. (1971) "La diaspora Thrace," *RSA* 1: 3–18.

(ed.) (1978) *Pulpudeva. Semaines philoppopolitaines de l'histoire et de la culture thrace, Plovdiv, 4–19 octobre 1976*. Vol. 2. Sofia.

(1983a) "The Thracians," in *Ancient Bulgaria. Papers Presented to the International Symposium on the Ancient History and Archaeology of Bulgaria, University of Nottingham, 1981*. Vol 1, ed. A. G. Poulter. Nottingham: 213–16.

(1983b) "Interpraetatio Thracica," *JIES* 11: 217–30.

(ed.) (2002) *Thrace and the Aegean*. Proceedings from the Eighth International Congress of Thracology. Vol. 1. Sofia.

Fol, A. and I. Marazov (1977) *Thrace and the Thracians*. New York.

Fol, A., J. Lichardus, and V. Nikolov (2004) *Die Thraker. Das goldene Reich des Orpheus*. Mainz.

Fol, A. and V. Fol (2005) *The Thracians*. Sofia.

Fontenrose, J. E. (1988) *Didyma, Apollo's Oracle, Cult and Companions*. Berkeley.

Fornara, C. W. (1971) "Themistokles' Archonship," *Historia* 20: 534–40.

Forrest, W. G. (1957) "Colonization and the Rise of Delphi," *Historia* 6: 160–75.

Fortunelli, S. (2007) *Il deposito votivo del santuario settentrionale*. Gravisca: scavi nel santuario greco. Vol. 1.2. Bari.

Foucault, M. (1978) *The History of Sexuality*. Vol. 1. *An Introduction*. Transl. R. Hurley. New York.

Fourrier, S. (2001) "Naucratis, Chypre et la Grèce de l'Est: le commerce des sculptures 'chypro-ioniennes,'" in *Naukratis. Die Beziehungen zu Ostgriechenland, Ägypten und Zypern in archaischer Zeit. Akten der Table Ronde in Mainz. 25.-27. November 1999*, ed. U. Höckmann and K. Detlev. Möhnesee: 39–54.

Francis, E. D. and M. Vickers (1984) "Amasis and Lindos," *BICS* 31: 119–30.

(1985) "Greek Geometric Pottery at Hama and its Implications for Near Eastern Chronology," *Levant* 17: 131–8.

Fränkel, C. (1912) "Korinthische Posse," *RhM* 67: 104–5.

Fraser, P. M. (1993) "Thracians Abroad: Three Documents," in Αρχαία Μακεδονία V. Ανακοινώσεις κατά το πέμπτο διεθνές συμπόσιο. Θεσσαλονίκη, 10–15 Οκτωβρίου, 1989. Vol. 2. Thessaloniki: 443–54.

(1995) "Citizens, Demesmen and Metics in Athens and Elsewhere," in *Sources for the Ancient Greek City-State*, ed. M. H. Hansen. Copenhagen: 64–90.

Fraser, P. M. and E. Matthews (eds.) (1987–2005) *A Lexicon of Greek Personal Names*. 4 vols. Oxford.

Frau, B. (1982a) "Graviscae: porto Greco di Tarquinia," in *Gli antichi porti di Tarquinia*, ed. B. Frau. Rome: 1–81.

(ed.) (1982b) *Gli antichi porti di Tarquinia*. Rome.

Friesinger, H. and F. Krinzinger (eds) (1999) *100 Jahre österreichische Forschungen in Ephesos: Akten des Symposions Wien 1995*. Vienna.

Froidefond, C. (1971) *Le Mirage égyptien dans la literature grecque d'Homère à Aristote*. Aix-en-Provence.

Gabrielsen, V. (2000) "The Synoikized Polis of Rhodes," in *Polis and Politics: Studies in Ancient Greek History*, ed. P. Flensted-Jensen, T. H. Nielsen, and L. Rubinstein. Copenhagen: 177–205.

Galli, V. (2004) *Le lucerne greche e locali.* Gravisca: scavi nel santuario greco. Vol. 11. Bari.

Galvagno, E. and C. Molè Ventura (eds.) (1991) *Mito, storia, tradizione: Diodoro Siculo e la storiografia classica. Atti del Convegno internazionale Catania-Agira 7–8 dicembre 1984.* Catania.

Gantès, L.-F. (1992) "La Topographie de Marseille grecque. Bilan des recherches (1829–1991)," in *Marseille grecque et la Gaule*, ed. M. Bats, G. Bertucchi, G. Congès, and H. Tréziny. Études Massaliètes 3. Aix-en-Provence: 71–88.

Garcia, D. (1987) "Observations sur la production et le commerce des céréales en Languedoc méditerranéen durant l'Âge du Fer. Les formes de stockage des grain," *RAN* 20: 43–98.

García-Bellido, P. (1994) "Las relaciones económicas entre Massalia, Emporion y Gades a través de la moneda," in *Iberos y Griegos: lecturas desde la diversidad*, ed. P. Cabrera, R. Olmos, and E. Sanmartí. Huelva Arqueologica 13. Huelva: 115–49.

García-Bellido, P. and R. M. S. Centeno (eds.) (1995) *La Moneda hispánica. Ciudad y territorio.* Madrid.

García y Bellido, A. (1935) "Los Iberos en Cerdeña, según los textos clásicos y la arqueología," *Emerita* 3: 225–67.

(1954) "Expansión de la cerámica ibérica por la Cuenca Occidental del Mediterráneo," *AEA* 27: 246–54.

Gardner, E. A. with an appendix by F. L. Griffith (1888) *Naukratis: Part II.* Rpt. 1992. Chicago.

Garlan, Y. (1993) "Εἰς ἐμπόριον dans le timbrage amphorique de Chersonèse," in *L'Emporion*, ed. A. Bresson and P. Rouillard. Paris: 99–102.

Garland, R. (1992) *Introducing New Gods. The Politics of Athenian Religion.* London. (2001) *The Piraeus: From the Fifth to the First Century B.C.* 2nd edn. Ithaca, NY.

Gat, A. (2002) "Why City-States Existed? Riddles and Clues of Urbanisation and Fortifications," in *A Comparative Study of Six City-State Cultures*, ed. M. H. Hansen. Copenhagen: 125–39.

Gaultier, Ph. and D. Briquel (eds.) (1999) *Les Étrusques, le plus religieux des hommes.* Paris.

Gauthier, P. (1972) *Symbola. Les Étrangers et la justice dans les cités grecques.* Nancy.

(1981) "De Lysias à Aristote (Ath. Pol., 51,4): le commerce du grain à Athènes et les fonctions des sitophylakes," *RD* 59: 5–28.

(1988) "Métèques, périèques, et *paroikoi*: bilan et points d'interrogation," in *L'Étranger dans le monde grec*, ed. R. Lonis. Nancy: 23–46.

(1993) "Décrets d'Érétrie en l'honneur de juges étrangers," *REG* 106: 589–98.

(1994) "Rois hellénistiques et juges étrangers," *JS* 2: 165–95.

(1995) "Bulletin épigraphique," *REG* 108: 432.

(1999) "'Symbola' athénienne et tribunaux étrangers à l'époque hellénistique," *BCH* 123: 157–74.

Georgi, S. (1982) "La massicciata frangiflutti e l'avamporto," in *Gli antichi porti di Tarquinia*, ed. B. Frau. Rome: 23–7.

Gerardo, P. M. (ed.) (1988) *Actes del I congreso peninsular de historia antigua.* Santiago.

Gianfrotta, P. A. (1975) "Le ancore votive di Sostrato di Egina e di Faillo di Crotone," *PP* 30: 311–18.

(1977) "First Elements for the Dating of Stone Anchor Stocks," *IJNA* 6.4: 285–92.

Gill, D. W. J. (1991) "Pots and Trade: Spacefillers or objets d'art?," *JHS* 111: 29–47.

(1994) "Positivism, pots and long distance trade," in *Classical Greece. Ancient Histories and Modern Archaeologies*, ed. I. Morris. Cambridge: 99–101.

Gindin, L. A. (1982) "La Thrace et le monde méditerranéen d'après les données linguistiques," in *Festschrift für Johannes Hubschmid zum 65. Geburtstag. Beiträge zur allgemeinen, indogermanischen und romanischen Sprachwissenschaft*, ed. M. Braisch and O. von Winkelmann. Bern: 323–6.

Giudice, G. (2007) *Il tornio, la nave, le terre lontane. Ceramografici attici in Magna Grecia nella seconda metà del VI sec. a.C. Rotte e vie di distribuzione.* Rome.

Giuffrida, M. (1996) "Afrodite Euploia a Cipro?," *Kokalos* 42: 341–8.

Gjerstad, E. (1934) "Studies in Archaic Greek Chronology," *Annals of Archaeology and Anthropology* 21: 67–84, pl. 9–10.

(1959) "Naukratis Again," *AArch* 30: 147–65.

Glinister, F. (2006) "Reconsidering 'Religious Romanization'," in *Religion in Republican Italy*, ed. C. E. Schultz and P. B. Harvey, Jr. Cambridge: 10–33.

Gómez Espelosín, J. (2009) "Iberia in the Greek Geographical Imagination," in *Colonial Encounters in Ancient Iberia: Phoenician, Greek, and Indigenous Relations*, ed. M. Dietler and C. López-Ruiz. Chicago: 281–97.

Gori, S. (ed.) (2006) *Gli Etruschi da Genova ad Ampurias. Atti del XXIV Convegno di Studi Etruschi ed Italici, Marseille-Lattes, 26 settembre – 1 ottobre 2002.* 2 vols. Rome.

Gorton, A. F. (1996) *Egyptian and Egyptianizing Scarabs: A Typology of Steatite, Faience and Paste Scarabs from Punic and Other Mediterranean Sites.* Oxford.

Graf, F. (1979) "Apollon Delphinios," *MH* 36: 2–22.

(1985) *Nordionische Kulte: Religionsgeschichtliche und epigraphische Untersuchungen zu den Kulten von Chios, Erythrai, Klazomenai und Phokaia.* Rome.

(2004) "What is Ancient Mediterranean Religion?," in *Religions of the Ancient World: A Guide*, ed. S. Iles Johnston. Cambridge, MA: 3–16.

Graham, A. J. (1970) "The Colonial Expansion of Greece," *Cambridge Ancient History.* III. 3. Cambridge.

(1978) "The Foundation of Thasos," *ABSA* 63: 61–98.

(1982) *Colony and Mother City.* 2nd edn. Chicago.

(1986) "The Historical Interpretation of Al Mina," *DHA* 12: 51–65.

(2001) *Collected Papers on Greek Colonization*. Leiden.

Grallert, S. (2001) "Akkulturation im ägyptischen Sepulkralwesen. Der Fall eines Griechen in Ägypten zur Zeit der 26. Dynastie," in *Naukratis. Die Beziehungen zu Ostgriechenland, Ägypten und Zypern in archaischer Zeit. Akten der Table Ronde in Mainz, 25–27 November 1999*, ed. U. Höckmann and D. Kreikenbom. Möhnesee: 182–95.

Gras, M. (1985a) "Aspects de l'économie maritime étrusque," *Ktema* 10: 149–59.

(1985b) *Trafics tyrrhéniens archaïques*. Rome.

(1993) "Pour une Méditerranée des *emporia*," in *L'Emporion*, ed. A. Bresson and P. Rouillard. Paris: 103–12.

(2000) "Les Étrusques et la Gaule méditerranéenne," in *Mailhac et le premier Âge du Fer en Europe occidentale: Hommages à Odette et Jean Taffanel*, ed. T. Janin. Lattes: 229–42.

Greco, E. (1994) "Pithekoussai: empório o apoikía," *AION(archeol)* 1: 11–18.

Griffith, F. L. (1888) "Egyptological Notes from Naukratis and the Neighbourhood," in *Naukratis II*, ed. E. A. Gardner. Rpt. 1992. Chicago: 77–84.

Grimal, N. and B. Menu (eds.) (1998) *Le Commerce en Égypte ancienne*. Cairo.

Grmela, L. (2007) "Lamps from Pistiros III," in *Pistiros III: Excavations and Studies*, ed. J. Bouzek, L. Domaradzka, and Z. H. Archibald. Prague: 120–204.

Groningen, B. A. van (1960) *Pindare au banquet*. Leiden.

Grove A. T. and O. Rackham (2003) *The Nature of Mediterranean Europe. An Ecological History*. New Haven.

Gschnitzer, F. (1990) "Die Stellung der Polis in der politischen Entwicklung des Altertums," *OA* 27: 287–302.

(1993) "Phoinikisch-karthagisches Verfassungsdenken," in *Anfänge politischen Denkens in der Antike*, ed. K. Raaflaub. Munich: 187–98.

Gunn, B. G. (1943) "Notes on the Naucratite Stela," *JEA* 29: 55–9.

Guralnick, E. (1997) "The Egyptian-Greek Connection in the 8th to 6th Centuries B.C.: An Overview," in *Greeks and Barbarians: Essays on the Interactions between Greeks and non-Greeks in Antiquity and the Consequences for Eurocentrism*, ed. J. E. Coleman and C. A. Walz. Bethesda, MD: 127–54.

Guy, M. (1999) "Le Parcellaire autour d'Emporion: colonisations et continuité de l'occupation," *Pallas* 50: 327–38.

Gwynn, A. (1918) "The Character of Greek Colonisation," *JHS* 38: 88–123.

Haack, M.-L. (2007) "Phocéens et Samiens à Gravisca," *BABesch* 82: 29–40.

Hackens, T. and R. Weiller (eds.) (1982) *Actes du IXe congrès international de numismatique, Berne, septembre 1979*. Louvain-la-Neuve.

Hadzisteliou Price, T. (1978) *Kourotrophos. Cults and Representations of the Greek Nursing Deities*. Leiden.

Hägg, R. (ed.) (1996) *The Role of Religion in the Early Greek Polis*. Stockholm.

Haider, P. W. (2001) "Epigraphische Quellen zur Intergration von Griechen in die ägyptische Gesellschaft der Saïtenzeit," in *Naukratis. Die Beziehungen* zu Ostgriechenland, Ägypten und Zypern in archaischer Zeit. Akten der Table Ronde in Mainz. 25–27 November 1999, ed. U. Höckmann and D. Kreikenbom. Möhnesee: 197–209.

Hales, S. and T. Hodos (eds.) (2009) Material Culture and Social Identities in the Ancient World. Cambridge.

Hall, E. (1989) Inventing the Barbarian: Greek Self-Definition Through Tragedy. Oxford.

Hall, J. (1997) Ethnic Identity in Greek Antiquity. Cambridge.

(2002) Hellenicity. Chicago.

(2003) "'Culture' or 'Cultures'? Hellenism in the Late Sixth Century," in The Cultures Within Ancient Greek Culture. Contact, Conflict, Collaboration, ed. C. Dougherty and L. Kurke. Cambridge: 23–34.

(2004) "How 'Greek' were the Early Western Greeks?," in Greek Identity in the Western Mediterranean, ed. K. Lomas. Leiden: 35–54.

Hamon, P. (1999) "Juges thasiens à Smyrne," BCH 123: 175–94.

Hansen, M. H. (1995) "The 'Autonomous City-State:' Ancient Fact or Modern Fiction?," in Studies in the Ancient Greek Polis, ed. M. H. Hansen and K. Raaflaub. Stuttgart: 21–43.

(ed.) (1996a) Introduction to an Inventory of Poleis. Acts of the Copenhagen Polis Centre. Vol. 3. Copenhagen.

(1996b) "ΠΟΛΛΑΧΩΣ ΠΟΛΙΣ ΛΕΓΕΤΑΙ (Arist. Pol. 1276a23). The Copenhagen Inventory of Poleis and the Lex Hafniensis de Civitate," in Introduction to an Inventory of Poleis. Acts of the Copenhagen Polis Centre. Vol. 3, ed. M. H. Hansen. Copenhagen: 7–72.

(1996c) "City-Ethnics as Evidence for Polis Identity," in More Studies in the Ancient Greek Polis, ed. M. H. Hansen and K. Raaflaub. Stuttgart: 169–96.

(1997) "Emporion: A Study of the Use and Meaning of the Term in the Archaic and Classical Periods," in Yet More Studies in the Ancient Greek Polis, ed. T. H. Nielsen. Stuttgart: 83–105.

(2000a) "Introduction. The Concepts of the City-State and City-State Culture," in A Comparative Study of Thirty City-State Cultures, ed. M. H. Hansen. Copenhagen: 11–34.

(2000b) "The Hellenic Polis," in A Comparative Study of Thirty City-State Cultures, ed. M. H. Hansen. Copenhagen: 141–87.

(2000c) "Conclusion: The Impact of City-State Cultures on World Histories," in A Comparative Study of Thirty City-State Cultures, ed. M. H. Hansen. Copenhagen: 597–623.

(ed.) (2000d) A Comparative Study of Thirty City-State Cultures. Copenhagen.

(ed.) (2002) A Comparative Study of Six City-State Cultures. Copenhagen.

(2004) "A Typology of Dependent Poleis," in An Inventory of Archaic and Classical Poleis. An Investigation Conducted by the Copenhagen Polis Centre for the Danish National Research Foundation, ed. M. H. Hansen and T. H. Nielsen. Oxford: 87–95.

(2006a) "*Emporion.* A Study of the Use and Meaning of the Term in the Archaic and Classical Periods," in *Greek Colonization: An Account of Greek Colonies and Other Settlements Overseas.* Vol. 1, ed. G. Tsetskhladze. Leiden: 1–39.

(2006b) *Polis. An Introduction to the Ancient Greek City-State.* Oxford.

(2007a) "Herodotus," in *The Return of the Polis. The Use and Meanings of the Word Polis in Archaic and Classical Sources,* ed. M. H. Hansen. Stuttgart: 104–34.

(ed.) (2007b) *The Return of the Polis. The Use and Meanings of the Word Polis in Archaic and Classical Sources.* Stuttgart.

Hansen, M. H. and T. Fischer-Hansen (1994) "Monumental Political Architecture in Archaic and Classical Greek Poleis. Evidence and Significance," in *From Political Architecture to Stephanus Byzantius,* ed. D. Whitehead. Stuttgart: 23–90.

Hansen, M. H. and T. H. Nielsen (eds.) (2004) *An Inventory of Archaic and Classical Poleis: An Investigation Conducted by the Copenhagen Polis Centre for the Danish National Research Foundation.* Oxford.

Hansen, M. H. and K. Raaflaub (eds.) (1995) *Studies in the Ancient Greek Polis.* Stuttgart.

(1996) *More Studies in the Ancient Greek Polis.* Stuttgart.

Harris, W. V. (2005) "The Mediterranean and Ancient History," in *Rethinking the Mediterranean,* ed. W. V. Harris. Oxford: 1–42.

(ed.) (2005) *Rethinking the Mediterranean.* Oxford.

Harrison, R. J. (1988) *Spain at the Dawn of History: Iberians, Phoenicians and Greeks.* London.

Harrison, T. (ed.) (2002) *Greeks and Barbarians.* Edinburgh.

Harvey, F. D. (1976) "Sostratos of Aigina," *PP* 31: 206–14.

Hasluck, F. W. (1910) *Cyzicus.* Cambridge.

Hauvette-Besnault, A.M. and M. Dubois (1881) "Antiquités de Mylasa," *BCH* 5: 95–119.

Haynes, S. (2000) *Etruscan Civilization. A Cultural History.* Los Angeles.

Head, B. C. (1911) *Historia Nummorum.* 2nd edn. Oxford.

Head, B. V. (1886) "The Coins," in *Naukratis. Part I,* ed. W. M. F. Petrie *et al.* Rpt. 1992. Chicago: 63–9.

Helly, B. (1971) "Décrets de Démétrias pour les juges étrangers," *BCH* 95: 543–59.

Helm, P. R. (1980) "'Greeks' in the Neo-Assyrian Levant and 'Assyria' in Early Greek Writers," Ph.D. Dissertation, University of Pennsylvania.

Helm, R. (ed.) (1956) *Eusebius' Werke 7. Die Chronik des Hieronymus I.* Leipzig.

Héra. Images, espaces, cultes. Actes du colloque international de Lille (1993). (1997) Naples.

Hermary, A. (2001) "Naucratis et la sculpture égyptisante à Chypre," in *Naukratis. Die Beziehungen zu Ostgriechenland, Ägypten und Zypern in archaischer Zeit. Akten der Table Ronde in Mainz. 25.-27. November 1999,* ed. U. Höckmann and D. Kreikenbom. Möhnesee: 27–38.

Hermary, A. and H. Tréziny (eds.) (2000) *Les Cultes des cités phocéennes. Actes du colloque international organisé par le Centre Camille-Julian (Aix-en-Provence/Marseille, 1999)*. Études Massaliètes 6. Aix-en-Provence.

Heurgon, J. (1957) "L'État etrusque," *Historia* 6: 63–97.

(1980) "À propos de l'inscripion 'tyrrhénienne' de Lemnos," *CRAI*: 578–600.

Heuzey, L. A. (1891) *Catalogue des figurines antiques de terre cuite du Musée du Louvre*. Paris.

Higbie, C. (2003) *The Lindian Chronicle and the Greek Creation of their Past*. Oxford.

Hill, D. K. (1932) "Some Boundary Stones from the Piraeus," *AJA* 36.3: 254–9.

Hind, J. G. F. (1972) "Pyrene and the Date of the 'Massaliote Sailing Manual,'" *RSA* 2: 39–52.

Hirschfeld, G. (1887) "Die Gründung von Naukratis," *RhM* 42: 209–25.

Höckmann, U. (2001) "Bilinguen: Zu Ikonographie und Stil der karisch-ägyptischen Grabstelen des 6. Jhs. v. Chr.," in *Naukratis. Die Beziehungen zu Ostgriechenland, Ägypten und Zypern in archaischer Zeit. Akten der Table Ronde in Mainz. 25–27 November 1999*, ed. U. Höckmann and D. Kreikenbom. Möhnesee: 217–32.

Höckmann, U. and A. Möller (2006) "The Hellenion at Naukratis: Questions and Observations," In *Naukratis: Greek Diversity in Egypt: Studies on East Greek Pottery and Exchange in the Eastern Mediterranean*, ed. A. Villing and U. Schlotzhauer. London: 11–22.

Höckmann, U. and D. Kreikenbom (eds.) (2001) *Naukratis. Die Beziehungen zu Ostgriechenland, Ägypten und Zypern in archaischer Zeit. Akten der Table Ronde in Mainz. 25–27 November 1999*. Möhnesee.

Hoffner, H. A. Jr. (ed.) (1973) *Orient and Occident. Essays Presented to Cyrus H. Gordon on the Occasion of his Sixty-Fifth Birthday*. Neukirchen-Vluyn.

Hogarth, D. G. (1898–9) "Excavations at Naukratis," *ABSA* 5: 26–97.

(1905) "Naukratis, 1903," *JHS* 25: 105–36.

Horden P. and N. Purcell (2000) *The Corrupting Sea: A Study of Mediterranean History*. Oxford.

(2005) "'Four Years of 'Corruption:' A Response to Critics," in *Rethinking the Mediterranean*, ed. W. V. Harris. Oxford: 348–75.

(2006) "HR Forum: The Mediterranean and 'the New Thalassology,'" *AHR* 11.3: 722–40.

Hornblower, G. D. (1926) "Phallic Offerings to Hathor," *MAN* 26: 81–3.

Horstmannschoff, H. F. J., H. W. Singor, F. T. van Straten, and J. H. M. Strubbe (eds.) (2000) *Kykeon. Studies in Honour of H. S. Versnel*. Leiden.

How, W. W. and J. Well. (1991) *A Commentary on Herodotus*. Vol. 2. Oxford.

Huber, K. (1999) *Le ceramiche attiche a figure rosse*. Gravisca: scavi nel santuario greco. Vol. 6. Bari.

Hurst, H. and Owen, S. (eds.) (2005) *Ancient Colonizations: Analogy, Similarity and Difference*. London.

Hurwit, J. M. (1985) *The Art and Culture of Early Greece, 1100–480 B.C.* Ithaca, NY.

Huxley, G. L. (1966) *The Early Ionians*. London.

Iacobazzi, B. (2004) *Le ceramiche attiche a figure nere*. Gravisca: scavi nel santuario greco. Vol. 5. 2 vols. Bari.

Iacopi, G. (1952) "Capo Cimmiti (Crotone). Iscrizione greca," *NSc* 6: 167–76.

Ilieva, P. (2009) "Samothrace: Samo – or Thrace?," in *Material Culture and Social Identities in the Ancient World*, ed. S. Hales and T. Hodos. Cambridge: 138–70.

Iriye, A. and P.-Y. Saunier (eds.) (2009) *The Palgrave Dictionary of Transnational History*. Basingstoke.

Isaac, B. (1986) *The Greek Settlements in Thrace Until the Macedonian Conquest*. Leiden.

Isager, S. and M. H. Hansen (1975) *Aspects of Athenian Society in the Fourth Century B.C.* Transl. J. H. Rosenmeier. Odense.

Izzet, V. (2007) *The Archaeology of Etruscan Society*. Cambridge.

James, P. (2003) "Naukratis Revisited," *Hyperboreus* 9.2: 235–64.

James, P., I. J. Thorpe, N. Kokkinos, and J. Frankish (1987) "Bronze to Iron Age Chronology in the Old World: Time for a Reassessment," *Studies in Ancient Chronology* 1: 1–147.

Janin, T. (ed.) (2000) *Mailhac et le Premier Âge du fer en Europe occidentale: Hommages à Odette et Jean Taffanel*. Lattes.

Jannaris, A. N. (1897) *A Historical Greek Grammar*. London.

Jannot, J.-R. (1995) "Les Navires étrusques, instruments d'une thalassocratie?," *CRAI* 3: 743–78.

  (2005) *Religion in Ancient Etruria*. Transl. J. Whitehead. Madison.

Jeffery, L. H. (1961) *The Local Scripts of Archaic Greece*. Oxford.

Jenkins, I. (2001) "Archaic Kouroi in Naukratis: The Case for Cypriot Origin," *AJA* 105: 163–79.

Johnston, A. W. (1972) "The Rehabilitation of Sostratos," *PP* 27: 416–23.

  (1979) *Trademarks on Greek Vases*. Warminster.

  (1982) "Fragmenta Britannica II: Sherds from Naukratis," *BICS* 29: 35–42.

  (1984) "Kyliphaktos, a New Vase-Name," *ABSA* 79: 125–8.

  (1991) "The Vase Trade: a Point of Order," *ActaHyp* 3: 404–6.

Johnston, A. W. and M. Pandolfini (2000) *Le iscrizioni*. Gravisca: scavi nel santuario greco. Vol. 15. Bari.

Johnston, A. W. and R. E. Jones (1978) "The 'SOS' Amphora," *BSA* 73: 103–41.

Johnston, J. E. (1998) "Pistyros – *Emporion* of the North Aegean," M.A. Thesis, University of Texas at Austin.

Johnston, S. I. (ed.) (2004) *Religions of the Ancient World: A Guide*. Cambridge, MA.

Jones, N. F. (1999) *The Associations of Classical Athens. The Response to Democracy*. Oxford.

Jones, R. E. (1986) *Greek and Cypriot Pottery: A Review of Scientific Studies*. BSA Fitch Laboratory Occasional Papers 1. Athens.

Jones, S. (1997) *The Archaeology of Ethnicity: Constructing Identities in the Past and Present*. London.

Jurina, P. (1996) "Lamps," in *Pistiros I: Excavations and Studies*, ed. J. Bouzek, M. Domaradzki, and Z. H. Archibald. Prague: 96–103.

Kaczmarczyk, A. and R. E. M. Hedges (1983) *Ancient Egyptian Faience: An Analytical Survey of Egyptian Faience from Predynastic to Roman Times*. Warminster.

Kammerzell, F. (2001) "Die Geschichte der karischen Minderheit in Ägypten," in *Naukratis: Die Beziehungen zu Ostgriechenland, Ägypten und Zypern in archaischer Zeit. Akten der Table Ronde in Mainz, 25–27 November 1999*, ed. U. Höckmann and D. Kreikenbom. Möhnesee: 233–55.

Karetsou, A. (ed.) (2000) *Κρήτη-Αίγυπτος. Πολιτισμικοί δεσμοί τριών χιλιετιών. Κατάλογος. Αρχαιολογικό Μουσείο Ηρακλείου, 21 Νοεμβρίου 1999– 21 Σεπτεμβρίου 2000*. Herakleion.

Kassel, R. and C. Austin (eds.) (1983–2001) *Poetae Comici Graeci*. 8 vols. Berlin.

Kearns, E. (1989) *The Heroes of Attica*. BICS Supplement 57. London.

Keesling, C. (2006) "Heavenly Bodies: Monuments to Prostitutes in Greek Sanctuaries," in *Prostitutes and Courtesans in the Ancient World*, ed. C. Faraone and L. J. McClure. Madison: 59–76.

Kinch, K. F. (1905) *Exploration archéologique de Rhodes. IIIe Rapport*. Copenhagen.

Kloppenborg, J. S. and R. S. Ascough (2011) *Greco-Roman Associations: Texts, Translations, and Commentary*. Vol. 1: *Attica, Central Greece, Macedonia, Thrace*. Berlin.

Knorringa, H. (1926) *Emporos: Data on Trade and Traders in Greek Literature from Homer to Aristotle*. Rpt. 1987. Chicago.

Kolarova, V. (1996) "Study on the Section of the Emporion's Fortifications as Discovered by the end of 1994," in *Pistiros I: Excavations and Studies*, ed. J. Bouzek, M. Domaradzki, and Z. H. Archibald. Prague: 35–42.

Koukouli-Chrysanthaki, C. (1972) "Αρχαιότητες και Μνημεία Ανατολικής Μακεδονίας," *Αρχαιολογικό Δελτίο* 27: 520–33.

Kraay, C. M. (1964) "Hoards, Small Change and the Origin of Coinage," *JHS* 84: 76–88.

Kron, U. (1984) "Archaisches Kultgeschirr aus dem Heraion von Samos. Zu einer speziellen Gattung von archaischem Trink- und Tafelgeschirr mit Dipinti," in *Ancient Greek and Related Pottery: Proceedings of the 2nd International Vase Symposium, Amsterdam 1984*. Amsterdam: 292–7.

Kurke, L. (1996) "Pindar and the Prostitutes, or Reassessing Ancient 'Pornography,'" *ARION* 4.2: 49–75.

(1999) *Coins, Bodies, Games, and Gold. The Politics of Meaning in Archaic Greece*. Princeton.

Kyrieleis, H. (1980) "Archaische Holzfunde aus Samos," *MDAI(A)* 95: 89–94.

(1981) *Führer durch das Heraion von Samos*. Athens.

(1990) "Samos and Some Aspects of Archaic Greek Bronze Casting," in *Small Bronze Sculpture from the Ancient World*, ed. M. True and J. Podany. Malibu: 15–30.

La Genière, J. de (ed.) (1991) *Épéios et Philoctète en Italie*. Naples.

La Magna Grecia e Roma nell' età arcaica. Atti dell'VIII convegno di studi sulla Magna Grecia, 1968. (1971) Naples.

Laín Entralgo, P. (ed.) (1971) *Estudios sobre la obra de Américo Castro.* Madrid.

Lambert, S. D. (1993) *The Phratries of Attica.* Ann Arbor, MI.

Lapatin, K. (ed.) (2008) *Papers on Special Techniques in Athenian Vases: Proceedings of a Symposium Held in Connection with the Exhibition "The Colors of Clay: Special Techniques in Athenian Vases," at the Getty Villa, June 15–17, 2006.* Los Angeles.

Laronde, A. (1993) "Les *Emporia* de la Cyrénaïque," in *L'Emporion*, ed. A. Bresson and P. Rouillard. Paris: 89–97.

Larsen, M. T. (2000) "The City-States of the Early Neo-Babylonian Period," in *A Comparative Study of Thirty City-State Cultures*, ed. M. H. Hansen. Copenhagen: 117–27.

Larson, S. (2007) *Tales of Epic Ancestry: Boiotian Collective Identity in the Late Archaic and Early Classical Periods.* Stuttgart.

Lattanzi, E. (1991) "Recenti scoperte nei santuari di Hera Lacinia a Crotone e di Apollo Aleo a Cirò Marina," in *Épéios et Philoctète en Italie*, ed. J. de La Genière. Naples: 67–73.

Lazarides, D. (1971) *Thasos and its Peraia.* Athens.

Lazov, G. (1996) "Decorated Clay Altars," in *Pistiros I: Excavations and Studies*, ed. J. Bouzek, M. Domaradzki, and Z. H. Archibald. Prague: 63–73.

Lazova, T. (1996) "Pistiros in the Ancient Lexicography," in *Pistiros I: Excavations and Studies*, ed. J. Bouzek, M. Domaradzki, and Z. H. Archibald. Prague: 217–19.

Le Rider, G. (1997) "Cléomène de Naucratis," *BCH* 121: 91–3.

Leahy, A. (1988) "The Earliest Dated Monument of Amasis and the End of the Reign of Apries," *JEA* 74: 183–99.

Leclère, F. (2008) *Les Villes de basse Egypte au Ier millénaire av. J.-C. Analyse archéologique et historique de la topographie urbaine.* Cairo

Lefkowitz, M. R. (1996) *Not out of Africa: How Afrocentrism Became an Excuse to Teach Myth as History.* New York.

    (2002–3) "Black Athena: The Sequel (Part I): Review Article," *IJCT* 9.4: 598–603.

Lefkowitz, M. R. and G. McL. Rogers (eds.) (1996) *Black Athena Revisited.* Chapel Hill, NC.

Lehmann-Hartleben, K. (1923) "Die antiken Hafenanlagen des Mittelmeeres," *Klio* Beiheft 14: 1–298.

Lejeune, M. (1991) "Ambiguïtés du texte de Pech-Maho," *REG* 104: 311–29.

Lejeune, M. and J. Pouilloux (1988) "Une transaction commerciale ionienne au Ve s. à Pech-Maho," *CRAI*: 526–36.

Lejeune, M., J. Pouilloux, and Y. Solier (1988) "Étrusque et ionien archaïque sur un plomb de Pech-Maho Aude," *RAN* 21: 19–59.

Leonard, A. (1997) *Ancient Naukratis: Excavations at a Greek Emporium in Egypt.* Annual of the American Schools of Oriental Research 54. Atlanta, GA.

Lepore, E. (1968) "Per una fenomenologia storica del rapport città-territorio in Magna Grecia," in *La città e il suo territorio. Atti dal VII convegno di studi sulla Magna Grecia.* Naples: 29–66.

 (2000) *La Grande Grèce: aspects et problèmes d'une "colonisation" ancienne. Quatre conférences au Collège de France (1982).* Naples.

Lévêque, P. (1993) "La Richesse foisonnante de l'*emporion*," in *L'Emporion*, ed. A. Bresson and P. Rouillard. Paris: 227–31.

Levy, E. (1988) "Métèques et droit de residence," in *L'Étranger dans le monde grec*, ed. R. Lonis. Nancy: 47–68.

Lilliu, G. (1971) "Navicella di bronzo protosarda da Graviscae," in M. Torelli, "Graviscae (Tarquinia). Scavi nella città etrusca e romana. Campagne 1969 e 1970." *NSc* 25: 289–98.

Lloyd, A. B. (1976) *Herodotus, Book II: Commentary 1–98.* Leiden.

Lo Schiavo, F. (2002) "Osservazioni sul problema dei rapporti fra Sardegna ed Etruria in età nuragica-II," in *Etruria e Sardegna cetto-settentrionale tra l'età del bronzo finale e l'arcaismo. Atti del XXI Convegno di studi etruschi ed italici.* Pisa and Rome.

Lomas, K. (ed.) (2004) *Greek Identity in the Western Mediterranean.* Leiden.

Lonis, R. (ed.) (1988) *L'Étranger dans le monde grec.* Nancy.

López Férez, J. A. (ed.) (1999) *Desde lo poemas homéricos hasta la prosa griega del siglo IV d.C.* Madrid.

López García, A. (1995) "Nota sulla lettera di piombo da Emporion," *Tyche* 10: 101–2.

Loprieno, A. (1988) *Topos und Mimesis. Zum Ausländer in der ägyptischen Literatur.* Wiesbaden.

Lordkipanidze, O. and P. Lévêque (eds.) (1999) *Réligions du Pont-Euxin. Actes du VIIIe symposium de Vanie (Colchide), 1997.* Transl. A. Fraysse and E. Geny. Paris.

Loukopoulou, L. (1983) "Colons et indigènes dans la Thrace propontique," *Klio* 71: 78–83.

 (1989). *Contribution à l'histoire de la Thrace propontique durant la période archaïque.* Athens.

 (1999) "Sur le statut et l'importance de l'*emporion* de Pistiros," *BCH* 123: 359–71.

Loukopoulou, L. and S. Psoma (2008) "Maroneia and Stryme Revisited. Some Problems of Historical Topography," in *Thrakika Zetemata* 1, ed. L. Loukopoulou and S. Psoma. Athens: 55–88.

Loukopoulou, L. and S. Psoma (eds.) (2008) *Thrakika Zetemata* 1. Athens.

Lücke, S. (2000) *Syngeneia: Epigraphisch-historische Studien zu einem Phänomen der antiken griechischen Diplomatie.* Frankfurt.

Lutz, H. L. E. (1943) "An attempt to Interpret the Name of the City of Naukratis," *University of California Publications in Semitic Philology.* 10.13: 281–6.

Lyons, C. L. and J. K. Papadopoulos (eds.) (2002) *The Archaeology of Colonialism*. Los Angeles.

Ma, J., N. Papazarkadas, and R. Parker (2009) *Interpreting the Athenian Empire*. London.

Macan, R. W. (1908) *Herodotus: The Seventh, Eighth, and Ninth Books with Introduction and Commentary*. London.

MacLachlan, B. (1992) "Sacred Prostitution and Aphrodite," *Studies in Religion* 21.2: 145–162.

Maiuri, A. (1925) *Nuova silloge d'iscrizioni di Rodi e di Cos*. Florence.

Malkin, I. (1987) *Religion and Colonization in Ancient Greece*. Leiden.

  (ed.) (1990a) *La France et la Méditerannée. Vingt-sept siècles d'interdépendance*. Leiden.

  (1990b) "Missionaires païens dans la Gaule grecque," in *La France et la Méditerannée. Vingt-sept siècles d'interdépendance*, ed. I. Malkin. Leiden: 42–52.

  (1998) *The Returns of Odysseus: Colonization and Ethnicity*. Berkeley.

  (2001) "Introduction" in *Ancient Perceptions of Greek Ethnicity*, ed. I. Malkin Washington, DC: 1–23.

  (ed.) (2001) *Ancient Perceptions of Greek Ethnicity*. Washington, DC.

  (2002) "A Colonial Middle Ground: Greek, Etruscan, and Local Elites in the Bay of Naples," in *The Archaeology of Colonialism*, eds. C. L. Lyons and J. Papadopoulos. Los Angeles: 151–81.

  (2003a) "Networks and the Emergence of Greek Identity," *MHR* 18: 56–74.

  (2003b) "Pan-Hellenism and the Greeks of Naukratis," in *La Naissance de la ville dans l'antiquité*, ed. M. Reddé, L. Dubois, D. Briquel, H. Lavagne, and F. Queyrel. Paris: 91–6.

  (2004) "Postcolonial Concepts and Ancient Greek Colonization," *MLQ* 65: 341–64.

  (2005a) "Herakles and Melqart: Greeks and Phoenicians in the Middle Ground," in *Cultural Borrowings and Ethnic Appropriations in Antiquity*, ed. E. Gruen. Stuttgart: 238–58.

  (ed.) (2005b) *Mediterranean Paradigms and Classical Antiquity*. London and New York.

  (2007) "Ethnicité et colonisation: le réseau d'identité grecque en Sicile," *Pallas* 73: 181–90.

  (2011) *A Small Greek World: Networks in the Ancient Mediterranean*. Oxford.

Marazov, I. (ed.) (1998) *Ancient Gold: The Wealth of the Thracians: Treasures from the Republic of Bulgaria*. New York.

Marcet, R. and E. Sanmartí-Grego (1989) *Empúries*. Barcelona.

Marcus, J. and G. M. Feinman (1998) "Introduction," in *Archaic States*, ed. J. Marcus and G. M. Feinman. Santa Fe, NM: 3–14.

  (eds.) (1998) *Archaic States*. Santa Fe, NM.

Marinatos, N. (1996) "Cult by the Seashore: What Happened at Amnisos?," in *The Role of Religion in the Early Greek Polis*, ed. R. Hägg. Stockholm: 135–9.

Markov, K. (1978) "La Présence thrace à l'île de Thasos du VIIe au IIIe s. av. n. è.," in *Pulpudeva. Semaines philoppopolitaines de l'histoire et de la culture thrace, Plovdiv, 4–19 octobre 1976.* Vol. 2, ed. A. Fol. Sofia: 185–91.

Marksteiner, T. (2002) "Städtische Strukturen im vorhellenistischen Lykien," in *A Comparative Study of Six City-State Cultures,* ed. M. H. Hansen. Copenhagen: 57–72.

Martelli, M. (1987) *La ceramica degli Etruschi.* Novara.

Martín, M. A. (1988) "Algunes precisions més sobre la ceràmica ibérica indiketa decorada amb pintura blanca," *Fonaments* 7: 47–56.

Massa-Pairault, F.-H. (1996) *La Cité des Etrusques.* Paris.

Masson, O. (1971) "Kypriaka," *BCH* 95: 305–34.

May, J. M. F. (1965) "The Coinage of Maroneia to 449 BC," *NC* 5: 27–56.

(1968) *The Coinage of Abdera, 540–354 B.C.* London.

McDonald, W. A. (1943) *The Political Meeting Places of the Greeks.* Baltimore.

McInerney, J. (1999) *The Folds of Parnassos: Land and Ethnicity in Ancient Phokis.* Austin.

Meritt, B. D. (1936) "Greek Inscriptions," *Hesperia* 5: 422.

Meritt, B. D, H. T. Wade-Gery, and M. F. McGregor (1939) *The Athenian Tribute Lists.* Vol. 1. Cambridge, MA.

Mesa redonda sobre termalismo antiguo (Madrid, Casa de Velázquez-UNED, 1991). Espacio, Tiempo y Forma, serie II. V. (1992).

Messineo, G. (1983) "Tesserae hospitales," *Xenia* 5: 3–4.

Metzler, J. (ed.) (1982) *Antidoron. Festschrift für Jürgen Thimme.* Karlsruhe.

Mihailov, G. (1972). *La Civilisation thrace.* Sofia.

Mikalson, J. D. (1998). *Religion in Hellenistic Athens.* Berkeley.

Miller, M. C. (2004) *Athens and Persia in the 5th Century BC: A Study in Cultural Receptivity.* Cambridge.

Miranda, E. (1989) "Osservazioni sul culto di Euploia," *MGR* 14: 133–7.

Mitchell, L. (2007) *Panhellenism and the Barbarian.* Swansea.

Mitchell, L. G. and P. J. Rhodes (eds.) (1997) *The Development of the Polis in Archaic Greece.* London.

Mitteis, L. and U. Wilcken (1912) *Grundzüge und Chrestomathie der Papyruskunde.* Vol.I.2. Leipzig.

Modes de contact et processus de transformation dans les sociétés anciennes. Actes du colloque de Cortone. (1983) Pisa-Rome.

Mohlo, A., K. Raaflaub, J. Emlen (eds.) (1991) *City-States in Classical Antiquity and Medieval Italy.* Stuttgart.

Möller, A. (2000) *Naukratis: Trade in Archaic Greece.* Oxford.

(2001a) "Naukratis – griechisches *emporion* und ägyptischer 'port of trade,'" in *Naukratis. Die Beziehungen zu Ostgriechenland, Ägypten und Zypern in archaischer Zeit. Akten der Table Ronde in Mainz. 25–27 November 1999,* ed. U. Höckmann and D. Kreikenbom. Möhnesee: 13–21.

(2001b) "Naukratis or How to Identify a Port of Trade," in *Prehistory and History: Ethnicity, Class, and Political Economy*, ed. D. W. Tandy. Montreal: 145–58.

Mommsen, H., M. R. Cowell, Ph. Fletcher, D. Hook, U. Schlotzhauer, A. Villing et al. (2006) "Neutron Activation Analysis of Pottery from Naukratis and Other Related Vessels," in *Naukratis: Greek Diversity in Egypt. Studies on East Greek Pottery and Exchange in the Eastern Mediterranean*, ed. A. Villing and U. Schlotzhauer. London: 69–76.

Moneo, T. (2003) *Religio Ibérica. Santuarios, ritos y divinidades (siglos VII-I a.C.)*. Madrid.

Montepaone, C. (1990) "Bendis tracia ad Atene: l'integrazione del nuovo attraverso forme dell'ideologia," *AION(archeol)* 12: 103–21.

Montserrat, D. (1996) *Sex and Society in Graeco-Roman Egypt*. London and New York.

Morel, J.-P. (1975) "L'Expansion Phocéenne en Occident: dix années de recherches (1966–75)," *BCH* 99: 853–96.

(1981a) "Le Commerce étrusque en France, en Espagne et en Afrique," in *L'Etruria mineraria: Atti del XII Covegno di Studi Etruschi e Italici, Firenze 1979*, ed. G. Camporeale. Florence: 463–508.

(1981b) "Empòrion en el marc de la colonització focea," *L'avenç* 38: 30–5.

Moreno, A. (2009) "'The Attic Neighbour:' the Cleruchy in the Athenian Empire," in *Interpreting the Athenian Empire*, ed. J. Ma, N. Papazarkadas, and R. Parker. London: 211–22.

Moretti, L. (1984) "Sulle iscrizioni greche di Gravisca," *RFIC* 112: 314–27.

Morgan, C. (2001) "Ethne, Ethnicity, and Early Greek States," in *Ancient Perceptions of Greek Ethnicity*, ed I. Malkin. Washington, DC: 75–112.

(2003) *Early Greek States Beyond the Polis*. London and New York.

Morris, I. (ed.) (1994) *Classical Greece. Ancient Histories and Modern Archaeologies*. Cambridge.

(2005) "Mediterraneanization," in *Mediterranean Paradigms and Classical Antiquity*, ed. I. Malkin. London and New York: 30–55.

Moscati, S. (1968) *The World of the Phoenicians*. Transl. A. Hamilton. London.

(ed.) (1988) *The Phoenicians*. Milan.

Moysey, R. A. (1976) "The Date of the Strato of Sidon Decree," *AJAH* 1: 182–9.

Muhs, B. (1994) "The Great Temenos at Naukratis," *JARCE* 31: 99–113.

Murray, O. (ed.) (1990) *Sympotica. A Symposium on the Symposion*. Oxford.

Musso, O. (1998) "Il piombo inscritto di Ampurias: Note linguistiche e datazione," *Empúries* 48–50: 156–9.

Musti, D. (1976) "Qualche considerazione sul problema della prostituzione sacra," in *Locri Epizefirii (Atti del sedicesimo convegno di studi sulla magna Grecia)*. Naples: 65–71.

Musti, D. and M. Torelli (1994) *Pausania. Guida della Grecia Libro II: La Corinzia e l'Argolide*. Milan.

Myres, J. L. (1899) *A Catalogue of the Cyprus Museum.* Oxford.

Najdenova, V. (1983) "Contribution à la religion en Thrace," in *Concilium Eirene XVI. Proceedings of the 16th International Eirene Conference,* ed. P. Oliva and A. Frolíkova. Vol. 2. Prague: 57–61.

Naso, A. (2006) "Etruscan and Italic Finds in North Africa, 7th-2nd Century BC," in *Naukratis: Greek Diversity in Egypt. Studies on East Greek Pottery and Exchange in the Eastern Mediterranean,* ed. A. Villing and U. Schlotzhauer. London: 187–98.

Nelson, C. and L. Grossberg (eds.) (1988) *Marxism and the Interpretation of Culture.* Urbana, IL.

Nick, G. (2001) "Typologie der Plastik des zyprischen und des 'Michstils' aus Naukratis," in *Naukratis. Die Beziehungen zu Ostgriechenland, Ägypten und Zypern in archaischer Zeit. Akten der Table Ronde in Mainz. 25-27 November 1999,* ed. U. Höckmann and D. Kreikenbom. Möhnesee: 55–68.

Nickels, A. (1982) "Agde grecque: les recherches récentes," *PP* 204–8: 269–79.

(1983) "Les Grecs en Gaule: l'exemple du Languedoc," in *Modes de contact et processus de transformation dans les sociétés anciennes. Actes du colloque de Cortone.* Pisa-Roma: 405–28.

Nielsen, T. H. (ed.) (1997) *Yet More Studies in the Ancient Greek Polis.* Stuttgart.

Niemeyer, H. G. (ed.) (1982) *Phönizier am Westen: die Beiträge des internationalen Symposiums über "Die phönizische Expansion im westlichen Mittelmeerraum" in Köln vom 24 bis 27 April 1979.* Mainz.

(2000) "The Early Phoenician City-States on the Mediterranean: Archaeological Elements for their Description," in *A Comparative Study of Thirty City-State Cultures,* ed. M. H. Hansen. Copenhagen: 89–115.

Nilsson, M. P. (1955) *Geschichte der griechischen Religion.* 2 vols. Munich.

(1960) "Bendis in Athen," *Opuscula selecta* III. Lund: 55–80.

O'Connor, D. (2003) "Egypt's Views of 'Others,'" in *'Never Had the Like Occurred': Egypt's View of its Past,* ed. W. J. Tait. London: 155–86.

Ober, J. (2008) *Democracy and Knowledge: Innovation and Learning in Classical Athens.* Princeton.

Oden, R. A. (1987) *The Bible Without Theology.* San Francisco: 131–53.

Oliva, P. and A. Frolíkova (eds.) (1983) *Concillium Eirene XVI. Proceedings of the 16th International Eirene Conference.* 2 vols. Prague.

Olmos, R. (1992) "Iconografía y culto a las aguas de época prerromana en los mundos colonial e ibérico," in *Mesa redonda sobre termalismo antiguo (Madrid, Casa de Velázquez-UNED, 1991). Espacio, Tiempo y Forma,* serie II, V.: 103–20.

(1995) "Usos de la moneda en la Hispania prerromana y problemas de lectura iconográfica," in *La moneda hispánica. Ciudad y territorio,* ed. P. García-Bellido and R. M. S. Centeno. Madrid: 41–52.

Olmos, R. and P. Rouillard (eds.) (1996) *Formes archaïques et arts ibériques – Formas arcaicas y arte ibérico.* Collection de la Casa de Velázquez 59. Madrid.

(2002) "Sculpture préromaine de la Péninsule Ibérique," *Documents d'Archéologie Méridionale* 25: 269–83.

Osborne, R. (1996) "Pots, Trade, and the Archaic Greek Economy," *Antiquity* 70: 31–44.

(1998) "Early Greek Colonization? The Nature of Greek Settlement in the West," in *Archaic Greece: New Approaches and New Evidence*, ed. N. Fisher and H. van Wees. London: 251–70.

(2001) "Why did Athenian Pots Appeal to the Etruscans?," *World Archaeology* 33: 277–95.

Owen, S. (2000) "New Light on Thracian Thasos: a Reinterpretation of the 'Cave of Pan,'" *JHS* 120: 139–43.

(2003) "Of Dogs and Men: Archilochos, Archaeology, and the Greek Settlement of Thasos," *PCPS* 49: 1–18.

Ozyigit, O. (1994) "The City Walls of Phokaia," *REA* 96: 77–109.

Padró i Parcerisa, J. (1980) *Egyptian-Type Documents. From the Mediterranean Littoral of the Iberian Peninsula Before the Roman Conquest.* 3 vols. Leiden.

Pages del Pozo, V. (1984) *Imitaciones de influjo griego en la cerámica ibérica de Valencia, Alicante y Murcia.* Madrid.

Pallas, D. (1958) "Ανασκαφή της Παλαιοχριστιανικής Βασιλικής του Λεχαίου," *Πρακτικά της εν Αθήνας Αρχαιολογικής Εταιρείας:* 119–35.

Pallottino, M. (1975) *The Etruscans.* Transl. K. Cremona. Bloomington.

Paoletti, O. and L. T. Perna (ed.) (2002) *Etruria e Sardegna centro-settentrionale tra l'Età del Bronzo Finale e l'Arcaismo. Atti del XXI Convegno di studi etruschi ed italici.* Pisa and Rome.

Pareti, L. (1956) "Basi e sviluppo della 'tradizione' antica sui primi popoli della Sicilia," *Kokalos* 2: 5–19.

Parke, H. W. (1967) *Greek Oracles.* London.

Parker, R. (1996) *Athenian Religion: A History.* Oxford.

(2002) "The Cult of Aphrodite Pandamos and Pontia on Cos," in *Kykeon. Studies in Honour of H. S. Versnel*, ed. H. F. J. Horstmannshoff, H. W. Singor, F. T. van Straten, and J. H. M. Strubbe. Leiden: 143–60.

Parker, R. and D. Obbink (eds.) (2000) "Aus der Arbeit der 'Inscriptiones Graecae' VI. Sales of Priesthoods on Cos I," *Chiron* 30: 415–49.

Pasqui, A. (1885) "Nota del predetto sig. A. Pasqui intorno agli studi fatti da lui e dal conte A. Cozza sopra l'ubicazione dell'antica Tarquinia," *NSc* 513–24.

Pébarthe, Ch. (1999) "Thasos, l'empire d'Athènes et les emporia de Thrace," *ZPE* 126: 131–54.

Pečírka, J. (1966) *The Formula for the Grant of Enktesis in Attic Inscriptions.* Prague.

Peden, A. J. (2001) *The Graffiti of Pharaonic Egypt. Scope and Roles of Informal Writings (c. 3100–332 BC).* Leiden.

Peek, W. (1966) "Ein milesisches Polyandrion," *Wiener Studien* 79: 218–30.

Pembroke, S. (1970) "Locres et Tarente: le rôle des femmes dans la fondation de deux colonies grecques," *Annales* 25: 1240–70.

Peña, M. J. (1973) "Artemis-Diana y algunas cuestiones en relación con su icono-grafía y su culto en Occidente, b) El problema de la Artemis ampuritana," *Ampurias* 35: 121–32.

(1985) "Le Problème de la supposée ville indigène à côté d'Emporion. Nouvelles hypothèses," *DHA* 11: 69–83.

(1988a) "Hipòtesis noves sobre Empúries a partir de l'analisi de les fonts literàries," *Fonaments* 7: 11–45.

(1988b) "El problema del estatuto juridico de Emporia(e). Analisis de la documentacion," in *Actes del I congreso peninsular de historia Antigua,* ed. P. M. Gerardo. Santiago: 455–66.

(1992) "Ampurias: dès la polis à la civitas," *Index* 20: 135–45.

(2000) "Les Cultes d'Emporion," in *Les Cultes des cités phocéennes. Actes du colloque international organisé par le Centre Camille-Julian (Aix-en-Provence/Marseille, 1999),* ed. A. Hermary and H. Tréziny. Études Massaliètes 6. Aix-en-Provence: 59–68.

Perreault, J. Y. (1993) "Les *Emporia* grecs du Levant: mythes ou réalité?," in *L'Emporion,* ed. A. Bresson and P. Rouillard. Paris: 59–83.

Petrie, W. M. F., C. Smith, E. Gardner, and B. V. Head (1886) *Naukratis: Part I.* Rpt. 1992. Chicago.

Petropoulos, E. K. (2005) *Hellenic Colonization in Euxeinos Pontos: Penetration, Early Establishment, and the Problem of the "Emporion" Revisited.* BAR International Series 1394. Oxford.

Pfiffig, A. J. (1975) *Religio etrusca.* Graz.

Pianu. G. (2000) *Il Bucchero.* Gravisca. scavi nel santuario greco. Vol. 10. Bari.

Picard, O. (1999) "Le Commerce de l'argent dans la charte de Pistiros," *BCH* 123: 332–46.

Pike, K. L. (1954) *Language in Relation to a Unified Theory of the Structure of Human Behavior.* Vol. 1. Glendale.

Pinch, G. (1993) *Votive Offerings to Hathor.* Oxford.

Pirenne-Delforge, V. (1994) *L'Aphrodite grecque.* Kernos Supplement 4. Liège.

Pirenne-Delforge, V. and E. Suárez de la Torre (eds.) (2000) *Héros et heroines dans les mythes et les cultes grecs. Actes du Colloque organisé à l'Université de Valladolid du 26 au 29 mai 1999.* Liège.

Pironti, G. (2007) *Entre ciel et guerre. Figures d'Aphrodite en Grèce ancienne.* Kernos Supplement 18. Liège.

Plana-Mallart, R. (1994a) "La Chora de Emporion," in *Homenaje a José María. Blázquez.* Madrid: 399–424.

(1994b) *La Chora d'Emporion: paysage et structures agraires dans le nord-est Catalan à la période pré-romain.* Paris.

(1999) "Cadastre et chôra ampuritaine," in *Territoires des cités grecques,* ed. M. Brunet. BCH Supplement 34. Paris: 199–215.

Polanyi, K. (1963) "Ports of Trade in Early Societies," *Journal of Economic History* 23: 30–45.

Polanyi, K., K. M. Arendberg, and H. W. Pearson (eds.) (1957) *Trade and Market in Early Empires: Economies in History and Theory.* Glencoe.

Pomey, P. (2006) "Les Navires étrusques: mythe ou réalité?," in *Gli Etruschi da Genova ad Ampurias. Atti del XXIV Convegno di Studi Etruschi ed Italici, Marseille-Lattes, 26 settembre – 1 ottobre 2002,* ed. S. Gori. 2 vols. Rome: 423–434.

Pope, H. (1935) *Non-Athenians in Attic Inscriptions.* New York.

Porten, B. (1984) "The Jews of Egypt," in *The Cambridge History of Judaism,* ed. W. D. Davies and L. Finkelstein. Cambridge: 372–400.

Porter, N. B. (ed.) (2000) *One God or Many? Concepts of Divinity in the Ancient World.* Bethesda, MD.

Potter, T. W. and C. Wells (1985) "A Republican Healing-Sanctuary at Ponte di Nona near Rome and the Classical Tradition of Votive Medicine," *JBAA* 138: 23–47.

Pouilloux, J. (1954) *Recherches sur l'histoire et les cultes de Thasos.* Part I. Études Thasiennes III. Paris.

(1988) "Un texte commercial ionien trouvé en Languedoc et la colonisation ionienne," *Scienze dell'antichità* 2: 535–46.

Poulter, A. G. (ed.) (1983) *Ancient Bulgaria. Papers Presented to the International Symposium on the Ancient History and Archaeology of Bulgaria, University of Nottingham, 1981.* 2 vols. Nottingham.

Price, E. (1924) "Pottery of Naukratis," *JHS* 44: 180–222.

Pridik, E. M. (1908) "Inscriptions grecques de la collection de Golenitschev," *Journal du Ministère de l'Instruction Publique* n.s. 13: 19 no. 12.

Prinz, H. (1908) "Funde aus Naukratis. Beiträge zur Archäologie und Wirtschaftsgeschichte des VII. und VI. Jahrhunderts v. Chr. Geb.," *Klio* Beiheft 7: 1–153.

Pritchard, J. B. (1943) *Palestinian Figurines in Relation to Certain Goddesses Known through Literature.* New Haven.

Pritchett, W. K. (1941) "Greek Inscriptions," *Hesperia* 10: 280.

Pryce, F. N. (1928) *Catalogue of Sculpture in the Department of Greek and Roman Antiquities of the British Museum.* Vol. 1, Part 1. London.

Psoma, S., C. Karadima, and D. Terzopoulou (2008) *The Coins from Maroneia and the Classical City at Molyvoti: A Contribution to the History of Aegean Thrace.* Meletemata 62. Athens.

Pugliese Carratelli, G. (1992) "Sul culto di Afrodite Euploia in Napoli," *PP* 262: 58–61.

Pujol y Camps, C. (1878) *Estudio de las monedas de Ampurias y Rhodas, con sus imitaciones.* Seville.

Purcell, N. (2005a.) "The Boundless Sea of Unlikeness? On Defining the Mediterranean," in *Mediterranean Paradigms and Classical Antiquity,* ed. I. Malkin. London and New York, 9–29.

(2005b.) "Colonization and Mediterranean History," in *Ancient Colonizations: Analogy, Similarity and Difference,* ed. H. Hurst and S. Owen. London: 115–39.

Py, M. (1985) "Les Amphores étrusques de Gaule méridionale," in *Il commercio etrusco arcaico. Atti dell'incontro di studio, 5–7 dicembre, 1983*, ed. M. Cristofani, P. Moscati, G. Nardi, and M. Pandolfini. Rome: 73–94.

(1995) "Les Étrusques, les Grecs, et la fondation de Lattes," in *Sur les pas des Grecs en Occident*, ed. P. Arcelin, M. Bats, D. Garcia, G. Marchand, and M. Schwaller. Études Massaliètes 4. Aix-en-Provence: 261–76.

Quilici, L. (1968) "Graviscae," *La Via Aurelia. Quaderni dell' Istituto di Topografia Antica* 4: 107–20.

Raaflaub, K. A. (2004) "Zwischen Ost und West: Phönizische Einflüsse auf die griechische Polisbildung?," in *Griechische Archaik. Interne Entwicklungen – Externe Impulse*, ed. R. Rollinger and Ch. Ulf. Innsbruck: 271–89.

Raptou, E. (1999) *Athènes et Chypre à l'époque perse (VIe-IVe s. av. J.-C.)*. Lyon.

Rathje, A. (1990) "The Adoption of the Homeric Banquet in Central Italy in the Orientalizing Period," in *Sympotica. A Symposium on the Symposion*, ed. O. Murray. Oxford: 279–88.

Reddé, M., L. Dubois, D. Briquel, H. Lavagne, and F. Queyrel (eds.) (2003) *La naissance de la ville dans l'antiquité*. Paris.

Reden, S. von (1995a) "The Piraeus – A World Apart," *Greece & Rome* 42.1: 24–37.

(1995b) *Exchange in Ancient Greece*. London.

Redfield. J. (2003) *The Locrian Maidens: Love and Death in Greek Italy*. Princeton.

Reed, C. M. (2003) *Maritime Traders in the Ancient Greek World*. Cambridge.

Remesal, J. and O. Musso (eds.) (1991) *La presencia de material etrusco en el ámbito de la colonización arcaica de la Península Ibérica*. Barcelona.

Ridgway, D. (1974) "Archaeology in Central Italy and Etruria," *AR* 20: 49–51.

(1984) *L'Alba della Magna Grecia*. Milan.

(1992) *The First Western Greeks*. Cambridge.

(1994) "Phoenicians and Greeks in the West: a view from Pithekoussai," in *The Archaeology of Greek Colonisation: Essays dedicated to Sir John Boardman*, ed. G. R. Tsetskhladze and F. de Angelis. Oxford: 35–46.

Riva, C. (2010) *The Urbanization of Etruria: Funerary Practices and Social Change, 700–600 BC*. Cambridge.

Robert, J. and L. Robert (1940) "Bulletin épigraphique," *REG* 53: 217 n. 89.

Robert, L. (1937) *Études Anatoliennes. Recherches sur les inscriptions grecques de l'Asie Mineure*. Paris.

(1963) *Noms indigènes dans l'Asie Mineure gréco-romaine I*. Paris.

(1970) Review of *Griechische Mauerbau inschriften*. T. 1: Texte und Kommentare, by F. G. Maier, *Gnomon* 42: 579–603.

(1989) "Les Juges étrangers dans la cité grecque," *Opera Minora Selecta*. Vol. 5. Amsterdam: 137–54.

Robins, G. (1995) "Women and Children in Peril: Pregnancy, Birth, and Infant Mortality in Ancient Egypt," *KMT* 5/4: 24–35.

Rodríguez Ramos, J. (2000) "La lectura de las inscripciones sudlusitano-tartesias," *Faventia* 22: 21–48.

(2002) "El origen de la escritura sudlusitano-tartesia y la formación de alfabetos a partir de alefatos," *Rivista di Studi Finici* 30: 81–116.

Rodríguez-Somolinos, H. (1996) "The Commercial Transaction of the Pech-Maho Lead: A New Interpretation," *ZPE* 111: 74–8.

Roebuck, C. (1951) "The Organization of Naucratis," *CP* 46: 212–20.

(1959) *Ionian Trade and Colonization.* New York.

Romero Recio, M. (2000) *Cultos marítimos y religiosidad de navegantes en el mundo griego antiquo.* BAR International Series 897. Oxford.

Rosenzweig, R. (2004) *Worshipping Aphrodite: Art and Cult in Classical Athens.* Ann Arbor.

Rosner, B. S. (1998) "Temple Prostitution in 1 Corinthians 6:12–20," *Novum Testamentum* 40: 336–51.

Rouillard, P. (1991) *Les Grecs et la Péninsule Ibérique du VIIe au IVe siècles avant J.-C.* Paris.

(1993) "L'*Emporion* chez Strabon: les *emporia* straboniens: fonctions et activités," in *L'Emporion*, ed. A. Bresson and P. Rouillard. Paris: 35–46.

(2009) "Greeks and the Iberian Peninsula: Forms of Exchange and Settlements," in *Colonial Encounters in Ancient Iberia: Phoenician, Greek, and Indigenous Relations*, ed. M. Dietler and C. López-Ruiz. Chicago: 131–153.

Rowe, A. (1938) "New Light on Objects Belonging to the General Potasimto and Amasis in the Egyptian Museum,"*Annales du service des antiquités d'Égypte* 38: 157–95.

Rubinstein, L. (2004) "Ionia," in *An Inventory of Archaic and Classical Poleis. An Investigation Conducted by the Copenhagen Polis Centre for the Danish National Research Foundation*, ed. M. H. Hansen and T. H. Nielsen. Oxford: 1053–1107.

Ruby, P. (2006) "Peuples, fictions? Ethnicité, identité ethnique et sociétés anciennes," *REA* 108: 25–60.

Ruiz, A. and M. Molinos (eds.) (1998) *The Archaeology of the Iberians.* Transl. M. Turton. Cambridge. Orig. 1993.

Ruiz de Arbulo Bayona, J. (1984) "Emporion y Rhode. Dos asentamientos portuarios en el golfo de Roses," in *Arqueología espacial: coloquio sobre distribución y relaciones entre los asentamientos del Bronce Final a Epoca Ibérica.* Vol. 4. Teruel: 115–40.

Saba, S. (in press) "A Problem of Historical Geography: Orthagoreia in Thrace Reconsidered," *Gephyra.*

Saffrey, H. D. (1985) "Aphrodite à Corinthe: Réflexions sur une idée reçue," *RB* 92: 359–74.

Said, E. (1978) *Orientalism.* New York.

Salmon, J. B. (1997) *Wealthy Corinth: A History of the City to 338 BC.* Oxford.

Salomon, N. (1997) *Le cleruchie di Atene: caratteri e funzione.* Pisa.

Salviat, F. (1999) "Le Roi Kersobleptès, Maronée, Apollonia, Thasos, Pistiros et l'histoire d'Hérodote," *BCH* 123: 259–73.

(2000) "La Source ionienne: Apatouria, Apollon Delphinios et l'oracle, l'Aristarchéion," in *Les Cultes des cités phocéennes. Actes du colloque international organisé par le Centre Camille-Julian (Aix-en-Provence/Marseille, 1999)*, ed. A. Hermary and H. Tréziny. Études Massaliètes 6. Aix-en-Provence: 25–31.

Sancisi-Weerdenburg, H. (2001) "Yaunā by the Sea and across the Sea," in *Ancient Perceptions of Greek Ethnicity*, ed. Irad Malkin. Washington, D.C.: 323–46.

Sandberg, N. (1954) ΕΥΠΛΟΙΑ. *Études épigraphiques*. Göteborg.

Sanmartí, J. (2009) "Colonial Relations and Social Change in Iberia (Seventh to Third Centuries BC)," in *Colonial Encounters in Ancient Iberia: Phoenician, Greek, and Indigenous Relations*, ed. M. Dietler and C. López-Ruiz. Chicago: 49–88.

Sanmartí, J., D. Asensio, and A. Martin (2002) "Les relacions commercials amb el món mediterrani dels pobles indígenes de la Catalynua sudpirinenca durant el periode tardoarcaic (*ca.* 575–450 AC)," *Cypsela* 14: 69–106.

Sanmartí-Grego, E. (1982) "Les Influences méditerranéennes au nord-est de la Catalogne à l'époque archaïque et la réponse indigène," *PP* 204–208: 281–303.

(1988) "Una carta en lengua ibérica escrita sobre plomo procedente de Emporion," *RAN* 21: 95–113.

(1990) "Emporion, port grec à vocation ibérique," in *La Magna Grecia e il lontano occidente: Atti del ventinovesimo convegno di studi sulla Magna Grecia.* Taranto: 389–410.

(1992) "Massalia et Emporion: une origine commune, deux destines different," in *Marseille grecque et la Gaule*, ed. M. Bats, G. Bertucchi, G. Congès, and H. Tréziny. Études Massaliètes 3. Aix-en-Provence: 27–41.

Sanmartí-Grego, E. and R.-A. Santiago (1987) "Une lettre grecque sur plomb trouvée à Emporion (Fouilles 1985)," *ZPE* 68: 119–27.

(1988a) "Notes additionelles sur la lettre sur plomb d'Emporion," *ZPE* 72: 100–2.

(1988b) "La Lettre grecque d'Emporion et son contexte archéologique," *RAN* 21: 3–17.

(1989) "Une nouvelle plaquette de plomb trouvé à Emporion," *ZPE* 77: 36–8.

Sanmartí-Grego, E., P. Castanyer i Masoliver, J. Tremoleda i Trilla (1992) "Nuevos datos sobre la historia y la topografía de las murallas de Emporion," *MDAI(M)* 33: 102–12.

Santiago, R.-A. (1990a) "Encore une fois sur la letter sur plomb d'Emporion (1985)," *ZPE* 80: 79–80.

(1990b) "Notes additionelles au plomb d'Emporion 1987," *ZPE* 82: 176.

(1990c) "Quelques corrections à *ZPE* 80, 1990, pp. 79–80," *ZPE* 84 (1990): 14.

(1994) "El Texto de Estrabón en torno a Emporion a la luz de los nuevos descubrimientos arqueológicos y epigráficos," *Emerita* 62: 61–74.

Santos Velasco, J. A. (1997) "The Iberians in Sardinia: A Review and Update," in *Encounters and Transformations: The Archaeology of Iberia in Transition*, ed. M. S. Balmuth, A. Gilman, and L. Prados-Torreira. Sheffield: 161–6.

Scheid, J. (1995) "*Graeco ritu*: A Typically Roman Way of Honoring the Gods," *HSPh* 97: 15–31.

(2004) "Religions in Contact," in *Religions of the Ancient World: A Guide*, ed. S. Iles Johnston. Cambridge, MA: 112–25.

Schindler, R. K. (1998) "The Archaeology of Aphrodite in the Greek West, *ca.* 650–480 BC," Ph.D. Dissertation, University of Michigan.

Schlotzhauer, U. and A. Villing. (2006) "East Greek Pottery from Naukratis: The Current State of Research," in *Naukratis: Greek Diversity in Egypt. Studies on East Greek Pottery and Exchange in the Eastern Mediterranean*, ed. A. Villing and U. Schlotzhauer. London: 53–68.

Scholtz, A. (2002/2003) "Aphrodite Pandemos at Naukratis," *GRBS* 43: 231–42.

Schultz, C. E. and P. B. Harvey, Jr. (eds.) (2006) *Religion in Republican Italy*. Cambridge.

Schweigert, E. (1940) "Greek Inscriptions," *Hesperia* 9: 332–3.

Serra Ridgway, F. R. (1990) "Etruscans, Greeks, Carthaginians: the Sanctuary at Pyrgi," in *Greek Colonists and Native Populations*, ed. J.-P. Doscœudres. Oxford: 511–30.

Shachar, I. (2000) "Greek Colonization and the Eponymous Apollo," *MHR* 15.2: 1–26.

Shafer, B. E., J. Baines, L. H. Lesko, and D. P. Silverman (eds.) (1991) *Religion in Ancient Egypt. Gods, Myths, and Personal Practice*. Ithaca, NY.

Shapiro, H. A. (1983) "Amazons, Thracians, and Scythians," *GRBS* 24: 105–14.

(1993) *Personifications in Greek Art: The Representation of Abstract Concepts 600–400 B.C.* Kilchberg/Zürich.

(2000) "Modest Athletes and Liberated Women: Etruscans on Attic Black-figure Vases," in "*Not the Classical Ideal*": *Athens and the Construction of the Other in Greek Art*, ed. B. Cohen. Leiden: 313–37.

Shaw, I. (2004a) "Egypt and the Outside World," in *The Oxford History of Ancient Egypt*, ed. I. Shaw. Oxford: 314–29.

(ed.) (2004b) *The Oxford History of Ancient Egypt*. Oxford.

Shefton, B. B. (1982) "Greeks and Greek Imports in the South of the Iberian Peninsula: The Archaeological Evidence," in *Phönizier im Westen: die Beiträge des internationalen Symposiums über "Die phönizische Expansion im westlichen Mittelmeerraum" in Köln vom 24 bis 27 April, 1979*, ed. H. G. Niemeyer. Mainz: 337–70.

(1994) "Massalia and Colonization in the North-Western Mediterranean," in *The Archaeology of Greek Colonisation. Essays Dedicated to Sir John Boardman*, ed. G. R. Tsetskhladze and F. de Angelis. Oxford: 61–85.

Sherwin-White, S. (1978) *Ancient Cos: A Historical Study from the Dorian Settlement to the Imperial Period*. Göttingen.

Shipley, G. (2004) "Lakedaimon," in *An Inventory of Archaic and Classical Poleis. An Investigation Conducted by the Copenhagen Polis Centre for the Danish National Research Foundation*, ed. M. H. Hansen and T. H. Nielsen. Oxford: 569–98.

Siebert, G. (1968) "Sur l'histoire du sanctuaire des dieux syriens à Délos," *BCH* 92: 359–74.

Simms, R. R. (1985) "Foreign Religious Cults in Athens in the Fifth and Fourth Centuries B.C.," Ph.D. Dissertation, University of Virginia.

(1988) "The Cult of the Thracian Goddess Bendis in Athens and in Attica," *AW* 18: 59–76.

Simon, E. (2006) "Gods in Harmony: The Etruscan Pantheon," in *The Religion of the Etruscans*, ed. N. T. de Grummond and E. Simon. Austin: 45–65.

Sinn, U. (1982) "Zur Wirkung des Ägyptischen 'Bes' auf die griechische Volksreligion," in *Antidoron. Festschrift für Jürgen Thimme*, ed. D. Metzler. Karlsruhe: 87–94.

Skarlatidou, E. (1984) "Ο Ελληνικός αποικισμός στην Αιγιακή Θράκη," *Αρχαιολογία* 13: 50–8.

Skon-Jedele, N. J. (1994) "Aigyptiaka: A Catalogue of Egyptian and Egyptianizing objects from Greek Archaeological Sites, *ca.* 1100–525 B.C. with Historical Commentary." Ph.D. Dissertation, University of Pennsylvania.

Slaska, M. (1985) "Le anfore da trasporto a Gravisca," in *Il commercio etrusco arcaico. Atti dell'incontro di studio, 5–7 dicembre, 1983*, ed. M. Cristofani. Rome: 19–21.

Slater, W. J. (1999) "Hooking in Harbors: Dioscurides XIII Gow-Page," *CQ* 49.2: 503–14.

Slings, S. R. (1994) "Notes on the Lead Letters from Emporion," *ZPE* 104: 111–17.

Smith, A. D. (1986) *The Ethnic Origins of Nations*. Oxford.

Smith, E. M. (1926) *Naukratis. A Chapter in the History of the Hellenization of Egypt*. Vienna.

Solin, H. (1981) "Sulle dediche greche di Gravisca," *PP* 36: 185–7.

Souzourian, H. and R. Stadelmann (2005) "Die ältesten Erwähnungen von Ioniern und Danaern," *AW* 2005.6: 79–83.

Sourvinou-Inwood, C. (1974) "The Votum of 477/6 B.C. and the Foundation-Legend of Locri Epizephyrii," *CQ* 24: 186–98.

(2000) "What is Polis Religion?," in *Oxford Readings in Greek Religion*, ed. R. Buxton. Oxford: 13–18.

Spivak, G. C. (1988) "Can the Subaltern Speak?," in *Marxism and the Interpretation of Culture*, ed. C. Nelsson and L. Grossberg. Urbana, IL.

Spivey, N. and S. Stoddart (1990) *Etruscan Italy*. London.

Stein, G. (2002) "Colonies without Colonialism: A Trade Diaspora Model of Fourth Millennium B.C. Mesopotamian Enclaves in Anatolia," in *The Archaeology of Colonialism*, ed. C. L. Lyons and J. K. Papadopoulos. Los Angeles: 27–64.

Straten, F. T. van (1981) "Gifts for the Gods," in *Faith, Hope, and Worship: Aspects of Religious Mentality in the Ancient World*, ed. H. S. Versnel. Leiden: 105–43.

Stroud, R. S. (1974) "An Athenian Law on Silver Coinage," *Hesperia* 43.2: 157–88.

Sullivan, R. D. (1996) "Psammetichos I and the Foundation of Naukratis," in *Ancient Naukratis. Volume II. Part I: The Survey at Naukratis*, ed. W. D. E. Coulson. Exeter: 177–95.

Tacheva-Hitova, M. (1983) *Eastern Cults in Moesia Inferior and Thracia (5th century BC–4th century AD)*. Leiden.

Tait, W. J. (ed.) (2003) *'Never Had the Like Occurred': Egypt's View of its Past*. London.

Tandy, D. W. (1997) *Warriors into Traders: The Power of the Market in Early Greece*. Berkeley.

(ed.) (2001) *Prehistory and History: Ethnicity, Class, and Political Economy*. Montreal.

Tang, B. (2005) *Delos, Carthage, Ampurias: The Housing of the Three Mediterranean Trading Centers*. Rome.

Tanner, J. (2003) "Finding the Egyptian in Early Greek Art," in *Ancient Perspectives on Egypt*, ed. R. Matthews and C. Roemer. London: 115–43.

Teixidor, J. (1980) "L'Assemblée législative en Phénicie d'après les inscriptions," *Syria* 57: 453–64.

(1993) "Un terme ouest-sémitique pour *emporion*?," in *L'Emporion*, ed. A. Bresson and P. Rouillard. Paris: 85–7.

Theodossiev, N. (2000a) *North-Western Thrace from the 5th to the 1st Centuries BC*. BAR International Series 859. Oxford.

(2000b) "Monumental Tombs and Hero Cults in Thrace during the 5th–3rd centuries B.C.," in *Héros et heroines dans les mythes et les cultes grecs. Actes du Colloque organisé à l'Université de Valladolid du 26 au 29 mai 1999*, ed. V. Pirenne-Delforge and E. Suárez de la Torre. Liège: 435–47.

Thein, A. (1999) "The Urbanism of Athens and the Piraeus: Sea or Land?," Paper presented at *Negotiating Ideologies: An Interdisciplinary Conference Exploring the Culture of Antiquity, 15–17 October 1999*.

Thelamon, F. (ed.) (1989) *Aux sources de la puissance: sociabilité et parenté*. Rouen.

Thompson, D. J. (1988) *Memphis under the Ptolemies*. Princeton.

Titz, P. (2002) "Transport Amphorae from Pistiros," in *Pistiros II: Excavations and Studies*, ed. J. Bouzek, L. Domaradzka, and Z. H. Archibald. Prague: 133–234.

Todorov, Y. (1987) *Thracian Culture*. Sofia.

Torelli, M. (1971a) "Gravisca (Tarquinia). – Scavi nella città etrusca e romana. Campagne 1969 e 1970," *NSc* 25: 195–299.

(1971b) "Il santuario di Hera a Gravisca," *PP* 26: 44–67.

(1976) "I culti di Locri," in *Locri Epizefirii (Atti del sedicesimo convegno di studi sulla magna Grecia)*. Naples: 147–56.

(1977) "Il santuario greco di Gravisca," *PP* 32: 398–458.

(1982) "Per la definizione del commercio greco-orientale: il caso di Gravisca," *PP* 37: 304–25.

(1988) "Riflessioni a margine dell'*emporion* di Gravisca," *PACT* 20: 181–90.

(1996) "The Encounter with the Etruscans," in *The Western Greeks*, ed. G. P. Carratelli. London: 567–76.

(1997) "Les Adonies de Gravisca. Archéologie d'une fête," in *Les Étrusques, le plus religieux des hommes*, ed. Ph. Ghautier and D. Briquel. Paris: 233–91.

(2000a) "The Etruscan City-State," in *A Comparative Study of Thirty City-State Cultures*, ed. M. H. Hansen. Copenhagen: 189–208.

(ed.) (2000b) *Gli Etruschi/The Etruscans*. Venice.

Tovar, A. (1971) "Un nuevo epigrama griego de Córdoba: ¿Arriano de Nicomedia, proconsul de Bética?," in *Estudios sobre de la obra de Américo Castro*, ed. P. Laín Entralgo. Madrid: 403–12.

Traill, J. S. (1975) *The Political Organization of Attica*. Hesperia Supplement 14. Athens.

Trillmich, W. (1990) "Early Iberian Sculpture and 'Phocaean Colonization,'" in *Greek Colonists and Native Populations*, ed. J.-P. Doescœdres. Oxford: 607–11.

True, M. and J. Podany (eds.) (1990) *Small Bronze Sculpture from the Ancient World*. Malibu.

Trümper, M. (2006) "Negotiating Religious and Ethnic Identity: The Case of Club-houses in Late Hellenistic Delos," *Hephaistos* 24: 113–40.

Truszkowski, E. (2003) "Réflexions sur la sculpture funéraire et votive du Sud-Est de la Péninsule Ibérique," *MDAI(M)* 44: 311–32.

Tsetskhladze, G. (ed.) (1998) *The Greek Colonisation of the Black Sea Area*. Stuttgart.

(ed.) (1999) *Ancient Greeks West and East*. Leiden.

(2000) "Pistiros in the System of Pontic Emporia," in *Pistiros et Thasos: structures économiques dans la péninsule balkanique aux VIIe-IIe siècles avant J.-C*, ed. M. Domaradzki, L. Domaradzka, J. Bouzek, and J. Rostropowicz. Opole: 233–46.

(ed.) (2006) *Greek Colonisation: An Account of Greek Colonies and Other Settlements Overseas*. Vol. 1. Leiden.

Tsetskhladze, G. R. and F. De Angelis (eds.) (1994) *The Archaeology of Greek Colonisation. Essays Dedicated to Sir John Boardman*. Oxford.

Tsiafaki, D. (1998) *Η Θράκη στην Αττική εικονογραφία του 5ου αιώνα π.Χ.: προσεγγίσεις στις σχέσεις Αθήνας και Θράκης*. Komotini.

Tsiafakis, D. (2000) "The Allure and Repulsion of Thracians in the Art of Classical Athens," in *Not the Classical Ideal: Athens and the Construction of the Other in Greek Art*, ed. B. Cohen. Leiden: 364–489.

Tsirkin, Y. B. (1986) "The Greeks and Tartessos," *Oikoumene* 5: 163–71.

Turfa, J. MacI. (2005) *Catalogue of the Etruscan Gallery of the University of Pennsylvania Museum of Archaeology and Anthropology*. Philadelphia.

(2006) "Votive Offerings in Etruscan Religion," in *The Religion of the Etruscans*, ed. N. T. de Grummond and E. Simon. Austin: 90–115.

Turfa, J. MacI. and A. G. Steinmayer (1999) "The Earliest Foresail on Another Etruscan Vase," *IJNA* 28.3: 292–6.

(2001) "Sewn hulls and self-defence," *IJNA* 30.1: 122–7.

Tušlová, P., S. Kučová, B. Wissová (2010) "Greek and Black Sea Transport Amphorae in Emporion Pistiros. Quantified Analysis of Material Excavated until 2009," in *Pistiros IV: Excavations and Studies*, ed. J. Bouzek, L. Domaradzka, and Z. H. Archibald. Prague: 205–20.

Tyrrell I. (2007) *Transnational Nation: United States History in Global Perspective since 1789*. Basingstoke.

Ulbrich, A. (2008) *Kypris: Heiligtümer und Kulte weiblicher Gottheiten auf Zypern in der kyproarchaischen und kyproklassichen Epoche (Königszeit)*. Münster.

Untermann, J. (1995) "Zum Stand der Deutung der 'tartessischen' Inscriften," in *Hispano-Gallo-Brittonica: Essays in Honor of Professor D. Ellis Evans on the Occasion of his Sixty-Fifth Birthday*, ed. J. F. Eska, R. Geraint Gruffydd, and N. Jacobs, Cardiff: 244–59.

Untermann, J. and F. Villar (eds.) (1993) *Lengua y cultura en la Hispania prerromana: Actas del V coloquio sobre lenguas y culturas prerromanas de la Península Ibérica*. Salamanca.

Ustinova, Y. (1999) *The Supreme Gods of the Bosporan Kingdom: Celestial Aphrodite and the Most High God*. Leiden.

Valbelle, D. (1990) *Les Neufs arcs. L'Égyptien et les étrangers de la préhistoire à la conquête d'Alexandre*. Paris.

Valentini, V. (1993) *Le Ceramiche a vernice nera*. Gravisca: scavi nel santuario greco. Vol. 9. Bari.

Vallet, G. (1968) "La Cité et son territoire dans les colonies grecques d'occident," *Atti dal VII convegno di studi sulla Magna Grecia*. Naples: 67–142.

Vanoyeke, V. (1990) *La Prostitution en Grèce et à Rome*. Paris.

Vasunia, P. (2001) *The Gift of the Nile: Hellenizing Egypt from Aeschylus to Alexander*. Berkeley.

Vatin, C. (1976) "Jardins et services de voirie," *BCH* 100: 555–64.

Veligianni-Terzi, Ch. (2004) *Οι Ελληνίδες Πόλεις και το Βασίλειο των Οδρυσσών*. Thessaloniki.

Vélissaropoulos, J. (1980) *Les Nauclères Grecs: recherches sur les institutions maritimes en Grèce et dans l'Orient hellénisé*. Genève.

(1982) "Les symboles d'affaires. Remarques sur les tablettes archaïques de l'île de Corfou," in *Symposion 1977. Vorträge zur griechischen und hellenistischen Rechtsgeschichte*. Akten der Gesellschaft für griechische und hellenistischen Rechtsgeschichte 3, ed. J. Modrzejewski and D. Liebs. Cologne: 71–83.

Velkov, V. (1967) *Le Travail servile en Thrace et en Mésie dans l'antiquité*. Sofia.

Velkov, V. and L. Domaradzka (1994) "Kotys I (383/2–359 av. J.C.) et l'emporion Pistiros de Thrace," *BCH* 118: 1–15.

(1996) "Kotys I (383/2–259 av. J.C.) and emporion Pistiros in Thrace," in *Pistiros I: Excavations and Studies*, ed. J. Bouzek, M. Domaradzki, and Z. H. Archibald. Prague: 205–16.

Velkova, Z. (1986) *The Thracian Glosses: Contribution to the Study of the Thracian Vocabulary*. Amsterdam.

Venit, M. S. (1988) *Greek Painted Pottery from Naukratis in Egyptian Museums*. Cairo.

Versnel, H. S. (ed.) (1981) *Faith, Hope, and Worship: Aspects of Religious Mentality in the Ancient World*. Leiden.

Veyne, P. (1965) "Quid dedicatum poscit Apollinem?," *Latomus* 24: 932–48.

Villaronga, L. (1977) *The Aes Coinage of Emporion.* Transl. E. Weeks. BAR Supplementary Series 23. Oxford.

(1991) "Les Rapports numismatiques entre Massalia et Emporion," *NAC* 20: 85–92.

(1998) "Metrologia de les monedes antiques de la Península Ibérica," *Acta Numismatica* 28: 53–74.

Villing, A. (2006) "'Drab Bowls' for Apollo: The Mortaria of Naukratis and Exchange in the Archaic Eastern Mediterranean," in *Naukratis: Greek Diversity in Egypt. Studies on East Greek Pottery and Exchange in the Eastern Mediterranean,* ed. A. Villing and U. Schlotzhauer. London: 31–46.

Villing, A. and U. Schlotzhauer (eds.) (2006) *Naukratis: Greek Diversity in Egypt. Studies on East Greek Pottery and Exchange in the Eastern Mediterranean.* London.

Vinogradov, Y. (1998) "The Greek Colonisation of the Black Sea Region in the Light of Private Lead Letters," in *The Greek Colonisation of the Black Sea Area,* ed. G. R. Tsetskhladze. Stuttgart: 153–78.

Vives y Escuedero, A. (1926) *La moneda hispánica.* Madrid.

Vlahov, K. (1982) "Die thrakische Religion nach den sprachlichen Angaben," *AUS* 76.1: 3–97.

Walters, H. B. (1903) *Catalogue of the Terracottas in the Department of Greek and Roman Antiquities in the British Museum.* London.

Webb, V. (1978) *Archaic Greek Faience. Miniature Scent Bottles and Related Objects from East Greece, 650–500 BC.* Warminster.

Welles, C. B. (1966) *Royal Correspondence in the Hellenistic Period. A Study in Greek Epigraphy.* Rome.

Welter, G. (1938) "Aeginetica XIII-XXIV," *JDAI* 53: 480–540.

Wendel, C. (ed.) (1936) *Scholia in Apollonium Rhodium vetera.* Berlin.

West, A. B. (1929) *Fifth and Fourth-Century Gold Coins from the Thracian Coast.* New York.

West, M. L. (1966) *Hesiod. Theogony.* Oxford.

(ed.) (1991–92) *Iambi et elegi Graeci ante Alexandrum cantati.* 2 vols. 2nd edition. Oxford.

(1997) *The East Face of Helicon.* Oxford.

White, R. (1991) *The Middle Ground: Indians, Empires, and Republics in the Great Lakes Regions, 1650–1815.* Cambridge.

Whitehead, D. (1977) *The Ideology of the Athenian Metic.* Cambridge.

(1986) *The Demes of Attica 508/7-ca. 250 B. C.* Princeton.

(1994a) "Site-Classification and Reliability in Stephanus of Byzantium," in *From Political Architecture to Stephanus Byzantium,* ed. D. Whitehead. Stuttgart: 99–124.

(ed.) (1994b). *From Political Architecture to Stephanus Byzantium.* Stuttgart.

Wilamowitz, U. von (1873) "Scavi nelle Curti," *Bulletino dell' Istituto*: 145–52.

Williams, D. (2006) "The Chian Pottery from Naukratis," in *Naukratis: Greek Diversity in Egypt. Studies on East Greek Pottery and Exchange in the Eastern Mediterranean*, ed. A. Villing and U. Schlotzhauer. London: 127–32.

Williams, D. and A. Villing (2006) "Carian Mercenaries at Naukratis?," in *Naukratis: Greek Diversity in Egypt. Studies on East Greek Pottery and Exchange in the Eastern Mediterranean*, ed. A. Villing and U. Schlotzhauer. London: 47–8.

Wilson, J.-P. (1997) "The Nature of Greek Overseas Settlements in the Archaic Period," in *The Development of the Polis in Archaic Greece*, ed. L. G. Mitchell and P. J. Rhodes. London and New York: 199–207.

  (1997–8) "The Illiterate Trader," *BICS* 42: 29–56.

Winter, I. J. (1995) "Homer's Phoenicians: History, Ethnography, or Literary Trope? [A Perspective of Early Orientalism]," in *The Ages of Homer: A Tribute to Emily Vermeule*, ed. J. B. Carter and S. P. Morris. Austin: 247–71.

Wolters, P. (1925) "Ausgrabungen am Aphroditentempel in Ägina 1924," *Gnomon* 1: 46–9.

Yamauchi, E. M. (1973) "Cultic-Prostitution: A Case Study in Cultural Diffusion," in *Orient and Occident. Essays Presented to Cyrus. H. Gordon on the Occasion of his Sixty-Fifth Birthday*, ed. H. A. Hoffner, Jr. Neukirchen-Vluyn: 213–22.

Yordanov, S. (2002) "Notes on the Etymology of the Name Pistiros," in *Pistiros II: Excavations and Studies*, ed. J. Bouzek, L. Domaradzka, and Z. H. Archibald. Prague: 331–3.

Youroukova, Y. (1976) *Coins of The Ancient Thracians*. Transl. V. Athanassov. BAR Supplementary Series 4. Oxford.

  (1982) "Les Invasions macédoniennes en Thrace et les trouvailles monétaires," in *Actes du IXe congrès international de numismatique, Berne, septembre 1979*, ed. T. Hackens and R. Weiller. Louvain-la-Neuve: 215–25.

Yoyotte, J. (1982–3) "L'Amon de Naucratis," *Revue d'Égyptologie* 34: 129–36.

  (1991–2) "Naucratis, ville égyptienne," *ACF* 92: 634–44.

  (1993–4) "Les Contacts entre Égyptiens et Grecs (VIIe-IIe siècles avant J.C.): Naucratis, ville égyptienne (1992–1993, 1993–1994)," *ACF* 94: 679–92.

  (1994–5) "Les Contacts entre Égyptiens et Grecs (VIIe-IIe siècles avant J.-C): Naucratis, ville égyptienne," *ACF* 95: 669–83.

Zaccagnini, C. (1993) "In margine all'*emporion*: modelli di scambio nelle economie del Vicino Oriente antico," in *L'Emporion*, ed. A. Bresson and P. Rouillard. Paris: 127–43.

Zahrnt, M. (2008) "Gab es in Thrakien zwei Städte Namens Mesambria? Überlegungen zur samothrakischen Peraia," in *Thrakika Zetemata* 1, ed. L. Loukopoulou and S. Psoma. Athens: 87–100.

Index

For EU product safety concerns, contact us at Calle de José Abascal, 56–1°, 28003 Madrid, Spain or eugpsr@cambridge.org.